WHO'S WHO IN FASHION

WHO'S IN FA
1700
1790
1820
1850
1870
1900
1920

1920
1947
1960
1980
2010

WHO'S WHO IN FASHION

FIFTH EDITION

Holly Price Alford

A.A.S., B.A., AND M.F.A.
VIRGINIA COMMONWEALTH UNIVERSITY

Anne Stegemeyer

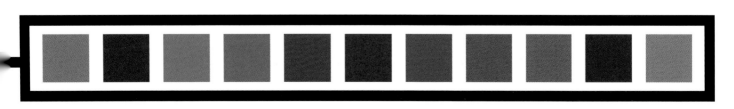

FAIRCHILD BOOKS
NEW YORK

*This book is dedicated in loving memory to my uncle Rufus Holley, Jr.,
whose creative talent I have been blessed with, and who always put
me on a pedestal. I miss you.*

—*Holly Price Alford*

EXECUTIVE EDITOR	Olga T. Kontzias
EDITORIAL DEVELOPMENT DIRECTOR	Jennifer Crane
ASSOCIATE DEVELOPMENT EDITOR	Justine Brennan
ANCILLARIES EDITOR	Noah Schwartzberg
ASSOCIATE ART DIRECTOR	Erin Fitzsimmons
PRODUCTION DIRECTOR	Ginger Hillman
SENIOR PRODUCTION EDITOR	Elizabeth Marotta
TIMELINE	Anne Sanow
COPYEDITOR	Anne Marie Calzolari
COVER DESIGN	Erin Fitzsimmons
PHOTO EDITORS	Sarah Silberg, Carly Grafstein, Alexandra Rossomando, and Andrea Lau
TEXT DESIGN AND COMPOSITION	Dutton & Sherman Design

Library of Congress Catalog Card Number: 2008939046
ISBN: 978-1-56367-710-6
GST R 133004424
Printed in the United States of America
CH12, TP08

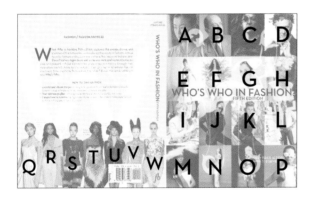

COVER ART CREDITS

A: Doo-Ri Chung, page 84 (© Jason Frank Rothenberg/Art + Commerce)
B: Jean Dessès, page 117 (© Sylvia Salmi/Bettmann/Corbis)
C: Catherine Malandrino, page 246 (Courtesy of the designer)
D: Cecil Beaton, page 34 (Traeger/© 1966 Condé Nast Publications)
E: Pierre Balmain design, page 25 (Jerry Schatzberg/© 1960 Condé Nast Publications)
F: Oscar de la Renta design, page 108 (© Condé Nast Publications)
G: Adolfo design, page 5 (Karen Radkai/© 1960 Condé Nast Publications)
H: Karl Lagerfeld for Chanel design, page 219 (Courtesy of Fairchild Publications, Inc.)
I: Anne Klein, page 209 (© Condé Nast Publications)
J: Tom Ford, page 149 (© Sølve Sundsbø/Art + Commerce)
K: Coco Chanel, page 78 (Horst P. Horst/© 1937 Condé Nast Publications)
L: Derek Lam, page 221 (© Jason Frank Rothenberg/Art + Commerce)
M: John Galliano for Christian Dior design, page 155 (Courtesy of Fairchild Publications, Inc.)
N: Hubert de Givenchy design, page 163 (William Klein/© 1966 Condé Nast Publications)
O: Rei Kawakubo for Comme des Garçons design, page 202 (Courtesy of Fairchild Publications, Inc.)
P: André Courrèges design, page 94 (Courtesy of the designer)
Q: Doo-Ri Chung design, page 84 (Courtesy of Fairchild Publications, Inc.)
R: Peter Som design, page 353 (Courtesy of Fairchild Publications, Inc.)
S: Lela Rose design, page 324 (Courtesy of Fairchild Publications, Inc.)
T: Tracy Reese design, page 317 (Courtesy of Fairchild Publications, Inc.)
U: Diane von Furstenberg design, page 391 (Courtesy of Fairchild Publications, Inc.)
V: Alexander McQueen design, page 258 (Courtesy of Fairchild Publications, Inc.)
W: Albert Kriemler for Akris design, page 215 (Courtesy of Fairchild Publications, Inc.)

CONTENTS

The Profiles

The Profiles

EXTENDED TABLE OF CONTENTS

Preface

In the full-color fifth edition of *Who's Who in Fashion*, you will discover fashion legends as well as newcomers, a collection of biographies that are as current as can possibly be in the fast-changing world of fashion, and also historically broad. This book is designed to help both students and fashion aficionados understand what's happening now, and understand who got us here. After all, where would fashion be today without pioneers such as CHARLES FREDERICK WORTH, COCO CHANEL, and YVES SAINT LAURENT?

The biographies in *Who's Who* trace the careers of women and men who have contributed to fashion; in addition to their career beginnings and highlights, important basic information such as dates of birth and death, nationality, and any major fashion awards won is included. Readers also will learn who has worked with whom. This is important in terms of explaining how influences and innovation work together in the dynamic field of fashion—and how they persist. Was DIOR solely responsible for the post-World War II New Look? Who is re-interpreting these styles today? Major fashion contributions and significant life events are also discussed.

This new edition of *Who's Who* includes major expansions and changes. In addition to designers of clothing, designers of accessories—shoes, jewelry, handbags, and luggage—are featured. Equally important are those who influence fashion by working behind the scenes, such as photographers, illustrators, editors, and writers, and this edition profiles them as well.

Another major enhancement for this edition is the use of full color illustrations and photos of people, designs, and merchandise throughout the text. Also new to the fifth edition is the fashion timeline. Far

from occurring in a vacuum, fashion is very much integrated with the times. Beginning in 1616, when Native American Pocahontas travelled to England wearing European clothing, through 2009 when Michelle Obama wore an ISABEL TOLEDO design for Barack Obama's inauguration as president, the timeline spans nearly 400 years of notable moments in fashion and culture—and shows how they are related. The French Revolution (1789–1795) produced the deadly mechanical invention the guillotine, and inspired a style trend for wearing red ribbons around the neck in imitation of those who were decapitated. World War II, and later the terrorist attacks of September 11, 2001, led to American designs created in patriotic colors of red, white, and blue. Sometimes just one person can cause a fashion upheaval. When the actor Clark Gable appeared bare-chested in *It Happened One Night* in 1934, sales of men's undershirts dropped, and never quite recovered. Princess Diana set off a major trend for flounced "meringue"-style wedding and prom dresses following her wedding to Prince Charles in 1981. The timeline places fashion in sequence and in context, and features many of the designers included later in the book as well as many other style makers, icons, and significant historical moments.

The awards and reference materials have been updated for this new edition; here readers will find lists of major fashion awards, by designer and year; a list of who is included in the Fashion Walk of Fame; photo credits and a bibliography of sources; and a full index. All of these elements, combined with the biographies and timeline, help to round out an understanding of who has contributed what, and when, and how.

Fashion is subjective, so too is the list of people included in this book. How did he or she impact fashion? What was the person or company's contribution to fashion? Did a designer leave a lasting imprint on the industry? Did an innovative design philosophy secure a place in fashion history? These are some of the questions that were asked as this list was compiled. Readers will have their own opinions about who should or shouldn't be included here—that kind of critical thinking and intense debate about the industry is part of what this book is meant to inspire.

I hope this book will prove useful—to students, to professionals, to those everywhere who share my passion for this extraordinary, maddening, ever-changing business.

Acknowledgments

To write a book requires a lot of effort and support from other people. For this new edition, I'd like to thank all of the designers, stylemakers, and companies who provided me with key information and some of the beautiful photographs that appear in this book. I also want to thank Karen Videtic, chair of the department of Fashion Design and Merchandising at Virginia Commonwealth University. From Fairchild Books, thanks to Olga Kontzias, executive editor; Justine Brennan, associate development editor; Liz Marotta, senior production editor; and Erin Fitzsimmons, associate art director, for their guidance and support. Thank you also to the people who provided editorial support and photo research assistance: Daniel Alfred, Chris Billias, Amy Butler, Anne Marie Calzolari, Marianne Camarda, Rob Carzone, Ashley Deiser, Dan Floros, Julie Gerstein, Carly Grafstein, Jeff Klingman, Andrea Lau, Mariah Macgregor, Adrienne Margolis, Justin Richards, Alexandra Rossomando, Anne Sanow, Sarah Silberg, and Max Wastler. On a personal note, I want to thank my husband, Thurmond Alford, Jr., for his patience and advice; my mother, Branda Price, who helped with my children when necessary; and my father, Dr. James E. Price, who gave me guidance, advice, and support.

Finally, to anyone I forgot to acknowledge, I offer you my sincere thanks.

—Holly Price Alford

My warmest thanks to the many people who have helped me with the earlier editions of this project. Thanks to the designers and their public relations representatives who returned questionnaires and supplied supplementary material; to my friends and acquaintances in the fashion field who generously shared reminiscences and personal experiences; and to all those at Fairchild, from Beth Applebome, former production editor, to Liz Marotta, senior production editor, who've moved the project from start to finish. And to Olga Kontzias, executive editor, long my editor and source of moral support, my special appreciation.

—Anne Stegemeyer

INTRODUCTION
Fashion—All About Change

The Rise of the Designer

Because the emphasis in this book is on contributions to fashion, it is important to understand something about how the role of designers has developed over time. Before designers existed, "fashion" meant that men and women followed the dress conventions of their time, which often were dictated by cultural and religious concepts, and very much by the constraints of social class. For example, a farmer's wife in eighteenth-century rural England or the new American colonies might wear a corset, but it would hardly be the elaborate version worn by royalty. Women were their own dressmakers—it was a necessary and basic skill. It was at the French court in the 1700s that the first designer to be known by name rose to prominence. ROSE BERTIN, dressmaker and confidante to Marie Antoinette, was responsible for launching many of the elaborate dress and hairstyles of that period. Bertin was exiled during the French Revolution, however, and it would be decades before the next name emerged.

CHARLES FREDERICK WORTH was from England, but he set up shop in France in 1857 and quite simply forever changed the way that dressmaking and design was done. Instead of making a few dresses at a time for individual clients, he designed entire collections; instead of displaying his designs on dress forms or miniature dolls, he showed them on live mannequins (his wife, in fact, could be considered the first fashion model). As the first truly *grand couturier*, Worth reflected a period of prosperity and conspicuous consumption in fashion and influenced other couture houses that proliferated during that period. The idea of couture and well-known designers was born.

The end of the nineteenth century and the opening years of the twentieth continued a period of prosperity that lasted until World War I. Couture houses continued to open, and name designers continued to emerge, such as PAUL POIRET, who worked with several fashionable couturiers before setting up on his own in 1904. With a genius for publicity equaled only by his talent, he became the best-known designer of his era but he was by no means the only one—JEANNE-MARIE LANVIN, CALLOT SOEURS, and COCO CHANEL were among the many designers who appeared on the scene during this time. A number of English designers—LUCILE, for example, and the tailors REDFERN and CHARLES CREED—also established themselves in Paris.

After World War I ended, there was a burst of creativity in the arts matched in fashion by an explosion of fresh design talent—MADELEINE VIONNET, Coco Chanel, ELSA SCHIAPARELLI, and NINA RICCI were among the most prominent. Most had begun working before the war but came fully into their own in the heady days of peace. War rationing of materials ended and designs became more elaborate. The exuberance of the times, reflected in the designs of the trendsetters such as Chanel and Vionnet, was a relief after the ravages of war. Fashion designers were still centered in Paris, but their designs became more accessible through copies and patterns available to people almost everywhere.

Translating Haute Couture

Although styles may have seemed to have been dictated from on high (Paris) up to this point, they also began to be created in reaction to events and inventions. After the exuberance following World War I and the 1920s, the economy of the 1930s meant that fashion had to adapt. Wealthy women might still be able to travel to Paris for their clothes during the Depression, but others needed cheap imitations made with inexpensive fabrics like cotton and rayon. The rise of leisure activities such as bicycling and boating—and, later, automobile driving—required less restrictive clothing for both men and women. In general, this period saw a rise in the demand for ready-to-wear apparel, which became possible with the invention of the sewing machine, increasing automation in manufacturing, and an absolute necessity when people went to work in factories and offices.

Democratization of Fashion

World War II (1939–1945), especially the occupation of Paris, the world's fashion capital, and the closure of many couture houses during the war under the Nazi regime changed fashion. The fashion houses in Paris had set the styles for France and other western nations, including the United States. With those houses closed, and materials being rationed during the war, Americans had to find their inspiration elsewhere. And find it they did. Designer CLAIRE MCCARDELL's work was informed by the American woman's need for practical, streamlined clothing that would allow for a more active lifestyle. CLARE POTTER, another seminal figure in American sportswear, also preferred simplicity to the ornamentation of European fashions. Streamlined and simpler designs also required less fabric, which was being rationed for wartime uniforms and other fabric needs. The military's need to manufacture uniforms and other clothing also led to the capability to mass produce clothing at cheaper prices after the war.

During this time there was Hollywood to consider too: film stars like Gary Cooper and Jane Russell and costume designers including ADRIAN and TRAVIS BANTON cast their indelible influence on what people wore. Couture rose to prominence again after the war years when French designers such as CHRISTIAN DIOR, BALENCIAGA, and GIVENCHY re-introduced glamour, but the broadening and accessibility of design that had begun would not reverse course. Boutique or diffusion collections known as *prêt-a-porter* (ready-to-wear) were a way for haute couture designers to compete and also established a new tradition of showing fashion collections at annual shows.

The stage was set for the particular call-and-response relationship between fashion design and fashion necessity, which took off in new directions in the twentieth century. The biographies and timeline included in this edition of *Who's Who* trace the path of this democratization of fashion as the twentieth century progressed.

Youthquake: The Shock Worn 'Round the World

Perhaps no period can be said to have caused so much social upheaval as the one that began in the early 1960s, when a new generation made its rebellious presence felt around the world. Fashion shifted its focus from the mature, elegant client of couture and refined design to the young and irreverent customer who wanted to wear nothing that would be suitable for her mother. Young British designers such as MARY QUANT and OSSIE CLARK gained attention and customers with their anti-establishment creations. New York's BETSEY JOHNSON introduced her playful, punkish designs for a youthful clientele and has never stopped. In Italy, designers in Milan rose as a fashion force. French design didn't entirely lose its luster, but adapted to the changing times. Powerhouse YVES SAINT LAURENT, for one, was able to craft not only the ladylike dresses worn by Catherine Deneuve in *Belle du Jour*, but also incorporated elements of Pop Art into his designs and even glamorized the hippie look with rich, flowing fabrics.

The aftershocks of the youthquake era may have diminished over time, but several concepts remain and flourish. Ideas for fashion circulate in all directions—Paris and New York are still central, but have had to recognize to the innovations coming from Italy, Spain, Belgium, England, Japan, and others. Pop culture continues to have an enormous influence on what we wear—especially the music business, from rock & roll to punk to pop to hip hop, and everything in between. Youthful styles may currently seem less extreme than they did during the 1960s, but the *idea* of youth has been fully embraced: we want to dress young even if we aren't, and the concept of "dressing for your age" has shifted dramatically.

Fashion Gone Global

Today, only a few thousand women in the world buy couture, and only a tiny number of them buy more than a piece or two and make regular purchases. This begs the question, how relevant is haute couture in today's globalized society? Certainly this not the first time the future of haute couture has been unclear. In fact, in 1965 the *New York Times* declared, "Every 10 years, the doctors assemble at the bedside of French haute couture and announce that death is imminent." But while the House of LACROIX's May 2009 decision to file for bankruptcy protection seems to be a direct nod at haute couture's demise, there are signs of its prevailing influence on today's fashion world. As an article in the September 2009 issue of *Vanity Fair*, "Toujours Coutures," stated, "At the end of January, reversing the direction of the plummeting stock market, the two grandest fashion houses in Paris, Chanel and Dior, were posting sales increases of 20 and 35 percent. As a Paris insider noted, 'Haute couture is still the best way for a designer to get noticed.'"

Haute couture may no longer be the sole incubator of new ideas, but it might not matter all that much: KARL LAGERFELD revamped Chanel in the 1990s, but he also designed a limited edition line for the mass-market clothing chain H&M. Other haute couture designers have since partnered with retailers and created signature collections with lower price points. Collaborations include THAKOON, ALEXANDER MCQUEEN, and ANNA SUI for Target, VERA WANG for Kohl's, and JIL SANDER for UNIQLO.

Fashion's customers have changed. The wealthy society women who once set the standards have been supplanted by newer role models—film stars, pop music divas, rapper entrepreneurs, and celebrities of all kinds. Indeed, branching out into designing from some other field of entertainment has become almost commonplace and yet another way for fashion and culture to continue their conversation. Designers have become celebrities themselves, no longer secluded in their studios but out in the open appearing as guests and judges on shows such as *Project Runway* and *America's Next Top Model*. There's some concern that this wide-open, increasingly global fashion market may be moving too fast, and lowering its standards. If the person interested in cutting-edge fashion today is either ignorant of or uninterested in the finer points of dressmaking, then what becomes of quality and creativity? Is the expert couture seamstress from the twentieth century irrelevant in the twenty-first? The timeline and biographies in this book suggest that this isn't the case, that the expert seamstress is now honing her skills at companies like the Los Angeles T-shirt design firm American Apparel as well as in historic fashion houses like CHLOÉ and LOUIS VUITTON. The new stylesetter of today is a young actress who designs a line of vegan shoes, who has launched her own T-shirt line on the side, seen wearing a blouse from the Gap with a GUCCI skirt. *Who's Who in Fashion* demonstrates how traditions are adapted and respect for quality and innovation persist.

Fashion is driven by our thirst for creativity and informed by social change. As designer Ossie Clark once said, "Fashion isn't just clothes. It's what's happening in everything." The changes on the fashion scene are obviously not in a class with those in the real world, but attitudes change, new talents arrive, established designers retire, and meanwhile the lowly rag trade has been transformed into a very big business.

PRE-1700 MILESTONES: 1600-1690

1616

Pocahontas travels to England dressed in European clothing

1666

England's King Charles II reforms male dress by introducing the three-piece suit

1672

First fashion magazine, *Mercure Galant*, begins publication in France

1690

The tricorne hat is introduced, to be a staple for the next 100 years

1693

London bookseller begins publication of *The Ladies' Mercury*, the first women's magazine with articles and fashion news

1698

Russian Tsar Peter the Great enforces Western styles on nobility after visiting Europe

THE EIGHTEENTH CENTURY: 1700-1790

1700

Full coats and breeches for men

Fitted bodice with stomacher, heavy trains for women

"Dressed" fashion prints show current fashions with actual fabrics glued in place

Women and men wear stays

Wigs worn by adults of all classes

Children dress like miniature adults

1704

Isaac Newton's *Opticks: Or a Treatise on the Reflections, Refractions, Inflections, & Colors of Light* explains color theory

1705

The sack dress emerges as the predominant fashion for women

1708

Import of printed silk textiles banned in England

1709

Panniers introduced

1712

London newspapers report the arrival of French fashion dolls

1715

Men's dress coats wired at the hem to stand out

Wide, circular hoops for women's skirts

Decorative Rococo style popular in architecture, fashion, and interior design, 1715–1775

1720

Painter Jean Watteau features Parisian aristocrats in plunging décollatage and gowns

The sack dress *à la française* features pleats falling loose from the neckline in back, which become known as "Watteau folds"

1725

Panniers become larger and oval-shaped, holding skirts out wide at sides

1730

Frock coat for fashionable men

1732

Hat Act forbids the export of beaver felt hats from the American colonies

1733

Development of the flying shuttle dramatically increases weaving speed

New England Weekly Journal advertises viewing of fashion dolls for two shillings at Boston dressmaker's shop

1734

Pinned and draped trains featured for mantua gowns

1735

Men's knee breeches feature ornamental buckles and buttons

Tapestry shoes for women

1740

Elaborately embroidered vests and coat cuffs for fashionable men

Women's decorated stomachers are removable to be worn with different dresses

Hair oiling and powdering is increasingly popular

1745

Blue indigo dye grown commercially in England

1748

Discovery of ruins in Pompeii prompts neoclassical revival

1750

Narrower coats and breeches for men

1752

Irish artisan uses copper plates to print illustrations on fabrics, resulting in *toile de Jouy*

1755

Louis IV's mistress Madame de Pompadour reknowned for her high hairstyle

French women adopt the less structured, English-influenced dress style *à l' anglaise*

1756

Construction resumed on the Louvre museum in Paris

Wolfgang Amadeus Mozart born in Salzburg, Germany

1759

Sumptuary laws established in China

1760

Hoops begin to be replaced by hip pads to support skirts

1762

Buckingham Palace acquired by King George III as the official residence of the British monarchy

Catherine the Great becomes ruler of Russia

Cherokee Indians visiting London combine Native American and European clothing styles

Jean-Jacques Rousseau publishes *Emile*, promoting the idea of less restrictive dress for children

1763

French coiffure show features 30 fashion dolls

1764

Fashionable young men adopt the dandy style at London's Macaroni Club

1765

Spinning jenny invented

Women's folding hoods, the calash

1769

First steam-powered automobile invented in France

1770

Soap and perfume company established by the Cleaver family in London, soon to be taken over by relative Yardley

Publication of *The Degradation of the Human Species Due to Whalebone Corsets*

Law passed in England punishing women who lured men into marriage using "false aids" such as wigs and padding to appear more beautiful

Men begin padding their calves to achieve the desired full shape

1772

French milliner ROSE BERTIN is appointed to the French court and becomes Marie Antoinette's designer and confidante

Elaborate tall hair styles all the rage in French court

Chinoiserie ornamentation style increases in popularity

1773

Doctors excuse French court women from wearing the restrictive *corps baleine* whalebone corset

1774

Looped-skirt polonaise style for women's overdresses

1776

Declaration of Independence

Philadelphia upholsterer Betsy Ross purportedly creates the first American flag

American navy introduces its first full uniform

American Revolution, 1776–1783

1778

France ships brown and blue uniform coats to the American army

Thomas Taylor of Nottingham patents the point-net machine, allowing mass production of lace

Women's panniers reach widths of 5 feet in French court

1780

Elaborately painted fans, plumes, gloves, and parasols for accessories

Simple mob caps increasingly worn indoors

1781

Marie Antoinette's hairdresser creates the "coiffure à l'Indépendance ou le Triomphe de la liberté," a high hairstyle complete with ship and masts, in celebration of American naval victories

1783

Marie Antoinette painted in "back-to-nature" thin muslin dress

Hot air balloon invented

Roller printing for fabric developed

1785

British inventor Edmund Cartwright creates the steam-powered loom

Point-net machine smuggled into France, used in Lyon and Nimes to produce silk net tulle

Trend for the *robe en chemise* dress gains popularity

1786

Germany enters the style and fashion magazine business with *Journal des Luxus und der Moden*

Commercial bleaching of fabrics begins

1787

Steamboat invented

1788

Parisian milliner Madame Eloffe creates life-size fashion doll in court dress

Europeans begin colonizing Australia

Poufed "hedgehog" hairstyle for women and men

1789

French revolutionaries called *sans-culottes*, for wearing trousers instead of knee breeches

French Revolution, 1789–1795

George Washington is sworn in as first U.S. president, in a suit of American-made fabric

Tricorne hat falls out favor to the bicorne

Boned corsets banned by law in France for health reasons

THE DIRECTOIRE PERIOD AND THE EMPIRE PERIOD: 1790–1820

1790

First U.S. census counts 3.9 million Americans

Tailcoats worn with knee breeches or trousers for men

Women's waistline begins elevating to the empire line

1792

English feminist Mary Wollstonecraft observes that "an air of fashion is but a badge of slavery"

Trousers rather than breeches become the norm for French and English men

Monarchy abolished in France

1793

Eli Whitney's cotton gin cleans more cotton in one day than a person can clean in one year

Over 16,000 executed by guillotine in French Reign of Terror, 1793–1794

Marie Antoinette executed in Paris

The guillotine inspires fashion *à la victime*, wearing loose dresses, shorn hair, and red ribbons around the neck

1794

French borrow from simpler British and Greek styles in reaction to excess of pre-Revolution period

Rebellious young French men and women flaunt comic exaggeration of above styles

1795

Brief fad for short Titus haircut among French women

Australian convicts issued cheap, ready-made clothing called "slops"

Wig powder taxed in England

1796

John Adams elected as second U.S. president

Steam engine invented

1797

Scrub board invented

1798

The Country Dyer's Assistant instructs women in home-dying cloth

1800

Josephine Bonaparte purchases Marie Antoinette's pearls for 250,000 francs

Indian word "pajama" introduced to the English language

Geometric Greek-inspired designs decorate gowns

Thomas Jefferson elected president

1801

Richer colors and heavier fabrics for women's empire-style dresses

Invention of mechanized loom for weaving patterned fabrics

1802

Women wear the hip- or knee-length pelisse coat

1803

U.S. gains territory with the Louisiana Purchase

1804

U.S. abolished slavery in states north of the Mason-Dixon Line

Napoleonic Wars, 1803–1815

Lewis & Clark make first land expedition to the Pacific Ocean, 1803–1806

French Empire declared, with Napoleon Bonaparte as Emperor and Josephine as Empress

Egyptian design popular after Napoleon's expeditions

1805

Arc de Triomphe completed in Paris

1806

Floral embroidery popular for women's gowns, scarves, and hats

1807

High-waisted Spencer jackets for women

Internal combustion engine invented in Switzerland

Trousers begin replacing knee breeches

1808

Empress Josephine is fashionable model in empire-waist chemise dresses

Military-style decoration in women's and men's dress

James Madison elected president

1809

Invention of bobbin-net machine improves machine-made lace

First Lady Dolly Madison becomes fashion icon

Empress Josephine's inventory reveals 676 dresses, 413 pairs of stockings, and 60 cashmere shawls

Brief fashion for women's laced and tucked pantalettes

1810

The pelisse coat becomes full-length

Napoleon Bonaparte divorces Empress Josephine

1811

Gothic and medieval influences appear for women

Luddite Revolt by English weavers

> War of 1812 between U.S. and England, 1812–1815

1813

Jane Austen published *Pride and Prejudice*

1814

Cossak-style trousers with foot straps for men

Napoleon defeated at Waterloo

1815

English dandy Beau Brummell declares that "the less a gentleman is noticeable, the more he is elegant"

Wellington boots popular after Duke of Wellington's victory over Napoleon

Skirts stiffened with horsehair to hold shape

1816

House of DOUCET established in Paris as a lace and bonnet business

Women's skirts begin to widen

James Monroe elected president

1817

Empire waist at its highest

1818

What goes up must come down: women's waistline begins to lower

First Brooks Brothers store opens in New York City

Women adopt the tailored redingote as outerwear

1819

U.S. gains Florida from Spain

THE ROMANTIC PERIOD: 1820–1850

1820

Missionaries introduce Western-style clothing to Hawaiian islands

Early settlers in Western U.S. adopt Native American moccasins and buckskin clothing

Corsets return with the lower, slender waistline

Gored, paneled skirts are introduced

> Number of American textile workers increases from 12,000 to over 55,000, 1820–1830

1821

Skirts begin to widen

1822

Number of slaves in U.S. has tripled since invention of cotton gin

1823

Scottish chemist Charles Macintosh patents method for waterproofing fabric

Metal eyelet holes patented

U.S. announces Monroe Doctrine, declaring no further colonization in the Western hemisphere

1824

King George IV of England has corsets made for his 50-inch waist

Female weavers in Pawtucket, Rhode Island, are first women involved in U.S. labor strike

Women's skirts become more bell-shaped

Introduction of the full gigot sleeve

John Quincy Adams elected president

1825

First public steam trains in operation

First women-only strike in New York when tailors strike for better wages

U.S. begins commercial production of calico cloth

Fashionable English men create slim waistline with stays

1826

Women's dresses feature lower waistlines

Lord & Taylor established as first major store on New York's Fifth Avenue

1827

Invention of glass-pressing machine, leading to larger store display windows

Women walk out in protest of bare-legged ballerina in New York City performance

Fan producer La Maison Duvelleroy opens in Paris

T. S. Whitmarch of Boston advertises "fashionable ready-made garments" for men

1828

The Art of Tying the Cravat is an essential guide for men

Parisian chef Marie-Antoine Carême sets fashion for double-breasted white jackets

Full pleated and gathered skirts

Wide hats and bonnets

Andrew Jackson elected president

1829

Establishment of the first regular police force in London

Publication of *The American Frugal Housewife* by Lydia Maria Child

1830

Godey's Lady's Book begins publication in Philadelphia, with articles, poetry, music, illustrations, fashion advice, and patterns

Charles Macintosh expands his Mackintosh coat business

First ready-to-wear apparel available in Parisian shops

Wide white Pelerine collars keep women's dresses modest

60% of U.S. textile workers are women

Men's slim silhouette goes out of fashion

1831

Women wear down-filled hip pads over layers of petticoats

French Foreign Legion founded, with blue tailcoat uniforms

1832

Omnibus passenger service begins in New York

Parasols increased in popularity

1833

V-shaped points introduced for dress bodices

1834

Wider, shorter skirts show off bright silk slippers

Female shoe binders across U.S. form union

1835

Beau Brummell lands in debtor's prison

French novelist George Sand (otherwise known as the Baroness Dudevant) scandalizes Parisian society by divorcing her husband and wearing men's clothing in public

Small bonnets replace large hats

1836

Women's sleeves become tighter at the top, fuller at the elbow

Sarah Hale becomes editor of *Godey's Lady's Book*, and promotes piety, purity, and domesticity

Martin Van Buren elected president

1837

Godey's Lady's Book states that "moral taste and goodness" are reflected in fashion choices

Thierry Hermès opens his harness workshop in Paris

Jewelry store Tiffany & Co. opens in New York, with the revolutionary policy of non-negotiable prices and the distinctive blue box

18-year-old Queen Victoria assumes English throne

Captain of the British ship *HMS Blazer* outfits his men in a short, boxy jacket

Collapsible silk top hat for the opera patented

18,000 women in New England are employed in shoe and boot manufacturing

1838

The blazer becomes popular with men for boating and tennis

Dark frock coats worn with colorful waistcoats for men

1839

The first successful photographic process, the daguerreotype, is introduced

1840

Queen Victoria sets the trend for white wedding dresses upon her marriage to Prince Albert

World's first postage stamp is issued, with Queen Victoria's picture

Seal coats become popular in Europe

Cashmere shawls reintroduced as larger wraps

William Henry Harrison elected president

1841

Oberlin College is first to grant university degrees to women

William Henry Harrison dies of pneumonia after not being dressed warmly enough for his inauguration; succeeded by John Tyler

1842

Frock coats and top hats for men

English writer James Bulwer-Lytton popularizes the color black for men's formal and everyday wear

Fashion periodical *Peterson's Magazine* begins publication in U.S.

Wider skirts demand more petticoats underneath

1843

Flounces and overskirts become more elaborate

Modest dark greens and browns the most popular dress colors for women

1844

First news dispatch via electric telegraph

English Factory Act limits women to 12-hour workday

Publication of *Dressmaking for Ladies: Universal Pattern Journal* published in Dresden, Germany

Women now wear an average of 15–20 pounds of clothing

James Polk elected president

1845

Elias Howe invents the sewing machine

Population of San Francisco increases from 400 to 50,000, 1845-1860

Brooks Brothers introduces ready-made suits for men, popular with gold rush prospectors

First police force established in New York City

Fashion for tight sleeves set in small armholes restricts women's movement

U.S. annexes Texas from Mexico

Paisley prints popular for men's dressing gowns

Boned bodice elongated for women

1846

First patent for the hoop skirt issued in the U.S.

Buckskin remains a staple of Western pioneer clothing

Sailor suits fashionable for boys after Queen Victoria's son has his portrait painted in one

Henry Poole transforms family's shop on London's Savile Row into high-class bespoke tailoring business

1847

Jeweler Louis-François Cartier establishes a workshop in Paris

British Factory Act reduces women's workday to 10 hours

1848

First women's rights convention held in Seneca Falls, New York

European revolutions engulf France, Austria, the German states, and Italy

U.S. gains California from Mexico

Zachary Taylor elected president

1849

Amelia Jenks Bloomer launches the Rational Dress Campaign by wearing full, ankle-length trousers topped with a short dress, thus dubbed "bloomers"

Abolitionist and slave Harriet Tubman escapes to Philadelphia

London hatmaker William Bowler invents the derby hat

Invention of the safety pin

"49ers" swarm into California for the gold rush

THE CRINOLINE PERIOD: 1850–1869

1850

First department store, Le Bon Marché, opens in Paris

U.S. population reaches 23 million

2 million slaves work in U.S. cotton fields

Women are less than 8% of the population of San Francisco

The average U.S. woman has 5.92 children

Isaac Singer invents the sewing machine with foot treadle

Zachary Taylor dies; succeeded as president by Millard Fillmore

1851

CHARLES FREDERICK WORTH marries his model and muse, Marie Vernet

R.H. Macy opens dry goods store in Haverhill, Massachusetts, serving the whaling community

London specialty grocer Charles Henry Harrod opens small shop in the exclusive Knightsbridge district

Singer sewing machines go on the market

Exhibition in London displays new inventions, including rubber

1852

Franklin Pierce elected president

1853

Bavarian immigrant Levi Strauss uses heavy French cotton cloth called "serge de Nimes" to create waist overalls for California gold rush prospectors

New York's police force adopts blue frock coats with brass buttons

Crimean War between European powers and Ottoman Empire, 1853–1856

First foreign merchants permitted in Japan

1854

LOUIS VUITTON founded in Paris as designer of quality luggage

Japan opens for trade with the West

Prince Albert is model for fashionable English men

1855

State visits between France and England result in vogue for English fashions in France

Godey's Lady's Book reaches monthly circulation of 150,000

Knitted waistcoat called the "cardigan" becomes popular after the Earl of Cardigan's successful campaign during the Crimean War

Singer expands operations to Paris

The Panama hat displayed at Paris exhibition

1856

Thomas Burberry opens his first shop in Basingstoke, England

Punch magazine ridicules the crinoline skirt when it arrives in London

Singer introduces installment buying plan

Young English chemist William Henry Perkin accidentally creates the first synthetic dye

Nurse Florence Nightingale becomes heroine in England after her service in the Crimean War

James Buchanan elected president

1857

CHARLES FREDERICK WORTH establishes his design house in Paris

New York Omnibus Co. raises fares from 7 to 12 cents for "ladies wearing hoops"

New purple "mauveine" color all the rage for women's clothing

Fringe trimming for women's dresses

Police attack women in New York protesting working conditions

Expansion of the Louvre in Paris under Napoleon III

1858

Godey's introduces gymnastics costumes for women

Manual washing machine invented

Brooks Brothers expands to a new New York location, proclaiming the store to be "the most extensive and magnificent clothing house on either continent"

"Fancy dry goods" store R.H. Macy & Co. opens in New York

1859

New England dressmaker "Madame Demorest" introduces the first paper patterns, which sell millions

Central Park opens in New York

The hoop skirt travels west with the pioneer wagon

Charles Darwin publishes *On the Origin of Species*

1860

11-year-old girl writes to candidate Abraham Lincoln, urging him to grow a beard

Subscriptions to *Godey's Lady's Book* reach 160,000

Men's loose, three-piece sack suit introduced

Luxury fashion house Emile Pingat established in Paris

Gored skirts drape over crinolines wider at the back

Nurses at London's Nightingale School of Nurses wear long dresses with starched white aprons

Invention of the band knife speeds manufacturing by cutting through several layers of cloth at one time

Red-shirted volunteer army in Italy sets trend for leader's "Garibaldi" shirt

Abraham Lincoln elected president

1861

Former slave ELIZABETH KECKLEY becomes Mary Todd Lincoln's personal dressmaker after designing her inaugural gown

Southern cotton production decreases dramatically

U.S. Civil War: 1861–1865

Due to naval blockades, Southern ladies wait for news of French fashions to reach them via Mexico and Texas

John Wanamaker opens first store in Philadelphia, selling military goods

Loose-fitting Garibaldi blouse with bishop sleeves for women

Death of her husband Prince Albert results in Queen Victoria wearing only black for the rest of her life

1862

Tiffany & Co. supplies the Union Army with swords, flags, and surgical implements

Japanese motifs appear in fabric design after exhibition in London

Northern factories record soldiers' measurements, leading to standardized patterns and ready-to-wear clothing for men

Macy's features the first department-store Santa

1863

Ebenezer Butterick begins selling clothing patterns in Massachusetts

Ladies restricted to wearing mourning colors of grey, lilac, or mauve at the English royal wedding of Prince Edward to Princess Alexandra of Denmark

J.B. Stetson designs his eponymous Western hat

Mount Holyoke College adopts overskirt and Turkish trousers as appropriate dress for women's physical education

Emancipation Proclamation abolishes slavery in U.S.

1864

Worth's famous peacock gown and headdress for the Princess de Sagan

Quick success results in New York office for Butterick Patterns

Macy's introduces elaborate window displays

Worth declares the crinoline obsolete and introduces the bustle

Lord & Taylor opens "mourning store" to dress Civil War widows

Policemen in London adopt the tall helmet hat

Abraham Lincoln reelected president

1865

Abraham Lincoln wears a custom-made Brooks Brothers coat to his second inauguration; he is assassinated wearing the same coat just over a month later

Immigration to U.S. swells: 33 million will arrive between 1865 and 1930

Andrew Johnson assumes presidency

Large, colorful, sloppy ties popular for men

The Mad Hatter in Lewis Carroll's *Alice in Wonderland* wears his signature top hat

1866

Cost of factory-made suit for men (coat, vest, trousers): $9.50

English women copy Princess Alexandra'a choker and high neckline look

Margaret Getchell becomes the first woman retail executive when she is promoted to store superintendent at Macy's

1867

Empress Eugenie of France wears a WORTH dress at the Universal Exhibition in Paris

Harper's Bazaar launches as weekly fashion newspaper

Butterick launches first magazine, *Ladies Quarterly of Broadway Fashions*

Russia sells Alaskan territory to the U.S.

1868

First rubber and canvas shoes for men's sports, later known as "sneakers"

Modernization in Japan popularizes Western-style dress

The Englishwoman's Domestic Magazine cautions against combining more than two bright colors in clothing

Narrower cage crinoline frees women's legs in front

Steam-moulding process developed to shape corsets

Ulysses S. Grant elected president

1869

Transcontinental railroad completed in U.S.

Modern bicycles invented

Baseball caps worn by first professional baseball team, the Cincinnati Red Stockings

THE BUSTLE PERIOD AND THE NINETIES: 1870-1900

1870

Celluloid is patented and used for buttons, washable collars, and cuffs

A sewing machine costs an average of $64

Franco-Prussian War, 1870–1871

20% of U.S. population is illiterate

Small black bow ties for men

Population of England reaches 26 million

1871

Tiffany introduces the "Audubon" sterling silver flatware design

JOHN REDFERN establishes English couture House of Redfern on the Isle of Wight

Great Chicago Fire

Civil war in France

1872

Mail order begins in U.S. with Montgomery Ward

Bloomingdale's opens, selling a wide variety of European fashions

Wider range of synthetic dyes results in bright, contrasting colors and patterns for women's clothing

Looser "tea gowns" introduced for women to wear at home

Narrower, elbow-length sleeves for dresses

1873

First cable cars in San Francisco

Public kindergartens open in U.S.

Levi Strauss and Nevada tailor Jacob Davis patent the first denim blue jeans with rivets and pocket stitching

Butterick launches *The Delineator* to market patterns and fashion

Economic depression in U.S.

Sears, Roebuck, and Co. catalogue offers canvas sport shoes for just 60 cents a pair

Rise in popularity of men's inexpensive ready-to-wear apparel

Remington manufactures the first typewriter

1874

Massachusetts passes 10-hour workday law

Chicago sporting goods company Sharp & Smith markets the first jockstrap

Edward Degas' painting *The Dance Class* depicts gauzy white costumes

Lawn tennis becomes a popular sport in England and U.S.

1875

Fabric and clothing emporium Liberty of London opens

Pale complexion fashionable for women

Western cowboys wear leather chaps during cattle drives

1876

Alexander Graham Bell patents the telephone

Butterick has 100 offices in the U.S. and Canada, and branches in Paris, London, Vienna, and Berlin

Rutherford B. Hayes elected president

1877

Wanamaker's expands to include both men's and women's clothing and dry goods

House of Doucet transformed into leading couture house by JACQUES DOUCET, grandson of the founders

Phonograph invented

Photography book *Street Life in London* depicts secondhand clothing store

1878

Fitted Princess dresses feature elaborate ruched bodices

1879

Hermès expands its business to saddelry

Actress Sarah Bernhardt's dramatic style all the rage upon her arrival in London with the Comédie Française

Soap maker at Proctor & Gamble accidentally invents bubble bath

Wanamaker's becomes first department store with a telephone

Thomas Edison invents the lightbulb

1880

Burberry invents waterproof gabardine, which becomes popular for mountain climbers and explorers

Harrods in London boasts over 100 employees

Rise in office employment increases demand for ready-to-wear business attire for men and women

Price of pair of store-bought cowboy boots: $7

Magazine *The Queen* depicts illustrations of the latest designs from the House of WORTH

James Garfield elected president

1881

Marshall Field & Co. established on State Street in Chicago

Boater hats popular for men

James Garfield assassinated; succeeded as president by Chester A. Arthur

Bulgari jewelry boutique established in Rome

1882

New York City gets electric lights

10,000 workers in New York City participate in the first Labor Day parade

Writer Oscar Wilde proclaims fashion to be "torture" for women

1883

Brooklyn Bridge opens in New York

Alice Vanderbilt wears diamond-encrusted white satin ballgown and battery-operated hat with lights in honor of Edison's invention

The wide "shelf bustle" becomes fashionable

Walking dresses for women feature adjustable overskirts

1884

Peter Carl Fabergé presents his first jeweled eggs to the Russian court

London clothing store Dr. Jaeger's Sanitary Woollen System opens, featuring "healthful" wovens of fine animal fibers

George Eastman invents the box camera

Maud Watson, winner of first Wimbledon ladies' title, shocks by wearing ankle-length dress for play

The Gentleman's Fashion Magazine dictates white flannels, striped coat, and straw hat for boating

Grover Cleveland elected president

1885

Oscar Wilde and George Bernard Shaw endorse Jaeger clothing

Marshall Field's department store in Chicago opens "budget floor" in its cellar

Little Lord Fauntleroy sets off fad for boys' black velvet suit with lace collar

Elaborate laced flounces adorn evening gowns

Emile Pingat produces dolman-sleeved jackets to be worn over bustle skirts

Women's bodices feature men's-style lapels and high collars

First sleeveless bathing costumes for women

1886

Tiffany introduces the diamond solitaire setting, which becomes the standard for engagement rings

Skintight bodywear designated the "leotard," after French acrobat Jules Leotard

Man is ejected from a ball at the Tuxedo Club in New York for wearing English-style dinner jacket without long tails

Statue of Liberty erected in New York City

1887

Electric trolleys introduced; operate in more than 200 cities by 1889

Macy's ad declares that the store's wares are "suitable for the millionaire, at prices in reach of the millions"

1888

Sears, Roebuck & Co. issues first mailer for jewelry and watches

Jack the Ripper terrorizes London's East End

Invention of Mum, the first deodorant

Benjamin Harrison elected president

1889

Eiffel Tower built in Paris

Impressionist painter Claude Monet begins his series of water lilies paintings

Singer introduces electric sewing machine

1890

Men adopt the belted Norfolk jacket for sports and leisure

Wasp-waisted, spirited, sporty, and feminine Gibson Girl makes her debut

Oscar Wilde declares 19th-century clothing "dreary" and adopts satin knee breeches with silk stockings

Feather boas for evening wear

Population of New York increases by 1 million, 1890–1900

Number of U.S. women working outside the home rises from 3.7 million to 5.3 million, 1890–1900

Art Nouveau design influences fabrics for evening gowns, 1890–1910

1891

JEANNE PAQUIN opens her couture house in Paris next to the House of WORTH

Creases and cuffs for men's pants become predominant

1892

First form of rayon introduced in France

Vogue magazine begins publication as a weekly New York society gazette

FAIRCHILD Publications formed in New York with men's clothing business newspaper

First zip fastener invented

Grover Cleveland elected for his second term as president

1893

Harper's Weekly praises the "evolution of sensible dress"

Shirtwaist blouse increases in popularity for women

First gas-powered car tested in Springfield, Massachusetts

Sigmund Freud begins publishing on psychoanalysis

Off-the-shoulder line popular for evening gowns

Liberty & Co. in London features flowing, smocked gowns

1894

First motion-picture parlors open in New York City, Chicago, and San Francisco

Cover of Sears catalogue emblazoned with "Book of Bargains: A Money Saver for Everyone"

LUCILE "LADY DUFF" GORDON opens her dressmaking shop Maison LUCILE in London's West End

Circular lace machine patented

Wide, puffed gigot sleeves emphasize women's shoulders

1895

Bicycling is a national craze: bloomers for women, knickers for men

Three lace-expert sisters establish the House of CALLOT SOEURS in Paris, specializing in intricate eveningwear

CHARLES WORTH dies; succeeded by his sons, Gaston and Jean Philippe

CHARLES DANA GIBSON marries Southern belle Irene Langhorne, who becomes his Gibson Girl muse and model

Full "leg-of-mutton" sleeves adorn women's shirtwaists and dresses

1896

U.S. Postal Service begins Rural Free Delivery, bringing catalogs to rural consumers

Massachusetts Audubon Society condemns feathered plumes on women's hats as "barbarous fashion"

Brooks Brothers introduces the button-down polo collar shirt for men

First modern Olympic Games in Athens

William McKinley elected president

1897

Tailor-made suits for women increase in popularity

LUCILE GORDON stages the first "catwalk"-style fashion shows and trains professional models

1898

Spanish–American War

U.S. annexes Hawaii

Trumpet skirt for women

Bloused dress front for women

1898–1907: the average adult wears 20 pounds of clothing

Palmolive hand soap introduced

Creased, cuffed trousers for men

Klondike Gold Rush attracts prospectors to the Yukon territory

Harrods department store installs the first escalator, and offers brandy to nervous customers upon reaching the top

1899

Population of New York City nears 3.5 million

Vogue initiates its pattern service

Theodore Veblen discusses fashion in his book *The Theory of the Leisure Class*

Boer War (1899–1902) introduces khaki for uniforms

Actress Sarah Bernhardt dons men's hose to play the title role in *Hamlet*

Cartier moves to the exclusive rue de la Paix, establishing it as the center of Parisian jewelery

Single-cylinder Oldsmobile introduced

THE EDWARDIAN PERIOD AND WORLD WAR I: 1900–1919

1900

Illiteracy in U.S. declines to 10.7%

U.S. population is 76 million

60% of U.S. population still lives on farms

462 shirtwaist factories operating in New York City

Average work week is 57.3 hours

Couture houses display *belle epoque* designs at the Exposition Universalle in Paris

First electric clothes washers appear

Blocky silhouette for men

S-bend "health corset" shifts women's posture forward

Spaulding makes uniforms for Olympic Games in Paris

Average cost of ready-made women's suit: $10

Japanese art on display at the World's Fair in Paris

William McKinley reelected president

1901

Jergens hand lotion introduced

Hot summer induces men to wear lighter shirts without jackets

Harper's Bazaar shifts to monthly magazine format

President McKinley assassinated; succeeded by Theodore Roosevelt

Queen Victoria of England dies, ending 63-year reign; Edward VII assumes throne

Ruff necklines popular for women

1902

Flatiron building opens in New York

1902–1910: women working outside the home rises to 25%

National Women's Trade Union League founded

Tea gowns feature the long bishop sleeve

Lunchbox and thermos invented

First Daughter Alice Roosevelt becomes famous for her outfits and antics

Macy's moves to Herald Square flagship location

1903

Viscose rayon fabric introduced

Actress Lillie Langtry appears in *Vogue*

Wright brothers fly first airplane at Kitty Hawk, North Carolina

The front-button negligee shirt for men is worn for sports and casual activities

Butterick building at Spring and MacDougal Streets in downtown Manhattan opens

Motoring gear includes duster coats, caps, brimmed hats with veils, goggles, gloves, and boots

Ehrlich Brothers store in New York holds fashion show to attract middle-class customers

The Great Train Robbery is first full-length feature film

1904

Colgate launches first toothpaste

Isadora Duncan makes her U.S. debut

Women's sleeves become elbow length and fuller cut

Dressmaker Lane Bryant opens New York boutique specializing in women's maternity dresses

First permanent wave at hair salon in London

Shetland sweaters for men by Brooks Brothers

Cartier designs the first wristwatch for Brazilian aviator Alberto Santos-Dumont, and the "Santos" style becomes a hit

Theodore Roosevelt reelected president

1905

Spiegel catalogue launched

Vanderbilt Cup Race establishes automobile racing as a society event

Slimmer princess silhouette for women appears

Rolex Watch Company established in Geneva, Switzerland

Fashionable Arrow Collar Man debuts as advertising campaign for detachable collars

Albert Einstein announces the theory of relativity

1906

San Francisco earthquake and fire

MARIANO FORTUNY designs his pleated silk Delphos gown

Pompadour hair style for women

Filmy, lacy afternoon frocks featured in *The Delineator*

Short jackets and circular skirt suits

Van Cleef & Arpels jewelry business established in Paris

1907

U.S. financial panic

Sears catalogue circulation reaches 3.6 million

Loosely-cut wraps and kimono coats for women

Swimmer Annette Kellerman arrested for wearing a one-piece sleeveless swimsuit on a beach near Boston

Number of movie houses in U.S. reaches 5,000

44,000 automobiles manufactured in U.S.

Cincinnati surgeon invents Odo-Ro-No deodorant

Straight-line corsets edge out the S-shaped curve

Gored skirts

1908

Ford introduces the Model T, which sells for $850

U.S. unemployment rate at 8%

Good Housekeeping features the shirtwaist dress

Filene's department store in Boston opens the Automatic Bargain Basement

Maytag patents first electric washing machine

15,000 women march in New York demanding higher pay, shorter hours, voting rights, and abolition of child labor

William Taft elected president

1909

The Ballets Russes debut in Paris with exotic costumes

Orientalism influence in women's fashion

Vogue's first cover featuring a photograph

First newsreel film shown in Paris

HATTIE CARNEGIE opens her first dress and millinery shop in New York

Young publisher Condé Nast buys *Vogue* and shifts its focus to fashion

National Association for the Advancement of Colored People (NAACP) founded by group of multiracial activists

Fortuny patents his pleating process

Selfridges department store opens on London's Oxford Street, with innovative displays and entertainment

1910

High-waisted empire line popular for women

Women's Wear Daily begins publication

1910s: shift to slimmer and lighter clothing for both men and women

George V becomes King of England after Edward's death

Mexican Revolution, 1910–1920

U.S. colleges and universities now enroll 350,000 students

PAUL POIRET becomes first designer to launch a fragrance

LUCILE GORDON introduces the slit skirt

Boy Scouts of America founded, with uniforms based on those of the U.S. Army

Cloakmakers' strike leads to increased union power for garment industry workers

Brooks Brothers brings the English polo coat to the U.S.

1911

Poiret creates the hobble skirt

Women adopt empire styling

Cubist exhibit in Paris

Triangle shirtwaist factory fire kills 146 working women and girls; factory owners acquitted

Vogue speculates whether women's trousers are "audacicous and sensational" or "demure and coquettish"

Men's silhouette begins to slim

Small dogs become a fashion accessory

1912

20,000 textile workers strike in Lawrence, Massachusetts, leading to public outcry and congressional investigation

LUCILE GORDON survives the sinking of the *Titanic*

Poiret tours Europe and the U.S. to show his designs, 1912–1914

MADELEINE VIONNET establishes her Paris couture house

Vernon and Irene Castle's "Castle Walk" is a U.S. dance craze

Dark, pin-striped suits for men's business attire

Film fan magazines proliferate

Lucien Vogel launches French fashion magazine *La Gazette du Bon Ton*, featuring illustrations of couture

Slim line for men's suits featured in *Haberdasher*

Ford introduces the assembly line for mass-producing automobiles

Florence Nightingale Graham introduces European cosmetics to American women through her new Elizabeth Arden business, along with the idea of "makeovers" in her salon

Woodrow Wilson elected president

1913

Income tax begins in U.S.

Marcel Duchamp's painting "Nude Descending a Staircase" causes furor at the Armory Show in New York

Gideon Sundback invents the slide fastener (later called the zipper)

PRADA founded as a leather-goods company in Milan

LUCILE GORDON shows draped tea gowns and evening dresses for the spring season

Orientalism reflected in POIRET's harem and lampshade look

1914

World War I: 1914–1919

Panama Canal opens

WWI begins in Europe

Black, white, tan, & blue fashionable due to wartime color dye rationing

American Mary Phelps Jacobs patents the brassiere; later sells patent to Warners for just $1,500

JEANNE LANVIN designs the *robe de style*

Irene Castle shows off her bobbed hair and short, swirly LUCILE dresses in Broadway ragtime hit *Watch Your Step*

EDNA WOOLMAN CHASE becomes editor of *Vogue*

Russian artist and costume designer ERTÉ creates illustrations for *La Gazette du Bon Ton*

Charlie Chaplin makes his film debut in *Making a Living*

Thomas Burberry designs the trench coat for the British War Office

1915

Skirts rise to the ankles

Trench coats and greatc oats for soldiers on the Western front

Belted pullover sweater for women credited to CHANEL

Explorer Sir Ernest Shackleton wears Jaeger on artic expedition

Theda Bara portrays "The Vamp" in *A Fool There Was*

Military influence in women's coats and caps

Maybelline introduces first cake mascara

First electric clothes dryers in use

Invention of lipstick in round metal tube

Lane Bryant expands with stores in Brooklyn, Chicago, and Detroit

1916

British *Vogue* begins publication

The brassiere arrives from France

German army issues body armor to soldiers

Margaret Sanger opens first U.S. birth control clinic

English tailor JOHN REDFERN creates the first women's uniform for the Red Cross

First U.S. shopping center opens in Lake Forest, Illinois

Keds canvas sneakers introduced

Max Factor markets first commercial eye shadow and brow pencil

ERTÉ joins *Harper's Bazaar* as fashion illustrator

Congress votes to put $75 million into highway construction

Woodrow Wilson reelected president

1917

U.S. enters WWI

Converse launches its All-Star athletic shoe

LUCILE GORDON designs ready-to-wear dresses for Sears, Roebuck & Co.

Women join the armed services; uniforms include ankle-length skirts

"Womanalls" popular in home-front factories

Cloche hat debuts in Paris

Exotic dancer Mata Hari executed for treason in France

Metal shortage influences corset designs

Russian Revolution topples monarchy; succeeded by Communists

1918

Compulsory schooling laws become nationwide

Increase in sales of women's cosmetics

Wartime production decreases U.S. unemployment rate to 1.3%

FENDI established in Rome, specializing in furs, handbags, and luggage

LUCILE GORDON's fashion empire grosses over $2 million

Worldwide influenza epidemic kills more than war; practical fashion for gauze masks

Russian royal family executed

Women's Wear Daily depicts safety veil as protection against flu

1919

Congress approves Prohibition

Bauhaus center for contemporary design established in Germany

Actress Mary Pickford's frilly, little-girl style

Mass-produced machine-made lace relegates handmade to the past

General Motors introduces installment buying

WWI ends in November

High U.S. war casualties puts American women into black mourning, followed by a decline of the custom

THE TWENTIES, THIRTIES, AND WORLD WAR II: 1920-1946

1920

American women granted the right to vote

Prohibition, 1920-1933

First commercial radio station begins broadcasting

French *Vogue* begins publication

Fictional Arrow Collar Man is receiving over 17,000 fan letters a day

Ready-to-wear clothing for women increases in popularity

CHANEL introduces yachting trousers for women

The dress of the decade makes its film debut in *The Flapper*

First diagonally-striped "repp" ties from Brooks Brothers

Warren G. Harding elected president

1921

Bathing suits are part of the first Miss America pageant

Consumer prices plunge

Kotex appears on the market

Basketball star Chuck Taylor hired by Converse to promote its All-Star shoe

GUCCI company founded in Florence, Italy

Actor Rudolph Valentino stars in *The Sheik*

James Joyce's *Ulysses* banned in the U.S. as "obscene"

First birth-control clinic opened in England

1922

King Tut's tomb discovered, leading to Egyptian fashion craze

POIRET introduces pyjamas as leisure wear

Vogue's first fashion shoot

Mussolini establishes fascist regime in Italy

MAN RAY begins fashion photography for *Vogue*

1923

Economic upswing begins

Suntanning becomes fashionable

Tube silhouette for women

HATTIE CARNEGIE opens her own boutique, where VIONNET knockoffs can be had for $50

The Arrow Collar Man inspires the Broadway musical *Helen of Troy, New York*

Dance craze "the Charleston" demands shorter skirts

Warren G. Harding dies of heart attack; succeeded as president by Calvin Coolidge

Lane Bryant's plus-size clothing outsells maternity wear

Hugo Boss establishes men's wear company in Metzingen, Germany

Chuck Taylor's name added to the Converse All-Star logo

Purchasing power of the dollar doubles, 1923-1927

1924

Liquor smuggling profits reach $40 million

Maiden Form popularizes the contour bra

JEAN PATOU designs Wimbledon champion Suzanne Lenglen's tennis clothes

Women adopt the short shingle bob

Peacock feather fans

Stretch fabric for bathing suits

The Burberry check print is created

Opening of Saks Fifth Avenue

French designer LILLY DACHÉ opens shop in New York

André Breton founds the surrealist movement

MAN RAY creates his image *Le Violin d'Ingres*

First Macy's Thanksgiving Day parade

Calvin Coolidge reelected president

Height of Harlem Renaissance, 1924-1929

1925

Josephine Baker dances braless at the Folies Bergère

VIONNET's gown with geometric inserts

Jazz thrives with Louis Armstrong's Hot Five

Fitzgerald's *The Great Gatsby* published

Acetate fabric introduced

Art deco exposition in Paris

"Oxford Bags" wide trousers for men

"Zipper" trademarked by B.F. Goodrich

1926

John Powers modeling agency opens

CHANEL introduces the little black dress

Number of American millionaires reaches 11,000

Raccoon coats popular for men

Buying on credit reaches all-time high in U.S.

"Plus-fours" knickers and Fair Isle sweaters worn by Prince of Wales

Gertrude Ederle is first woman to swim the English Channel

Rudolph Valentino dies, causing mass hysteria among female fans

Women's dresses rise above the knee

1927

Charles Lindburgh's nonstop transatlantic flight

The Jazz Singer is first "talkie" film

First Academy Awards presented

Pointed handkerchief hemlines for women's gowns

ELSA SCHIAPARELLI opens her Paris boutique and makes her *Vogue* debut with the "trompe l'oeil" sweater

Clara Bow dubbed the "It Girl"

Babe Ruth becomes first baseball player to hit 60 home runs in one season

Women rush to copy the Louise Brooks bob

Female tennis stars try men's trousers on the court

1928

Disney debuts Mickey Mouse

Jeans appear as fashion apparel

Men's Wear explains the cummerbund to American men

Billboard Magazine launches its first weekly music charts

Cocktail of the moment is Dubonnet and gin

Women copy Greta Garbo's slouch hat in *A Woman of Affairs*

Hemlines begin to lower

Penicillin introduced

Speedo introduces the racerback swimsuit

Women granted the right to vote in England

Over 400,000 Americans travel abroad

"Double Bubble" bubble gum invented

Herbert Hoover elected president

1929

U.S. divorce rate climbs past 16%

Gang violence results in Saint Valentine's Day massacre in Chicago

Sears catalogues sent to 15 million U.S. homes

Mies van der Rohe designs the Barcelona chair

CHANEL's wool jersey suits promote a "total look"

First sunglasses sold by Foster Grant company

PATOU returns women's waistlines to their natural position in his collection

CECIL BEATON photographs heiress Nancy Cunard with her signature stacked bangle bracelets

U.S. unemployment rate climbs from 8.5% to 29.9%, 1929–1932

Publication of *A Room of One's Own* by Virginia Woolf

U.S. stock market crash in October

1930

Over 1,300 U.S. banks have failed

Preshrunk fabric process patented

CHANEL signs contract with United Artists to design costumes for Hollywood stars

Drought and dust storms plague central U.S., 1930–1939

Marlene Dietrich wears a man's suit in *Morocco*

Chrysler building opens in New York

Max Factor invents lipgloss

Philadelphia tailors Marliss and Max Rudolphker produce the first mass-market, ready-to-wear tuxedos

Neoprene invented

1931

Elastic yarn introduced

Empire State Building opens in New York

U.S. Rubber Company introduces Lastex

Edward G. Robinson displays the gangster look in *Little Caesar*

New and improved Technicolor used in feature film *The Runaround*

VIONNET's bias-cut gowns

Vogue depicts women's naval-style, bell-bottom trousers

1932

Joan Crawford's frilly *Letty Lynton* dress (designed by ADRIAN) inspires sales of a half-million knockoffs at Macy's

Stretch cuffs for sportswear featured at the Winter Olympics in Lake Placid, New York

Lord & Taylor begins promoting American designers

Hit song "Brother Can You Spare a Dime"

Fashion editor CARMEL SNOW creates fashion world furor when she leaves *Vogue* for *Harper's Bazaar* after just three years

Founding of the Fashion Originators Guild of America to protect designers from copying and piracy

Amelia Earhart is first woman to make solo transatlantic flight; designs flying clothes for female pilots

Pablo Picasso's painting *Girl Before a Mirror*

Bras begin to feature cup sizing and adjustable straps

Franklin Delano Roosevelt elected president

1933

Platinum blonde Jean Harlow stars in *Bombshell*

Tennis star Alice Marble wears shorts at Wimbledon

French tennis star René Lacoste starts his eponymous company featuring the embroidered crocodile logo

Grant Wood's painting *American Gothic* is a sensation at the Chicago World's Fair

Breck introduces shampoo for different hair types: dry, normal, and oily

Gold Diggers of 1933 provides Depression escapism

Amelia Earhart designs clothing for "the woman who lives actively," sold in Macys and other department stores

Roosevelt's New Deal legislation announced

Hitler assumes power in Germany

Hugo Boss designs uniforms for Nazi troops and Hitler Youth

End of Prohibition

1934

Increasing acceptance of trousers for women leads to the panty girdle

Clark Gable appears bare-chested in *It Happened One Night*, causing steep drop in sales of men's undershirts

Wider shoulders for women's clothing

Implementation of Hays Code for films, including the ban on nudity, "suggestive dancing," vulgar language, or illicit sex

Dionne quintuplets born in Canada and set off media frenzy

Esquire lauds the English drape suit for men

Fred Astaire and Ginger Rogers dance away in *The Gay Divorcee*

Jazz singer and bandleader Cab Calloway performs in white tie and tophat at The Cotton Club in Harlem

Introduction of "Lady Levi's," the first jeans for women

National Recovery Act limits work week to 40 hours, sets minimum employment age at 16, and specifies minimum wage

1935

Social Security established

SCHIAPARELLI's hooded Grecian gowns

Revolution in men's underwear when Jockey shorts are patented

DuPont patents nylon

Katherine Hepburn glamorizes trousers

Child star Shirley Temple sets off copycat fashion craze for girls

Works Progress Administration establishes sewing shops

Germany begins first television broadcasts

Italy invades Ethiopia

1936

Jesse Owens wins 4 gold medals at the Olympic Games in Berlin

Edward VIII abdicates the throne to marry American divorcee Wallis Simpson; her simple dress is designed by MAINBOCHER

DIANA VREELAND begins her fashion editorial career at *Bazaar* with her column "Why Don't You"

LILLY DACHÉ's glamorous hats

Tampax patented

Spanish Civil War, 1936–1939

Magli brothers establish Bruno Magli shoe factory in Bologna, Italy

Franklin Roosevelt reelected president

1937

Debut of the Hermès scarf

MAINBOCHER designs bias-cut dress for Wallis Simpson's wedding to the Duke of Windsor

The peplum suit

SCHIAPARELLI collaborates with artist Salvador Dali on her "lobster" dress

Golden Gate Bridge opens in San Francisco

Cole Porter's "I've Got You Under My Skin" is song hit of the year

Japanese forces invade northern China

JACQUES FATH opens couture house in Paris

First fully automatic washing machine introduced

Esquire declares the zipper fly to be the "newest tailoring idea for men"

Amelia Earhart disappears during her flight over the Pacific

Disney's *Snow White* is first full-length animated film

1938

Nylon stockings introduced

NORMAN HARTNELL becomes official dressmaker to the British royal family

FERRAGAMO introduces the platform shoe

Vogue publishes its first annual American edition

Tourism now the third largest U.S. industry

Debutante Brenda Frazier appears on the cover of *Life* magazine in a white strapless dress

Germany annexes Austria and part of Czechoslovakia

1939

WWII begins in Europe when Germany invades Poland

Nylon fibers on display at the "world of tomorrow" World's Fair in Flushing, New York

NBC television broadcasts the opening of the World's Fair, and televisions go on sale to the public

Large sunglasses emulate Hollywood glamour

Publication of John Steinbeck's *The Grapes of Wrath*

Gone With the Wind encourages new interest in the crinoline and snoods

Marlene Dietrich ignores pleas to return to her native Germany and becomes a U.S. citizen

1940

Nylon bras and girdles marketed

German army occupies the fashion capital of Paris; many couture houses close for the duration of the war

American designers gain prominence due to Parisian fashion shutdown

U.S. registers 32 million cars on the road

Publication of Ernest Hemingway's *For Whom the Bell Tolls*

California's population expands by 70%, 1940s

Carmen Miranda makes her Hollywood debut in her signature platform sandals and fruit headdress in *Down Argentine Way*

Eleanor Lambert inaugurates the U.S. Best-Dressed List

Roosevelt elected president for third term

1941

British chemists invent polyester

HATTIE CARNEGIE protégé NORMAN NORELL teams up with Anthony Traina to form Traina-Norell

Clothing rationing in England, 1941–1948

Coach leather goods founded in New York, inspired by the baseball glove

U.S. enters WWII after Japan bombs Pearl Harbor

Red, white, and blue clothing becomes popular

1942

CLAIRE MCCARDELL's "popover" dress is a hit

Women adopt hairnets, scarves, and the "Victory Roll" hairdo

Humphrey Bogart's trench coat and hat in *Casablanca*

U.S. Navy issues the T-shirt

Rosie the Riveter becomes a fashion icon with "We Can Do It!" poster

U.S. clothing rationing forbids pleats, pockets, ruffles, zippers, wide lapels, and trouser cuffs, 1942–1946

Y-front opening added to men's underwear

Elizabeth Arden creates "Montezuma Red" lipstick to match red trim on women's armed forces uniforms

CLAIRE MCCARDELL shows models in black Capezio ballet flats

British designers team up to create the "Utility Collection"

MAINBOCHER designs uniforms for U.S. Navy WAVES

Betty Grable cheers up servicemen worldwide in her iconic pinup shot

Sales of women's slacks increase

U.S. marriage rate at all-time high

1943

Hawaiian and Polynesian prints popular

Eisenhower jacket for men

The one-piece playsuit

Fashion magazines give tips for drawing "stocking seams" on legs

MCCARDELL brings the leotard into fashion

Film director Howard Hughes uses aircraft cantilever techniques to design Jane Russell's steel underwire push-up bra in *The Outlaw*

Photographer IRVING PENN begins working for *Vogue*

First known use of the term "supermodel"

Fashion house of ALIX GRÈS closed in Paris after she defiantly shows first collection in French patriotic red, white, and blue

First Coty American Fashion Critics award for millinery bestowed on LILLY DACHÉ

Lena Horne showcases her glamorous style in *Stormy Weather*

Baggy zoot suits flaunt wartime fabric restrictions

American soldiers wear Levi's jeans and jackets overseas

1944

D-Day invasion in Normandy

American troops liberate Paris

Traveling exhibit *Théâtre de la Mode* featuring two-foot-tall mannequins wearing French couture helps raise funds for war relief

"Bobby-soxers" wear ankle socks and saddle shoes

Bomber jackets inspired by fighter pilots

Maidenform designs pigeon-carrier vests for paratroopers

Seventeen magazine begins publication

Roosevelt elected president for fourth term

1945

Dirndl skirts

SCHIAPARELLI launches her perfume Shocking, coining the term "shocking pink"

French designers JACQUES HEIM and Louis Reard introduce the bikini

PIERRE BALMAIN opens his Paris couture house

RICHARD AVEDON becomes staff photographer for *Harper's Bazaar*

Roosevelt dies; Harry Truman becomes president

U.S. drops atomic bombs on Hiroshima and Nagasaki, Japan

WWII ends

PIERRE BALMAIN shows bell-shaped skirts with small waists; later claims first credit for fashion's postwar "new look"

Car ownership in U.S. doubles, 1945–1955

Frozen foods become available on the consumer market

1946

Returning soldiers bring duffle coats and cotton T-shirts back to the homefront

Postwar explosion in U.S. birth rate, 1946–1964

Rita Hayworth wears a black strapless satin gown by designer JEAN LOUIS in *Gilda*

Men's pant legs become cuffed again

Minnetonka Moccasin company established

MAINBOCHER designs Girl Scout uniforms

Physician Klaus Maertens develops a lace-up boot with an air-padded sole to help him recovery from a skiing injury

First edition of Dr. Benjamin Spock's *Common Sense Book of Baby and Child Care* published

THE NEW LOOK: FASHION CONFORMITY PREVAILS: 1947–1960

1947

CHRISTIAN DIOR's first solo collection is a smash hit with his "New Look"

McCall's declares "the short skirt is out of the running"

Nylon becomes available again after war rationing

First commercial microwave ovens

Princess Elizabeth of England marries Prince Philip wearing a gown by NORMAN HARTNELL

U.S. House Committee on Un-American Activities begins hearings

Planned suburb of Levittown in New York

United Nations approves establishment of Israel

England grants independence to India

Women in New York picket stores selling Dior's New Look

First H&M store opens in Sweden

1948

Polaroid camera invented

Berlin Airlift

Marshall Plan begins in Europe

German shoe mogul brothers Adi and Rudi part ways, resulting in the formation of separate Adidas and Puma brands

Copies of New Look dresses sell for $24.95 in New York stores

Invention of Velcro

JACQUES FATH quadruples sales after U.S. publicity tour

Harry Truman reelected president

1949

People's Republic of China founded

Cheongsam banned in China in favor of the unisex Mao suit

Vogue features the Brooks Brothers pink button-down shirt for women

Alaska becomes the 49th U.S. state

Abstract expressionist painter Jackson Pollock featured in *Life* magazine

LILLY DACHÉ launches clothing line

DIOR shows strapless evening gowns with full skirts

Russia detonates its first atomic bomb

North Atlantic Treaty Organization (NATO) formed

1950

30% of global population is urban

U.S. population is 161 million

HARDY AMIES designs Princess Elizabeth's wardrobe for her first royal tour of Canada

Korean War: 1950–1953

DuPont produces acrylic

ALIX GRÈS sculpts Grecian-style pleated gowns directly on live models

HATTIE CARNEGIE designs uniforms for the Women's Army Corps

PIERRE CARDIN couture house opens in Paris

Diner's Club issues the first credit card

IRVING PENN collaborates with fashion model wife Lisa Fonssagrives for photographs of the Paris collections

1951

First collective couture show by Italian designers held in Florence

Premiere of *I Love Lucy*

Marlon Brando sports the "wife-beater" in *A Streetcar Named Desire*

Chinos

Publication of J.D. Salinger's *Catcher in the Rye*

JAMES GALANOS opens his fashion company in California

Teens and young men choose between the crew cut or the "D.A."

1952

Women's coats with batwing sleeves

The tight "sweater girl" look returns with patterns and embellishments

Dr. Maertens and partner open a factory in Munich to meet the demand for their boots

EDNA WOOLMAN CHASE retires as editor-in-chief of *Vogue* after a 56-year tenure at the magazine

Queen Elizabeth II assumes the British throne

Dwight D. Eisenhower elected president

1953

Eisenhower wears homburg to inauguration rather than customary top hat

First color TVs available

Teenage girls popularize felt circle skirts

Joseph Stalin dies

Pregnant Lucille Ball on *I Love Lucy* wears maternity fashions

GUCCI opens first store in New York City

Queen Elizabeth II wears NORMAN HARTNELL dress to her coronation

Marlon Brando wears the biker look in *The Wild One*

Discovery of DNA structure

Debut of *TV Guide* and *Playboy* magazine

1954

CHANEL reopens her Paris design house

Knee-length Bermuda shorts for women and men

Pedal-pushers

First Holiday Inn opens

Interest in western wear sparked by increasing number of Americans taking car trips

U.S. Supreme Court declares school segregation to be unconstitutional in landmark case *Brown v. the Board of Education*

Americans wear cardboard glasses to enjoy the 3-D effects of *The Creature from the Black Lagoon*

Bill Haley and the Comets have a smash hit with "Rock Around the Clock"

First color television broadcast in U.S.

DIOR introduces men's suiting features to women's clothes

Dorothy Dandridge is first African American to be nominated for Best Actress for her performance in *Carmen Jones*

CHARLES WORTH's great-grandson sells the fashion house to PACQUIN

1955

Bus boycott in Montgomery, Alabama, instigated by Rosa Parks

Sportswear designer CLAIRE MCCARDELL appears on the cover of *Time*

Disneyland opens in Anaheim, California

MARY QUANT opens youth-oriented Bazaar boutique in London

James Dean sports the T-shirt, jeans, and leather jacket look in *Rebel Without a Cause*

"A-line" introduced by DIOR

SALVATORE FERRAGAMO debuts the stiletto heel

LILLY DACHÉ appears as mystery guest on TV's popular *What's My Line*

Pat Boone's white buck shoes

Marilyn Monroe's white dress flies up over the subway grate in *The Seven Year Itch*

Grace Kelly embodies cool glamour in *To Catch a Thief*

McDonald's opens for business

Polio vaccine

1956

CRISTÓBAL BALENCIAGA creates the sack dress

Gregory Peck portrays *The Man in the Gray Flannel Suit*

Grace Kelly marries Prince Rainier of Monaco in a dress designed by Hollywood costume designer Helen Rose

PIERRE CARDIN is first European designer to establish a business in Japan

Fashion magazines depict models in colored eye shadow

Fedora hat for men

Publication of Allen Ginsberg's poem "Howl"

Leotards, ballet flats, and "sloppy joe" sweaters typify the beatnik look for young women

Elvis Presley debuts his rock n' roll look on *The Ed Sullivan Show*

PIERRE BALMAIN designs Brigitte Bardot's clothing for *And God Created Woman*

Hermès "Kelly bag" becomes a classic after the new Princess of Monaco is photographed with one

Eisenhower reelected president

1957

Publication of Jack Kerouac's *On the Road*

21-year-old apprentice YVES SAINT LAURENT takes over at House of Dior when DIOR dies

American women buy knock-offs of CHANEL's collarless wool suit by the thousands

European Common Market established

French designer Ted Lapidus opens both haute couture studio and unisex boutique

Hip-huggers first introduced by Ardee

Doris Day shows off her good-girl style in *The Pajama Game*

Eisenhower sends federal troops to protect black students at newly desegretated schools in Little Rock, Arkansas

USSR launches Sputnik, the first satellite to orbit the earth

Ed Sullivan broadcasts "Elvis the Pelvis" from the waist up only

Audrey Hepburn glamorizes the beatnik look in *Funny Face*

Peak of U.S. baby boom, with a baby born every seven seconds

1958

Bank of America introduces the Visa card

Jeans displayed as part of the American exhibit at the World's Fair in Brussels

London's "Teddy Boys" adopt drainpipe trousers

Founding of the American Football League

American NORMAN NORELL is first designers elected to the Coty Hall of Fame

First Ebony Fashion Fair travels to ten U.S. cities, with proceeds going to charity

Skirts begin to shorten

Elizabeth Taylor's white silk slip in *Cat on a Hot Tin Roof*

1.4 million Americans travel abroad

Charles de Gaulle becomes president of France

1959

Mattel Co. introduces the Barbie doll

Spandex invented

DuPont trademarks Lycra

Hawaii becomes the 50th state

Revolution in Cuba brings Fidel Castro to power

Guggenheim Museum designed by Frank Lloyd Wright opens in New York

Dancing to the "twist"

Sandra Dee stars in surfer film *Gidget*

S.I. Newhouse purchaes controlling interest in Condé Nast publishing business

Pantyhose introduced

1960

U.S. population is 176 million

MARC BOHAN assumes takes over at House of DIOR after SAINT LAURENT suffers a nervous breakdown

Birth control pills approved by the Food and Drug Administration

Invention of optical light laser

Barbie gets a boyfriend, Ken

The song "Itsy-Bitsy, Teeny-Weeny, Yellow Polka-Dot Bikini" is a hit

Italian designer Princess Irene Galitzine introduces palazzo pajamas

NORMAN NORELL introduces the mermaid dress

Levi's opens racially integrated plant in Blackstone, Virginia

Dr. Martens boots arrive in England and become a hit with postmen, police officers, and factory workers

Estimated one million American families have bomb shelters

80% of Americans own televisions

Debut of designer Richard Blackwell's "Ten Worst Dressed Women" list includes Brigitte Bardot, Shelley Winters, and Lucille Ball

John F. Kennedy elected president

THE SIXTIES AND SEVENTIES: STYLE TRIBES EMERGE: 1961–1979

1961

Kennedy is first president to be sworn in without a hat; sales drop and the and the custom fades

OLEG CASSINI appointed as Jackie Kennedy's official dressmaker

Women copy Jackie Kennedy's bouffant hair and pillbox hat

Soviets erect the Berlin Wall

Bay of Pigs invasion of Cuba

Butterick purchases Vogue Patterns from Condé Nast

Russians put first man in space; Americans follow less than a month later

Jeans and sneakers exemplify gang style in *West Side Story*

HUBERT DE GIVENCHY designs Audrey Hepburn's clothes in *Breakfast at Tiffany's*

Audrey Hepburn inducted into the International Best-Dressed List Hall of Fame

Disposable diapers introduced to the market

1962

First overseas television broadcast

SAINT LAURENT launches his own design house

Pop art exhibit at the Museum of Modern Art in New York

Marilyn Monroe sings happy birthday to President Kennedy wearing a flesh-toned, skin-tight rhinestone dress by costume designer JEAN LOUIS

Andy Warhol's *Campbell's Soup Cans* painting

FENDI hires KARL LAGERFELD to design furs

First Target store opens in Roseville, Minnesota

BONNIE CASHIN designs Coach purse inspired by the paper shopping bag

Council of Fashion Designers of America (CFDA) is founded

Marilyn Monroe dies in August

DIANA VREELAND becomes editor of *Vogue*

Ursula Andress wears a white bikini in the James Bond film *Dr. No*

Cuban Missile Crisis brings U.S. and USSR to the brink of war

1963

Betty Friedan publishes *The Feminine Mystique*

Weight Watchers is founded

GALANOS presents the smock dress

London's MARY QUANT launches her Ginger Group line of less expensive separates

Martin Luther King, Jr. delivers his "I have a dream" speech during civil rights march in Washington, D.C.

Comfort-oriented ECCO footwear is founded in Denmark

Poet Sylvia Plath's autobiographical novel *The Bell Jar* fictionalizes her experience as an intern at *Mademoiselle*

Ted Lapidus scandalizes couture world by opening mass-market boutique in the Belle Jardiniere department store

President Kennedy assassinated in Dallas; Lyndon B. Johnson becomes president

1964

The Beatles arrive in the U.S. with "mop top" haircuts

Vietnam War, 1964–1975

ANDRÉ COURRÈGES shows skirts well above the knee in his futuristic, space-age collection

Monokini by RUDI GERNREICH

Trendy, inexpensive Biba boutique opens in London

Bell-bottoms make first appearance as flamenco pants

First *Sports Illustrated* swimsuit issue features the bikini

Civil Rights Bill passed by Congress

Martin Luther King, Jr., becomes youngest man to win Nobel Peace Prize at age 35

Dr. Strangelove satirizes the atomic bomb scare

Levi's introduces Sta-Prest slacks

Boxer Muhammad Ali defeats Sonny Liston for the World Heavyweight Championship

SAINT LAURENT opens first ready-to-wear line and boutique, Rive Gauche

Fashion-forward H&M expands to open stores in England, Denmark, Norway, Switzerland, and Germany

Johnson reelected president

1965

MARY QUANT raises hemlines higher, making the miniskirt official

Race riots in Los Angeles spread to other U.S. cities

Vidal Sassoon creates his famous angled bob

California group The Beach Boys have three #1 hits

SAINT LAURENT's geometric "Mondrian" shift dresses bring pop art to haute couture

"Swinging" London centered on Carnaby Street

"Mod" clothes for men introduced to the American market

Diana Rigg wears a leather catsuit designed by John Bates on *The Avengers*

Seamless pantyhose introduced

Levi's expands to Europe and Asia

Voting Rights Act enacted

Debutante Edie Sedgwick is fashion icon and Andy Warhol muse

Seventeen magazine states that teenage girls purchase 20% of all apparel and 23% of all cosmetics sold in the U.S.

BILL BLASS appears in his own ad, captioned "Who needs Paris when you can steal from yourself?"

GERNREICH patents the "no-bra" bra

1966

America's apparel industry is worth $15 billion

The shift dress

Nancy Sinatra sings "These Boots Are Made for Walkin'"

MARY QUANT launches cosmetics line

National Organization for Women founded

Black Panther Party founded; adopt military-style uniform & berets

Kevlar patented, later used in bulletproof vests

Paper dress fad

Brigitte Bardot sets off fad for ROGER VIVIER's patent-leather Pilgrim Buckle shoe

SAINT LAURENT creates the "Le Smoking" tuxedo pant suit for women

PACO RABANNE shows dresses made of linked plastic discs

Star Trek debuts on television

Female reporter denied entry to fashionable New York restaurants for wearing a pantsuit

Stick-thin English model Twiggy is dubbed "The Face of '66"

1967

Green Bay Packers win the first Super Bowl

"Summer of Love" in Haight-Ashbury, San Francisco

Newsweek declares that "the hippies are antagonizing the squares"

Vietnam War demonstrations

Nehru suit jackets for men

GUCCI expands to London

RALPH LAUREN creates his first Polo tie collection

MISSONI shows first colorful knitwear collection in Florence

Faye Dunaway makes Depression-era fashion cool in *Bonnie and Clyde*

Dustin Hoffman gets more than a glimpse of Anne Bancroft's stockings in *The Graduate*

YVES SAINT LAURENT creates Catherine Deneuve's ladylike look for *Belle du Jour*

1968

Rock musical *Hair* showcases long locks and love beads

Student riots in Europe and the U.S.

PUCCI's colorful print collection features a stretch bikini and matching velvet robe

Credit card sales rise from $1 billion to more than $7 billion, 1967-1970

SAINT LAURENT introduces the trapeze dress

SONIA RYKIEL opens her first Paris boutique, specializing in knitwear

Olympic skier Susie Chaffee competes in a silver unitard

Jimi Hendrix releases *Electric Ladyland*

Jackie Kennedy wears Valentino dress for her wedding to Aristotle Onassis

American designer Ken Scott features the "hippie gypsy look" in his collection

The Beatles champion Indian-inspired fashion

Puma introduces the suede basketball shoe

Civil rights leader Martin Luther King assassinated

Democratic presidential candidate Robert Kennedy assassinated

First heart transplant performed

Safari jackets for men and women

Richard Nixon elected president

1969

Barbra Streisand wears see-through, bell-bottom pajama outfit by SCAASI to Oscars

Stonewall Riots in New York launch the gay rights movement

Children's television show *Sesame Street* debuts, including appearances by Carol Burnett, James Earl Jones, and singer Grace Slick

Hemlines fall with the maxi-skirt

PALOMA PICASSO, daughter of painter Pablo, launches career designing jewelry for YVES SAINT LAURENT collection

Rolling Stones affect eyeliner and dangling earrings for their *Gimme Shelter* tour

The Gap opens its first store in San Francisco, selling Levi's jeans, records, and cassette tapes

Richard Burton buys 69-carat pear-shaped diamond for wife Elizabeth Taylor

Woodstock music festival

American astronaut Neil Armstrong becomes first man to walk on the moon

JESSICA MCCLINTOCK invests $5,000 in small California company called Gunne Sax, streamlining and prettifying the granny dress

Men's ties widen to at least 4 inches

Cary Grant inducted into the International Best-Dressed List Hall of Fame for his classic style

1970

Ohio National Guard kills 4 students at Kent State University

80% of shirts manufactured by Arrow are colored or patterned

Women's pant styles include knickers, midis, and gauchos

Women's Wear Daily declares that the midiskirt will replace the mini

First Earth Day celebration

Singer Neil Young brings back the fringed buckskin jacket

FAIRCHILD Publications begins publishing *W*

Rolling Stones singer Mick Jagger wears colorful, flowing GIORGIO SANT'ANGELO trousers

Floppy disks introduced

Twiggy retires from modeling at age 20, claiming "you can't be a clothes hanger for your entire life!"

1971

Athletic footwear company Nike founded

The fad for hot pants

ZHANDRA RHODES begins producing her flamboyant, pattern-based designs

Lip gloss makes its debut

Levi Strauss wins the Coty Fashion Critics Award for world fashion Influence

Flowing caftans for both women and men

Twin Towers completed at New York's World Trade Center

Sonny and Cher wear matching bell-bottoms on their hit TV show

Mick and Bianca Jagger marry in YVES SAINT LAURENT suits

Anti-war march in Washington, D.C. draws over 200,000

Constitutional amendment grants 18-year-olds the right to vote

1972

King Tut museum tour inspires Egyptian-themed jewelry

OSSIE CLARK commissions the unknown MANOLO BLAHNIK to design shoes for his collection

Ms. magazine begins publication

Jackie Onassis and her trademark sunglasses

Rosie Casals wears decorated tennis dress at Wimbledon, ending the all-white tradition

David Bowie's glam-rock look for concept album *Ziggy Stardust*

Israeli team massacred at the Olympic Games in Munich

Video cassette recorders introduced, to little success

Break-in at the Democratic headquarters in the Watergate hotel in Washington, D.C.

Elvis makes the switch to jumpsuits for his fall tour

Nixon reelected president

1973

Cease-fire agreed upon in Vietnam

Benefit fashion show at Versailles widens audience for American designers

Yom Kippur War, 1973-1974

Bodysuits popular as outerwear

Revlon debuts Charlie perfume with ads depicting men's wear look for women

U.S. Supreme Court rules that abortion is legal in *Roe v. Wade*

David Bowie poses with Twiggy for the cover of his album *Pin Ups*

Blaxploitation spoof *Cleopatra Jones* features outrageous stretch chiffon outfits by GIORGIO SANT'ANGELO

Motorola inventor creates first cell phone

Passage of Endangered Species Act spurs manufacturing of fake fur

Oil crisis, 1973-1974

L'eggs introduces Sheer Energy pantyhose

1974

Nixon resigns after Watergate hearings; Gerald Ford becomes president

RALPH LAUREN designs Robert Redford's wardrobe for *The Great Gatsby*

Beverly Johnson is first black model to be featured on the cover of *Vogue*

Renowned writer and Nobel Prize winner Aleksander Solzhenitsyn exiled from Soviet Union

Montgomery Ward catalogue features do-it-yourself ear-piercing device

String bikinis

First barcode reader installed in Ohio supermarket

ELIE TAHARI opens his Madison Avenue boutique

Pam Grier shows off her afro in *Foxy Brown*

Spanish designer FERNANDO SANCHEZ uses dress construction techniques for lingerie

1975

John T. Molloy publishes *Dress for Success*

HALSTON's collection features ultrasuede separates and slinky disco dresses

Men's wear-inspired separates for women by CALVIN KLEIN and RALPH LAUREN

REI KAWAKUBO shows her first collection for Comme des Garçons in Tokyo

Arthur Ashe defeats Jimmy Connors to become first African-American to win Wimbledon

Microsoft founded by Bill Gates

Patti Smith goes androgynous on the cover of her debut album *Horses*

The Gap creates its own line of basic clothing

Computer-aided design (CAD) begins to be used for pattern-making

Polyester comes into its own with leisure suits for men

Clogs, platform shoes, and chunky boots

Singer Diana Ross creates her own costumes for her role in *Mahogany*

First Zara store opens in Spain with knockoffs of popular fashions

1976

Skimpy Dallas Cowboy Cheerleader uniforms attract attention at the Super Bowl

Farrah Fawcett's feathered hair—and the braless look—translate to high ratings for *Charlie's Angels*

Knee-length T-shirt dresses

Divorce rates double

Digital watch introduced

Olympic gold medal figure skater Dorothy Hamill's wedge-cut bob

U.S. celebrates its bicentennial

LIZ CLAIBORNE establishes her ensemble-oriented sportswear line for women

Cover of *Punk* features illustration of Ramones wearing Converse All-Stars

GEOFFREY BEENE is first American designer to show in Milan

DIANE VON FURSTENBERG's wrap dress makes the cover of *Newsweek* magazine

MARY MCFADDEN revives FORTUNY-style pleats in her first collection

Jimmy Carter elected president

1977

John Travolta struts in his three-piece white suit in *Saturday Night Fever*

VIVIENNE WESTWOOD pioneers the ripped, slashed, and pinned punk look at her SEX shop in London

Punk style includes Dr. Martens boots

Diane Keaton's men's wear look in *Annie Hall* styled by RALPH LAUREN

Miniseries *Roots* sparks interest in African designs

Queen Elizabeth II celebrates her Silver Jubilee in a pink HARDY AMIES dress

Bianca Jagger rides white horse into Studio 54 wearing white and gold HALSTON

Elvis Presley dies

Premiere of *Star Wars*

Slim, no-nonsense suits for women are dictated by *The Woman's Dress for Success Book*

Baggy fatigue pants with high, wrapped waist by WILLI SMITH are a much-copied hit from the designer's first collection

ZHANDRA RHODES uses safety pins and chains in her punk-inspired "Conceptual Chic" collection

ISSEY MIYAKE shows oversized sweaters with narrow leggings

1978

RALPH LAUREN's "Prairie" collection

Gore-Tex patented

Sportswear designer PERRY ELLIS launches his line of loose, oversized clothing

Inflation soars to 10%

98% of U.S. households own at least one television

U.S. and China establish diplomatic relations

Italian manufacturer Tecnica trademarks the Moon Boot

World's first test tube baby is born in England

Over 900 cult members die in mass suicide in Jonestown, Guyana

The Complete Book of Running causes sales of running shoes to skyrocket

1979

Sony Walkman first introduced in Japan

Arab-Israeli peace treaty

Illiteracy rate in U.S. drops below 1%

Margaret Thatcher becomes first female prime minister of England

Bo Derek wears her hair cornrowed as an object of desire in *10*

Peasant blouses

Blondie singer Deborah Harry combines New Wave/disco look

Revolution in Iran; Shah overthrown, American hostages taken

Sculptor David Yurman launches jewelry line with braided gold and silver bracelet

Target stores earn $1 billion in annual sales

Nuclear power plant failure at Three-Mile Island in Pennsylvania

DIEGO DELLA VALLE turns his father's cobbler business into luxury loafer brand J.P. Tod's

Heiress Gloria Vanderbilt licenses her name for designer jeans

THE EIGHTIES, NINETIES, AND A NEW MILLENNIUM: 1980-2009

1980

Richard Gere wears ARMANI suits in *American Gigolo*

NORMA KAMALI's gray sweatshirt material skirts and oversized tops

Volcano Mount St. Helens erupts in state of Washington, killing 57

Italian knitwear company Benetton opens first U.S. store in New York

American Association of Retired People has 12 million members and counting

Dallas and *Urban Cowboy* spark trend for cowboy hats and boots

14-year-old model Brooke Shields appears in controversial "nothing comes between me and my CALVINS" ad campaign for jeans

PALOMA PICASSO begins designing for Tiffany & Co.

VHS defeats Betamax as the VCR format of choice

The Preppy Handbook revives interest in Lacoste polo shirts and madras plaid

John Lennon assassinated

Ronald Reagan elected president

1981

MTV debuts on the air, launching the music video

JAMES GALANOS designs Nancy Reagan's one-shouldered inauguration gown

LAURA ASHLEY designs are a favorite of Lady Diana Spencer's "Sloane Ranger" set

Debut of TV's *Dynasty*, with Joan Collins and Linda Evans in glamorous costumes designed by Nolan Miller

John Hinckley, Jr., claims obsession with actress Jodie Foster prompted his assassination attempt on President Reagan

Invention of Polartec fleece

Coach opens flagship store in New York

First factory outlet center opens in Burlington, North Carolina

OSCAR DE LA RENTA updates the Boy Scouts uniform

GIORGIO ARMANI becomes the first designer to create a lower-priced "diffusion" line with the launch of Emporio

Princess Diana's romantic wedding dress designed by husband-and-wife design team EMANUEL

STEPHEN JONES opens first millinery shop in London and becomes a hit with clubgoers

VIVIENNE WESTWOOD's pirate collection ushers in the New Romanticism

AZZEDINE ALAÏA's first collection earns him the sobriquet "King of Cling"

Space shuttle *Columbia* is successfully launched

1982

THIERRY MUGLER features the wedge dress with exaggerated shoulder pads

Boy George of the band Culture Club lauded by *Vogue* as a "mover and shaker" of the new club scene

KENNETH COLE kick-starts his business by selling 40,000 pairs of shoes in two and a half days during New York's Market Week

Workout headbands become fashion fad after Olivia Newton-John wears one in her music video for "Physical"

Princess Diana affects the big-shouldered glam look

Photographer BRUCE WEBER shoots first ad campaign for CALVIN KLEIN underwear, featuring pole vaulter Tim Hintnaus

Vietnam Memorial, designed by Yale college student Maya Lin, is opened

First CDs manufactured

Grace Kelly dies in car crash

Jane Fonda's workout video sparks gymwear craze

Margaret Thatcher famous for her economic policies and power suits

1983

Time magazine substitutes the computer for "man of the year"

The Swatch wristwatch is launched

Flashdance sets off craze for leg warmers and drop-shouldered sweatshirts

Michael Jackson moonwalks while wearing one white glove in video for "Billie Jean"

President Reagan refers to the USSR as the "evil empire"

First commercial cell phone service available in the U.S.

The term "yuppie" first used to describe materialistic, professional baby boom generation

J. Crew catalogue launched

Princess Stephanie of Monaco apprentices at DIOR

KARL LAGERFELD becomes design director at CHANEL

VIVIENNE WESTWOOD creates designs using prints by graffiti artist Keith Haring

Elizabeth Taylor appears in Blackglama fur ad "What becomes a legend most?"

Sony markets first portable CD player, the Discman

REI KAWAKUBO's collection for Comme des Garçons is dubbed "post-holocaust" on its Paris debut

Tom Cruise instigates a run on Ray-Ban sunglasses after sporting them in *Risky Business*

Pop star Prince debuts his purple, ruffled romantic look in music video for "Little Red Corvette"

Gap Inc. buys Banana Republic, a two-store safari and travel clothing company

Dooney & Bourke develop the All-Weather Leather bag

U.S. embassy in Beirut bombed

1984

Apple introduces the Macintosh computer

AIDS virus identified by French and American researchers

CALVIN KLEIN launches Obsession perfume

Russell Simmons and Rick Rubin launch Def Jam Records

Debut of television show *Lifestyles of the Rich and Famous*

Retailer UNIQLO opens its first store in Japan

Founding of Design Industries Foundation Fighting AIDS (DIFFA)

Jay McInerney's book *Bright Lights, Big City* is first yuppie coming-of-age novel

MAC cosmetics launched to create makeup suitable for fashion photography

Miami Vice sets off the T-shirt under ARMANI jacket style for men

Surge in sales of Levi's 501 jeans

Nancy Reagan's ADOLFO suits become known as "Reagan red"

Movie *Amadeus* inspires eighteenth-century clothing revival in clubwear

Surfer-inspired Reef sandal company founded in California

Reagan reelected president

1985

Levi's introduces Dockers khakis

Madonna shows off her street style in *Desperately Seeking Susan*

DONNA KARAN launches her first collection, featuring the jersey body suit and wrap skirts

"High-thigh" one-piece swim suits for women

Anne White's skintight jumpsuit is banned from future Wimbledon matches as "not traditional"

WILLI SMITH designs uniforms for workers who help artist Christo wrap the Pont Neuf bridge in Paris

Wreckage of *Titanic* discovered

Benetton begins series of multi-ethnic, socially conscious ads

PRADA issues the black nylon backpack

Spanish chain Zara expands and accelerates "fast fashion" pace by decreasing design to distribution process to under two weeks

Rock Hudson, first celebrity to acknowledge he had AIDS, dies

ATM machines now widespread

Michael Jackson and other stars record "We Are the World" for famine relief in Ethiopia

Madonna channels Marilyn Monroe in "Material Girl" video

KARL LAGERFELD's summer collection for CHANEL features a Watteau-inspired suit

Mikhail Gorbachev becomes head of Soviet Union, proposes reform policies of *glasnost* and *perestroika*

1986

Cher wears black beaded, midriff-baring BOB MACKIE gown with feather headdress to the Academy Awards

Rap stars Run DMC perform in Adidas Super Stars

QVC home shopping network founded

Princess Stephanie launches swimwear line

Edwin Schlossberg wears blue linen suit with silver tie designed by WILLI SMITH for his wedding to Caroline Kennedy; her gown is by CAROLINE HERRERA

Explosion at nuclear power plant in Chernobyl sends radioactive fallout over the Soviet Union and Europe

MARC JACOBS launches his first collection and becomes the youngest designer to win the CFDA Award for New Fashion Talent at age 23

Reagan administration embroiled in Iran-Contra scandal

Professional women take up the THIERRY MUGLER power suit look

Stirrup pants and oversized geometric-patterned sweaters

Space shuttle *Challenger* explodes after liftoff

1987

Fashion Institute of Technology features "Three Women: KAWAKUBO, VIONNET, MCCARDELL" exhibit

Michael Douglas as Gordon Gekko in *Wall Street* asserts that "greed is good"

Hugo Boss suits exemplify "power dressing" for men

CHRISTIAN LACROIX introduces the pouf skirt

George Michael dances in ripped acid-washed jeans in his music video for hit song "Faith"

Men spend $1 billion on toiletries and grooming products, double the amount from a decade ago

Introduction of the debit card

Acid-washed jeans and matching jackets for women and men

Musée des Arts de la Mode in Paris holds a major DIOR retrospective

Merger between Moët Hennessy and LOUIS VUITTON results in LVMH luxury goods conglomerate

U.S. stock market crashes in October

1988

DONNA KARAN expands with less-expensive line DKNY

Working Girl depicts the yuppie wanna-be style of wearing high-top Reeboks and white socks with suits for the commute to work

More than 22 million computers sold

Track star Florence Griffith-Joyner competes at the Seoul Olympics wearing a lace bodysuit

Retail giant Wal-Mart posts $20 billion in sales

ANNA WINTOUR becomes editor of *Vogue*

South African businessman Johann Rupert establishes Richemont luxury goods group, including part ownership in Cartier and CHLOÉ

George H.W. Bush elected president

1989

MIUCCIA PRADA shows her first ready-to-wear collection

Leggings outselling jeans in some parts of the U.S.

Parsons School of Design honors Lena Horne for her contribution to fashion

First commercial production of microfibers in the U.S.

J. Crew opens first retail location in New York

Legendary *Vogue* editor DIANA VREELAND dies

U.S. invades Panama, 1989–1990

Berlin Wall falls

Opening of the glass pyramid at the Louvre, designed by I.M. Pei

1990

GIANNI VERSACE launches couture line

U.S. population reaches 248 million

Michelle Pfeiffer wears understated ARMANI to the Oscars

George Michael's hit video "Freedom" features lip-synching supermodels

New York Times runs front-page article "The Green Movement in the Fashion World"

RIFAT OZBEK's all-white collection

JEAN-PAUL GAULTIER designs Madonna's satin corset cone bra for her Blonde Ambition tour

Reunification of East and West Germany

Iraq invades Kuwait

Supermodel Linda Evangelista quoted as saying "I don't get out of bed for less than $10,000 a day"

Jockey introduces a string bikini for men

MC Hammer sports baggy pants in his music video "U Can't Touch This"

VERA WANG establishes her bridal business, featuring sleek, modern gowns

Introduction of babyGap

1991

Soviet Union collapses

Recession in U.S.

Princess Diana appears on the cover of *Vogue* wearing a plain black sweater

CHRISTIAN LOUBOUTIN opens his boutique in Paris, featuring his signature red-soled shoes

Seattle grunge band scene explodes with Nirvana's hit single "Smells Like Teen Spirit"

ANNA SUI shows first collection

Supermodel Christy Turlington signs $800,000 yearly contract with Maybelline

Balkan Wars in former Yugoslavia, 1991–2001

First Gulf War inspires yellow ribbon campaign

Modern art takes a new turn with Damien Hirst's shark suspended in formaldehyde

Fiction writer Douglas Coupland publishes his novel *Generation X*, coining a term for marketers everywhere

Elizabeth Taylor wears VALENTINO for her eighth trip down the aisle

1992

Mall of America opens in Bloomington, Minnesota with over 500 stores, movie theaters, and an amusement park

European Union formed

Vogue's April cover features supermodels in white shirts and jeans from The Gap

Minimalism takes over from 80s excess

Khaki camouflage pattern popular

Belgian deconstructionist designer Ann Demeulemeester debuts her first collection in Paris

Sicilian duo DOLCE & GABBANA revive the corset as the "bustier"

Benetton's controversial AIDS campaign depicts dying patient

Daymond John launches the FUBU urban gear line with a collection of hats produced in his house in Queens, New York

ALEXANDER MCQUEEN discovered by *Vogue* stylist Isabella Blow

Brief fad for men's skirts limited to trendy city neighborhoods

Rap impresario Russell Simmons launches Phat Farm Fashions

Sharon Stone eschews underwear in the white dress interrogation scene in *Basic Instinct*

GALLIANO shows goth-inspired outfits

Launch of DKNY menswear line

MARC JACOBS is fired from PERRY ELLIS following a critically panned grunge-inspired collection

Bill Clinton elected president

1993

DOLCE & GABBANA design costumes for Madonna tour

Waifish model Kate Moss featured in *Vogue*'s first grunge fashion shoot

OSCAR DE LA RENTA becomes first American to head a Paris couture house when he takes the helm at PIERRE BALMAIN

PETA runs anti-fur campaign featuring supermodels

PRADA launches lower-priced Miu Miu line

Retro and vintage revival

African kente cloth patterns used in contemporary clothing designs

Bare midriffs

Environmentally friendly fabric Lyocell developed

The term "fashionista" is coined

Husband and wife team Suzanne Clements and Ignacio Ribeiro launch line of whimsical separates under the name CLEMENTS RIBEIRO

KATE SPADE introduces her line of handbags

First Lady Hilary Clinton wears DONNA KARAN's cut-out shoulder gown

CALVIN KLEIN is voted both Men's- and Women's wear Designer of the Year

Terrorist bombing at the World Trade Center

Fortune magazine links popularity of baseball caps to balding baby boomers

Mosaic browser debuts, instigating wide-spread use of the Internet

1994

LAGERFELD sexes up the Chanel suit

Levi's introduces first computer-imaged, custom-fit jeans

Economic recovery begins

Rapper Snoop Dogg wears TOMMY HILFIGER rugby shirt to host *Saturday Night Live*

GAULTIER revives punk and body-piercing at the Paris summer shows

Rock singer Courtney Love popularizes the "kinderwhore" look

VIVIENNE WESTWOOD's bustle dress

Fashion Targets Breast Cancer campaign begins

ISSEY MIYAKE shows his colorful, pleated "Flying Saucer" dress

GUCCI hires TOM FORD to revamp its image

Nirvana frontman Kurt Cobain commits suicide

Actress Elizabeth Hurley's fame quotient skyrockets after she wears VERSACE's safety-pin dress

Supermodel Claudia Schiffer earns reported $12 million

The year of the Wonderbra

Slip dresses worn over T-shirts

Patent issued for the hair scrunchie

First Old Navy store opens in Colma, California

MAC debuts its first Viva Glam lipstick, with 100% of proceeds donated to sufferers of HIV and AIDS

3 million users connected to the Internet

1995

JOHN GALLIANO appointed to GIVENCHY, becoming the first British designer to head up a French couture house

RALPH LAUREN's long black halterneck dress

Media dubs use of emaciated models as "heroin chic"

Sheath dress and jacket combination popular

GUCCI Group formed with TOM FORD as creative director

Oklahoma City bombing

Wildly popular *Pride and Prejudice* miniseries inspires Austen regency-era touches in women's fashion

Rap star Jay-Z launches Rocawear

ISAAC MIZRAHI is featured in the documentary *Unzipped*

European Union removes border controls for member countries

Prime Minister of Israel Yitzhak Rabin assassinated

Accessories designer ERIC JAVITS introduces man-made "Squishee" straw

Amazon.com opens for online business

Online auction site eBay launched

Vintage Levi's sell for as much as $2,000 in Japan

Elvis' red jumpsuit sells at auction for $107,000

Bloody footprint left by a Bruno Magli shoe features in O. J. Simpson murder trial

H&M continues expansion with stores in France, Finland, Belgium, and Austria

1996

CALVIN KLEIN's long, lean, clean silhouette

Sharon Stone wears a Gap mock turtleneck to the Oscars

DRIES VAN NOTEN shows layered textures and colors

TOM FORD's collection for GUCCI evokes HALSTON

Slim, structured lines for men's suits

Cargo pants popular

Nokia introduces cell phones with e-mail access

90% of U.S. companies have "Casual Fridays"

Courtney Love makes herself over with help from VERSACE

Platform shoes come around again for women

Princess Diana granted a divorce from Prince Charles

NARCISCO RODRIGUEZ shoots to stardom when he designs Carolyn Bessette Kennedy's dress for her wedding to JFK Jr.

Boris Yeltsin becomes Russia's first democratically elected president

Low-rise bootcut pants require thong underwear

Clinton reelected president

10 million users connected to the Internet

1997

"Dolly" becomes the first cloned sheep

ALEXANDER MCQUEEN replaces GALLIANO at GIVENCHY when Galliano jumps ship for DIOR

MICHAEL KORS appointed as chief ready-to-wear designer of Céline

FENDI's baguette bag

STELLA MCCARTNEY, Paul McCartney's daughter, takes the design helm at CHLOÉ, with a contractual clause accepting her decision to use no fur or leather

First DVD players available in U.S.

ELIE TAHARI establishes Theory brand

Height of dot-com boom

Yoga becomes wildly popular

Brighter colors take over from neutrals

MARC JACOBS becomes designer for LOUIS VUITTON

MARTIN MARGIELA becomes head designer for Hermès

DIANE VON FURSTENBURG revives her fashion business with a wrap-dress update

LVMH acquires French beauty chain Sephora and opens first New York store

China regains control of Hong Kong, ending 156 years of British rule

Princess Diana dies in paparazzi car chase in Paris

MCQUEEN admits first GIVENCHY collection is "crap" when panned by critics

Belgian designer Walter Van Beirendonck designs costumes for band U2's "PopMart" tour

Designer GIANNI VERSACE murdered in his Florida mansion; sister Donatella assumes control of his designs

Fashion journalist CARRIE DONOVAN appears in ads for Old Navy

1998

Sex and the City debuts, featuring clothing by PATRICIA FIELD

Sales of MANOLO BLAHNIK and JIMMY CHOO shoes increase due to influence of *SATC* star Sarah Jessica Parker

Rapper Sean Combs launches his SEAN JOHN line

Brazilian bikini wax becomes popular

Supermodel Cindy Crawford dons a body-baring slip dress by GALIANO for her second wedding

Human Genome Project announced

Soccer star David Beckham wears sarong-style skirt by JEAN PAUL GAULTIER

Washington intern Monica Lewinsky's stained blue dress becomes evidence during Clinton's impeachment trial

Skimpy schoolgirl look in teen singer Britney Spears's "Baby One More Time" video

Actress Gwyneth Paltrow channels Grace Kelly

Hilary Clinton wears OSCAR DE LA RENTA on the cover of *Vogue*

Young designers VIKTOR & ROLF make their debut with the "atomic bomb" evening dress collection

Fashionable women eschew pantyhose for bare legs

1999

American Express funds ALEXANDER MCQUEEN's $1 million fashion show

Shootings at Columbine High School in Colorado

Luggage company Samsonite enters the fashion business with functional jackets

The Matrix renews interest in the long trench coat

Soccer star Brandi Chastain pulls off her jersey at the World Cup finals to reveal her Nike sports bra

Sex and the City fans copy character Carrie Bradshaw's name necklace

Invention of the Blackberry personal digital assistant

Vladimir Putin named Acting President of Russia

JFK Jr. and Carolyn Bessette die in plane crash

PRADA Group acquires JIL SANDER

GUCCI Group acquires YVES SAINT LAURENT

GUCCI's collection includes a pair of embellished jeans priced at $3,096

Rapper Jay-Z becomes first to reference Jacob the Jeweler in his song "Girl's Best Friend"

Nike Town opens in London, with 70,000 feet of retail space

Target introduces designer line of products by Michael Graves

Netflix launches online DVD rental service

FAIRCHILD Publications becomes part of Condé Nast

NAACP honors founders of FUBU with Entrepreneurs of the Year Award

Coach launches men's and women's footwear line

Y2K panic rings in the New Year

2000

Guggenheim in New York features an Armani retrospective

Dot-com boom takes a downturn

Reality TV kicks off with *Big Brother* and *Survivor*

U.S. population is 291.4 million

Latino population in U.S. reaches 35.5 million

Kmart introduces line of clothing names for Mexican singer Thalia

Speedo invents Fastskin, a new swimsuit material based on sharkskin

HEDI SLIMANE launches streamlined DIOR Homme line

Pashmina shawls

Entrepreneur Sara Blakely invents Spanx

Stock market begins to fall

Rap star Lil Kim becomes spokesperson for MAC Viva Glam lipstick

PHILIP TREACY shows first haute-couture hat collection in Paris

Christy Turlington launches her collection of yoga wear

LVMH launches eLuxury

Zara chain has expanded into Europe, the U.S., South America, and the Middle East

Fashion fans line up overnight for opening of H&M's first U.S. store in New York City

JIL SANDER leaves her own fashion house over creative differences with owner Prada

Shoe designer KENNETH COLE expands with a women's clothing line

Gap introduces a maternity line

Deconstructionist fashion line Imitation of Christ holds first show in an East Village funeral parlor

STELLA MCCARTNEY designs Madonna's dress for her wedding to Guy Ritchie

George W. Bush declared president by U.S. Supreme Court after controversial election

GEOFFREY BEENE, BILL BLASS, CALVIN KLEIN, RALPH LAUREN, HALSTON, RUDI GERNREICH, CLAIRE MCCARDELL, and NORMAN NORELL are the first designers to be honored on the Fashion Walk of Fame in New York City

Condé Nast launches *Lucky*, the "magazine about shopping"

2001

Economic crisis in Japan

Singer Björk wears swan dress designed by Macedonian designer Marjan Pejoski to the Oscars

STELLA MCCARTNEY leaves CHLOÉ to launch her own line

CHRISTOPHER BAILEY joins Burberry as creative director

ALEXANDER MCQUEEN featured in Metropolitan Museum of Art's "Extreme Fashion" exhibit

Madonna revives the punk kilt look for her "Drowned World" tour

Young designer ZAC POSEN spurns conglomerates LVMH and GUCCI to open his own studio in Tribeca

Singer Jennifer Lopez launches her own fashion line

PRADA opens enormous store designed by architect Rem Koolhaus in New York's Soho neighborhood

Jaeger hires young designer Bella Freud to jazz up its traditional woolens line

WORTH court gown worn by George Washington's great-great-grandniece sells at auction for a record $101,500

Apple releases the first iPod

Former child star twins Mary Kate and Ashley Olsen launch "tween" fashion and product line with Wal-Mart

9/11 terrorist attacks in U.S.

Americans show their patriotism by wearing red, white, and blue

OSCAR DE LA RENTA, JAMES GALANOS, DONNA KARAN, PAULINE TRIGÈRE, BONNIE CASHIN, GIORGIO SANT'ANGELO, CHARLES JAMES, and ANNE KLEIN are added to the Fashion Walk of Fame

STEPHEN JONES hat featured on British postage stamp

2002

Almost 7 million cosmetic surgery procedures performed in the U.S.

"Everybody in khaki" ad campaign for the Gap

Sober black suits are the celebrity outfit of choice at the Academy Awards

TV show *What Not To Wear* debuts in U.K.

The Euro becomes the standard currency for the European Union

SAINT LAURENT revives his Mondrian dress

SAINT LAURENT retires

Design label PROENZA SCHOULER is started by young New Yorkers Lazaro Hernandez and Jack McCollough

U.S. invades Afghanistan

STEPHEN BURROWS, MARC JACOBS, BETSEY JOHNSON, NORMA KAMALI, LILLY DACHÉ, PERRY ELLIS, MAINBOCHER, and WILLI SMITH are added to the Fashion Walk of Fame

Juicy Couture track suits

605 million users connected to the Internet

2003

Teen consumer market estimated to have reached $70 billion

ISAAC MIZRAHI designs for Target

GAULTIER replaces MARGIELA at Hermès

JIL SANDER returns to designing her line under the PRADA Group

Debut of *Queer Eye for the Straight Guy*

Actor Johnny Depp appropriates Rolling Stone Keith Richards' eyeliner and dangling earring look to portray Jack Sparrow in *Pirates of the Caribbean*

AIDS estimated to have infected 42 million people worldwide

Ex–ANNA WINTOUR assistant publishes bestselling novel *The Devil Wears Prada*

T-shirt wholesaler American Apparel enters the retail market

The South Beach Diet is introduced

VERSACE glams up the biker look in fall collection

Portugese designer Fátima Lopes opens first U.S. store in Los Angeles

Pop star Gwen Stefani launches her clothing and accessories line L.A.M.B.

U.S. invades Iraq

Fashion publicist Eleanor Lambert dies at the age of 100

2004

Sarah Jessica Parker becomes spokesperson for Gap

Singer Janet Jackson causes furor over exposed breast "wardrobe malfunction" at Super Bowl halftime show

MICHAEL KORS launches line of high-end career clothes he calls "carpool couture"

Popularity of "status bags" results in $1.3 billion in sales for Coach

Men sport closely-cropped facial stubble

The Fug Girls launch their fashion-commentary Weblog

TOM FORD leaves GUCCI Group over business disagreements

NASCAR commissions Tiffany design for its trophy

French ban on Muslim headscarves in schools causes controversy

Cartier files trademark infringement suit against Jacob the Jeweler

Tennis star Serena Williams starts her own line of clothing

JIL SANDER leaves PRADA Group for second time

Limited-edition collection by KARL LAGERFELD for H&M sells out within an hour

George W. Bush reelected president

2005

Model Heidi Klum debuts as host of *Project Runway*

VIVIENNE WESTWOOD creates a stir with T-shirts declaring "I am not a Terrorist, please don't arrest me"

Singer Beyoncé and her mother Tina Knowles launch fashion business House of Deréon

STELLA MCCARTNEY designs collection for H&M

Shopping mall in Dubai includes indoor skiing

Launch of Portland Fashion Week, featuring sustainable designs and apparel

Blonde, tan, and skinny is the starlet style of choice, by stylist Rachel Zoe

Bride and Prejudice sparks interest in Bollywood fashion

Leggings return, in capri length worn under miniskirts

Women's proportion shifts to short-over-long

UNIQLO opens first U.S. stores in New Jersey

HELMUT LANG walks away from his label owned by PRADA Group

Raf Simons takes over design for JIL SANDER brand

2006

Hollywood stylist Rachel Zoe blamed for promoting anorexic chic

Fug Girls begin covering fashion week shows for *New York* magazine

Avant-garde designers VIKTOR & ROLF are H&M's featured designers for fall line

Target launches its Go International guest designer program, beginning with LUELLA BARTLEY, Sophie Albou, and BEHNAZ SARAFPOUR

Former Vice President Al Gore's global-warning film *An Inconvenient Truth* is a hit

The Devil Wears Prada comes to the big screen, with Meryl Streep in the title role

Katie Couric debuts as first female evening news anchor on CBS and is criticized for wearing a white jacket after Labor Day

Accessories company Coach launches knitwear collection

Trendsetters favor skinny jeans tucked into boots

Clunky, colorful Crocs are a hit

Ugg boots worn with shorts

UNIQLO establishes global flagship store in New York's Soho

Size 0 models banned from Spanish runways after a model collapses and dies from heart failure brought on by fasting

HELMUT LANG brand sold to Japanese group Link Theory

George Clooney, channeling Cary Grant, is named sexiest man alive by *People* magazine

MAC's Viva Glam products reach $70 million in donations to HIV/AIDS support fund

Online clothing sales top computer sales for first time

2 billion cell phones now in use worldwide

2007

Apple introduces the iPhone

Madonna designs spring collection for H&M

Disney teen star Miley Cyrus inspires fan Web site "dresslikemiley.net"

VERA WANG debuts her Simply Vera line for Kohl's department store

ROBERTO CAVALLI's fall H&M line flies off the shelves

STELLA MCCARTNEY starts 100% organic skincare line

Supermodel Kate Moss designs collection for U.K. chain Topshop

VALENTINO Fashion Group invests in PROENZA SCHOULER

Target features guest designers PROENZA SCHOULER, Patrick Robinson, Alice Temperley, and Erin Fetherston

Leggings for men shown in Marni fall fashion collection

Mary Kate and Ashley Olsen launch high-end line The Row in London

Converse issues the All-Star high-top Ramones shoe

2008

Best Actress winner Marianne Cotillard wears a mermaid gown by JEAN PAUL GAULTIER to the Oscars

DIANE VON FURSTENBERG and LIZ CLAIBORNE are added to the Fashion Walk of Fame

Actress Natalie Portman designs collection of vegan shoes

Olsen twins launch young contemporary line Elizabeth and James

First Dubai Fashion Week

Controversy over whether purported plus-size winner of *America's Next Top Model* is actually plus-sized

Target features guest designers Jovovich-Hawk, Richard Chai, Jonathan Saunders, and THAKOON

ANNA WINTOR bestowed with Order of the British Empire (OBE) by Queen Elizabeth II

Sarah Jessica Parker designs low-priced fashion line Bitten for mall retailer Steve & Barry's

Troubled starlet Lindsay Lohan launches her own line of leggings, one version featuring kneepads

ZAC POSEN releases capsule collection for Target in Australian stores

JOHN GALLIANO and Commes des Garçons attempt another run at men's skirts for the spring '09 season

Jacob the Jeweler sentences to 2½ years in prison for money laundering

Benetton runs Microcredit Africa Works ad campaign

American Apparel has over 200 retail outlets worldwide

Limited Comme des Garçons collection for H&M inspires 14-hour waits in Japan

Kate Moss begins second ad campaign for David Yuman jewelry

More than 173 million iPods have been sold worldwide

Fashionistas try to remain stylish as "recessionistas"

Suri Cruise declared Hollywood's most fashionable toddler

Fashion critic Richard Blackwell dies

Recession forces store closures and layoffs by Lane Bryant, Eddie Bauer, Timberland, and Ann Taylor

JIL SANDER brand purchased by Japanese company Onward

Barack Obama becomes first African-American to be elected U.S. President; wife Michelle wears NARCISCO RODRIGUEZ dress on election night

Over 20% of world population connected to the Internet

2009

U.S. unemployment rate tops 7%

CHANEL announces cutback of 200 jobs in Paris

New First Lady Michelle Obama wears ISABEL TOLEDO's suit and coat for inauguration ceremony and a white dress by JASON WU to the inaugural ball

J. Crew sees popularity in kids' collection surge after Sasha and Malia Obama wear coats from the Crewcuts line to the inauguration

MATTHEW WILLIAMSON is guest designer for H&M's summer line

Target features guest designer Tracy Feith

ISAAC MIZRAHI debuts his first collection as designer for LIZ CLAIBORNE

Unfinished Burj Dubai skyscraper to be world's tallest

Joseph ABBOUD
Amsale ABERRA
Reem ACRA
ADOLFO
ADRI
ADRIAN
AGNÈS B.
Azzedine ALAÏA
Sir Hardy AMIES
John ANTHONY

ANTONIO
ARKADIUS
Giorgio ARMANI
Laura ASHLEY
Richard AVEDON

Joseph Abboud

Designer Joseph Abboud.

BORN Boston, Massachusetts, May 5, 1950

AWARDS Cutty Sark Men's Fashion Award *Most Promising Menswear Designer*, 1988 • Woolmark Award for Distinguished Fashion, 1989 • Council of Fashion Designers of America (CFDA) *Menswear Designer of the Year*: 1989, 1990

Joseph Abboud (Ah–bOOd) brings a fresh viewpoint to the conservative realm of men's clothing, fusing a European aesthetic with American practicality. His clothes are exceptionally well made of beautiful fabrics, classic but with a contemporary attitude, combining colors and textures to give classicism a modern edge.

Of Lebanese descent, Abboud came to designing with a strong retail background—12 years in buying, merchandising, and sales promotion at Louis of Boston. He went to work there part time in 1968 during his freshman year at the University of Massachusetts, and worked full time after graduation. He also studied at the Sorbonne in Paris, where he fell in love with the European sense of style. He left Louis in 1981 for a job as sales representative at Polo/RALPH LAUREN, joined the design team, and became associate director of men's wear. Following a year at Barry Bricken, Abboud was ready to form his own company in 1986.

In addition to the signature Abboud collection, there are shirts and ties, casual sportswear and golf clothes, loungewear, sleepwear, robes, rainwear, and men's scarves, as well as home products ranging from bedding to bath accessories to flatware. The label is sold at fine specialty stores and in Abboud boutiques around the United States. Internationally it is distributed in Canada, Great Britain, Japan, and Taiwan.

In the spring of 2005, after creative differences with Chief Executive Marty Staff, Joseph Abboud left the company to pursue outside interests. His name is recognized and respected in the fashion world to this day.

Above: Wool suit, 2008.

Right: Look from Black Brown 1826 for Lord & Taylor, 2009.

BORN Ethopia, 1955

Amsale Aberra is known for creating elegant, understated, and sophisticated wedding gowns. After emigrating to the United States to pursue a degree at New York City's Fashion Institute of Technology, Aberra took a position as an assistant designer at Harve Bernard. It was while planning her own wedding that she realized the dearth of the wedding dress market. Aberra's struggle to find a simple and modern gown for her own wedding—to her college sweetheart in 1986—lead her to pursue designing wedding dresses.

Aberra began her business out of her small New York loft apartment, but it quickly outgrew the space. Aberra's philosophy is to produce gowns that are timeless and elegant. She focuses on updating her gowns with modern bustles, colors, and silhouettes. "People shouldn't be able to look at your pictures and tell what year you got married," she said in a 2001 interview. "When women look at their wedding pictures 50 years from now, I don't want them to say, 'What did I do?'"

Her bridal-wear designs became so popular that she introduced an eveningwear line in 1998, designed with a similar ethos in mind. Her eveningwear line has garnered praise from fashion critics and celebrities, including Vanessa Williams, Halle Berry, Julia Roberts, Selma Blair, Salma Hayek, and Lucy Liu.

In 2001, Aberra opened a 5,000 square foot boutique on Madison Avenue. The boutique offers all lines developed by the Amsale group, including Amsale Bridesmaids, Christos, and Kenneth Pool, which is designed by season one *Project Runway* contestant Austin Scarlett. Aberra continues to serve as creative director for the Christos and Amsale lines. With sales reaching upwards of $25 million a year, she is considered the top couture wedding dress designer in the world.

Amsale Aberra

Designer Amsale Aberra.

Spring 2007.

BORN Beruit, Lebanon

A leader in luxury bridal and eveningwear, Reem Acra has always had a passion for design. While studying at the American University in Beruit, she attended a party wearing a silk embroidered dress she'd made out of one of her mother's tablecloths. The dress attracted the attention of a fashion editor who was so impressed that she hosted a fashion show featuring Acra's designs ten days later.

Acra then came to the United States to attend the Fashion Institute of Technology in New York City and later completed her studies at Esmond in Paris. Once out of school, she traveled the world, drawing inspiration from the varied cultures to which she was exposed. After working as an interior designer for several years, she returned to her first craft, fashion design. Acra later made a splash in the fashion world when a wedding dress she made for a high-society friend grabbed the attention of attendees. Shortly thereafter, her glamorous, sophisticated and meticulously made designs gained international recognition.

In 1997, Reem Acra launched her first collection, Reem Acra Bridal, which used classical elements of design and intricate beadwork and embroidery to fuse an exotic look with romantic appeal. By 2002, she launched her eveningwear collection, which drew from both European and American styles. In 2008, she launched her first ready-to-wear collection.

Designer Reem Acra.

Resort 2008.

Spring 2008.

Designer Adolfo.

BORN Adolfo Sardina; Havana, Cuba, February 13, 1933

AWARDS Coty American Fashion Critics' Award *Special Award* (millinery): 1955, 1969

When Adolfo announced his retirement in March 1993, he had been established in fashion for 25 years. First as a milliner, then with custom-made and ready-to-wear, he turned current trends into wearable, elegant clothes for countless socially prominent women and notables such as Nancy Reagan. His knitted dresses and especially his knit suits became daytime uniforms, while for evening he created extravagant gowns in luxurious fabrics and characteristically subtle color combinations.

Adolfo demonstrated an early interest in fashion, encouraged by an aunt, Maria Lopez. She took him to Paris to see the designer showings and introduced him to both CHANEL and BALENCIAGA, where he began his career as an apprentice. After a year's apprenticeship, he came to New York in 1948 as designer for Danish-born milliner Bragaard. In 1953 he moved to the milliner Emme where he quickly gained recognition; in 1956 his name appeared on the label as Adolfo of Emme.

In 1962 he opened his own millinery firm with the help of a $10,000 loan from BILL BLASS. Among his many successes were the Panama planter's hat in 1966 and the shaggy Cossack hat in 1967, plus huge fur berets and such non-hats as fur hoods, kidskin bandannas, and long braids entwined with flowers attached to the wearer's hair. His declining interest in hats coincided with their disappearance from the heads of fashionable women and Adolfo gradually added clothing, finally switching entirely into apparel.

In addition to knits and the suit homages to Chanel, each collection included classic silk print dresses, often paired with the suit jackets, and one or two beautifully tailored coats and suits. His twice-a-year showings invariably brought out a large audience of faithful clients, usually with three or four of them in the same suit or dress. He also faithfully promoted his clothes with trips to stores around the country.

Since closing his apparel business, he has concentrated on his licenses, including perfume, men's wear, luggage, handbags, sportswear, furs, and hats.

Bow from Adolfo of Emme, 1960.

BORN Mary Adrienne Steckling; St. Joseph, Missouri; November 7, 1934

DIED New York, November 5, 2006

AWARDS Coty American Fashion Critics' Award "*Winnie,*" 1982

Adri specializes in soft, reality-based clothes in the best American sportswear tradition, giving simple, wearable shapes an unexpected edge, using unusual fabrics in interesting mixes. Her supple, weightless fabrics—such an integral part of her designs—came largely from Italy's finest mills, with some selections from specialized French, American, and Irish houses. These are truly investment clothes to be worn and appreciated indefinitely.

Adri studied design at Washington University in St. Louis and was a guest editor at *Mademoiselle* magazine during her sophomore year. She continued her studies at Parsons School of Design in New York City where CLAIRE MCCARDELL was her critic. McCardell, with her belief in functional, comfortable clothes, proved an important and lasting influence. In October 1971 Adri's clothes were included in a two-designer showing at the Smithsonian Institution in Washington, D.C. The theme was Innovative Contemporary Fashion; the other designer honored was Claire McCardell.

Striped shirt under sashed cardigan over a tweed skirt, 1973.

Designer Adri, third from right, with models wearing looks from ready-to-wear, fall/winter 1972.

She also worked at retailed B.H. Wragge up until the launch of her own collection for Adri Designs Inc. in 1966. Adri launched many sportswear lines from that point forward under several different labels, including Collectors Items and Clothes Circuit.

Adri opened Adri Studio Limited on Seventh Avenue in 1976, which made women's designers sportswear. The business remains today but is now a private client, buy-and-order-based business run out of Adri's loft on West 20th Street.

She died at her home in New York of Parkinson's disease at the age of 71.

BORN Adrian Adolph Greenburg; Naugatuck, Connecticut, March 3, 1903

DIED Los Angeles, California, September 13, 1959

AWARDS Neiman Marcus Award, 1943 • Coty American Fashion Critics' Award "*Winnie*," 1945 • Parsons *Medal for Distinguished Achievement*, 1956

A top Hollywood studio designer of the 1920s and 1930s, Adrian was also successful at made-to-order and ready-to-wear.

In 1921 he began studies at The New York School of Fine and Applied Arts, now Parsons The New School for Design. In 1922, he transferred to the school's Paris branch. After six months in Paris he met Irving Berlin, who saw a costume Adrian had designed for a classmate to wear to the annual Bal du Grand Prix. Berlin offered him a job designing for the *Music Box Revue*. He then returned to New York, where he continued to work on stage productions, including the Greenwich Village *Follies* and George White's *Scandals*. In 1923, Rudolph Valentino's wife, director Natacha Rombova, lured Adrian to Hollywood to design costumes for her screen idol husband.

In 1926 he started working for Cecil B. DeMille, and in 1928 moved with DeMille to MGM where he soon began designing for that studio's films.

Above: Designer Adrian.

Bottom left: Coat of Raymond-Holland satin, 1948.

As the studio's chief designer, Adrian created costumes for such stars as Greta Garbo, Joan Crawford, Katharine Hepburn, Rosalind Russell, and Norma Shearer—nearly 200 films in all.

The association with MGM lasted until 1941, when he left the studio to open his own business, Adrian Ltd., for couture and top-ticket ready-to-wear. He closed his Beverly Hills salon in 1948 but continued in wholesale until a 1952 heart attack forced his retirement. Following his recovery, he and his wife, actress Janet Gaynor, retired to their farm in Brazil where he concentrated on landscape painting, a longtime avocation.

Adrian returned to Hollywood in 1959 to design the costumes for the Lerner and Loewe New York production of *Camelot*. It was while working on the production that he died suddenly of a cerebral hemorrhage.

In general, the Adrian look was sleek and modern, a silhouette marked by exaggeratedly wide shoulders tapering to a small waist. He was a master of intricate cut—stripes were worked in opposing directions on shapely, fitted suits, and color patches and bold animal prints were set into sinuous black crepe evening gowns. Diagonal closings, dolman sleeves, and floating tabs were recurring details. In addition, he did draped, swathed late-day dresses and romantic organdy evening gowns such as the gown from *Letty Lynton* designed for Joan Crawford, which was widely copied. It is said that more than 50,000 were sold at Macy's alone.

In addition to women's clothes and stage costumes, Adrian also produced several men's wear collections, and had two perfumes, Saint and Sinner.

Agnès B.

BORN Agnès Andrée Marguerite Troublé; Versailles, France, 1941

Agnès B. is the inspiration for a generation of laid-back sportswear dressing. After graduating from the École des Beaux-Arts in Versailles and an editorial stint at *Elle* magazine, she worked as an assistant to Dorothée Bis and as a freelance designer for several clothing firms before going into business for herself. She initiated her style in the early 1970s as a reaction to what she felt were the too-dressy, too-trendy clothes available at the time in Paris. Her unforced,

Designer Agnès B.

airy, low-key clothes, essentially sports separates and accessories for women, men, and children, are sold primarily in her own stores around the world, including New York, Amsterdam, London, and Tokyo. Her output now includes perfume, skin care and cosmetics products, and a maternity collection.

In 2008, after winning a bid in a national design contest, she designed the uniforms for the guards at the Palace of Versailles in France.

Spring 2007.

BORN Tunis, Tunisia, 1935

Fashion connoisseurs now consider him a genius and one of the last true couturiers but until 1980 when Azzedine Alaïa presented his first ready-to-wear collection, he worked in obscurity, known only to a select group of adventurous customers who also bought from the great couture houses. For the previous 18 years he had worked out of his apartment, with a list of knowledgeable clients ranging from Paloma Picasso to Dyan Cannon and Raquel Welch.

Raised in Tunis by his grandmother, Alaïa studied sculpture at the École des Beaux-Arts of Tunis, and while in art school worked for several dressmakers. In 1957 he went to Paris where he had been promised a job with DIOR. Arriving a few months before Dior's death, he did indeed get a job in the Dior cutting room but lasted only five days. For the next few years he supported himself by working as an *au pair*, at the same time making clothes for his fashionable young employers and their friends. By 1984, he had become so commercially successful that he bought his own townhouse in the Marais section of Paris.

Alaïa's first international notice was for an accessory—black leather gauntlets studded with silver rivets. His original clothes, said to be the sexiest in Paris, were seamed, molded, and draped to define and reveal every curve of a woman's body. Translating these techniques from woven cloth to knits is probably his greatest ready-to-wear achievement.

After 1992, Alaïa stopped doing runway shows and essentially dropped off the fashion radar. Although he continued to design for a few select customers, his deliveries to retail establishments were so sporadic that few stores were willing or able to cope. He has reappeared in the new century as if reborn, both in his influence on younger designers toying retrospectively with the 1980s, and in his own collections. These, while unmistakably Alaïa, are totally without nostalgia and entirely contemporary.

In 2001 he sold a minority share of his business to PRADA, and in July of that year staged a showing of just 22 pieces in his own home and headquarters to a select audience of barely 100 people. It was considered one of the most exhilarating and influential collections of the year—only his fourth showing in ten years—and confirmed his standing as probably the least derivative designer of our time.

Alaïa's unique draping, inspired by the work of the great MADELEINE VIONNET, is the heart of his style—the key to his design is his belief that fashion should be timeless.

Working with Prada saw him through a second renaissance, and in July 2007, he successfully bought back his house and brand name from the group.

Above: Designer Azzedine Alaïa (left) working on French Revolution 200th anniversary costume.

Left: Spring 2003.

Sir Hardy Amies

BORN Edwin Hardy Amies; Maida Vale, London, England, July 17, 1909

DIED English Cotswolds, March 5, 2003

AWARDS KCVO (Knight Commander of The Royal Victorian Order), 1989

Dressmaker to Queen Elizabeth II for over 50 years, Sir Hardy Amies has always specialized in tailored suits and coats, and cocktail and evening dresses. The house also makes breezy, more contemporary women's clothes such as pantsuits and casual classics. Men's wear has become a major part of its business.

Amies succeeded in fashion without formal design training; his mother, however, worked for a London dressmaker and as a child he was sometimes taken there as a treat. After leaving school, he spent several years in France and Germany, becoming fluent in both languages, returning to England when he was 21 to work for a manufacturer of scales.

In 1934 he became designer for Lachasse, a London couture house owned by his mother's former employer, and within a year was managing director. He left Lachasse in 1939 to serve in the British Army Intelligence Corps. During his Army career he gained the rank of lieutenant colonel and in 1944 was head of the Special Forces Commission to Belgium.

While in the service Amies was given two months' leave at the request of the Board of Trade to make a collection of clothes for South America. These, designed in his spare time at the War Office, were his first steps toward his own business. In 1945 he was mustered out to take part in a government-sponsored collection designed in accordance with the rules of the wartime Utility Scheme. In 1946 he opened his own dressmaking business, added a boutique line in 1950, and men's wear in 1959. Starting with ties and shirts, the men's wear business progressed to made-to-measure suits and soon extended to firms in the United States, Canada, and Japan.

In 1984, at age 75, Amies announced plans to leave his multimillion dollar fashion business to the members of his staff but denied any intention of an early departure. Ten years later he was still actively engaged in his businesses.

In May 2001 he sold his business to Luxury Brands Group, which also acquired NORMAN HARTNELL, another classic British house that had dressed the queen. In November of that year Amies announced his retirement, at age 93, and Jacques Azagury, a Moroccan-born designer with his own label, was made head of couture for the house. A new ready-to-wear line was also planned. Besides the men's wear, licensing agreements have included jewelry, small leather goods, luggage, and bed linens. Among Sir Hardy's publications are: *Just So Far*, 1954; *ABC of Men's Fashion*, 1964; *Still Here*, 1984.

Upon his death, his former studio assistant, Ian Garlant, was appointed director. Garlant presented his first couture collection in 2006. In 2007, the Victoria and Albert Museum held an exhibition entitled "The Golden Age of Couture," which featured Amies's work.

Designer Sir Hardy Amies (right) photographing models wearing his creations.

At the School of Industrial Art (now High School of Art and Design) Anthony won three European scholarships. He spent one year at the Accademia di Belle Arti in Rome before returning to New York and attending two years at the Fashion Institute of Technology.

His first job was a nine-year stint with Devonbrook, followed by three years with Adolph Zelinka. John Anthony, Inc. was established in January 1971 and closed in 1979.

After a number of years spent in made-to-order fashion and in recovering the use of his own name, Anthony reopened for fall 1986, showing a small ready-to-wear collection out of his couture salon.

Since then he has been in and out of ready-to-wear, in recent years concentrating entirely on custom work with its emphasis on luxurious materials, impeccable handwork, and the perfect fit that comes only with clothes made on the person who wears them.

Designer John Anthony (right) dressing a model for his show.

BORN Gianantonio Iorio; New York City, April 28, 1938

AWARDS Coty American Fashion Critics' Award "*Winnie*," 1972; *Return Award*, 1976

John Anthony's strength is in sophisticated, feminine clothes of refined elegance, marked by a feeling for asymmetry, a sensuous suppleness, and masterly tailoring. In each collection he has confined himself to a few lean, simple shapes in luxurious fabrics, a limited color palette, and a small group of key textures.

Ivory cotton shirt with drawstring neck, 1977.

Antonio

BORN Antonio Lopez; Puerto Rico, 1943
DIED Los Angeles, California, March 17, 1987

Antonio was an illustrator of protean talent, sensitive to every social shift and art movement, changing styles innumerable times over his 24-year career. At the start, his work was elegant and relatively conventional fashion illustration, but by 1965 pop art had become the essence of his drawings, followed by surrealism and by monumental figures clearly inspired by French artist, Fernand Léger. He later moved to a more fluid style, but each period was never less than flamboyant, and always dramatic in its use of black and white or color. In addition to women's and men's fashion, he also brought his unique point of view to bear on children's clothes.

When his family moved to New York, Antonio was nine-years-old but already committed to art—even as a very small child he would sketch little dresses to please his mother, a dressmaker. He attended the High School of Industrial Art (now the High School of Art and Design) and the Fashion Institute of Technology, from which he dropped out at 19 to join *Women's Wear Daily*. He left *WWD* after only four months when he was refused permission to freelance and began working for the *New York Times*. During the 1960s he traveled back and forth to Europe working for *Elle* and *British Vogue* among others, eventually spending so much time in Europe that at the end of the decade he decided to move to Paris. Seven years later he moved back to New York. Other publications he worked for were *Harper's Bazaar*, *Vogue*, and *Interview*.

In 1964, Antonio undertook what became a five-year project, recording the life work of CHARLES JAMES under the direct supervision of the designer. He also was a molder and maker of fashion models, advising them on makeup and hairstyles to fit his ideas of their best looks. He became interested in education and gave lectures and workshops to students of fashion illustration in the United States and in the Dominican Republic. A retrospective of his work, 1963 to 1987, was mounted at FIT in 1988.

Illustration of model wearing a long, pleated dress, 1973.

Illustration of Yves Saint Laurent design, 1973.

Designer Arkadius.

BORN Arkadiusz Weremsczuk; Lublin, Poland, July 5, 1969

AWARDS British Fashion Council *New Generation Award*, September 2000 • *Elle* Awards, Warsaw, Poland *Best Designer of the Year*, October 2000

From the start Arkadius has amused, and sometimes enraged, fashion onlookers with wildly creative shows of clothes that are alternately calmly wearable and provocatively outrageous; his fine tailoring skills and imaginative cutting go hand-in-hand with a taste for ornate decoration and eccentric presentations. Half creator, half businessman, he has been described as bizarrely talented and hailed as the next JOHN GALLIANO.

Born into a family of teachers, Arkadius set his sights on London and on fashion while still in college in Krakow, leaving before graduation to pursue his dream. He reached London in 1994—after side excursions to Tuscany and Munich—with his goal to attend Central St. Martins College of Art and Design. He first had to learn enough English to walk through its doors but managed to enroll in September of that year. During his third year he was invited to work in ALEXANDER MCQUEEN'S design studio, and his July 1999 graduation collection earned both a double first and a sponsor for his debut collection that September at London Fashion Week.

Appearing to have found a happy medium between commercialism and art, Arkadius has since added ready-to-wear, men's wear, and jeans.

Spring 2004.

Giorgio Armani

Designer Giorgio Armani.

BORN Emilia-Romagna, Italy, July 11, 1934

AWARDS Neiman Marcus Award, 1979 • Council of Fashion Designers of America (CFDA) *International Award*, 1983

After brief tries at medicine and photography, Giorgio Armani began his fashion career in 1964, first as a window dresser, then as assistant buyer of men's clothing for La Rinascente, a large Italian department store. During the seven years he spent there he developed his ideas on men's dress and a dislike for what he considered a stiff, formal look that disguised individuality.

His next job, as designer for a men's wear company of the Cerutti Group, gave him even greater knowledge of the practical and commercial aspects of the clothing business. From there he went on to design for a number of companies including Ermenegildo Zegna and UNGARO.

Armani produced his first men's wear collection under his own label in 1974, incorporating the

ideas he had developed while working for others. An unconstructed blazer was his first attention-getter. He moved into the area of women's wear in 1975, bringing to it the same perfectionist tailoring and fashion attitude applied to his men's clothes.

From day into evening, Armani's emphasis is on easy, uncontrived shapes cut from exquisite Italian fabrics, tailored with absolute mastery. Color and fabric are primary considerations. His preference is for neutrals such as taupe, beige, black, and infinite tones of gray. He claims to have taught women to dress with the ease of men but always with a feminine turn to even the most masculine cut. His work is not intended to shock and he is not interested in trends; he aims for a soft, light silhouette, emphasizing femininity and gently disguising imperfections.

Armani business interests now include perfumes and accessories for men and women sold in fine retail stores and free-standing shops in Italy and around the world. The Emporio label and shops were developed to bring Armani styles to young men and women who could not afford the regular line,

Look from Armani Prive, spring 2008.

and A/X: Armani Exchange is younger and sportier still. He has also done film work.

Armani devotes himself to work singlemindedly, supervising every aspect of his collections, which are shown in his own theater. He does not use stylists and insists on complete control, down to such details as the models' hairstyles and makeup.

In October 2000, a 25-year Armani retrospective opened at the Guggenheim Museum in New York, moving in March 2001 to the museum's outpost in Bilbao, Spain, and in 2003 to Berlin, Germany.

Currently Giorgio Armani owns 305 stores in 35 countries. The company offers five different brands for age groups from 18 to 60, and it has an estimated net worth of $2 billion.

Armani has extended his style and name to hotels and residences, beginning in 2007 with 144 private residences in Dubai in the world's tallest building, Burj Dubai. The first Armani hotel opened in the same building in 2008.

Designer Giorgio Armani with model, 1979.

Men's wear, fall 2008, with women's wear, pre-fall 2008.

Ready-to-wear, spring 2010.

Laura Ashley

BORN Merthyr Tydfil, Wales, 1926

DIED Coventry, England, September 17, 1985

Romantic and innocent, the Laura Ashley look consisted of dresses with long, soft skirts in small flower prints, sweetly trimmed with lace. It would appear to have little connection with life and fashion in the twenty-first century yet its influence can still be seen on city streets, worn in ways the designer would probably not have imagined—with backpacks and work boots—and in the collections of cutting-edge designers from Italy to the United States.

In 1953 Ashley and her husband, Bernard, began printing textiles on the kitchen table of their London flat. The couple began with towels, scarves, and placemats, which Bernard carried around to the major London stores and sold so successfully that the Ashleys formed their first company in 1954. As their business and family expanded, they moved from London to Wales, setting up a factory at Carno, Montgomeryshire. In the early 1980s the family moved into an eighteenth-century chateau in

Flower print dress, 2005.

Northern France, although the business remained centered in Wales.

Laura Ashley died in 1985 as a result of a fall, but the company endured. Reaching its apogee in the 1960s, 1970s, and early 1980s, it went public in 1985. At its height, there were Laura Ashley stores in cities as diverse as New York, Paris, Geneva, and San Francisco, dispensing the distinctive prints in decorative fabrics and clothes, bringing the cozy warmth of an English cottage into the harsh city environment.

In 1989, the company launched its "Mother and Child" collection of coordinated apparel and home furnishings, which became a great success. In 1993, Laura Ashley celebrated its 40th anniversary. That same year Sir Bernard Ashley, who had served to that time as chairman, stepped down to become honorary president, a position he held until 1998.

The final 3 percent of the company owned by the family and the Ashley trust was sold in June 2001.

Designer Laura Ashley (left).

BORN New York City, May 15, 1923
DIED San Antonio, Texas, October 1, 2004

AWARDS Pratt Institute, *citation of dedication to fashion photography*, 1976 • Council of Fashion Designers of America (CFDA) *Lifetime Achievement Award*, 1989

The son of a retail store owner, Richard Avedon (Av-ah-don) received his first photographic training in the Merchant Marines. He took a class in experimental photography at the New School for Social Research, taught by Alexey Brodovitch, art director of *Harper's Bazaar*, and in 1945 joined the staff of the magazine. Thus began his long and distinguished career in fashion and commercial photography and an association with *Harper's Bazaar* that endured for 20 years. During that time he had nonfashion assignments from other publications, including *Theatre Arts*. In 1966 he moved to *Vogue*, remaining there until 1990.

His fashion photography, notable for its sense of style, freedom, and drama, captured the tone of the 1960s and recorded the sexual revolution. He took the action photography of Martin Munkacsi to a more sophisticated level, working in the studio, and, for his simulated photojournalism, on location. He also did photo-collages using the illustrations of Katerina Danzinger, a visual consultant on the Fred Astaire film, *Funny Face*, and has been a TV consultant. Since leaving *Vogue*, he has been a staff photographer at *The New Yorker*—their first—providing them with aggressively anti-glamour portraits. One-man shows of his work have been held at, among other venues, the Museum of Modern Art in 1975, the Metropolitan Museum of Art in 1978 and 2002, and in 1994 at the Whitney Museum. This last was a retrospective placing emphasis on his non-fashion work, which presumably, he considered more serious than the fashion.

In September of 2004, Avedon suffered a stroke while taking pictures in San Antonio, Texas, for *The New Yorker*. He died a month later.

Photographer Richard Avedon.

BADGLEY MISCHKA

Laura BIAGIOTTI

Christopher BAILEY

Dirk BIKKEMBERGS

Glenda BAILEY

Manolo BLAHNIK

Cristóbal BALENCIAGA

Bill BLASS

Pierre BALMAIN

Kenneth Paul BLOCK

Jeffrey BANKS

B. MICHAEL

Travis BANTON

Ozwald BOATENG

George BARBIER

Marc BOHAN

Shane BARNES

Monica BOTKIER

Neil BARRETT

Louise BOULANGER

Scott BARRIE

Veronique BRANQUINHO

John BARTLETT

Tom BRIGANCE

Luella BARTLEY

Donald BROOKS

Cecil BEATON

Thom BROWNE

Geoffrey BEENE

BRUCE

Gilles BENSIMON

Barbara BUI

Christian BÉRARD

Tory BURCH

Eric BERGÈRE

Stephen BURROWS

Rose BERTIN

Badgley Mischka

BORN Mark Badgley; East St. Louis, Illinois, January 12, 1961

James Mischka; Burlington, Wisconsin, December 23, 1960

AWARDS Mouton Cadet, *Young Designer Award*, 1989

Mark Badgley (Badge-lee) attended UCLA and James Mischka (Meesh-Ka) earned a B.A. in Managerial Science at Rice University in Houston. They met at Parsons School of Design where both graduated with B.F.A. degrees in Fashion Design. After Parsons, their paths diverged, and they both became design assistants. Badgley worked for Jack Rogers and DONNA KARAN, and Mischka went to YVES SAINT LAURENT and WILLI SMITH. The two young designers teamed up in 1988 to form their own company. In January 1992 the firm was acquired by Escada, the large German fashion company, but the two designers retained creative control and a financial stake in the business.

The designers are best known for their beaded eveningwear, favored by celebrities from New York to Hollywood. They describe their clothes as modern and sleek, appropriate for dinner and dancing. However, they have broadened their focus to include day wear, separates, and a collection of bridal gowns with the clean, elegant lines and the luxurious beading and ornamentation that distinguish their clothes for eve-

Designers James Mischka (left) and Mark Badgley (right).

Spring 2009.

Fall 2008.

ning. In October 2004, Iconix Brand Group acquired Badgley Mischka from Escada. Since that date, Badgley Mischka has been hailed by *Vogue* as being among the top ten American designers.

BORN Yorkshire, England, 1971

AWARDS British Fashion Awards *Designer of the Year*, 2005; *Men's wear Designer of the Year*, 2007, 2008 • *GQ Designer of the Year Award*, 2008

Although today he is one of Britain's most influential young designers, Christopher Bailey (Bay-lee) once wanted to be a veterinarian. After winning a student competition at age 18 for a coveted spot in a two-year fashion course at London's Royal College of Art, however, his career path was set in motion. DONNA KARAN visited the school and offered Bailey a job after seeing his portfolio. He worked with her design team in New York for more than two years, and then joined TOM FORD at Gucci. In 2001 he was hired as the creative director at Burberry and tasked with revamping the venerable label's image. His runway debut a few months later was a laid-back and playful "return to the British roots" of the company.

Today Bailey oversees design for all of Burberry's collections, including Burberry London, Burberry Prorsum, and Thomas Burberry, as well as all other licensed products, advertising, art, and store design. And while the designs for both men and women have evolved as fresh and forward-thinking—and the ad campaigns feature the likes of supermodel Kate Moss—Bailey

Men's wear, fall/winter 2009.

Designer Christopher Bailey.

Spring 2009.

never forgets that it all began with the trench coat that Thomas Burberry invented in 1890. They remain a staple of every collection, a classic made cool again for the twenty-first century.

Glenda Bailey

BORN Derbyshire, England, 1958

AWARDS *Adweek* magazine, *Editor of the Year*, 2001

After earning a degree in fashion design from the University of Kingston, future magazine editor Glenda Bailey (Bay-lee) dabbled briefly in the fashion industry herself. In 1983, she produced a collection for Guisi Slaverio in Italy. Soon, though, she found her true calling in publishing, launching and editing a series of successful fashion magazines. The style of magazine that she envisioned, and that she found missing in English publishing, was a mix of hard-hitting reportage, chic fashion, and lifestyle features.

She became editor of *Honey* magazine in 1986 and was assigned to launched *Folio* magazine soon after. Her in-depth knowledge of fashion and trends, combined with a penchant for bucking convention and trying new ideas, made hers a sort of Midas touch in the publishing world. In 1988, she was appointed launch editor of British *Marie Claire*, which she turned into the biggest-selling fashion magazine in the United Kingdom. She crossed the Atlantic in 1996 to become editor of the American *Marie Claire*. Perhaps her most renowned issue of that magazine was the "celebrity challenge" issue, for which celebrities agreed to, in lieu of interviews, perform extraordinary tasks such as living in an igloo or surviving in the desert.

In 2001, Bailey became editor of *Harper's Bazaar*, maintaining her highly relevant and news-tinged perspective on fashion publishing. Sales of the magazine surged 38 percent from 2001 to 2007. Her approach to fashion is atypically populist, and her magazine features in *Harper's Bazaar* often have an instructional angle to them. "We have these beautiful aspirational images so people can dream," Bailey says, "but at the same time we also know that even the most fashionable, knowledgeable woman wants ideas."

Editor Glenda Bailey.

BORN Guetaria, Spain, January 21, 1895
DIED Valencia, Spain, March 24, 1972

Master tailor and dressmaker, Cristóbal Balenciaga (Bah-len-see-AH-gah) was a great originator, possibly the greatest couturier of all time. Of them all, only he could do everything—design, cut, fit, and sew an entire garment. He worked alone, using his own ideas, putting together with his own hands every model that later appeared in his collections. His clothes, so beautiful and elegant, were also so skillfully designed that a woman did not have to have a perfect figure to wear them. They moved with the body and were comfortable as well as fashionable.

The facts of Balenciaga's origins and early life are so obscured by legend that it is difficult to know where reality begins and myth ends. His father, for example, has been said to have been both captain of the Spanish royal yacht and captain of a fishing boat. It is known that after his father's death, he and his mother moved to San Sebastián where she became a seamstress. Balenciaga followed in her footsteps to become a skilled tailor. As the story goes, his career in fashion began when the Marquesa de Casa Torres allowed him to copy a DRÉCOLL suit he had admired on her, later sending him to Paris to meet the suit's designer. The Marquesa encouraged him to study design and in 1916 helped him set up his own shop in San Sebastián. This

Designer Cristóbal Balenciaga.

was the first of three houses named Eisa; the others were in Madrid and in Barcelona.

Balenciaga moved to Paris in 1937, returning to Spain at the beginning of World War II. After the war he reopened in Paris on avenue George V, where he established himself as the preeminent designer of his time, one of the most imaginative and creative artists of Paris couture.

Red-skirted evening dress with braided top, 1946.

Black lace dress with pink sash, 1951.

Balenciaga, continued

A great student of art, he understood how to interpret his sources rather than merely copy them. The somber blacks and browns of the old Spanish masters were among his favorite colors and the influence of such early moderns as Monet and Manet can also be found in his work. His interest in the post-cubists and abstract expressionists can be seen in his late designs.

His innovations, especially during the 1950s and 1960s, are still influential: the revolutionary semi-fitted suit jacket of 1951; the 1955 middy dress, which evolved into the chemise; the cocoon coat; the balloon skirt; and the flamenco evening gown cut short in front and long in back. To achieve his sculptural effects he worked with the Swiss fabric house, Abraham, to develop a heavily sized silk called gazar, very light but with a capacity for holding a shape and floating away from the body.

In 1968 Balenciaga abruptly closed his house and retired to Spain. There has been speculation concerning his reasons but perhaps he was simply tired—he was 75 years old. He came out of retirement to design the wedding dress of Generalissimo

Henri de Toulouse Lautrec inspired designs, 1951.

Red velvet stole over an ivory satin gown, 1952.

Franco's granddaughter, whose marriage took place in 1972 just two weeks before Balenciaga died.

A shy and private man who loathed publicity, Balenciaga was seldom photographed, never appeared in his own salon, and, except for his perfumes, refused to have anything to do with commercial exploitation. Since his death, he has been honored by a number of exhibitions: in New York in 1973 at the Metropolitan Museum of Art; in 1986 at the Fashion Institute of Technology; and in France in 1985 at the Museum of Historic Textiles in Lyon, the center of the French silk industry. The label was revived for ready-to-wear in the 1990s as Balenciaga Le Dix, with Joseph Thimister as head designer (1992–1997), and upon his departure with NICOLAS GHESQUIÈRE. In July 2001, the house was bought by Gucci, which allotted a 9 percent share to Ghesquière as creative director.

Balenciaga's sense of proportion and balance, his mastery of cut, his touches of wit, the architectural quality and essential rightness of his designs still inspire awe and admiration. He is rightly considered one of the giants of twentieth-century couture.

BORN Pierre Alexandre Claudius Balmain; St. Jean-de-Maurienne, France, May 18, 1914
DIED Paris, France, June 29, 1982

AWARDS Neiman Marcus Award, 1955 • Drama Desk Award for Outstanding Costume Design, 1980

Pierre Balmain claimed credit for beginning the New Look—critics and writers divided it between him, DIOR, FATH, and BALENCIAGA. It is true that his first collections accentuated the femininity of the figure with a small waist, high bust, rounded hips, and long, full skirts—all New Look characteristics. He continued making clothes of quiet elegance, and at his death had just completed the sketches for his fall collection.

An only child, Balmain was only seven when his father died. He was raised by his mother, who later worked with him in his couture salon. In 1934, while studying architecture at the École des Beaux Arts in Paris, he began sketching dresses and took his designs to CAPTAIN EDWARD MOLYNEUX. The British-born designer, who allowed the 20-year-old to work for him in the afternoons while continuing school in the mornings, finally advised him to devote himself to dress design. Molyneux then gave him a job and Balmain remained with the house until called into

Designer Pierre Balmain.

the Army in 1939. After the fall of France in 1940, Balmain returned to Paris to work for LUCIEN LELONG, where he stayed until 1945 when he left to open his own house.

In 1951 he opened a New York ready-to-wear operation, for which he designed special collections, and he also did theater and film work. In addition to Balmain boutiques there were perfumes, Vent Vert and Jolie Madame, and over 60 licenses including men's wear, jewelry, luggage, and accessories. The fragrance business was bought by Revlon, which introduced new fragrances Ivoire in 1981 and Opera in 1994.

After Balmain's death in 1982, the business continued until January 1990 with Erik Mortensen in charge of couture. When the house was sold, Mortensen, who had been there for 42 years, was replaced. When ownership changed once more, OSCAR DE LA RENTA moved in as couture designer. His first collection was for spring 1993, his last for fall/winter 2002–2003. He was succeeded by Frenchman Laurent Mercier who was fired in June 2003. On August 2, 2003, French designer Christophe Lebourg was made creative director. Due to financial difficulties at the company, Balmain filed bankruptcy in 2004. After a two year hiatus, Balmain returned in the fall of 2006 under the direction of Christophe Decarnin.

Strapless ball dress, 1960.

Jeffrey Banks

BORN Washington, D.C., November 3, 1955

AWARDS Coty American Fashion Critics' Award, 1977, 1982 • *Earnshaw* magazine *Earnie* Award for boys' wear, 1980 • Cutty Sark *Designer of the Year*, 1987

Jeffrey Banks began his illustrious career as a precocious child of ten when he designed an Easter outfit for his mother consisting of a raw silk dress and a side-buttoned wool jersey coat. By age 15, he was selling men's wear at Britches of Georgetown where he was already a regular customer. He received his formal education at Pratt Institute in Brooklyn, New York, and graduated from the Parsons School of Design, New York, in 1977. Following stints as assistant to Ralph Lauren, and then to CALVIN KLEIN, Banks designed for Alixandre, Concorde International, Merona Sport, and Nik Nik. At Merona Sport in the late seventies, he introduced new colors and innovative fabrics, increasing sales by more than half.

Jeffrey Banks men's wear and boy's wear labels were launched in 1980. In 1988, Japanese investor Tomio Taki bought a one-third interest in a joint venture with Banks, allowing Banks more time to design. He designed for Hartz & Company in 1984 and consulted for Herman Geist in 1990. Licensing agreements were signed with Bloomingdale's for men's wear, Neema Clothing for fine tailored clothing, and

Designer Jeffrey Banks.

Watson Brothers for hosiery and belts. Jeffrey Banks Ltd. and Jeffrey Banks International would register sales of over $20 million by the late nineties.

Following a hiatus ending in 1998, Banks signed on as design director of the Johnnie Walker Collection of sportswear and accessories, and creative design director for Bloomingdale's labels The East Island and Metropolitan View. Designing woven shirts and knits for Haggar Clothing Company, Haggar Cool 18 increased sales at department stores. With Alixandre, Banks won a special Coty Award for his collection of men's furs.

With a penchant for plaid and old world charm Jeff Banks's designs are classic, handsome, and mature, even when catering to his younger audiences. The palette for his boy's wear is perhaps reactionary to that of his mentors with brighter playful primary and secondary colors. His men's wear collections are formalist, yet warm and comfortable, and exude confidence at every turn.

Banks has served on the board of trustees at the Fashion Institute of Technology and is an executive board member of the Council of Fashion Designers of America. He is also vice chair of the board of the Hetrick-Martin Institute.

Male model (right) wearing a look from Jeffrey Banks, 1981.

Travis Banton

BORN Waco, Texas, August 18, 1894

DIED Los Angeles, California, February 2, 1958

Travis Banton worked for Paramount Pictures for 14 years, designing elegant, sophisticated clothes for some of the screen's most legendary actresses— Claudette Colbert, Marlene Dietrich, Carole Lombard, and Mae West among them. He favored glow and shimmer over sparkle and shine and was especially partial to the bias cut. With an extraordinarily long career, Banton is remembered particularly for what became known as "The Paramount look." He produced clothes of the highest quality, often cut on the bias, superb in fabric, workmanship, and fit. The effect was dreamy, elegant, understated.

His parents moved to New York City when Banton was two years old. He briefly attended Columbia University, transferred to the Art Student's League and then to the School of Fine and Applied Arts. His apprenticeship to Madame Frances, a successful New York custom dressmaker, was interrupted by naval service in World War I, but not before he established himself as a designer. On his return he worked for a number of custom houses, including LUCILE, training ground for Howard Greer and a number of other designers, then opened his own salon. There his designs included elaborate costumes for the *Ziegfeld Follies*.

At the instigation of Walter Wanger, he went to Hollywood in 1924 to design costumes for Leatrice Joy in Paramount Pictures's *The Dressmaker From Paris*. He stayed on at Paramount and in 1927, when

Howard Greer left to open his own custom business, became the studio's head designer. At the expiration of his Paramount contract in 1938, Banton joined Howard Greer as a private couturier. A year later he went to 20th Century Fox, then worked off and on for Universal Studios. Meanwhile, he conducted his own dressmaking business, turning to ready-to-wear in the 1950s. He designed Rosalind Russell's wardrobe for the stage production of *Auntie Mame*, and dressed Dinah Shore for both her television appearances and her private life.

At the end of his career he had designed costumes for more than 122 movies. Banton is also credited with teaching the craft of costume design to legendary Edith Head.

Designer Travis Banton (center) with models.

George Barbier

BORN Nantes, France, October 10, 1882
DIED Paris, 1932

George Barbier began his career as a set and costume designer for the Ballet Russes after finishing the École de Beaux-Arts in Paris. His illustrations gracefully captured the essence of art deco, the prevailing art movement of the time. Barbier's first paid work as an illustrator was with the elite fashion journal, *Journal de Dames et Des Modes*. Although the publication folded only two years after its inception, his work there would establish him in the fashion industry as both a designer and an illustrator. He later began illustrating for the *Gazette du Bon Ton*, and when *Vogue* took over the journal, his contract continued with Condé Nast's premier fashion magazine. Barbier was commissioned to illustrate for some of the most popular design houses of his generation—WORTH, LANVIN, and POIRET. Although he never actually owned his own design house, Barbier created flamboyant, celebratory, and decorative original designs through his illustrations, which catered to the

Designer/illustrator George Barbier.

exotic designer as well as the liberated French fashion consumer.

After World War I, Barbier began designing for the theater. Along with ERTÉ, he designed costumes and sets for the *Follies Bergére* in France, and subsequently for the *Ziegfield Follies* in the United States. He also designed costumes for Valentino's 1924 film, *Monsieur Beaucaire*. The last show Barbier worked on was *Paris Shakes* at the Casino de Paris, which starred actress Josephine Baker.

Barbier died in 1932 at the age of 50. His legacy continues through his influence on many popular designers of the twentieth century, including BOB MACKIE and JOHN GALLIANO, both groundbreaking designers in their own right.

Illustration of woman in a Paquin evening dress, 1913.

BORN Jane Barnes; Maryland, 1954

AWARDS Coty American Fashion Critics Award *Men's Wear*, 1980; *Men's Apparel*, 1981; *Men's Wear Return Award*, 1984 • Council of Fashion Designers of America (CFDA) *Outstanding Menswear Designer*, 1981 • Good Design Award, 2007

Jhane Barnes established her own company in 1977 when she was 23. While known mainly for men's sportswear, she has also made sportswear for women. Her designs are unconstructed, beautifully tailored in luxurious and original fabrics, many of which she designs herself. They are marked by innovative details, carefully thought out and carried through. She is original and creative, with architectural insight into clothing, now confined exclusively to men's wear, from belts and neckwear to sportswear, suits, and outerwear, sold through a few fine stores and her own website.

Designer Jhane Barnes.

Other design commitments include textiles, carpets, furniture, upholstery, drapery, and a collection of throws for the home.

In 2002, Barnes made her textile company private under the Jhane Barnes Textiles label. She is continually inspired by the relationship between technology and environmental sustainability. Barnes created an environmentally-friendly line of office furniture for Jofeo, an Indian-based manufacturer. The line, Tahke, is made from bamboo. She has also furnished businesses such as Google, Delta Air Lines, and SONY.

In 2007 Barnes applied her signature techniques used in her men's wear line to design resin wall panels and tabletops for Lumicar. She won the Good Design Award for this creation.

"Mental block" men's wear design.

Neil Barrett

BORN South Devon, England, 1965

Nail Barrett grew up in southwestern England on the stormy English Channel, as he describes himself, "a very practical kid who went out dressed for all kinds of rough weather." His family, master tailors, made uniforms for British naval officers.

In 1989 after college (Central St. Martins and the Royal College of Art), Barrett went to work, first for Gucci then for Prada Uomo, before joining the Belgian luggage company Samsonite. There he designed a collection of men's clothes intended specifically for travelers. These included the time-travel jacket with built-in watch, a travel jacket with built-in earplugs and inflatable neck pillow, and multipocket, crease-resistant pants. Intended not as fashion but as

Designer Neil Barrett.

practical things for travel, they were greeted enthusiastically by the fashion press.

Barrett's first collection to appear under his own name was strictly men's wear—described as haute utilitarian—spare, durable clothes designed not just for the runway but to be worn. His first capsule collection for women appeared in Milan in January 2000, shown with his men's collection. Before that women would raid men's stores for items such as his motorcycle jackets and sweaters. For both women and men, Barrett thinks not of the ultrafit, ultrathin model but of the real people with less-than-perfect bodies who will be wearing the clothes. His strength lies in fabric innovation (he has been a consultant to the Italian textile industry), in subtle colors and clever details, and an ability to make clothes that are individual fashion and also wearable.

In 2003, Neil Barrett was named creative director for Puma, and in 2006, he launched his Indigo Denim Collection for men and women.

Left: Men's wear, fall 2008.
Right: Women's wear, pre-spring 2009.

BORN Nelson Clyde Barr; Alessandria, Italy, January 16, 1946

DIED Alessandria, Italy, June 8, 1993

Scott Barrie attended Philadelphia Museum College of Art and the Mayer School in New York. He started creating fashion on his grandmother's sewing machine at age ten—inspired by his godmother, a successful designer for jazz singers Dinah Washington and Sarah Vaughan—and eventually became part of a group of brash young designers establishing themselves on Seventh Avenue in New York in the late 1960s. Barrie began designing in 1966, selling to small boutiques, and reached success when Henri Bendel and Bloomingdales placed orders for

Designer Scott Barrie (right).

his sexy, outrageous designs. In 1969, he established his company, Barrie Sport, with offices on Seventh Avenue, designing skinny evening wear dresses using matte jersey, with high slits and modern draping that appealed to a young audience. His clients included Lee Traub, the wife of the then-president of Bloomingdales, and model Naomi Sims. By the early 1970s, his designs included furs, loungewear, and accessories in addition to his elegant and risqué eveningwear.

In the early 1980s, Barrie stopped designing under his own name and moved to Milan to design for the Italian high-fashion house of Krizia. He stayed in Italy to design a collection of Italian-influenced sportswear, knits, and leather clothes—with only a hint of his signature matte jersey eveningwear—under his own name, for the Japanese company Kinshido. In 1993, he died of brain cancer at the age of 47.

Tweed sweater suit, 1974.

John Bartlett

BORN Columbus, Ohio, March 22, 1963

AWARDS Woolmark *Cutting Edge Award*, 1992 • Fashion Institute of Technology *Alumni Award*, 1994 • Council of Fashion Designers of America (CFDA) *Perry Ellis Award for New Fashion Talent*, 1993; *Men's wear Designer of the Year*, 1997

John Bartlett has, from the beginning of his career, put an unconventional spin on his approach to men's wear, giving familiar pieces a fresh, younger look with altered scale and proportions and unexpected mixes of texture and pattern. His body-conscious clothes, while firmly grounded in the American sportswear

Designer John Bartlett.

tradition, are not for the timid or unimaginative, but rather for freethinking men with minds of their own. He has also produced collections for women with the same edgy viewpoint as his clothes for men.

Bartlett graduated from Harvard in 1985 with a B.A. in Sociology, went on to the Fashion Institute of Technology's men's wear program, graduating in 1988 with the Bill Robinson Award. He interned with WILLI SMITH, Bill Robinson, and RONALDUS SHAMASK—spending a year as men's designer for WilliWear from 1988 to 1989, and was design director for Shamask from 1989 to 1991. He established his own label in 1992. Despite critical acclaim, he has struggled over the years to find stable financial backing to build his business, and in November 2002, announced he was closing down and leaving fashion.

Left: Spring 2007.
Right: Fall 2006.

BORN Stratford Upon Avon, England

AWARDS *Elle Young Designer of the Year Award,* 2000 • British Fashion Council *Designer of the Year Award,* 2008

Before launching her fashion label Luella in 1999, Luella Bartley had already been involved in the world of fashion as a successful journalist and as a fashion editor for British *Vogue.* Once having said that she wanted to make "the kind of clothes you can get drunk and fall over in," her first collection embraced a whimsical girly/punk aesthetic and was presented in a friend's apartment. The designs caught the attention of the press and were a hit with both critics and "It Girls" alike. Frilly dresses, cropped jackets, and graffiti accents are some of the hallmarks of her young, upbeat designs.

Bartley's business acumen has also served her well. In 2001 she took her collections to Milan and New York, where she remained for six years. Global distribution soon followed for her ready-to-wear and then accessories lines. Target chose her as their debut guest designer for the store's Go International line in 2006, and the following year Bartley returned to her

Above: Spring/summer 2009.
Below, right: Fall/winter 2008.

London home and opened her first flagship store in Mayfair. In 2008 she expanded her profile with a limited edition line of handbags in Hong Kong and a collaboration on four designer T-shirts with the globally-conscious group Tonic. Her 2009 spring ready-to-wear collection, which she termed both "ladylike" and "psychedelic," was a noted hit. In November 2009 the Luella fashion label ceased trading after a key financier, Club 21, pulled out.

Designer Luella Bartley.

Cecil Beaton

BORN London, England, January 14, 1904
DIED Brood Chalke, Wiltshire, England, January 18, 1980

AWARDS Antionette Perry (*Tony*) Award: *Quadrille*, 1955; *My Fair Lady*, 1957; *Coco*, 1970. Neiman Marcus Award, 1956 • Commander of the British Empire (C.B.E.), 1957 • Motion Picture Academy Award: *Gigi*, 1958; *My Fair Lady* (sets and costumes), 1965, and *Légion d'Honneur*, 1960

Photographer, artist, costume and set designer, and writer, Cecil Beaton was educated at Harrow and at Cambridge University. In 1928 he began a long affiliation with *Vogue* magazine, where his first contributions were spidery sketches, caricatures of well-known London actresses, and drawings of clothes worn at society parties; photographs appeared later. In her memoirs, EDNA WOOLMAN CHASE of *Vogue* describes him at their first meeting as "... tall, slender, swaying like a reed, blond, and very young...." He gave an impression that was "an odd combination of airiness and assurance." And later, "What I like

Cecil Beaton.

best is his debunking attitude toward life and his ability for hard work." In photography he did both fashion and portraiture, and became the favored photographer of the British royal family. During World War II, he photographed for the Ministry of Information, traveling to North Africa, Burma, and China.

Beginning in 1935, Beaton designed scenery and costumes for ballet, opera, and theatrical productions in both London and New York. Among his credits: *Lady Windermere's Fan*, *Quadrille*, *The Grass Harp*, and *The School for Scandal* (Comédie Française). He did the costumes for the New York, London, and film productions of *My Fair Lady*, and costumes for the films *Gigi* and *The Doctor's Dilemma*. He also designed hotel lobbies and club interiors.

A prolific writer and diarist, Beaton published many books, illustrating them and those of others with drawings and photographs. He was knighted by Queen Elizabeth II in 1972. In 1975 he suffered a stroke, which left him partially paralyzed, but he learned to paint and take photographs with his left hand. From 1977 until his death, he lived in semi-retirement at his house in Wiltshire.

Audrey Hepburn wearing a costume photographed and designed by Cecil Beaton for *My Fair Lady*, 1963.

BORN Haynesville, Louisiana, August 30, 1927
DIED September 28, 2004

AWARDS Coty American Fashion Critics' Award
"*Winnie*," 1964; *Return Award*, 1966; *Hall of Fame*,
1974; *Hall of Fame Citation*, 1975; *Special Award
(jewelry)*, 1977; *Special Award (contribution to inter-
national status of American fashion)*, 1979; *Special
Award (women's fashions)*, 1981; *Hall of Fame
Citation*, 1982 • Neiman Marcus Award: 1964, 1965
• Council of Fashion Designers of America (CFDA)
Special Award, 1985; *Special Award Designer of the
Year*, 1986; *Special Award (for fashion as art)*, 1989

Designer Geoffrey Beene.

Mini shirtdress, 1968.

Long considered the most original and creative
designer in American fashion, Geoffrey Beene is
noted for his subtle cut, imaginative use of color,
and luxurious fabrics. Making clothes that fit the life
of the modern woman has been a major preoccu-
pation—he believes that clothes must not only look
attractive but also must move well, be comfortable to
wear, and easy to pack. Year by year he has refined his
style and continued to work toward greater simplicity, with increasing emphasis on cut and line and the
lightest, most unusual fabrics.

The grandson and nephew of doctors, Beene came
to fashion after three years in pre-med and medicine
at Tulane University in New Orleans. Deciding that
medicine was not for him, he went to California and
while waiting to enroll at the University of Southern
California, worked in window display at I. Magnin,
Los Angeles. There his talent was recognized by an
executive who suggested he make a career of fashion.

He attended Traphagen School of Fashion in
New York for one summer and in 1947 went to Paris
to study at L'École de la Chambre Syndicale and
Académie Julian. While in Paris he apprenticed with a
tailor who had worked for the couturier MOLYNEUX, a
master of tailoring and the bias cut. Returning to New
York in 1950, Beene designed for several small custom salons and for Samuel Winston and Harmay. In

Beene, continued

1958 he joined Teal Traina and for the first time had his name on the label. He opened his own business in 1962.

Beene's first collection, shown in spring 1963, had elements characteristic of his work throughout the 1960s: looser fit, eased waistlines, bloused tops, flared skirts. Each collection included at least one tongue-in-cheek style to stir things up, such as a black coat paved with wood buttons and a tutu evening dress with sequined bodice and feather skirt. Among the memorable Beene designs are long, sequined evening gowns cut like football jerseys complete with numerals, tweed evening pants paired with jeweled or lamé jackets, a gray sweatshirt bathing suit, and soft evening coats made of striped blankets from the Hudson's Bay Company.

He has, at various times, designed furs, swimwear, jewelry, scarves, men's wear, and Lynda Bird Johnson's wedding dress. He has had a boutique

Ready-to-wear, spring/summer 1973.　　Ready-to-wear, spring/summer 1⊙

collection, fragrances for women and men, and licensed his name for shoes, gloves, hosiery, eyeglasses, loungewear, bedding, and furniture. Beene has shown his clothes in Europe with great success—in Milan in 1975, and at the American Embassies in Rome, Paris, Brussels, and Vienna. In December 1989 he opened his first retail shop in the Sherry Netherland Hotel on Fifth Avenue.

In 1988 he was honored by a retrospective of his work at the National Academy of Design, "Geoffrey Beene: The First Twenty-Five Years," to celebrate the 25th anniversary of his business. In the fall of 1993, he commissioned a 30-minute film to mark his 30th year in his own business. In February 1994, The Fashion Institute of Technology mounted "Beene Unbound," a 30-year retrospective of his designs.

In late 2001 he gave up his wholesale operation, electing to sell only to private clients. Geoffrey Beene died from complications due to pneumonia in 2004. A biography of his life entitled, *Beene by Beene* written by Marylore Luther, Laura Jacobs, Pamela A. Parmel, and James Wolcott was published in 2005. In 2006, the Geoffrey Beene Cancer Research Center at Manhattan's Memorial Sloan-Kettering Cancer Center was established with funds from his estate.

Linen shirt and wool skirt, 1985.

BORN Paris, France, 1944

World famous fashion photographer Gilles Bensimon joined the staff at French fashion magazine *ELLE* in 1967. When American *ELLE* was launched in 1985, he moved to the United States to work as creative director. Bensimon soon established a reputation for shooting the best of the best, and in his time at *ELLE*, he took photographs of Christy Turlington, Claudia Schiffer, Lisa Snowdon, Cindy Crawford, Naomi Campbell, Tyra Banks, Rachel Williams, and Elle Macpherson, who Bensimon married in 1985 (and divorced four years later).

Bensimon eventually earned the title of international creative director at *ELLE*, thanks in no small part to his meticulous attention to detail. Bensimon was known to take his work extremely seriously, exerting control over models, hair, and clothing in every one of the magazine's photos. Bensimon would often shoot *ELLE*'s fashion features himself to ensure that they were up to his exact standards.

Bensimon made headlines with his third marriage, to former model Kelly Killoren who went on to serve as founding editor of *ELLE Accessories* and to work as a fashion and society journalist and reality television personality.

In 2003 he published his first-ever photo retrospective, *Gilles Bensimon Photography: No Particular Order*, a 200-page inventory of famous shots from his 30-year career.

In April 2009, Bensimon's photos of country singer Faith Hill (in which she posed as her favorite blonde icons: Grace Kelly, Twiggy, and Brigitte Bardot) made the cover of *Redbook*, marking the first time in 20 years that the photographer shot for a publication other than *ELLE*. The shoot supposedly was only the first of the photos that he planned to take for other outlets including *Marie Claire*.

Photographer Gilles Bensimon.

Gilles Bensimon

Christian Bérard

BORN Paris, France, 1902
DIED Paris, France, 1949

Christian Bérard's (Bayr-ard) fashion reputation is based largely on his work for *Vogue* in the 1930s but as artist, decorator, and costume designer, his life was intertwined with the creative lives of the Paris of his time and his influence extended far beyond his illustrations. In great demand for comments and suggestions as well as technical advice, he was a familiar figure in creative circles, rumpled and disheveled, a marked contrast to the refinement and beauty of his work.

Jean Cocteau was a close friend and Bérard, recognized as one of the great stage designers of his time in the French theater, designed many of Cocteau's productions—both scenery and costumes—from the

Artist Christian Bérard (right).

first *La Voix Humaine* (1930) to *La Folle de Chaillot* (1949). At the end of World War II, Bérard also worked with Cocteau on the creation of Théâtre de la mode, a touring exhibition of miniature fashion mannequins that featured designs from Paris's finest couturiers. In addition, he designed for the Comédie Française and also collaborated with actor-producer Louis Jouvet.

Illustration, 1935.

BORN Troyes, France, November 6, 1960

Eric Bergère (Bûr-ZHÂR) began his fashion career early, studying clothing techniques in his native Troyes, a center of the knitting industry, before moving to Paris where he further studied fashion design. He started working at Hermès when he was just 20 years old and stayed eight years, designing everything from women's sportswear to furs and swimwear.

In 1988 he began a seven-year period of freelance work—for Erreuno in Milan, LANVIN, Jun Ashida, and Inès de la Fressange in France—spanning the range from coats and suits to evening clothes and wedding dresses. He also designed eyeglasses, shoes, and collections of leather and fur for various firms.

His first collections under his own name were for both women and men and appeared for Summer 1996.

Designer Eric Bergère.

Subsequent collections—tailored clothing and sportswear for men, dresses, sportswear and career clothes for women—have been described as elegant clothes with clean, wearable shapes and subtle detail. In addition to his own Paris boutique, the clothes are sold in fine stores in Europe and Asia, and also on the Internet.

Spring 2002.

Rose Bertin

BORN Marie-Jeanne Rose Bertin; near Abbeville, France, July 2, 1747

DIED Épinay-sur-Seine, France, September 22, 1813

At 16, Rose Bertin became an apprentice in the Paris millinery shop of a Mlle. Pagelle. When sent to deliver hats to the royal princesses at the Conti Palace, she was noticed by the Princesse de Conti, who became her sponsor. Nine years later in 1772, having become a partner in the shop, Bertin was appointed court milliner. She was introduced to Marie Antoinette and became her confidante.

With such connections her establishment, *Au Grand-Mogol*, became extremely successful, not only with the French court but with the diplomatic corps. She executed commissions for dresses and hats to be sent to foreign courts, thus becoming one of the early exporters of French fashion. She also produced fantastic headdresses reflecting current events, enormously costly and symbolic of the excesses that led to the French Revolution.

Easter bonnet decorated with a bird, 1943.

Hat designed for Easter, 1943.

Bertin could be considered the first "name" designer. She was celebrated in contemporary memoirs and encyclopedias and has left behind a reputation for pride, arrogance, and ambition. So influential was she that she was dubbed "The Minister of Fashion." With the onset of the Revolution, she fled to England to escape the Terror but remained loyal to the Queen. She returned to France in 1800, retaining and transferring the business to her nephews. She died in 1813 at her home in Épinay-sur-Seine.

BORN Rome, Italy, 1943

Laura Biagiotti graduated from Rome University with a degree in archaeology, then went to work at her mother's clothing company where she began producing clothes for other designers. Her first collection under her own label appeared in Florence in 1972. Soon afterwards she bought a cashmere firm and thus discovered her true métier.

She became known as the "Queen of Cashmere," producing beautiful sweaters in the precious fiber for both men and women. Exceptional in their

Designer Laura Biagiotti (right).

colorings and quality, the sweaters were sold under the MacPherson label.

For her label Laura Biagiotti Roma, Biagiotti has collaborated with her daughter, Lavinia Cigna, to produce women's clothes that are feminine and wearable, interestingly detailed, and of excellent workmanship, with a refined mastery of knitwear. Her first fragrance Fiori Bianchi appeared in 1982, followed over the years by numerous others for women and men.

In the fall of 2001, she launched a new fragrance line, Laura Biagiotti Roma.

Biagiotti has been honored by her government for her consistent support of Italian culture and trade, both at home and abroad.

Spring/summer 2008.

Dirk Bikkembergs

BORN Cologne, Germany, January 2, 1959

AWARDS Golden Spindle award for *Best Young Designer in Fashion*, 1985 • Moët & Chandon *Esprit du Siècle* award, 2000

A 1982 graduate of the Royal Academy of Fine Arts in Antwerp, Dirk Bikkembergs is one of the wave of designers to come out of Belgium since the early 1980s. He first worked at various Belgian fashion firms before the Golden Spindle award led to a collaboration with a Belgian shoe manufacturer and his first collection of men's shoes in 1986. Men's clothing followed, then knits, and in 1988 his first full collection in Paris.

His first women's collection in 1993 shared the runway with the men's—essentially the same garments but fitted for a woman's body. The collection now spans the range from outerwear to evening. In 2000, he launched Bikkembergs Sport and a diffusion line for both men and women. Bikkembergs sees the same person wearing pieces from each collection.

His aim is to make clothes and shoes that are beyond fashion and will not be dated after six months but will endure for years.

Designer Dirk Bikkembergs.

Above: Pitti Uomo Men's Fashion Week, 2007.

Right: Men's wear, fall 2006.

Designer Manolo Blahnik.

BORN Santa Cruz de la Palma, Canary Islands, November 27, 1942

AWARDS Council of Fashion Designers of America (CFDA) *Special Award (Outstanding Excellence in Accessory Design)*: 1987, 1989; *Stiletto Award*, 1997

One of the world's most creative and influential shoe designers, Manolo Blahnik is based in London, where he turns out four collections a year of his fantastical, elegant shoes. His designs are sold through a very few fine specialty stores worldwide and in his own boutiques to such celebrity customers as Bianca Jagger, Cher, Madonna, PALOMA PICASSO, and Sarah Jessica Parker. They have frequently been chosen for runway presentations by designers as different in approach as ZANDRA RHODES and BILL BLASS. He has done collections for PERRY ELLIS, CALVIN KLEIN, and ANNE KLEIN, and men's shoes for SAINT LAURENT.

Blahnik's father was Czech and his mother was Spanish, an elegant woman who shopped for clothes in Paris, Monte Carlo, and Madrid. His mother exposed Blahnik to the great designers of the day—DIOR, BALENCIAGA, and Spain's famous cobbler, Rius. He attended the University of Geneva, first studying politics and law, soon switching to literature and architecture. He then moved on to Paris where he studied art for two years at l'École du Louvre, and moved to London around 1968.

Early in 1971 Blahnik traveled to New York, where his friend Paloma Picasso arranged for him to show his stage designs to *Vogue* editor DIANA VREELAND.

She was so impressed by the shoes in his sketches that she urged him to go into shoe design and helped him connect with an Italian manufacturer. Now he employs four Italian factories, spending nearly three months a year in Milan supervising the translation of his ideas into reality. As a designer he works alone without assistants, drawing as many as 300 designs a year, often even whittling the original lasts. The shoes are fantastically expensive, each pair made by hand from the costliest fabrics and finest leathers, with a few rare designs studded with diamonds and other precious gems. While he does make a few low-heeled designs, Blahnik is mainly identified with the extravagantly high, spiky heel.

A man of prodigious energy, Blahnik personally cuts 80 or more samples each season, a skill that took him seven years to acquire. He draws and paints, but mainly he thinks about shoes. He has filled two floors and the attic of his weekend house in Bath, England, with his collections: one shoe of each pair he has ever made. He is constantly traveling between London, Milan, the United States, and Asia. An avid movie buff, he uses his New York business trips to catch up, sometimes seeing as many as four movies in a day. In 2003, the Design Museum of London opened a major Blahnik exhibit; a book showcasing his drawings was published in conjunction. In 2005, Eric Boman published *Blahnik by Boman*, a splashy photographic celebration of the designer's shoes. In 2006, Sophia Coppola invited Blahnik to design the footwear for her film, *Marie Antoinette*, which went on to win the Academy Award for best costume design. Blahnik is also known for his designs worn by Sarah Jessica Parker in *Sex and the City*. They appeared in the TV series (1998) and played a key role in the 2008 film.

Blue pump and original sketch from the movie *Sex and the City*, 2008.

Bill Blass

BORN Fort Wayne, Indiana, June 22, 1922
DIED New Preston, Connecticut, June 12, 2002

AWARDS Coty American Fashion Critics' Award *"Winnie,"* 1961; *Return Award*, 1963; First Coty Award for *Men's Wear*, 1968; *Hall of Fame*, 1970; *Hall of Fame Citation*, 1971, 1982, 1983; *Special Award (furs for Revillon America)*, 1975 • Neiman Marcus Award, 1969 • Council of Fashion Designers of America (CFDA) *Lifetime Achievement Award*, 1986; *Dom Pérignon Award*, 1995; *Special Award The Dean of American Fashion*, 2000

In late 1999 when Bill Blass announced his retirement and the sale of his business, anguished cries went up

Designer Bill Blass.

Zebra print wrap pajama, 1974.

from members of the New York social establishment, of which he was an acknowledged member. For these women and their sisters around the country, he had produced high-priced, high-quality clothes, for more than 30 years, first for other labels and finally under his own name.

Blass was a quintessentially American designer, and his work, from the most glamorous evening clothes to simple, elegant daytime fashions, reflected that attitude. Evening clothes could resemble dressy sportswear with skirts of crisp taffeta or sheer chiffon topped by cashmere twin sets. Interesting mixtures of patterns and textures were expertly coordinated to create a polished, worldly look, investment clothes for women with active social lives.

Blass graduated from Fort Wayne High School in 1939, then studied fashion in New York for six months. He got his first fashion job in 1940 as sketch artist for David Crystal, resigning to enlist in the Army in World War II, where he was assigned to the 602nd Camouflage Battalion engaged in counter intelligence. After the war he worked briefly for ANNE KLEIN (who informed him that he had good manners but lacked talent), and in 1946 became a designer at Anna Miller & Co. When the company merged with Maurice Rentner, Blass quickly rose to head designer; his name went on the label when Rentner died in

1960. Ten years later Blass bought the company and renamed it Bill Blass Ltd.

In addition to his designer clothes for women, the Blass design projects have included Blassport women's sportswear, rainwear, *Vogue* patterns, loungewear, scarves, and men's clothing. His name has also been licensed for automobiles, uniforms for American Airlines flight attendants, even chocolates. Bill Blass perfume for women was introduced in 1978.

Blass gave time and support to his industry and was an early vice president of the Council of Fashion Designers of America. He was also a perceptive and generous supporter of design talent in others. In January 1994, he donated $10 million to the New York Public Library.

Blass died of cancer in 2002 shortly after finishing his memoir, *Bare Blass*. The label continues to put out new collections with the help of designers PETER SOM and Michael Bastian.

Actress Candice Bergen wearing kimono dress, 1970.

Silk toga, 1965.

Blazer, skirt, vest, and scarf, 1972.

Kenneth Paul Block

BORN Larchmont, New York, July 26, 1924
DIED Manhattan, April 23, 2009

Even when fashion magazines began using photographers instead of illustrators, Kenneth Paul Block remained in demand. Indeed, Block was an illustrator—and, for a time, chief features artist—for *Women's Wear Daily* for nearly 40 years. He later worked for *W* as well.

One of three sons to Goodman and Elizabeth Block—his father a lawyer and his mother a piano teacher—Block graduated from the Parsons School of Design. His first job was in 1945 as a sketch artist for McCall's Patterns. It was in the mid-1950s that he joined *WWD*, where he became known for his sketches of designer clothes as well as celebrities and socialites. Over the years, Block sketched a number of high-profile subjects including Babe Paley, Gloria Vanderbilt, Catherine Deneuve, and Sophia Lauren. His illustrations coincided with the magazine's rising interest in society, giving him the opportunity to gain notoriety as the magazine became more influential. Block became famous for capturing intricate details that made his glamorous subjects look even more alluring. He was known for capturing small gestures—particulars in the way his subjects would sit or hold an object—that gave him an edge above other illustrators. Block's style was so influential that he ended up the subject of a 2008 book, *Drawing Fashion: The Art of Kenneth Paul Block.*

Despite the prevalence of photography, Block was so well respected that some say he singlehandedly kept illustration in fashion publications. He was known to sketch the runway shows and previews of all of the major designers from the time of COCO CHANEL up through the psychedelic designs of the 1960s and 1970s, although Block himself was famous for never changing his own style of wearing an ascot, brightly colored jacket, and white buck shoes.

Before his death in 2009 at the age of 84, Block donated 1,844 of his illustrations to Boston's Museum of Fine Arts, ensuring that his work will always be on view.

Illustration of Italian coats from Ferragamo, Genny, Versace, and Krizia, 1990s.

Illustration of black dress from Ungaro, 1973.

Designer B. Michael.

BORN Durham, Connecticut

B. Michael's career began not on Fashion Avenue but on Wall Street, where the University of Connecticut graduate worked as an account executive. He ultimately left finance, though, to work for OSCAR DE LA RENTA, and he later launched a successful millinery line. His hat collection expanded to include accessories and clothing, and in 1998, B. Michael became a member of the Council of Fashion Designers of America. He unveiled his first couture collection in 1999, and today offers extensive collections for both women and men.

B. Michael has worked as a fashion critic and frequent guest lecturer at New York's Fashion Institute of Technology. His celebrity clients include Cicely Tyson, Halle Berry, Cate Blanchett, and Lynn Whitfield. His gowns are colorful and elegant but most often simple. One notable exception was the "kaleidoscope" dress, which comprised of sewn-together pieces.

B. Michael is one of the only black male designers on the New York Fashion Week scene. He has said that in order for black designers to make headway in fashion, they need to disregard their own minority status. "The most important point for me," he says, "is that the industry sees us as American designers that dress a diverse mainstream market." In February 2003, B. Michael partnered with Wayne Demar to form Dm Fashion Group, which markets and perpetuates the b. Michael brand.

Spring 2009.

Ozwald Boateng

BORN London, November 28, 1968

AWARDS Trophees de la Mode, *Best Male Designer*, 1996 • British Fashion Awards, *Top Men's wear Designer*, 2000 • Cologne Fashion Awards, *Best Male Designer*, 2002 • Order of the British Empire (OBE) (for services to the clothing industry), 2006 • Mayfair Times Awards, *Fashion Personality of the Year*, 2008

Born in London to Ghanaian parents, Ozwald Boateng learned how to sew at an early age. He studied computing at Southwark College, where his girlfriend asked him to help design clothes for her college fashion show. When he was 23, he quit his job in IT to sell his designs along the Portobello Road.

Boateng opened his own store on Vigo Street near Savile Row in 1995. By 1996, he was winning awards and in 1997 he showcased his first men's wear line—the first men's wear show of its kind to be held during women's London Fashion Week. In 1999 he was included in *The New Alchemists* by Charles Handy, profiled as one of 12 people predicted to have a huge impact on society. In 2002 the Ozwald Boateng headquarters opened at 12A Savile Row, and his suits were

Designer Ozwald Boateng.

seen on the red carpet at the Oscars worn by Will Smith ("best dressed" in 2002) and Daniel Day-Lewis in 2003. He was interviewed in *Live Forever*, a 2003 film highlighting the conception of Cool Britannia and Britpop. Also in 2003 he introduced his new perfume Parfum Bespoke at Bundespresident residence, Berlin.

Appointed creative director for GIVENCHY Homme in 2003, Boateng brought his unique brand of Savile Row tradition and contemporary design to this French men's wear brand. His first hugely successful collection was shown in July 2004 in Paris. Boateng left Givenchy in 2006.

Boateng's suits have been described as a perfect hybrid of tradition and modernity. Credited with revolutionizing the most famous street in the world for men's tailoring, he redefined the cut of the traditional suit and combined expert cutting skills with bold color, slim-fitting silhouettes, and luxurious fabrics. His contemporary approach to men's wear design has also helped to draw in a younger demographic to Savile Row.

To date Boateng has written and directed more than ten short films. He produces two ready-to-wear collections to great critical acclaim each season in addition to bespoke suits.

Spring/summer 2007.

Designer Marc Bohan.

BORN Paris, France, August 22, 1926

Chief designer and artistic director of CHRISTIAN DIOR from 1960 to 1989, Marc Bohan was responsible for the couture and ready-to-wear collections, as well as accessories, men's wear, and bed linens. Refined and romantic, his clothes were also very wearable, notable for beautiful fabrics and exquisite workmanship. He always maintained that elegance consists of adapting dress for the place, the atmosphere, and the circumstance.

The son of a milliner who encouraged his early interest in sketching and fashion, Bohan had a solid background when he took over design direction at Dior. He was assistant to ROBERT PIGUET from 1945 to 1953, worked with CAPTAIN EDWARD MOLYNEUX and MADELEINE DE RAUCH, and had his own couture salon that closed after one season due to undercapitalization. He was head designer at JEAN PATOU starting in 1954; after a few years he left Patou to freelance, working briefly in New York for Originala.

In August 1958 Bohan went to work for Dior, designing the London, New York, and South American collections. When SAINT LAURENT was drafted into the Army in September 1960, Bohan was chosen to design the January collection. In 1989, after 29 years as chief designer, Bohan left Christian Dior and in September of the same year became fashion director for NORMAN HARTNELL, the British fashion house. His first collections were couture, followed by ready-to-wear in fall 1991. He left Hartnell when the house closed in 1992.

Short overcoat, 1974.

Little black evening dress, 1984.

Monica Botkier

BORN Brooklyn, New York

Monica Botkier (BOUGHT-key-air) began her career as a fashion photographer for magazines such as *Surface* and *Mademoiselle*. An aficionado of accessories, Botkier began making leather bags for herself. She would wear them to photo shoots, where they intrigued editors, and models would ask where they could get the bags. Only a few months later, in the summer of 2003, items from her first collection were on sale at Barneys. In 2007, she was inducted into the Council of Fashion Designers of America.

Her bags are luxurious and decorated accessories that nevertheless remain highly functional. The image of an elephant—a good luck symbol in India, where Botkier traveled in her youth—recurs subtly in her handbags. She released her first shoe collection, which she said was influenced by Miu Miu and LOUBOUTIN, in 2008. In her shoes as well as her handbags, Botkier employs leather and hardware to give many of these items a postured, urban edge. Her accessories decorate such celebrities as Angelina Jolie, Heidi Klum, and Lindsey Lohan. In 2008, she designed a line of bags for Target Brands, Inc., joining a lengthening list of designers who work with the megastore. Botkier continues to take photographs for her own ad campaigns.

Designer Monica Botkier.

Limited edition Bianca bag, 2008.

BORN Louise Melenot; France, 1878
DIED 1950

When she was 13 years old, Louise Melenot worked as an apprentice in a dressmaking shop. She went on to partner with the esteemed Paris dressmaker MADELEINE CHÉRUIT, and the pair worked together for several years. In 1927, she left the House of Chéruit to open a salon with her husband, Louis Boulanger (BOO-lan-jer). Briefly, in 1933, she closed down her own couturier shop and went to work for the Callot sisters at their reknowned design house, CALLOT SOEURS, which was known for its exotic detail and its innovative use of gold and silver lamé. She soon reopened her salon at a new location on the Rue Royale in Paris. During World War II, when the German army invaded France, she was forced to close down her shop.

Boulanger's trademarks were taffeta and bold colors. She favored printed textiles over the popular embroidery of the time. A characteristic dress of Boulanger's was cut along the bias, or diagonal, with a back hem that flowed down to the wearer's ankles and a front hem that stopped at the knees. In the mid-1920s, she introduced the "pouf." The pouf was an evening gown that pressed its wearer tightly around the torso and waist but fanned out in elaborate pleats at the hips, creating a sort of bouffant effect.

Embroidered-tulle and satin dress, 1935.

Veronique Branquinho

BORN Vilvoorde, Belgium, June 6, 1973

AWARDS VH1 *Fashion Award for Best New Designer,* 1998 • Moët & Chandon *Fashion Award,* 2000

One of the many fresh talents nurtured and based in Belgium, Veronique Branquinho (Bran-kee-no) first studied painting at the Saint Lucas School of Art in Brussels before switching to fashion studies at the Royal Academy of Fine Arts in Antwerp. She graduated in 1995, and worked briefly for several commercial labels before opening her own business in 1997. In August of that year she showed her first collection in the trendy Paris store, Colette, attracting both favorable press notice and orders. Since then she has designed two collections for the Italian leather firm Russo Research, which routinely hires young designers for limited stints. She has also participated in fashion events in Italy at the Venice Biannale, in Japan, South Korea, and at the Fashion Institute of Technology in New York. She also designs shoes.

Branquinho works with a light touch in the designer range, very much aware of current trends while going her own distinctive way. Even the most tailored pieces—jackets, pants, coats, or leathers— have a relaxed, easy assurance, while the dresses, blouses, and knit pieces are fluid and feminine with

Designer Veronique Branquinho.

a certain mysterious elegance. Far from imposing a certain look, she is pleased to see women make her clothes personal by mixing them with things they already own. In 2003, she launched a men's wear line in Paris and opened a flagship store in Antwerp. She celebrated her brand's tenth anniversary in 2007 and was invited to preside over the Art of Fashion Foundation International Symposium and fashion student competition the same year. In 2008, the Momu in Antwerp presented the exhibition, "Moi, Veronique Branquinho TOuTe NUe" a showcase of her designs spanning from 1998 to 2008. She announced in 2009 that the label would close due to a decline in sales. She is working as the artistic direc-tor at the Belgian leather-goods brand Delvaux.

Spring 2007.

Printed swimming culottes, 1960.

store's designer. He spent the war years in Air Corps Intelligence in the South Pacific, returning to Lord & Taylor in 1944. In 1949 he opened his own firm on Seventh Avenue. In the 1960s and 1970s he concentrated primarily on swimwear, designing for Sinclair, Water Clothes, and Gabar. He retired in the late 1970s but continued to lecture extensively on fashion throughout the United States before his death.

Brigance trained as a couturier in Paris and sold sketches to French and English designers, but whatever he designed bore an unmistakably American viewpoint. In an interview in 1960, he said that "the secret of a woman being well dressed lies in her being appropriately dressed for her way of life."

BORN Thomas Franklin Brigance; Waco, Texas, February 4, 1913
DIED New York City, October 14, 1990

AWARDS Coty American Fashion Critics' Award "*Winnie*" (for revolutionizing the look of American women at the beach), 1953 • International Silk Citation, 1954 • National Cotton Fashion Award, 1955 • Italian Internazionale delle Arti (for foreign sportswear), 1956

Probably best known for his swimwear, Tom Brigance designed everything from coats and suits to day and evening dresses and blouses, before finding his true calling in sportswear. His early beach outfits could be ultrafeminine with ruffles and frills or ultrasophisticated in fabrics such as grey flannel and black velvet. At Brigance's death in 1990, the head of Gabar, where he worked for two years prior to his retirement, said that a Brigance-designed, skirted swimsuit was still one of his company's best-selling styles.

The son of an English mother and French father, Brigance studied at Parsons School of Design and the National Academy of Art in New York, and later at the Sorbonne in Paris. On his return to New York his talent was recognized by Dorothy Shaver, president of Lord & Taylor, and in 1939 he became the

Plaid swimsuits, 1953.

Donald Brooks

Designer Donald Brooks.

Draped jersey evening gowns, 1972.

BORN New York City, January 9, 1928

DIED Stony Brook, Long Island, August 1, 2005

AWARDS National Cotton Fashion Award, 1962 • Coty American Fashion Critics' Award *Special Award* (influence on evening wear), 1958; "*Winnie*," 1962; *Return Award*, 1967; *Special Award* (lingerie design), 1974 • New York Drama Critics' Award for costumes (for *No Strings*), 1963 • International Silk Association Award, 1954 • Parsons *Medal for Distinguished Achievement*, 1974 • *Emmy Award*, 1982

Noted for romantic evening designs and uncluttered day clothes, Donald Brooks has also designed extensively for theater and film. He is known for his use of clear colors in unexpected combinations, careful detailing, and dramatic prints of his own design.

Brooks studied at the School of Fine Arts of Syracuse University and at Parsons School of Design in New York City. He had his own company from 1964 to 1973 and has freelanced extensively, specializing in better dresses. He has designed collections for Albert Nipon and exclusive designs for Lord & Taylor. He costumed Diahann Carroll in the Broadway musical, *No Strings*, and Liza Minelli in *Flora the Red Menace.* His ten movie credits between 1963 and 1987 include costumes for Julie Andrews in *Star* and *Darling Lili.* He won an Emmy for his designs for Lee Rimick in the 1982 television film *The Letter.* He has also designed furs, bathing suits, men's wear, shoes, costume jewelry, wigs, and bed linens. Brooks died in 2005 at the age of 77.

Purple-print seraglio pajamas, 1967.

Designer Thom Browne (front) and models.

BORN Allentown, Pennsylvania, 1965

AWARDS Council of Fashion Designers of America (CFDA) *Men's Wear Designer of the Year*, March 2006 • *GQ Designer of the Year Award*, 2008

In 2006, Thom Browne inked a contract with Brooks Brothers to design a high-end unisex collection for the outlet called Black Fleece. The deal was the culmination of a rags-to-riches narrative arc that had Browne moving to New York with the proceeds and his used car. Later, a job in a GIORGIO ARMANI showroom landed him a high profile position for Club Monaco, owned by Polo RALPH LAUREN. Browne then left Club Monaco in 2001 to start the Thom Browne label. So, the legend goes, Browne sewed up five narrow suits and declared war on casual Fridays which, by the end of the dot-com boom had become the dominant Wall Street culture.

Whatever the origins of the Thom Browne suit—as his eponymously named creation was dubbed—it caught the attention of the fashion press and trendsetting weeklies. His muted flannel-square silhouette-suit cut an instantly recognizable shape on catwalks; narrow waist and high pegged trousers topped with a proportionately slender jacket. Browne's style—depending on who one talks to—is either celebrated as an outré riff on 1950s corporate America or derided as a sly, if too pricey, wink. Indeed, approaching $6,000, the creations are an expensive statement.

The designer has toned down some of his more outrageous impulses with a sportswear line and renewed his contract with Brooks Brothers through 2011.

Fall 2006.

Bruce

BORN Daphne Gutierrez, 1972
Nicole Noselli; New Jersey, 1972

AWARDS Council of Fashion Designers of America (CFDA) *Perry Ellis Award for Women's wear*, 2001

The designing partners of Bruce met while studying at New York City's Parsons School of Design and started their collaboration soon after graduation in 1995. Their day jobs in and out of the fashion industry convinced them that they wanted to follow a more individualistic route, designing clothes unique to the wearer and with details and shape that require a closer look. They presented their first capsule collection for fall 1997, and their first formal show for spring 1998, receiving a positive critical response while keeping hype to a minimum.

Designers Daphne Gutierrez (left) and Nicole Noselli (right).

The pair is lauded for skillful cutting techniques, immaculate execution, and an absorption with fit, producing clothes with a subtle edge of sensuality. They do not design for an ideal Bruce woman but expect their customers to be as individual as their designs. They would never expect a woman to wear Bruce head to toe. The clothes are in the upscale sportswear category and are sold at fashion-forward stores such as Barneys in New York, Wilkes Bashford in San Francisco, and Harrod's in London. The duo took a break between 2004 and 2007 but made a comeback in 2008 with Bruce II ready-to-wear.

Spring 2008.

BORN Paris, France, 1957

Barbara Bui (BOO-ee) came to fashion self-taught and by a route as diverse as her French-Vietnamese origins—first studies in literature then classes in theater. It was in her theater classes that she met her future partner, William Halimi. When they tired of theater in the 1980s, the pair opened a boutique to sell her designs and called it Kabuki, later renaming it Barbara Bui.

After successful showings in Paris, Bui withdrew from runway presentations until the mid-nineties, when she showed in New York. Her collections

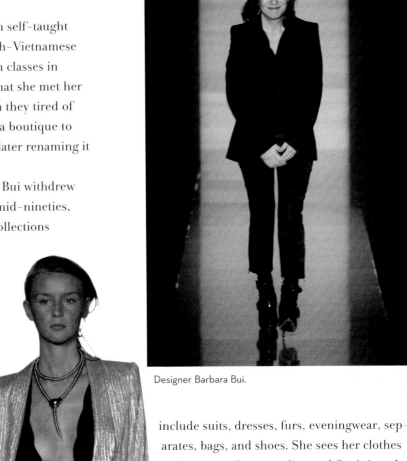

Designer Barbara Bui.

include suits, dresses, furs, eveningwear, separates, bags, and shoes. She sees her clothes as balancing the masculine and feminine, the delicate and the assertive, for women with a strong point of view who feel themselves citizens of the world.

In addition to a boutique and a café in Paris there are shops in Milan and in New York. In 2004, she launched the first perfume Barbara Bui Le Parfum. In 2007, she collaborated with the legendary rock-and-roll photographer David Bailey to create artwork for a print ad campaign in the United States.

Left: Spring 2009.
Right: Spring 2006.

Tory Burch

BORN Tory Robinson; Valley Forge, Pennsylvania, June 15, 1966

AWARDS Accessories Council of Excellence, *Accessory Brand Launch of the Year Award*, 2007 • Council of Fashion Designers of America (CFDA), *Accessory Designer of the Year Award*, 2008

Coming out of the tradition of Ralph Lauren, Tory Burch is one of the most successful examples of marketing a stylized version of oneself as a ready-to-wear lifestyle. Her breezy early-1960s Palm Beach meets Upper East Side style has won her a niche among a cross-section of women. Tory Burch launched in 2004 and includes ready-to-wear, handbags, shoes, and jewelry. Burch's popularity then wound through Oprah Winfrey to land masscult audience by 2005.

Burch is also a well-known New York socialite and mother. With a sophisticated American aesthetic, upper-middle class professional women are known for wearing her double T-logo embossed lifestyle accessories. Celebrity fans include Cameron Diaz, Jennifer Lopez, Uma Thurman, and Hilary Swank.

Burch grew up on a farm in Valley Forge, Pennsylvania, and studied art history at the University of Pennsylvania. She also cut her teeth doing PR for Ralph Lauren and Vera Wang. Burch's mid-priced off-the-rack collections usually center on a classical

Designer Tory Burch.

silhouette—such as a slit necked tunic—that is updated with embroidery and detail. She has stated that her mother Reva Robinson—a 1960s socialite—is the muse for these updates of such 1960s iconography. The Tory Burch Reva line, which features shoes and handbags, is named after her mother. There are 16 stand-alone Tory Burch boutiques in the United States, and more than 400 department and specialty stores worldwide that carry the company's merchandise.

The popular Reva line.

Designer Stephen Burrows (center) and models.

BORN Newark, New Jersey, September 15, 1943

AWARDS Coty American Fashion Critics' Award *Special Award (lingerie)*, 1974; "Winnie," 1977 • Council of Fashion Designers of America, *Board of Directors' Special Tribute*, 2006

Stephen Burrows has always gone his own way in fashion, favoring soft, clinging fabrics such as chiffon and matte jersey, and with a partiality for the asymmetrical. He used patches of color for a mosaic effect in the early 1960s, top-stitched seams in contrasting thread, and finished edges in a widely copied, fluted effect known as "lettuce hems."

The first African-American designer to gain international acclaim started making clothes as a young boy under the tutelage of his grandmother. He later honed his design skills at the Philadelphia Museum College of Art and the Fashion Institute of Technology in New York City. In 1968 he and an FIT classmate, Roz Rubenstein, joined forces to open a boutique. The next year both went to work for Henri

Bendel—Rubenstein as accessories buyers, Burrows as designer in residence. In 1973 they formed a partnership and a firm on Seventh Avenue. In November of the same year Burrows was one of five American designers to show in France at a benefit for the Versailles Palace, an event which proved a smash success for the Americans. A few years later KARL LAGERFELD declared him to be "the most original American talent since CLAIRE MCCARDELL."

Burrows and Rubenstein returned to Bendel's in 1977, remaining until 1981 when the store was sold. Since then, Burrows has been in and out of business a number of times, ascribing his lack of commercial success at least partly to a lack of business skills. He has supported himself by making theater costumes, designing for the licensing divisions of other designers, and for the occasional private client. He has also done furs.

In January 2002 he was back as house designer at Bendel's, with an in-store studio and staff; a small collection sold only at the Fifth Avenue store. In 2006, the fortieth anniversary of Burrows's clothing line, he won the Council of Fashion Designers of America (CFDA) *Board of Directors' Special Tribute* award.

Stephen Burrows's clothing is sold in fine stores in the United States, Europe, and the Middle East.

Spring 2007.

CALLOT SOEURS
Giuliana CAMERINO
Ennio CAPASA
Albert CAPRARO
Roberto CAPUCCI
Pierre CARDIN
Hattie CARNEGIE
Bonnie CASHIN
Oleg CASSINI
Consuelo CASTIGLIONI
Edmundo CASTILLO
Roberto CAVALLI
Nino CERRUTI
Sal CESARANI
Hussein CHALAYAN
Gabrielle "Coco" CHANEL
Edna Woolman CHASE
Madeleine CHÉRUIT
CHLOÉ
Jimmy CHOO
Doo-Ri CHUNG
Liz CLAIBORNE
Ossie CLARK

CLEMENTS RIBEIRO
Anne COLE
Kenneth COLE
Sybil CONNOLLY
Jasper CONRAN
Esteban CORTAZAR
Francisco COSTA
André COURRÈGES
Patrick COX
Jules-François CRAHAY
HOUSE OF CREED
Bill CUNNINGHAM

Callot Soeurs

FOUNDED 1895

CLOSED 1937

Founded by four sisters—Marie Callot Gerber, Martha Callot Bertrand, Regina Callot Tennyson-Chantrell, and Joséphine Callot Crimont—the couture house of Callot Soeurs (Cal-low Soor) was noted most particularly for formal eveningwear of intricate cut and rich color. It was famous for its delicate lace blouses, and use of gold and silver lamé, floating fabrics such as chiffon, georgette, and organdy, flower embroidery, and embroidery in Chinese colors. The high standard of excellence maintained in collection after collection over many years built the Callot reputation, and the world's most fashionable women went there to dress. Among them was the noted Spanish-American beauty Rita de Acosta Lydig, who was rumored to be a financial backer of the house.

The sisters were daughters of an antiques dealer who specialized in fabrics and lace. He was also said to be a painter. All were talented, but it was Marie Callot Gerber, the eldest, who was the genius. Tall and gaunt, her hair dyed a brilliant red, she was usually dressed in a baglike costume covered with oriental jewelry and ropes of freshwater pearls. Gerber possessed great technical skill—she was also an artist of impeccable taste, an originator. Her sisters eventually retired and she became the sole proprietor of the house, which at one time had branches in London and New York.

Henri Bendel was a great admirer of Gerber, referring to her as the backbone of the fashion world of Europe. She was an early influence on MADELEINE VIONNET, who worked for some time at Callot. During the 1920s the house produced every up-to-the-minute look, always with such taste, subtlety, and superb workmanship that the clothes had the timelessness and elegance of classics. Gerber's son, Pierre Gerber, took over the business in 1928; it was absorbed into Calvet in 1937.

Evening dress, 1910-1914.

Designer Giuliana Camerino (center).

BORN Italy, ca. 1920

AWARDS Neiman Marcus Award, 1956

Giuliana Camerino began designing and making handbags during World War II in Switzerland, where she had taken refuge with her banker husband and infant son. When they returned to Venice in 1945 the family established a firm to produce her designs, which she named "Roberta," after her favorite movie.

The Roberta name was established with beautiful and original handbags, especially the striped velvet satchels and pouches with carved motifs and the exceptional leathers. At its peak, the business, which began with one employee, employed over 200, plus more than 3,000 freelance artisans. Velvets were woven and cut by hand in the ancient, time-consuming manner; frames, handles, and locks were produced in Camerino's own factories. She operated a tannery for her leathers, a fabric-printing plant, and factories producing clothes and umbrellas. The business expanded to include ready-to-wear, knitted fashions, furs, fragrances, and luxurious accessories for women and men. Camerino was praised by Stanley Marcus for her creativity and constant flow of new ideas.

Her handbags were revived in the early twenty-first century in a new age of opulence. Once again, the elegance of the designs, the beauty of the materials, and the perfection of workmanship were recognized for the precious rarities that they are. Her name can be found on sunglasses, jewelry, handbags, car interiors, motorboats, and makeup.

Autumn/winter 2005-2006.

Ennio Capasa

BORN Lecce, Italy, 1960

Ennio Capasa's parents owned upscale boutiques in Lecce, a city on the heel of the Italian boot. Growing up there he hated fashion, which he considered to be for "tired rich people." But after graduating from the Milan Academy of Fine Arts in 1982 and wanting to avoid Italy's mandatory military service, Capasa looked for work in industrial design in Japan, and instead found a job in fashion design with YOHJI YAMAMOTO. It was there that he learned to drape, cut, and sew.

Designer Ennio Capasa.

After three years it was time to move on, and in 1987 he left Yamamoto with the older designer's suggestion that he start his own label. Rather than use his own name, Capasa chose CoSTUME NATIONAL, from the title of an antique book on French uniforms.

He felt that it was the moment for a new silhouette—more relaxed, closer to the body from the shoulder down—more style than fashion. His first collection for women was based on the skimpy proportions of Charlie Chaplin and was greeted with disdain by the Italian fashion press. Since then he has gone from success to success quietly, without the press hype usually considered necessary to gain recognition. The first men's collection was in 1993; there are now bags, belts, and leather goods. In 2004, C'N'C was launched. The streetwear line was produced by Itierre S.p.A.

His cool, hip clothes for women and men have found a receptive audience worldwide, sold by forward-thinking retailers such as Barneys New York and in his own boutiques in Milan, Rome, Tokyo, and New York.

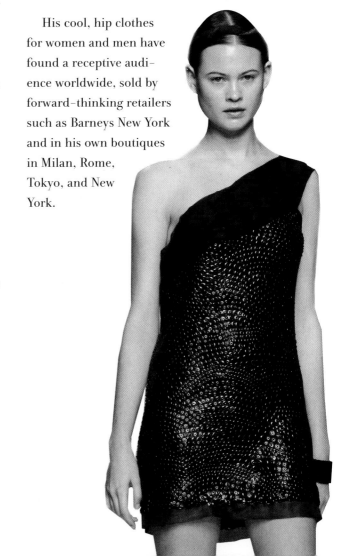

Left: Look from Costume National, spring 2009.
Right: Look from Costume National, spring 2008.

Designer Albert Capraro (center) and models.

BORN New York City, May 20, 1943

A graduate of Parsons School of Design, Albert Capraro worked for LILLY DACHÉ as an associate and from 1966 to 1974 as associate to OSCAR DE LA RENTA. He established his own business for designer ready-to-wear in 1975.

Capraro's first public notice came when Mrs. Gerald Ford, then First Lady, invited him to bring his collection to the White House. He closed the business in 1985, but continued to design for individual clients such as Mrs. Ford under the label Albert Capraro Couture. On the wholesale side, he designed exclusively for the specialty shop Martha, since closed.

In June 1990 he joined ADELE SIMPSON as designer of a new collection while continuing to design his private collections, but left in December of the same year when the future of the firm was uncertain. In recent years he has shown in Milan.

Betty Ford discussing her wardrobe with Albert Capraro, 1975.

Roberto Capucci

BORN Rome, Italy, December 2, 1929

Scion of a wealthy Roman family, Roberto Capucci first studied art at the Accademia di Belle Arti in Rome. In 1950, at the age of 21, he opened a small fashion house in Rome and showed successfully in Florence the same year. He opened a house in Paris in 1962 and moved back to Rome seven years later.

Considered a genius ranking with BALENCIAGA and CHARLES JAMES, Capucci has experimented daringly with cut and fabric to achieve dramatic sculptural and architectural effects. Fittingly, because he has raised dressmaking to the level of an art, his clothes are shown in total silence without histrionics. He does not use design assistants.

In early 2003, still doing couture on a limited basis, Capucci entered into an agreement for a ready-to-wear collection under his name. This was to be designed by three young designers, including the

Designer Roberto Capucci.

Spanish designer Sybilla and the American Tara Subkoff of Imitation of Christ, working not as a team but individually, in turn, and drawing on his archives for inspiration. The first showing was in Milan in February/March 2003.

Above: Evening gown.

Right: Pleated cocktail dress.

Designer Pierre Cardin surrounded by models.

Men's wear, spring 1969.

Pierre Cardin

BORN San Biago di Callalta, Italy, 1922

AWARDS *Golden Thimble of French Haute-Couture Award*, 1979, 1982

Pierre Cardin (Car-dan) is considered one of the most creative, intellectual, and avant-garde couturiers of the 1950s and 1960s. He showed the first nude look in 1966, followed by metal body jewelry, unisex astronaut suits, helmets, batwing jumpsuits, and other clothing then considered suitable for space travel.

The son of Italian immigrants, Cardin grew up in St. Etienne, France, and moved to Vichy at the age of 17. He worked there as a tailor, then left Vichy for Paris at the end of World War II and went to work at PAQUIN. At Paquin he executed costume designs based on sketches by CHRISTIAN BÉRARD for Jean Cocteau's film, *La Belle et la Bête*, and was introduced by Cocteau to CHRISTIAN DIOR. He worked briefly for SCHIAPARELLI, then as assistant to Dior, where in 1947 he headed the coat and suit workroom. He left Dior to form his own business, showing his first collection in 1950.

Boutiques followed for men and women—men's ready-to-wear appeared in 1958, children's apparel ten years later. From there he went on to label the world with the Cardin name—more than 600 licenses extending from wines to bicycles, jewelry to bed sheets, food to swimwear and toiletries. Cardin was the first couturier to make fashion accessible to the masses, and first to take advantage of a brand licensing system, as he did in 1960. Cardin was also a leader in expanding his company's operations throughout the world—most notably in Japan, China, and the USSR. In 1970 he established his own Paris theater, L'espace Pierre Cardin. Cardin now owns the famous Paris restaurant, Maxim's. In 1979 he entered into a trade agreement with the Peoples Republic of China to produce Cardin clothes there. A Maxim's has been established in Beijing.

In July 1987 he named his longtime collaborator, Andre Oliver, artistic director of the couture house, while continuing to share the design duties. In the wake of Oliver's death he reassumed artistic direction of the house.

In 1982, the Sogetsu Kaikan Museum in Tokyo held a Retrospective of Cardin's work, and in 1991, he was named Peace ambassador to UNESCO. In 1999, Cardin was decorated by the President of Ukrainian Republic with the Order of Merit. In 2002, he celebrated his 50-year anniversary in fashion.

Twiggy in short, pleated silk dress, 1967.

Hattie Carnegie

BORN Henrietta Kanengeiser; Vienna, Austria, 1889
DIED New York City, February 22, 1956

Hattie Carnegie began as a milliner, opening her first shop when she was just 20. By the end of her life, she had a multimillion dollar business, including two resort shops, made-to-order workrooms, ready-to-wear factories, millinery, jewelry, and perfumes. She is said to have been the first American custom designer to go into ready-to-wear. Her knack for discovering design talent was legendary—JAMES GALANOS, NORMAN NORELL, PAULINE TRIGÈRE, and CLAIRE MCCARDELL all worked for her.

Carnegie's designs were youthful and sophisticated, never faddish, never extreme, eternally Carnegie whatever the current trends might be. Less than 5 feet tall, she was noted for suits with nipped waists and rounded hips that were especially becoming to smaller women, as well as embroidered, beaded evening suits, theater suits, at-home pajamas, and long wool dinner dresses. Beautiful fabrics and excellent workmanship were hallmarks and anything but the best was abhorrent to her.

She arrived in America when she was 11 and started working in her early teens—first as a messenger at Macy's, then in a millinery workroom, and later as a

Designer Hattie Carnegie.

millinery model. In her spare time she designed hats for neighborhood women. She changed her name from Henrietta Kanengeiser to Carnegie in emulation of Andrew Carnegie, "the richest man in the world." In 1909 she opened her own hat shop, and in 1915, a custom dressmaking salon on West 86th Street near fashionable Riverside Drive. Her partner, Rose Roth, made dresses; Carnegie made hats and waited on customers. She did not know how to cut or sketch, and never learned. What she did have was great fashion flair and an acute business intelligence. In 1917 she bought out her partner.

Her first buying trip to Europe occurred in 1919, and from then on she went four times a year, bringing back quantities of Paris models, which she would adapt. She dressed society beauties, movie celebrities, and stage stars such as Constance Bennett, Tallulah Bankhead, and Joan Crawford. In the early 1930s, recognizing the hard facts of the depression, she opened a ready-to-wear department in her shop where a good Vionnet copy could be had for as little as $50.

She was married briefly in 1918, again in 1922. In 1928 she married Major John Zanft, who survived her. Her clothing business continued for some years after her death in 1956.

Black dress and white hat, 1953.

Designer Bonnie Cashin.

A third generation Californian, Cashin was raised in San Francisco where her father was an artist, photographer, and inventor; her mother was a custom dressmaker. She played with fabrics from an early age, was taught to sew, and her ideas were encouraged. She studied at the Art Students League of New York, then returned to California where she designed costumes for the theater, ballet, and motion pictures—*Anna and the King of Siam* and *Laura* are among her 60 film credits. She moved back to New York in 1949.

From 1953 Cashin freelanced, designing collections for sportswear houses Adler and Adler and Philip Sills, and bags for Coach Leatherware. In 1967 she started The Knittery, limited edition collections of hand knits and cashmeres from Scotland, also concentrating on coats and raincoats.

BORN Oakland, California, September 28, 1908
DIED New York City, February 3, 2000

AWARDS Coty American Fashion Critics' Award "*Winnie*," 1950; *Special Award* (for leather and fabric design), 1961; *Return Award*, 1968; *Hall of Fame*, 1972 • Neiman Marcus Award, 1950

Bonnie Cashin always worked in her own innovative idiom, uninfluenced by Paris. She especially believed in functional layers of clothing and showed this way of dressing long before it became an international fashion cliché. From the beginning she specialized in comfortable clothes for country and travel, using wool jersey, knits, canvas, leather, and tweeds in subtle, misty colors.

Some dominant Cashin themes were the toga cape, the kimono coat and the shell coat, a sleeveless leather jerkin, the poncho, the bubble top, the hooded jersey dress, and a long, fringed, plaid mohair at-home skirt. Signature details included leather bindings and the use of toggles and similar hardware for closings. Clothes were coordinated with hoods, bags, boots, and belts of her own design. Her clothes are included in the costume collections of museums, colleges, and design schools around the country.

Designer Bonnie Cashin in Hollywood.

Cashin, continued

In the early 1980s she established The Innovative Design Fund, a public foundation, with herself as president. Its purpose was to nurture uncommon, directional ideas in design—clothing, textiles, home furnishings, or other utilitarian objects—with awards to be used solely for producing prototypes. Another fund, "The James Michelin Distinguished Lecturer Program," at the California Institute of Technology at Pasadena began operation in 1992. Its purpose is to bring the arts and sciences together.

the mini-er the dress — the maxi-er the accessories —

Sketch by Bonnie Cashin.

Bonnie Cashin for Sills & Co. and Ballantyne Cashmere, 1966.

Shopping bag tote for Coach, 1964.

BORN Paris, France, April 11, 1913
DIED Long Island, New York, March 17, 2006

AWARDS Council of Fashion Designers of America, *Board of Directors' Special Tribute*, 2003

Perhaps best known as the designer to Jacqueline Kennedy and other glamor icons of the twentieth century, Oleg Cassini's origins are in Western Europe, where he was born to parents who were stripped of their nobility in the Russian Revolution. When he was young, his parents moved to Italy, where a young Cassini would help his mother in her dressmaking shop. He later studied fine art at the Academia di Belle Arte in Florence.

In 1936, Cassini moved to New York and worked as a junior designer. He soon relocated to Hollywood, where he worked at Paramount Studios designing costumes for B movies. By the 1950s, Cassini found himself back in mainstream fashion, designing glamorous ready-to-wear sheath dresses, cocktail dresses and knit suits. Some of his more high-profile clients included Joan Crawford, Joan Fontaine, Grace Kelly, Marilyn Monroe, and Gene Tierney—whom he later married.

In 1960, he became Jacqueline Kennedy's official dressmaker. As her iconic style garnered international acclaim, so did Cassini. Many of the outfits he

Designer Oleg Cassini.

Jacqueline Kennedy in apricot silk ziberline dress, 1962.

Jacqueline Kennedy in a red wool suit and beret, 1961.

created—including a high-necked silk ottoman evening dress and Kennedy's one-shoulder strapless gowns—became some of the most imitated pieces in U.S. history.

Among Cassini's other fashion innovations were the sheath evening dress, the A-line dress, the little white collar dress, and the women's military look. In the 1990s, he partnered with David's Bridal to create a line of Oleg Cassini bridal dresses. In 2001, Cassini's designs were showcased in the Metropolitan Museum of Art's exhibition titled "Jacqueline Kennedy: The White House Years."

Consuelo Castiglioni

BORN Italy, ca. 1959

Consuelo Castiglioni became a fashion designer more by chance than by plan when her husband's family firm was having difficulties. As Italy's foremost supplier of top-quality fur pelts to houses such as FENDI and PRADA, they were suffering from the antifur movement of the early 1990s. Although she had never been involved in fashion, Castiglioni decided in 1993 to design a small fur collection called Marni, to present to the press during the Milan ready-to-wear showings. Her first attempts attracted little or no attention and it wasn't until 1999, when she showed a colorful "deluxe hippy" collection of patchwork coats, tie-dyed crushed velvet dresses, and multi-colored fur jackets, that the firm took off. The house has since split off to become a separate fashion entity.

Using luxurious materials such as cashmere, silk, and fur, Castiglioni creates young, pretty clothes with a modern edge. They are sold in fine retail stores and, increasingly, in the company's own boutiques.

Spring 2009.

Designer Consuelo Castiglioni.

Fall 2009.

Designer Edmundo Castillo.

Castillo's focus is on feminine, sexy shoes designed along classic lines with a modern edge and made of only the finest materials—shoes that women want to wear and also collect. He views them as more makeup for the feet than mere foot-coverings. He says, "The beauty of a shoe is in how it transforms and takes life when it makes contact with the foot. . ."

Castillo currently designs the Edmundo Castillo brand for Sergio Rossi.

BORN San Juan, Puerto Rico, April 13, 1967

AWARDS Council of Fashion Designers of America (CFDA) *Perry Ellis Award for Accessories,* 2001

Even as a teenager, Edmundo Castillo was a shoe addict, obsessed with having the newest and best sneakers. He began his design studies with one year at the Altos de Chavon School of Design in the Dominican Republic before moving to New York and stints at both the Fashion Institute of Technology and Parsons. After a succession of jobs working in shoe stores where his passion blossomed, he began his real training in shoemaking in 1989 in the men's and women's footwear division at DONNA KARAN. "If it weren't for her, I wouldn't know half of what I know now. . . ." He stayed there eight years as a shoe designer, moved to Polo RALPH LAUREN for one year as senior design director before returning to Karan to design the Donna Karan and DKNY men's shoes. In 1999 he began work on his own line of women's shoes.

"Eco Pump" from Sergio Rossi, 2009.

Roberto Cavalli

BORN Florence, Italy, November 14, 1940

Born into a family richly endowed with artistic capability, Roberto Cavalli's fierce individualism and creativity were forged early on in life. His grandfather, Giuseppe Rossi, was a prolific impressionist painter with the Macchiaioli Movement, and his mother was a tailor. Following in their footsteps, Cavalli enrolled at the local art institute, where he created a series of flower prints on knit that immediately caught the attention of major Italian hosiery factories, opening the door to a long, innovative career. Soon thereafter, Cavalli's experimentation led to the development of a unique process of printing on lightweight leather. After patenting the process, he started piecing odd pieces of leather together to create what would become his signature patchwork pieces, which were commissioned by Hermès and PIERRE CARDIN.

Cavalli showcased his first namesake collection at the Salon for prêt-à-porter in Paris and then the White Room of Palazzo Pitti in Florence in 1970. In this revolutionary collection, Cavalli showcased his delicate, unique creations: jeans made of printed denim (formerly a fabric exclusively of the Italian working

Designer Roberto Cavalli.

class, and not the couture elite), intarsia leathers, and exotic prints. In 1980 Roberto Cavalli married Eva Duringer, former Miss Universe runner-up, who has become his lifelong companion and business partner. After a brief respite from the fashion world so that the couple could focus on raising a family and breeding horses, Cavalli relaunched his look at the Milano Collezion in the 1990s.

Cavalli is known internationally for his sensual rock-and-roll influenced couture, glamorous animal prints, and well-cut sensual pieces that flatter the figure, as well as partnerships with musicians and celebrities ranging from Christina Aguilera to Victoria Beckham. Cavalli aroused controversy when he announced that Kate Moss would be the face of his spring 2006 collection immediately following her drug scandal.

By 2007, he created a special collection for H&M, including women's wear, men's wear, lingerie, and accessories.

The Cavalli brand continues to gain international success and is distributed in more than 50 countries.

Pre-spring 2009.

BORN Biella, Italy, 1930

When he was 20 years old, Nino Cerruti (Che-ROO-tee) was forced to quit his philosophy studies and take over the family textile business after his father's death. Inspired to take the company in a more modern direction, he began designing men's wear and took an innovative approach to the trade. Cerruti is known for having deboned the formerly structured Italian men's jacket, creating supple, light, body-conscious suits. GIORGIO ARMANI worked under him from 1964 to 1970, and the younger designer often shares credit for taking the stuffiness out of Italian clothing.

In 1967, Cerruti opened a boutique in Paris, leaving the fabric production in Italy under the filial name Lanificio Fratelli Cerruti. He called his boutique Cerruti 1881, after the founding date of his family business. Cerruti 1881 was known for its classic wool suits and for furnishing costumes for over 150 movie productions. Some of Cerruti's most well-known subjects are Richard Gere's character in *Pretty Woman* and Clint Eastwood's in *In the Line of Fire.*

In efforts to secure global expansion of his company and the succession of his son, Cerruti sold 51 per-

Designer Nino Cerruti.

cent of his brand to the Italian corporation Fin.part in 2000. A year later, Fin.part took over the entire company, and Cerruti was forced to bow out. Still, he continues to control the fabrication end of his family textile business.

Richard Gere wearing a classic wool suit in the movie, "Pretty Women," 1990.

Sal Cesarani

BORN Salvatore J. Cesarani; New York City, September 25, 1939

AWARDS Coty American Fashion Critics' Award *Special Award (men's wear)*, 1975, 1976; *Men's Wear Return Award*, 1982 • Fashion Group of Boston Award, 1977

The son of Italian immigrant tailors, Sal Cesarani graduated from the High School of Fashion Industries and the State University of New York. He developed his color sense and knowledge of merchandising as fashion coordinator at the prestigious men's store Paul Stuart (1964–1969), then worked successively

Designer Sal Cesarani.

Wool suit.

at Polo RALPH LAUREN, Country Britches, and Stanley Blacker, before forming Cesarini Ltd. in 1976. He has produced women's fashion but has mainly concentrated on dressing men.

Essentially a traditionalist, Cesarani handles modern trends in a classic way. His cut and tailoring are impeccable: pants break at precisely the right point, jackets fit exactly with contemporary ease. As befits a classicist, he favors natural fibers—fine woolens and tweeds for fall and winter, linens and cottons for the warm months.

Cesarani has taught men's wear at the Fashion Institute of Technology and Fabric Selection and Design Styling Theory at Parsons School of Continuing Education, and has served on the Advisory Board of the Fashion Crafts Educational Commission of the High School of Fashion Industries. He is further involved with fashion education as a member of the advisory board of the Kent State University School of Fashion in Ohio. He has been recognized both nationally and by New York City for his distinguished design career and for his dedication to community service.

Designer Hussein Chalayan.

BORN Hüseyin Çağlayan; Nicosia, Cyprus, 1970

AWARDS British Designer of the Year, 1999, 2000

Hussein Chalayan (Sha-LIE-on) went to boarding school in England and to college in Cyprus. After college, he enrolled at London's Central St. Martin's College of Art and Design, and while still in school apprenticed with a Savile Row tailor. His highly eccentric 1993 graduation collection was featured in the window of one of London's most adventurous boutiques, which immediately established him as a hot new talent.

Subsequent collections have included unrippable paper clothes and sharply-tailored suits printed with illuminated flight patterns, showing his continuing interest in technology-inspired fabrics. In various financial ups and downs, Chalayan has been in and out of business but has managed to get new backing and continue producing collections.

Chalayan has shown the total dedication and complete self-belief necessary for survival in his chosen field. His work, with its clearly-defined, minimalist silhouettes, has ranged from the wildly conceptual to the highly wearable designs he produced for Tse, the New York-based cashmere house. In 2001 it was included in the exhibition "London Fashion" at New York City's Fashion Institute of Technology. He is admired by such unconventional fashion thinkers as REI KAWAKUBO and ALEXANDER MCQUEEN and has been mentioned as a possible designer for several major European houses.

In 2008, his pieces were exhibited in "Gothic: Dark Glamour" at The Museum at FIT, and "Superheroes: Fashion and Fantasy" at the Costume Institute of the Metropolitan Museum of Art.

Hussein Chalayan

Spring 2007.

LED dress, 2007.

Gabrielle "Coco" Chanel

BORN Gabrielle Bonheur Chanel; Saumur, France, August 19, 1883

DIED Paris, France, January 10, 1971

AWARDS Neiman Marcus Award, 1957

In evaluating Gabrielle "Coco" Chanel, some place her alongside such giants as VIONNET and BALENCIAGA, while others see her as more personality than creator, with an innate knack for knowing what women would want a few seconds before they knew it themselves. Certainly her early designs exerted a liberating influence and even the evening clothes had a youthful quality that was all her own.

She purposely obscured the details of her early life, but it is now said that she was one of five children born to an unmarried mother. By the time Chanel was 12, her mother was dead, her father had deserted his family, and she had been sent to an orphanage run by nuns. There she spent six years and there she learned to sew. She started in fashion making hats—first in a Paris apartment in 1910, later in a shop in Deauville. In 1914 she opened a shop in Paris, making her first dresses of wool jersey, a material at that time not considered suitable for fashionable clothes.

Designer Coco Chanel.

Her business was interrupted by World War I but she reopened in 1919, by which time she was famous in the fashionable world. Slender and vital, with a low, warm voice, she was a superb saleswoman and undoubtedly her personality and private life contributed to her success. Misia Sert, the wife of the Spanish painter, Jose Maria Sert, was a friend and introduced her to such leading figures of the 1920s art world as Diaghilev, Picasso, Cocteau, dancer Serge Lifar, and decorator/designer Leon Bakst. She was famous for feuds with other designers, notably ELSA SCHIAPARELLI. Although she never married, there were many love affairs. Grand Duke Dmitri, grandson of Czar Alexander II, was a frequent escort, and a three-year liaison with the Duke of Westminster may have contributed to her longstanding use and appreciation of Scottish tweeds.

Chanel closed her couture house in September 1939 at the outset of World War II. During and after the Occupation she shared her life with a German officer, for which many refused to forgive her. She managed to leave Paris for Switzerland in 1945, remaining there in exile for eight years.

At the age of 70 she decided to go back into business, presenting her first postwar collection on February 5, 1954. A continuation of her original

Spaghetti-strapped sheer-lace dress, 1928.

themes of simplicity and wearability, it received a bru-
tal reception from both the French and English press,
still under the influence of the waist cinchers and
pads of the New Look. By the end of the year, however, it was clear that once again Chanel had seized
the moment when women were ready for change;
the dresses from the reviled collection sold very well,
especially in America but also in France. Her success
continued into the 1960s when her refusal to change
her basic style or raise hemlines led to a decline in her
influence. Inevitably, the pendulum swung back and
in 1969 her life was the basis for *Coco*, a Broadway
musical starring Katharine Hepburn.

Chanel's daytime palette was neutral—black,
white, beige, red—with pastels introduced at night.
Trademark looks included the little boy look, wool
jersey dresses with white collars and cuffs, pea jackets, bell-bottom trousers, and her personal touches of
suntanned skin, bobbed hair, and magnificent jewelry
worn with sportswear.

In her second, post–World War II period, she is
best remembered for her suits made of jersey or the
finest, softest Scottish tweeds. Jackets were usually
collarless and trimmed with braid, blouses soft and
tied at the neckline, skirts at or just below the knee.

Suits were shown with multiple strands of pearls and
gold chains set with enormous fake stones. In her
own case, these were mixed with real jewels. Other
widely-copied signatures were quilted handbags with
shoulder chains, beige sling-back pumps with black
tips, flat black hair-bows, and a single gardenia.

In addition to couture, Chanel's empire encom-
passed perfumes, a costume jewelry workshop, and
for a time, a textile house. Chanel No. 5 was created in
1922. In 1924 Parfums Chanel was established to market the perfumes, which have continued to proliferate.
A line of cosmetics was introduced after her death.

Chanel, "La Grande Mademoiselle," died on a
Sunday night in January 1971. The House of Chanel
has continued, directed by a succession of designers. Ready-to-wear was added in 1977 with Philippe
Guibourgé as designer. KARL LAGERFELD has since
taken over design duties for both the couture and
ready-to-wear and is credited with bringing the
house into the modern era.

Chanel remains a legend for her taste, wit, personal style, and for her unfaltering dedication to perfection. Hers was a luxury based on the most refined
simplicity of cut, superb materials, and workmanship
of the highest order.

Designer Coco Chanel, 1934.

Beige tweed skirt and plaid grey coat, 1970.

Edna Woolman Chase

Vogue editor Edna Woolman Chase (right) with Condé Nast (center).

BORN Asbury Park, New Jersey, March 14, 1877
DIED Locust Valley, New York, March 20, 1957

AWARDS *Légion d'Honneur*, 1935 • Neiman Marcus Award, 1940

The child of divorced parents, Edna Woolman Chase was raised by her Quaker grandparents, whose principles and plain style of dress were to prove a lasting influence. In 1895, when she was 18, she went to work in the Circulation Department of *Vogue*, then just two years old, with a salary of $10 a week. She was to spend 56 years at *Vogue*, 37 of them as editor.

She fell in love with the magazine immediately. As she was enthusiastic, hardworking, and willing to take on any and all chores, she acquired more and more responsibility. By 1911 she was the equivalent of managing editor. Her name first appeared on the masthead as editor in February 1914. British and French *Vogue* were born in 1916 and 1920, respectively; Chase was editor-in-chief of all three editions. During World War I she began to feature American designers in *Vogue's* pages and is credited with originating the modern fashion show in 1914 when *Vogue*

produced a benefit "Fashion Fête," sponsored by prominent society women.

During her tenure, *Vogue* survived two world wars, a depression, and tremendous social changes. With Condé Nast, who bought it in 1909, she helped shape the magazine according to her own strong sense of propriety and high standards of professionalism. She suffered the second-rate badly, respected talent and industriousness; she herself wrote directly to the point. Taste, business ability, and a capacity for hard work brought her to the top of her profession and kept her there for an amazing time span. She retired as editor-in-chief in 1952 and became chairman of the editorial board. Her requirements for success are still worth considering by those thinking of a career in fashion. They were: taste, sound judgment, and experience—the training and knowledge gained from actually working in a business, which she valued above formal course-taking.

She was married to and divorced from Francis Dane Chase and had one child, the writer and actress Ilka Chase. A second marriage in 1921 to Richard Newton ended with his death in 1950. She wrote her autobiography *Always in Vogue* in 1954 with her daughter Ilka and died a few years later in 1957 of a heart attack.

BORN France, 1880s
DEATH 1935

Madeline Chéruit (Sher-wee) began her business in 1906 after working for a Paris couturier by the name of Raudnitz. She was known for her heavily embroidered and beaded evening gowns, and her use of rich fabrics such as taffeta, lame, and silvery gauze. She was always fascinated with the way natural and artificial light hit fabrics, which helped her in choosing a particular fabric to compliment a dress. In 1914, she became well-known for her walking suits, as well as her afternoon dresses, and by 1925, she became fascinated with cubanistic art. This fascination led her to create hand-painted dresses that were influenced by the art form. The house closed in 1935, when ELSA SCHIAPARELLI took over the location for her own business.

Madeleine Chéruit

Black-net-and-sequin dress, 1927.

Cape of gossamer-gold tissue over a dress, 1921.

Chloé

FOUNDED Paris, France, 1952

Chloé was founded by Gaby Aghion, a fashion-forward Egyptian-born Parisian who rejected the stiff formality of 1950s fashion and struck off with business partner Jacques Lenoir to create the first luxury prêt-a-porter design house. Aghion favored soft silhouettes that clung to the body and emphasized the feminine form. She chose the house name after a close personal friend, for she felt the word Chloé evoked a warm, flowing femininity. Aghion and Lenoir defined the trademark of the house by hiring young, innovative designers whose collections would reflect the youthful and modern attitude of Paris's denizens. In this spirit, they launched their first collection in 1956 over breakfast at the Café de Flore, a local haunt of existentialists and artists that the pair also personally frequented.

This first group of Chloé's young Left Bank designers, whom Aghion had hand-selected to carry out her vision, defined the Paris ready-to-wear movement "Le Style." In 1966, KARL LAGERFELD became head designer and transformed Chloé into one of

Designer Gaby Aghion (left).

the most iconic fashion brands of the 1970s, attracting celebrities like Jacqueline Kennedy, Brigitte Bardot, Maria Callas, and Grace Kelly—with elegant daywear, flowing skirts, and romantic, airy blouses.

Chloé established the careers of MARTINE SITBON in the 1980s (during which it was acquired by the luxury conglomerate Richemont Group); STELLA MCCARTNEY in the late 1990s, who gave the brand a mix of vintage lingerie and custom tailoring; and PHOEBE PHILO who was the designer at the fashion house from 1997 through 2008. Currently, head designer Hannah MacGibbon, a former assistant to Phoebe Philo, has been credited with reenergizing the brand and bringing out Chloé's signature "girl naiveté."

Fall 2008.

Designer Jimmy Choo.

BORN Jimmy Choo Yeang Keat; Penang, Malaysia, 1961

AWARDS British Fashion Council, *British Accessory Designer of the Year*, 2000

Jimmy Choo was raised the son of a shoemaker in Malaysia, and he reportedly made his first pair of shoes when he was 11 years old. In the early 1980s, he studied fashion at Cordwainers College in London. He sold his first label, Lucky Shoes, out of a stall market on the city's South Bank in 1986.

A few years later, he was discovered by Princess Diana, who was obliged as a member of the royal family to use a British designer. Choo was suddenly cast into the fashion spotlight, and he began creating shoes for twice-yearly runway shows in Great Britain. To contend with the ballooning workload, he enlisted his niece, Sandra Choi, to join him in shoe production.

In England, the pair was deprived of the materials available to designers in fashion centers like Paris or Milan. So they would improvise their way to interesting toe shapes, "using the filler you'd use to fix your car," Choi told the *New York Times*. Choo and Choi

were soon approached by Tamara Mellon, a fashion enthusiast working for British *Vogue*, who convinced them to start a shoe label. Mellon came to work for them, and eventually they launched the first Jimmy Choo store near Harvey Nichols in London.

Mellon handled the business end of the operation while Choo strained to expand beyond his accustomed role of made-to-order shoe cobbler. Mellon made deals with Italian factories so they could increase volume. Soon, they were producing shoes for the stars of major Hollywood productions.

But Mellon and Choo found themselves increasingly at odds over the management of the Jimmy Choo line, of which Mellon appeared more and more to be the dominant party. In April 2001, Choo was bought out of the company by Equinox Luxury Holdings, part of a billion-dollar venture capital firm. Mellon and Choi now control Jimmy Choo, Ltd. Choo himself maintains a line of Jimmy Choo couture footwear, for which he licenses his own name from the larger company. These shoes are available, by appointment only, from a storefront off Oxford Street in London.

Advertisement for Jimmy Choo shoes and purses.

Doo-Ri Chung

BORN South Korea, 1973

AWARDS Swarovski's Perry Ellis Award for *Emerging Talent, Women's wear*, 2005; CFDA/*Vogue Fashion Fund Award*, 2006

Korean-American Doo-Ri Chung was raised in New Jersey, where her parents ran a dry-cleaning shop. Perhaps it was this early exposure to fabrics that led to her appreciation and skill with jersey knit. After graduating from the Parsons School of Design in 1995, she joined the design team at GEOFFREY BEENE, where she spent six years and eventually rose to the position of head designer.

Chung began producing her own line of draped jersey dresses in 2001, working from the basement below her parents' business. She made her runway debut in 2003 and quickly gained a loyal following among the younger fashion set. By 2006 she was noticed with two major awards, which netted her $200,000. She has since collaborated on capsule collections for J. Crew and the Gap, and sells her line to exclusive stores such as Barneys New York and

Designer Doo-Ri Chung.

Bergdorf Goodman. In addition to expanding her collection to produce accessories and resort wear, she launched a lower-price line, Under.Ligne, in early 2009.

Left: Fall 2008.
Right: Spring 2006.

Designer Liz Claiborne.

BORN Anne Elisabeth Jane Claiborne; Brussels,
Belgium, March 31, 1929
DIED New York, June 26, 2007

AWARDS Council of Fashion Designers of America
(CFDA) *Special Award*, 1985; *Humanitarian Award*
for the Liz Claiborne and Art Ortenberg Foundation,
2000 • Dallas Fashion Award, 1985

Liz Claiborne made her name in sportswear, where
her strength lay in translating new trends into under-
standable and salable clothes. They were simple and
uncomplicated with an easy, natural look and were in
the moderate price range. She was known for sensitive use of color and for excellent technical knowledge of fabric. As her company expanded into other
areas, such as dresses, men's wear, and children's
clothes, she came to function largely as editor of the
work of other designers.

The daughter of a banker, Claiborne spent her
early childhood in New Orleans and went on to study
painting in Belgium and France. Her career in fashion began in 1949 when she won a trip to Europe in
a *Harper's Bazaar* design contest. On her return to
the United States, she worked as a model sketcher,
as assistant to TINA LESER, Omar Kiam, and others.
She was top designer at Youth Guild for 16 years. In
February 1976 she formed Liz Claiborne, Inc., with
her husband, Arthur Ortenberg, as business manager.

She has served as critic at the Fashion Institute of
Technology and has received numerous awards from
retailers and industry associations. In 1989, she and
her husband retired from the company to devote
themselves to environmental issues. The company
has since expanded to giant size through acquisitions,
including KENNETH COLE and Ellen Tracy.

On June 26, 2007, Liz Claiborne died from complications related to a rare form of cancer found in
the abdomen.

ISAAC MIZRAHI took over as creative director for the
Liz Claiborne label in 2008.

Knee length pleated skirt, 1972.

Ossie Clark

BORN Raymond Oswald Clark; Lancashire, England, June 9, 1942

DIED London, England, August 6, 1996

In his heyday in the 1960s, Ossie Clark was the top designer for English film and rock stars, entirely in touch with everything going on: music, art, politics, film, and photography. He dressed Julie Christie and Brigitte Bardot, was painted by David Hockney, vacationed with the Rolling Stones, and put the Beatles in the front row of his shows, setting precedents that designers still try to follow. The difference was that those were his friends, not celebrities invited for their publicity value.

Clark entered Manchester Regional Art College at 16, immediately becoming part of a circle that included the actors Ben Kingsley and Celia Birtwell. Birtwell was a textiles student who created brightly-colored, naïve prints that Clark used in his designs; she later became his wife. In 1962 Clark won a scholarship to the Royal College of Art in London where he met David Hockney, also a student.

In 1965, Clark and Birtwell, with fellow designer Alice Pollock, started a shop called Quorum in Chelsea, just off the King's Road at the heart of

Designer Ossie Clark.

swinging London. Clark was the "King of King's Row." By the early 1970s, drugs, numerous affairs with women and men, and erratic work habits had undermined his life. Birtwell took their two sons and left him in 1973, and Quorum closed two years later. By the end of the decade, Clark was broke and living in a tiny public housing flat.

In the late 1980s Clark had become converted to Buddhism and began to rebuild his life. He was once again beginning to be recognized. CHRISTIAN LACROIX went to London to meet him and both RIFAT OZBEK and JOHN GALLIANO greatly admired him and invited him to their shows. In 1995, several of his pieces were included in an exhibition of street fashion at the Victoria and Albert Museum. Then in 1996 he was murdered—by a drug addict with whom he had lived for nearly a year and had kicked out.

Clark's success was based on two things: he loved women's bodies and made clothes for them that were sexy but not too obvious; his designs were based on his genius as a master cutter—he cut directly into the fabric, requiring neither patterns nor templates. He studied the masters—VIONNET, CHANEL, POIRET—and picked up ideas such as bias-cut bodices or Peter Pan collars, which he then translated into something entirely his own.

In July of 2003, the Victoria and Albert Museum featured his work in a retrospective exhibition. London fashion tycoons Marc and Julian Worth relaunched the Ossie Clark label in 2008 but announced plans to close in July 2009.

Model wearing a crepe playsuit from Ossie Clark's "Quorum" fashion show in London, 1973.

Designers Suzanne Clements (left) and Inacio Ribeiro (right).

BORN Suzanne Clements; England, 1969
Inacio Ribeiro; Brazil, 1963

Suzanne Clements and Inacio Ribeiro trained at Central St. Martins College of Art & Design in London, both graduating in 1991 with first class honors. They married a year later. Before moving to London to get formal training, Ribeiro had worked as a designer for several years; Clements had a fledgling knitwear line carried at Harrods and Liberty. After graduation, they went to Brazil where they worked as design consultants, returning to London in 1993.

Their first collection under the Clements Ribeiro label was in October 1993—crisp separates in cotton pique, hand-painted silk chiffons, and textured linen. They quickly became known for uncluttered, exuberant designs, featuring bold stripes of color and luxurious cashmeres. In 1995 they gave their first solo presentation at the Brazilian Embassy during London Fashion Week. A shoe collection was added in 1996. In 2001 the couple was hired by the French firm Cacharel, meanwhile continuing to design for their own label.

Spring/summer 2004.

Look from Amni Hot Spot-Minas Cult Fashion Show in Brazil, 2005.

Anne Cole

BORN Los Angeles, California, ca, 1930

AWARDS Dallas Fashion Award, 1987 • Otis College of Art and Design *Fashion Achievement Award*, 1993, 2001

The daughter of Fred Cole, one of swimwear's great innovators, Anne Cole was born into the beachwear business. She studied at UCLA and Holy Names College before joining the family firm in 1951, after a brief fling in the theater. Once in the company she had to work her way up, moving from the mailroom to posting orders to taking trunk shows on the road.

Being drafted into the family business was a Cole tradition; Fred Cole was starring in silent movies when his mother decided it was time he joined their firm, West Coast Knitting Mills. The factory made drop-seat underwear until Fred started them knitting women's swimsuits. Taking what had been a drab and shapeless garment, he lowered the back and defined the bust and waistline; these became the first fashion swimsuits. He also introduced brilliant colors. He continued to innovate, working with Margit Fellegi, a Hollywood costume designer. They introduced the cotton suit puckered with rubber threads, and during World War II

Anne Cole (center) with models.

when rubber was restricted, originated the two-piece "swoon suit" that laced up the sides of the trunks and had a tie bra. The name of the company was changed to Cole of California in 1941. After the war came plunging necklines, cut-outs, bare midriffs, suits in sequins, gold lamé jersey, and water-resistant velvets.

When her father sold Cole of California to Kayser-Roth in 1960, Anne Cole left the company but then went back to establish Cole's New York office and become stylist and company spokesperson. The firm has since had several owners, most recently Los Angeles-based Authentic Fitness, which also includes Speedo and Catalina.

The Anne Cole Collection, launched in 1982, is the expression of Anne Cole's most advanced fashion ideas. She sees swimsuits as existing somewhere between fashion and beauty aids, reflecting current trends but with the prime function of enhancing the appearance of the wearer. She is given credit for introducing the tankini, the popular two-piece suit with a tank top and bikini bottom.

The 2001 Otis award was in recognition of her design innovations and of her efforts as a mentor to fashion design students at the school. At that time she was still actively engaged in swimsuit design, as she put it, "the oldest living swimwear designer in the world."

Swimwear.

BORN Long Island, New York, March 23, 1954

AWARDS Council of Fashion Designers of America (CFDA) *Dom Perignon Award for Humanitarian Excellence*, 1996 • Fashion Footwear Association of New York (FFANY) *The Fashion Medal of Honor Award*, 1997

Kenneth Cole could be considered an example of creative entrepreneurship and downright chutzpah, valuable qualities in his chosen field. He grew up on Long Island, in his spare time working as a stock boy at the local shoe store. After graduation from Emory University in 1976, he worked for the shoe business his family owned in Brooklyn before deciding he was ready to go on his own. In 1982, with limited money for an introductory splash, he launched his company Kenneth Cole Productions from a 40-foot trailer parked across the street from the hotel where the shoe show was taking place. While supposedly shooting a

Designer Kenneth Cole.

full-length film, he was actually showing his shoes and sold out his production quota in two and a half days. Since then, the company has expanded beyond shoes for men and women to clothing for men, women, and children as well as luggage, accessories, and fragrance. These are sold worldwide in fine stores and in his own retail shops. He has also designed uniforms for the W hotel chain.

Cole is nearly as well-known for his provocative, socially-conscious advertising and active participation in causes—from AIDS awareness to homelessness to abortion rights—as he is for his cool, hip fashions. He has been recognized for his fashion and humanitarian work by organizations ranging from New York Magazine to Amnesty International, and with honorary degrees from Manhattanville College and the University of Illinois School of Public Health.

WE ALL WALK IN DIFFERENT SHOES.

SONNY CABERVAL, PRACTICING SIKH AND ENTREPRENEUR SPEAKING OUT AGAINST FACIAL PROFILING.

KENNETHCOLE.COM 25 YEARS OF NON-UNIFORM THINKING.

Above: Advertisement, 2008.

Left: Ensemble from Kenneth Cole, 2008.

Sybil Connolly

Designer Sybil Connolly (front).

BORN Swansea, Wales, January 24, 1921
DIED Dublin, Ireland, May 16, 1998

America discovered Sybil Connolly in the early 1950s, thanks to CARMEL SNOW of *Harper's Bazaar* and to the Fashion Group of Philadelphia who were visiting Dublin. In 1953 she took a collection to the United States, where her one-of-a-kind designs and beautiful Irish fabrics made a strong impression. In 1957 she set up her own firm, with a special boutique for ready-to-wear. Her clothes were simple in cut, extremely wearable, notable for fabric and workmanship, especially the iridescent Donegal tweeds and the evening dresses made of gossamer Irish linen worked in fine horizontal pleats.

When she was 15 years old, Connolly's father died and her mother moved the family to Waterford in southern Ireland. In 1938 she went to work for Bradley's, a London dressmaker, returning to Ireland at the outset of World War II as buyer for Richard Alan, a Dublin specialty shop. By the time she was 22, she was a company director. She built the store's couture department into a thriving business and when their designer left in 1950 created a small col-

Dresses, 1954.

lection herself, the start of her designing career. Her clothes have been carried by fine specialty stores across the United States.

Jasper Conran

Designer Jasper Conran (right).

BORN London, England, 1959

AWARDS British Fashion Council *Designer of the Year*, 1986

As the son of Sir Terence Conran, the founder of Conran's Habitat stores, Jasper Conran would seem to have been predestined for a design career. He was educated at Bryanston School in England until the age of 16, when he was accepted at New York's Parson's School of Design. He studied there for 18 months, leaving in 1977 for a brief stint with Fiorucci, then returned to London the same year. In 1978 he produced his first independent show and the next year became a member of London Designer Collections.

Conran's continued success is solidly based on his technical ability—fine tailoring and thoughtful details—executed in luxurious fabrics. His clothes are original in cut, designed for a sophisticated and elegant woman, none of the legendary English dowdiness here. Other design projects have included fine crystal and a deluxe automobile model.

Left: Spring/summer 2009.
Right: Spring/summer 2009.

Esteban Cortazar

BORN Bogotá, Columbia, May 17, 1984

One of the youngest designers to emerge in the fashion industry, presenting his first collection at the age of 15, Esteban Cortazar credits his early family life for sowing the seeds of design inspiration. Born to jazz singer Dominique Vaughan and artist Valentino Cortazar, Esteban Cortazar was immersed early in the creative process, both in his native Columbia and in Miami Beach, where his family relocated when Esteban was 11 years old. Preteen Esteban flourished in the cultural landscape of Miami, becoming a local style icon, and soon he was recruited to window dress vintage shops.

When TODD OLDHAM opened a new boutique in South Beach in 1997, Cortazar saw his opportunity and approached the designer with a book of his own sketches. Oldham was so impressed that he invited Cortazar to be a guest at his upcoming Fashion Week show in New York. The experience only further cemented his passion and love for fashion.

His inspired 30-piece collection debuted unofficially at Miami International Fashion Week in 1999 as part of a group show, alongside established favorites in the fashion community, including CAROLINA HERRERA. Cortazar followed up by launching his label Cortazar in March 2002 with a 14-piece evening wear collection. His collection caught the eye of

Fall 2009.

Designer Esteban Cortazar (right) with model.

Bloomingdale's Kalman Ruttenstein, earning his designs the highly coveted window display at Bloomingdale's flagship New York store.

Cortazar asked retired supermodel and longtime supporter Cindy Crawford to open and close his 2004 spring/summer collection, adorning her in a dazzling floor-length gown constructed entirely of Swarovski Crystal mesh, much to the delight and surprise of his audience. This collection was so well-received, that 7th on Sixth's Fern Mallis invited him to open the Mercedes-Benz Los Angeles Fashion Week. In December 2007 he was appointed designer of EMANUAL UNGARO, but left the company in 2009.

Cortazar has attracted a large celebrity following and his designs have been worn on the red carpet by Beyoncé Knowles, Eva Longoria, and Paris Hilton. His pieces have also been selected by designer and stylist Patricia Field to be featured on HBO's *Sex and the City*.

BORN Guarani, Brazil, 1961

AWARDS Council of Fashion Designers of America Award *Women's wear Designer of the Year*, 2006 and 2008; Fashion Group International Award *Star Honoree in Fashion*, 2008

Francisco Costa grew up outside of Rio, Brazil, watching his parents successfully operate their own apparel business. Determined to carve his own niche in the fashion industry designing for a large fashion house, Costa moved to New York at the age of 21. After studying English as a second language at Hunter College, Costa enrolled in night classes at the Fashion Institute of Technology, where his talent and vision were quickly recognized when he was honored with the Idea Como/Young Designers of America Award. Post-graduation, Costa landed coveted jobs with Susan Bennett Studio and BILL BLASS before spending five years collaborating with OSCAR DE LA RENTA on his signature line, PIERRE BALMAIN haute couture, and colaunching the Oscar de la Renta Pink label. Costa then moved on to TOM FORD for GUCCI, where he served as senior designer focusing on eveningwear and custom client designs.

Designer Francisco Costa.

Francisco Costa

In 2002, Costa was hand-picked by CALVIN KLEIN to be his successor as creative director of the Calvin Klein Collection for women, just months before Klein sold the company to Phillips-Van Heusen in a $730 million deal. Hired to breathe complexity into the established minimalist aesthetic of Klein's structured designs, Costa's collections for the design house received some of the best reviews in the company's history, adding a new airy feminine je ne sais quoi. Costa muses in his artist's statement that his "collections are for women who are sexy, independent, and confident; and each piece represents effortless, sensual, timeless style."

Sequined jersey dress, 2004.

Look from Calvin Klein Collection, fall/winter 2009.

André Courrèges

Designer André Courrèges (center) with models.

BORN Pau, France, March 9, 1923

André Courrèges emerged on the fashion scene in 1962 as a brilliant tailor. Using fabrics with considerable body, he cut his coats and suits with a triangular flare that disguised many figure defects, the balanced silhouettes defined by crisp welt seaming. His aim was to make functional, modern clothes for active modern women. Among his successes—many of them widely copied—were all-white collections inspired by his Basque heritage and tunics worn over narrow pants with flared bottoms that slanted from front to back. There were squared-off dresses ending above the knee, short, white baby boots, industrial zippers, and zany accessories such as sunglasses with slit "tennis ball" lenses. He was called "the couturier of the space age."

Courrèges studied civil engineering before switching to textiles and fashion design. His first job was with Jeanne Lafaurie. From 1952 to 1960 he worked as a cutter for BALENCIAGA, whose influence showed

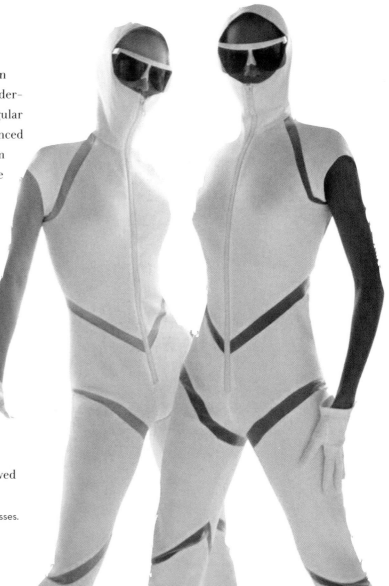

White jumpsuits and sunglasses.

White dress and sunglasses.

In 1996 the couple regained the company, which has continued in business with Madame Courrèges in active control. André Courrèges had retired in 1995 to devote himself to painting and sculpture. The clothes are still made in their own factory to the original patterns in the same fabrics and sold in their own shops and in fine specialty stores. Madame Courrèges has said that they were always designing for the year 2000, and in 2001 the Courrèges influence was noted in numerous collections by other designers.

clearly in his early designs. In 1961, with the blessing of the great designer, Courrèges and his wife Coqueline, who became his close collaborator, left Balenciaga to open their own business. Together they designed, cut, sewed, and presented their first collection in a small apartment on the Avenue Kléber.

Courrèges was so widely plagiarized that the couple sold the business in 1965, then spent two years working for private clients and setting up their own manufacturing and production. They returned in 1967 with Couture Future deluxe ready-to-wear and the distinctive "uc" logo displayed on the outside of the clothes, another fashion first. There were see-through dresses, cosmonaut suits, knitted "catsuits" with flowers appliquéd on the body, and knee socks. The Courrèges name also extended to accessories, luggage, perfumes, men's wear, and boutiques in the United States and other countries. These carried everything from sports separates to accessories to Couture Future. The name continued on a ready-to-wear line designed by Courrèges in collaboration with other designers.

Short, black sequin dress.

Patrick Cox

BORN Edmonton, Canada, March 19, 1963

AWARDS British Fashion Council, *Accessory Designer of the Year*, 1994 and 1995; Footwear Association of New York, *Fashion Medal of Honor*, 1996

Patricia Cox's shoe designs are known for their distinctive and often eccentric details—flourishes like a chainmail skirt over the heel of a black pump or a Union Jack symbol on a pair of loafers. "I am a magpie," said Cox. "My eye collects details."

A Canadian native, Cox traveled to London at the age of 19 to study footwear design at Cordwainers Technical College. In the early 1980s, he created shoes for well-known maverick designers like JOHN GALLIANO and VIVIENNE WESTWOOD. Cox gained renown for his attention to detail and, in 1985, had enough name recognition to start his own design company.

In 1991, he opened the first of several boutiques in London, but he would not achieve true fame until his Wannabe line in 1993, which began with a pair of Pee Wee Herman–inspired loafers. Cox's shoe designs are colorful and innovative showpieces that demand attention. In 2001, he presented the Light Boot, a disco boot that lit up using fiber-optic technology.

Advertising campaign, spring/summer 2006.

Handbag from luxury accessories line, 2006

In 2003, Cox was appointed creative director of the French shoe company Charles Jourdan, while continuing to design under his own label. In 2005 he decided to develop his own business further and refurbish his London boutique. He also launched a luxury accessories line in 2006. His work can be viewed at the Victoria and Albert Museum in London, at the museum at the Fashion Institute of Technology in New York City, and at the Bata Shoe Museum in Toronto, Canada.

Designer Patrick Cox.

BORN Liege, Belgium, May 21, 1917
DIED Monte Carlo, Monaco, January 5, 1988

AWARDS Neiman Marcus Award, 1962

Recognized for his thoughtful, interesting cuts, Jules-François Crahay (Krah-HAY) was deeply influenced by fabrics and liked to design his own. He was probably best known for his use of folklore themes, admiring their rich mixture of color, materials, and embroidery.

Crahay grew up in the fashion business, starting to work at age 13 as a sketcher in his mother's couture house. After studying couture and painting in Paris (1934–1935), he returned to Liege to work for his mother (1936–1938). His Army service during World War II ended in capture by the Germans and imprisonment in Germany from 1940 to 1944.

Designer Jules-François Crahay (right) with model wearing look from spring/summer 1974.

In 1951 he opened his own fashion house in Paris, which closed within a year. He then became chief designer at NINA RICCI, receiving his first credit as sole designer in 1959. He stayed at Ricci until 1964 when he moved to the House of LANVIN, succeeding Antonio del Castillo as head designer. According to published reports, he was the highest paid couturier of his time. For 20 years he created and maintained a recognizable Lanvin look with his own flair for original details. He retired from Lanvin in 1984 and the following year started a ready-to-wear collection under his own name in Japan.

Hard working and never satisfied, he is quoted as saying, "I like ready-to-wear. I want to have fun making dresses. It is my love, it is my life."

Lanvin dress of printed colors, 1967.

Jules-François Crahay

House of Creed

FOUNDED London, 1760

One of the world's oldest family businesses, the House of Creed has been producing fragrances for the world's elite for 239 years. Established in London by saddle maker James Henry Creed, the house quickly achieved its premiere status when Queen Victoria appointed it as official supplier to the court. Known for using the highest quality natural ingredients and exacting production methods, the House of Creed's fragrances were soon adopted by aristocracies across continental Europe.

In the 1850s, Henry Creed (James Henry's grandson) expanded the business to include tailoring. The House of Creed moved to Paris in 1854. Henry's son (also Henry) joined the house in the early 1900s and produced riding habits for European royalty. Fashionable women of leisure were drawn to his

Designer Henry Creed.

shapely Basque jackets (which feminized lines from menswear), full skirts, and fitted tweeds. Devotees of Creed's tailoring included glamorous accused German spy Mata Hari (who reportedly faced the firing squad in a Creed suit), and Alice Roosevelt, the trend-setting daughter of U.S. President Theodore Roosevelt.

Henry Creed passed the family business to his son Charles Creed in the 1930s. Having first opened his own house in London, Charles continued the family's tradition of tailoring by producing elegant women's suits and coats, sheer wool blouses, and evening dresses. Forced to close the Paris business with the advent of World War II, Charles later designed wholesale lines for firms in London and the United States. The clothing design arm of the House of Creed ended with Charles's death in 1966.

The company today is overseen by sixth-generation Olivier Creed, a perfectionist who is credited with reviving the ailing brand and re-establishing the House of Creed as masters of exclusive fragrance.

Designer Charles Creed (right) with model.

Retaining the highest standards, Creed fragrances today are worn by royalty, celebrities, and world leaders seeking scents that are unmistakably luxurious. In the spring of 2009 Creed introduced Acqua Florentina for women—the house's first new fragrance in years—and in the fall released a limited edition of Windsor, originally created for the Duke of Windsor in 1936. And in keeping with family tradition, Olivier is grooming his son Erwin to shepherd the House of Creed into its seventh generation.

Brown suede coat, 1948.

Bill Cunningham

BORN Boston, Massachusetts, ca. 1929

AWARDS Council of Fashion Designers of America (CFDA) *Eugenia Sheppard Award for Fashion Journalism*, 1993 • 2008, Chevalier deus lárde des Arts et de Lettres, French Ministry of Culture

A familiar New York figure in his beret, corduroys, and parka, camera unobtrusively at the ready, Bill Cunningham observes and records fashion, not as worn on the runway, but as it appears in the real world on real people. In fair weather or foul, from one of his favorite posts at 57th Street and Fifth Avenue, in SoHo, or at the GreenMarket or flea market, he catches the passing scene for his "On the Street" column in the Sunday *New York Times*; his second feature, "Evening Hours," chronicles benefits, art show openings, and other social events.

Cunningham's early attraction to fashion was totally alien to his conservative New England background. In Boston he worked after school at Bonwit Teller, and when he moved to New York after graduation, went to work for Nona Park and Sophie Shonnard in their Chez Ninon boutique at the New York Bonwit's. It was there he first saw the fashionable women who later became his photographic subjects. On his own time he made masks and headdresses for ladies attending the then-popular masked balls, and later opened his own hat shop called William J., backed by Rebecca Harkness, the noted ballet patron. Drafted into the Army, he was stationed in the South of France and was able to join his former employers, Nona and Sophie, in Paris when they were there shopping for their clients.

Once out of the Army, he was hired by *Women's Wear Daily*'s JOHN FAIRCHILD to write a twice-weekly

Photographer Bill Cunningham.

column, leaving after nine months to write about fashion for the *Chicago Tribune*. A friend, illustrator ANTONIO, suggested that he use a camera to make notes, a move that opened his world and was the beginning of a new career. In the mid '70s, he began freelancing at the *New York Times* and in 1993 went on staff. To attract his photographic attention, a subject must have more than mere perfection, which he finds uninteresting. For him, a person with style must have something extra: "something so personal—flawless but with a dash."

Lilly DACHÉ

Louise DAHL-WOLFE

Sandy DALAL

DARYL K

Jessica DAVES

Jean-Charles DE CASTELBAJAC

Oscar DE LA RENTA

Baron ADOLF DE MEYER

DE RAUCH

Giles DEACON

Louis DELL'OLIO

Diego DELLA VALLE

Patrick DEMARCHELIER

Pamela DENNIS

Jean DESSÈS

Collette DINNIGAN

Christian DIOR

DOLCE & GABBANA

Carrie DONOVAN

Jacques DOUCET

DRÉCOLL

DSQUARED2

Gilles DUFOUR

Randolph DUKE

Stephen DWECK

Lilly Daché

BORN Beigles, France, October 10, 1898
DIED Louvecienne, France, December 31, 1989

AWARDS Neiman Marcus Award, 1940 • Coty American Fashion Critics' Award *Special Award (millinery)*, 1943

Vivacious and feminine, Lilly Daché (Da-SHAY) brought an inimitable French flair to American fashion at a time when no woman was considered fully dressed without a hat. She left school at 14 to apprentice with a milliner aunt, at 15 was an apprentice in the workrooms of the famous Paris milliner Reboux, and later worked at Maison Talbot. She came to the United States in 1924, spent one week behind the millinery counter at Macy's, then, with a partner, opened a millinery shop in the West Eighties. When

Designer Lilly Daché.

her partner left, Daché moved to Broadway and 86th Street in the same neighborhood as HATTIE CARNEGIE.

Her next move was to Madison Avenue and, finally, to her own nine-story building on East 57th Street. This contained showrooms, workrooms, and a duplex apartment on the roof where she lived with her husband Jean Després, executive vice president of Coty. By 1949 Daché was designing dresses to go with her hats. She also undertook lingerie, loungewear, gloves, hosiery, men's shirts and ties, and even a wired strapless bra.

Her major design contributions were draped turbans, brimmed hats molded to the head, half hats, colored snoods, romantic massed flower shapes, and visored caps for war workers. She was considered America's foremost milliner and influenced many others in this country, including HALSTON. She closed her business in 1969 upon her husband's retirement.

Floral hats, 1945.

Louise Dahl-Wolfe

BORN San Francisco, California, November 19, 1895

DIED Allendale, New Jersey, December 13, 1989

Accomplished in both fashion and portrait photography, Louise Dahl-Wolfe attended the California School of Design (now San Francisco Institute of Design). Before buying her first camera in 1923, she worked at everything from designing electric signs to decorating. After travels to Europe and Africa, during which she met future husband, Mike Wolfe, she moved to San Francisco, then to the Great Smoky Mountains of Tennessee. Her first published photographs were documentary shots of her Tennessee neighbors, which were bought by Frank Crowninshield and appeared in *Vanity Fair* in 1933.

Dahl-Wolfe's first black-and-white fashion photography appeared in *Harper's Bazaar* in 1936, her first color in 1937; her elegant photographs graced the magazine until 1958. With dramatic lighting and backgrounds ranging from intricate Chinese screens to seamless paper, she caught the essence of individual fashions as simple as a CLAIRE MCCARDELL linen sundress and as structured as a pair of satin ball gowns by CHARLES JAMES. She was the first to use color effectively in fashion photography, driving both the color separators and Art Director Alexey Brodovitch to distraction with her insistence on perfection. Unlike many of her peers, she never considered photography as art but rather as a commercial medium. She left *Harper's Bazaar* after CARMEL SNOW and Brodovitch resigned, worked for a few months at *Vogue*, then retired to Frenchtown, New Jersey, with her artist husband.

Photograph for *Vogue*, 1959.

Photographer Louise Dahl-Wolfe (right) shooting a model for *Harper's Bazaar*, 1947.

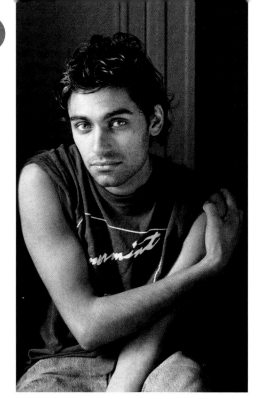

Designer Sandy Dalal.

breeding of 1960s Swinging London and colonial India, appealing to men with a sense of adventure and a taste for luxury. They have been well received by such stores as Barneys in New York and Fred Segal of Los Angeles. He has also worked for Italian and Japanese firms, including Onward Kashiyama and its International Concept Brand (ICB) label, while continuing to design for his own label.

BORN Sandy Agashiwala; Bronx, New York, 1977

AWARDS Council of Fashion Designers of America (CFDA) *Perry Ellis Award for New Talent in Men's wear*, 1998

Sandy Dalal first became interested in making clothes when he was ten years old and went with his mother on a trip to the Far East, where she was checking out factories to make clothing for designers. He himself started sewing at 14 and by his senior year in high school had made more than 30 pieces, mostly shirts and pants—any jacket designs were sent to a tailor to execute. At 18 he felt ready to begin a design career, but at his family's insistence enrolled at the University of Pennsylvania where he majored in international trade and marketing. He also was on the fencing team but always continued to sew.

In 1996 he made his first tailored suit by himself. The next year, using his mother's maiden name, Dalal, he established his own business called Sandy Dalal Ltd. This was financed with a few thousand dollars saved from summer jobs, plus the backing of family and friends. The clothes were cut with clean, simple lines, and made of beautiful fabrics—a cross-

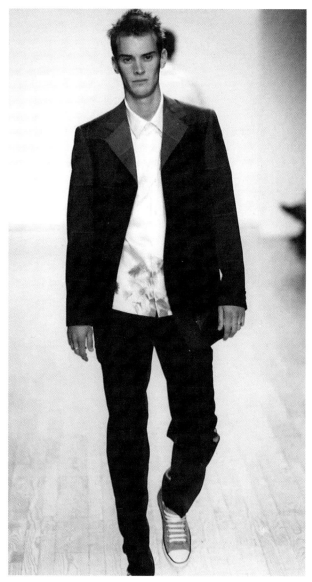

Spring/summer 2000.

Her original indie credibility has held up, however, and it seems to be how she works best. After a collaboration with Barneys New York for an in-store boutique in 2005, which increased the exposure of her line, she found her financial footing again. She has since sold her collections to other exclusive stores, and reopened in her original space on New York's Bond Stret where she today sells both her Daryl K and lower-priced Kerrigan lines.

Designer Daryl K.

BORN Daryl Kerrigan; Dublin, Ireland, 1964

AWARDS CFDA *New Talent Award*, 1996

Daryl K studied fashion at Dublin's National College of Art and Design, and moved to New York in 1986. Starting out by working in thrift shops and as a wardrobe consultant on films, she developed a hip, "downtown" aesthetic that she soon put to good use in her own designs. She established her own salon in the East Village in 1991. Her low-slung leather pants and lean T-shirts, produced under her Daryl K line, quickly earned her a cult following and made her a critic's darling.

Daryl K may have been the name on the lips of every cool girl, but large-scale success proved elusive. After being courted by French luxury line Céline and consulting for TOMMY HILFIGER, she sold her company to an investment firm in 2000 with the promise of expansion. When the deal collapsed, she was out of business and struggled to come up with the financing to produce new work.

Look from Daryl K, spring 2009.

Jessica Daves

BORN Cartersville, Georgia, February 20, 1898
DIED New York City, 1974

Jessica Daves (Dayvz) arrived in New York in 1921. She worked in the advertising departments of various New York City stores, including Saks Fifth Avenue, writing fashion copy and learning about fashion merchandising. In 1933 she went to *Vogue* magazine as a fashion merchandising editor, where her ability was spotted by EDNA WOOLMAN CHASE, then editor-in-chief. In 1936 she was made managing editor, and she became editor in 1946. Upon Mrs. Chase's retirement in 1952, Daves became editor-in-chief of American *Vogue*. She was also a director of Condé Nast Publications from 1946 until she retired in 1963, served as editorial consultant for a year, and then worked on specialized books until November 1966.

An accomplished writer and editor, Daves could fix a piece of ailing copy in minutes. She was known for clearheadedness, sound judgment, and was very astute at business. The years of her editorship coincided with a phenomenal growth of the American ready-to-wear industry. She recognized its increasing importance and broadened the magazine's coverage of domestic ready-to-wear, including more moderately priced clothes. Under her direction, *Vogue* assumed a more serious tone and ran more articles of intellectual interest than before.

Vogue editor Jessica Daves.

BORN Casablanca, Morocco, November 28, 1949

Part of the ready-to-wear movement that burgeoned in France in the 1960s and came into full flower in the 1970s, Jean-Charles de Castelbajac (CASSEL-bai-jack) is best known for the fashion flair he gives to survival looks—blanket plaids, canvas, quilting, rugged coats—and sportswear for both men and women. He has been called "the space age BONNIE CASHIN."

Castelbajac's parents moved to France when he was five. His mother started her own small clothes factory and he went to work for her when he was 18. He designed for Pierre d'Alby, joined a group of young designers in 1974, then opened his first retail shop. He has collaborated with COURRÈGES on ready-to-wear, designed for a number of manufacturers, including some in Italy, and has done theatrical costumes.

Designer Jean-Charles de Castelbajac.

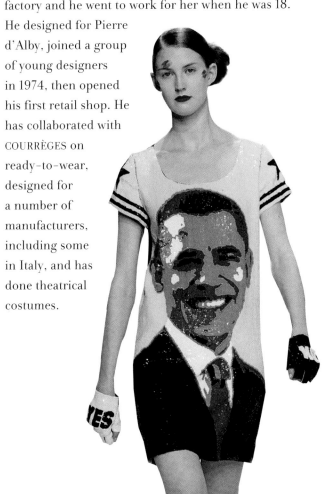

Ready-to-wear, spring/summer 2009.

Winter 2009.

Jean-Charles de Castelbajac

Oscar de la Renta

BORN Santo Domingo, Dominican Republic, July 22, 1932

AWARDS Coty American Fashion Critics' Award "*Winnie*," 1967; *Return Award*, 1968; *Hall of Fame*, 1973 • Neiman Marcus Award, 1968 • Council of Fashion Designers of America (CFDA) *Women's wear Designer of the Year*, 2000

Oscar de la Renta is known for sexy, extravagantly romantic evening clothes in opulent materials. His daytime clothes, sometimes overshadowed by the more spectacular evening designs, have a European flavor—sophisticated, feminine, and eminently wearable.

Educated in Santo Domingo and Madrid, de la Renta remained in Madrid after graduation to study

Designer Oscar de la Renta (right) and model.

Fall 2009.

art, intending to become a painter. His fashion career began when sketches he made for his own amusement were seen by the wife of the American ambassador to Spain, who asked him to design a gown for her daughter's debut. His first professional job was with BALENCIAGA'S Madrid couture house, Eisa. In 1961 he went to Paris as assistant to Antonio de Castillo at LANVIN-Castillo, and in 1963 went with Castillo to New York to design at Elizabeth Arden. He joined Jane Derby in 1965 and was soon operating as Oscar de la Renta, Ltd., producing luxury ready-to-wear.

A signature perfume introduced in 1977 has been enormously successful; a second fragrance, Ruffles, appeared in 1983. He has also done boutique lines, bathing suits, wedding dresses, furs, jewelry, bed linens, and loungewear. In 1992 he took over the design of the BALMAIN couture collection remaining until his

Above: Dress, 2004.

Right: Ready-to-wear, fall 2009.

retirement in late 2002. He continues to design his own New York collection.

Oscar de la Renta is considered the poster child of the Dominican Republic. In 1982, he built La Casa de Niño, an orphanage and school for children of La Romana. Over 1,200 kids occupy the orphanage each year. Today, Oscar de la Renta represents a home line, eyewear, and a bridal wear collection that was launched in 2006. Oscar's family now runs the business with Oscar de la Renta still at the helm. His son-in-law Alex Bolen operates as chief executive officer, his stepdaughter Eliza Bolen is creative director, and his adopted son Moises de la Renta is in the Design Studio.

Baron Adolf de Meyer

BORN Adolf Meyer-Watson; September 1, 1868
DIED Los Angeles, California, 1946

Baron Adolf de Meyer is considered the first true fashion photographer, the one who transformed fashion photography into a major artistic expression. He dropped the Watson from his last name, gained a Saxon title, and in 1899, married Olga Alberta Caracciolo, the godchild of Edward VII of England. The marriage opened society to de Meyer, and the couple devoted themselves to the pleasures and pursuits of the English upper crust. Upon the King's death in 1910, it became necessary that he earn some money. De Meyer soon established a reputation as a photographer in Paris and London; his early pictures of Diaghilev's Ballets Russes captured the dazzling splendor and drama that so captivated the European avant-garde. In 1913, the imminent onset of World War I persuaded de Meyer and his wife to leave for New York where he went to work for Condé Nast's, *Vogue* and *Vanity Fair*. In 1923 he was hired away

Photographer Baron Adolf de Meyer.

by Hearst and was given the opportunity to work in Paris.

De Meyer's primary interest was in creating an ideal of feminine beauty and softness, of luxury and romance. His photographs relied on glamorous backgrounds and elaborate settings, reflecting a life of opulent ease and aristocratic idleness. They embodied the painterly traditions of nineteenth-century art with their emphasis on glowing light and romantic atmosphere. He employed soft focus—using a lens that was sharp in the center, soft at the edges—and sometimes stretched silk gauze over the lens. He made much use of backlighting—his most famous and influential technique. Many other photographers imitated his approach but failed to achieve the same extravagantly flattering and glamorous results. His influence declined with the liberation of women. A new age had begun and he could not move with the times.

Photograph for Elizabeth Arden, 1940.

FOUNDED 1928

CLOSED 1973

Starting in 1928 with a single worker, de Rauch grew and stayed in business for 45 years. The house was known for beautiful, wearable, functional clothes. Soft fabrics were handled with great fluidity, draped close at the top of the figure. Wide necklines were often framed with folds or tucks. Plaids, checks, and stripes were treated with simplicity and precision, so perfectly done they seemed to have been assembled on a drawing board.

An accomplished sportswoman, founder Madeleine de Rauch began in the 1920s to design her own clothes for active sports. When friends persuaded her to make clothes for them, she opened a business called the House of Friendship in 1928, employing a single worker. With the help of her two sisters, the business grew and in the 1930s evolved into the House of de Rauch overlooking the Cours de Reine. It closed in 1973.

Dress and veiled black hat, 1956.

Jacket, hat, and skirt, 1958.

Giles Deacon

BORN Darlington, England

AWARDS British Designer of the Year, 2006

Giles Deacon (Dee-Kin) was raised in a remote area of the Lakes District in England, where the family home was three miles from the nearest village. He went to the Central St. Martins College of Art and Design in London to study art, but quickly gravitated to the spontaneous world of fashion. Deacon was part of a high-profile class at St. Martins that included LUELLA BARTLEY, ALEXANDER MCQUEEN, STELLA MCCARTNEY, and future stylist Katie Grand. He graduated in 1992 and for several years gained experience working for a diverse range of design teams such as JEAN-CHARLES DE CASTELBAJAC, LOUIS VUITTON, MARC JACOBS, and French Connection. After a brief but high-profile stint as head designer for Bottega Veneta in 2000 (he was fired when the GUCCI Group purchased the line a year later), he returned to fashion freelancing in London.

Designer Giles Deacon.

Deacon debuted his own line, Giles, at London Fashion Week in 2004, and received raves for his sexy yet "grown-up" designs. Recent collections have included beautifually constructed dresses with edgy embellishments such as bold prints, ripped suede, mohair, and safety pins. In addition to his couture pieces Deacon focuses his line on a more affordable middle range, and has also produced inexpensive capsule collections of skirts and T-shirts for New Look.

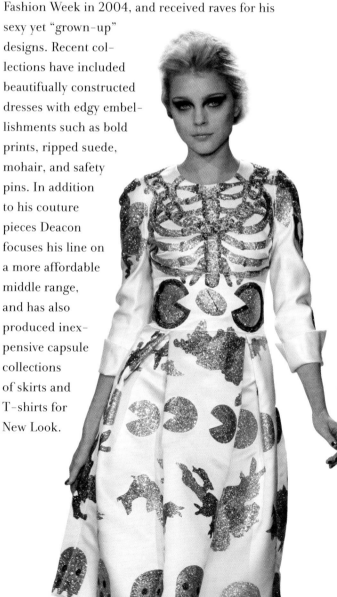

Above: Giles Deacon design, 2007.

Right: Pac-Man inspired design, spring 2009.

BORN New York City, July 23, 1948

AWARDS Coty American Fashion Critics' Award *"Winnie" (with Donna Karan)*, 1977; *Hall of Fame (with Donna Karan)*, 1982; *Special Award (women's wear, with Donna Karan)*, 1984

Louis Dell'Olio is best known for his years at ANNE KLEIN, first as codesigner with DONNA KARAN and then as sole designer when she left to open her own house. After her departure he continued the direction begun with Karan—a modern, sophisticated interpretation of the classic Anne Klein sportswear—clothes in the deluxe investment category marked by clean, sharp shapes in beautiful fabrics. His other design projects included furs for Michael Forrest.

In 1967 Dell'Olio received the Norman Norell Scholarship to Parsons School of Design, from which he graduated in 1969, winning the Gold Thimble Award for coats and suits. He assisted Dominic Rompollo at Teal Traina and was designer at the Giorgini and Ginori divisions of Originala. In 1974, he joined Karan, a friend from Parsons, as codesigner at

Designer Louis Dell'Olio (right).

Anne Klein & Co. Spring 1985 was their last joint collection. Dell'Olio continued as sole designer for Anne Klein until 1993, when he was replaced by RICHARD TYLER. He has continued to design on a freelance basis. In 2000, he agreed to sell a line of sportswear under the label LINE by Louis Dell'Olio for QVC. The line won the product star award by QVC during the label's first year. His design philosophy continues to be "to make women look and feel beautiful."

Beaded crochet dress from Louis Dell'Olio for Anne Klein, 1993.

Diego Della Valle

BORN San Elpidio a Mare, Italy; December 30, 1953

Diego Della Valle was the grandson of Filippo Della Valle, a cobbler who began a modest business in 1924 making fine shoes by hand. His son, Diego's father, developed the company to large-scale industrial production but it was Diego who gave it glamour.

He attended law school in Bologna, and spent a year in the United States before returning to Italy to enter the family business. With an excellent design sense and a flair for promotion he has expanded the business and brought the company international recognition, linking up with such prominent designers as GIANFRANCO FERRÉ, FENDI, LACROIX, and AZZEDINE ALAÏA.

Under the Diego Della Valle label the firm continues to make exquisite, one-of-a-kind shoes on special order, as well as fine, traditional, ready-to-wear footwear. It is, however, best known for J.P. Tod's, the leather driving shoe with the American-sounding name he introduced in 1987. This is a moccasin with 133 small leather pebbles, or *gommini*, set in the sole and running up the heel. Available in countless materials and colors, it's the casual shoe of choice for celebrities worldwide. The name was shortened to Tod's in 1999. The company also produces boots, loafers, and handbags, and a less expensive collection of casual shoes called Hogan.

Designer Diego Della Valle.

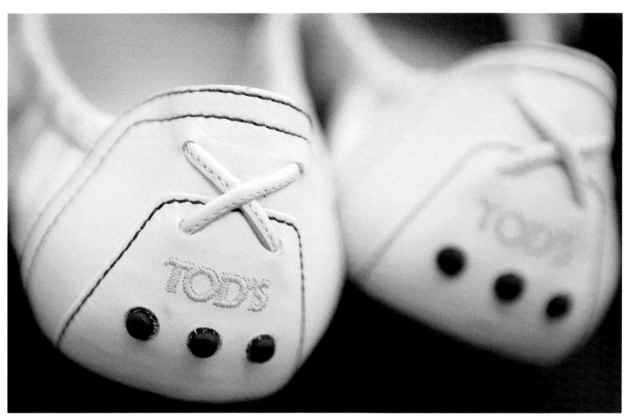

J.P. Tod's loafers.

Patrick Demarchelier

BORN Le Havre, France, August 21, 1943

AWARDS AND HONORS Council of Fashion Designers of America (CFDA) *Eleanor Lambert Award*, 2007 • Officier dans l'Ordre des Arts et des Lettres, 2007

Considered one of the top photographers of fashion, Patrick Demarchelier's photographs have graced the covers of hundreds of international beauty and fashion magazines. Already knowing he wanted to make his living as a photographer, Demarchelier requested a camera for his 17th birthday. He began working for a freelance photographer who taught him about fashion photography, and his work drew the attention of *Elle* and *Marie Claire* magazines in France, Italy, and Germany.

Demarchelier moved to New York in 1975 and learned to speak English from watching television and listening to people on the street. He worked for international magazines such as *Glamour*, *Mademoiselle*, *Vogue*, and *Harper's Bazaar*. In 1989, upon her request, he photographed Princess Diana, and shortly thereafter, became the first non-British photographer to the Royal family. In 2004, he signed a new contract with Condé Nast.

Demarchelier believes that society is too "perfection obsessed," and is credited with bringing out his subjects' natural beauty in his photographs. He achieves this by creating an environment of spontaneity during his shoots, and forming a bond of trust with his clients. Many of his famous photographs are nudes, of which he states that it captivates the "timid and nakedness" of the subject. His celebrity clients include Ronald Reagan, Bill Clinton, Elton John,

Photographer Patrick Demarchelier.

Madonna, Nicole Kidman, Paul Newman, and Britney Spears.

In 2007, the Council of Fashion Designers of America presented him with the "Eleanor Lambert Award" to honor his contribution to the world of fashion. On November 23, 2007, Patrick Demarchelier was honored as an Officier dans l'Ordre des Arts et des Lettres on the 50th anniversary of this prestigious award. In 2008, Le Petit Palais, Musée des Beaux Arts de la Ville de Paris, presented a comprehensive selection of 400 photographs in honor of Demarchelier.

Pamela Dennis

BORN Newark, New Jersey, August 24, 1960

Pamela Dennis has carved a distinctive niche for herself in the designer evening category. Without formal training, she came into design by chance when, invited to a wedding and with nothing to wear, she took a few yards of silk to a tailor and had him make it into a columnar dress. Another wedding guest, a photostylist, asked to use the dress in a diamond commercial, which led to three more commercials and inspired Dennis to design her first collection.

Her clothes are distinguished by simple shapes in luxurious fabrics—silk crepe, chiffon, georgette, charmeuse, wool bouclé, stretch crepe—enhanced with crystals or hand-beaded lace. They have been sold nationally and internationally to fine boutiques and specialty stores and worn by celebrities.

Designer Pamela Dennis.

In 2000, with the aim of adapting her signature styles for a more accessible price range, Dennis sold her company to a newly-formed luxury conglomerate. The move proved disastrous with an acrimonious parting of ways in early 2001. By March 2002, though still not yet able to use her own name, Dennis was back in business on a limited basis with plans for future expansion.

Currently, her Pamela Dennis Private Client Group sportswear line, which features couture finishing, is sold on QVC.

Spring 2001.

Designer Jean Dessès.

White dress with black lace trim, 1951.

BORN Alexandria, Egypt, August 6, 1904
DIED Athens, Greece, August 2, 1970

Jean Dessès is remembered primarily for draped evening gowns of chiffon and mousseline in beautiful colors, and for the subtlety with which he handled fur. Of Greek ancestry, he was as a child interested in beautiful clothes and designed a dress for his mother when he was only nine. He attended school in Alexandria, Egypt, studied law in Paris, and in 1925 switched to fashion design. For 12 years he worked for Mme. Jane on the Rue de la Paix and in 1937 opened his own establishment.

Dessès visited the United States in 1949. He admired American women and in 1950 designed a lower-priced line for them called Jean Dessès Diffusion. This is seen as the beginning of French couture expansion into ready-to-wear.

A gentleman of refined and luxurious tastes, Dessès was inspired in his work by native costumes he saw in museums on his travels, especially in Greece and Egypt. Customers included Princess Margaret, the Duchess of Kent, and the Queen of Greece. Other designers worked for him—VALENTINO in the 1950s, also GUY LAROCHE. Dessès gave up his couture business in 1960 due to ill health and continued the ready-to-wear until 1965, when he retired to Greece. With the recent renewed interest in vintage couture his beautiful classic gowns have had a second coming, no longer hidden in museum collections but showing up on the backs of celebrities such as Renée Zellweger, who wore one to the 2001 Academy Awards.

Actress Renée Zellweger wearing a Jean Dessès design at the Academy Awards, 2001.

Collette Dinnigan

BORN South Africa, September 24, 1965

AWARDS Australian Designer of the Year, 1996

Collette Dinnigan is regarded as one of the top Australian designers in the world. She is known for her use of luxurious fabrics, beads, and lace. She enrolled at Wellington Polytechnic, and decided to study fashion after she accidentally took a fashion course instead of a graphic design one. After graduation, she moved to Australia and worked at the Costume Department of the Australian Broadcasting Commission in Sydney for several years.

In 1990, she started her business. The line is currently sold in boutiques as well as fine stores such as Barneys New York, Nieman Marcus, and Joyce in Hong Kong. In 1995, she became the first Australian to mount a full scale ready-to-wear parade in Paris, and is still the only one to be invited by Chambre Syndicale du prêt-a-porter des couturiers et des créateurs de mode. She has been recognized with numerous awards for her business practices, including induction into the "Business Women's Hall of Fame"

Designer Collette Dinnigan.

and receiving the Leading Women's Entrepreneurs of the World Award in 2002.

In 2001 she teamed up with London retailer Marks and Spencer to launch a lingerie line entitled Wild Hearts. She was honored in 2005 with a stamp commemorating her and is the only Australian featured in an American Express commercial as well as their print ads in 2006. Her clothes are worn by celebrities such as Halle Berry, Naomi Watts, Elle McPherson, and Tori Spelling.

Ready-to-wear, spring 2009.

Designer Christian Dior (left).

BORN Granville, France, January 21, 1905
DIED Montecatini, Italy, October 24, 1957

AWARDS Neiman Marcus Award, 1947 • Parsons
Medal for Distinguished Achievement, 1956

The name Christian Dior is most associated with the New Look. This silhouette was, in essence, a polished continuation of the rounded line seen in the first postwar collections, appearing at the same time at a number of design houses. Dior's was a dream of flowerlike women with rounded shoulders, feminine busts, tiny waists, and enormous spreading skirts. Everything was exquisitely made of the best materials available.

Dress, fall/winter 1949-1950.

Dior was the son of a well-to-do manufacturer of fertilizer and chemicals from Normandy. He wished to become an architect, but his family wanted him to enter the diplomatic service. He studied political science at L'École des Sciences Politiques, performed his obligatory military service, and in 1928 opened a small art gallery with a friend. This was soon wiped out by the Depression, which also ruined Dior's family. In 1931 he traveled to Russia, returned disillusioned with Soviet Communism, and for the next few years lived from hand to mouth, eating little and sleeping on the floor of friends' apartments.

He became seriously ill in 1934 and had to leave Paris. During a forced rest in Spain and the south of France, he learned tapestry weaving and developed a desire to create. He returned to Paris in 1935, 30 years old and without means of support. Unable to find any kind of job, he started making design sketches and also did fashion illustrations for *Le Figaro*. That year he sold his first sketches for 20 francs each.

His early hat designs were successful, his dresses less so. In 1937, after a two-year struggle to improve his dresses, he sold several sketches to ROBERT PIGUET and was asked to make a number of dresses for an upcoming collection. He was hired by Piguet in 1938 but in 1939 went into the Army. The fall of Paris

Dior, continued

in June 1940 found him stationed in the south of France. Asked by Piguet to come back to work, Dior delayed his return until the end of 1941, by which time another designer had been hired. He then went to work for LUCIEN LELONG, a much larger establishment. At the end of 1946 he left Lelong to open his own house.

Dior was backed in his new project by Marcel Boussac, a French financier, race horse owner, and textile manufacturer, who originally was looking for someone to take over an ailing couture house he

Designer Christian Dior (center) with models.

owned. Instead, Dior persuaded Boussac to back him, and in the spring of 1947, presented his wildly successful first New Look collection.

He continued to produce beautiful clothes in collection after collection, each evolving from the one before, continually refining and expanding his talent. In 1952, with the sensuous line, he began to loosen the waist, freed it even more with the H-line in 1954, and the A- and Y-lines in 1955.

Dior described himself as silent, shy, and reticent by nature, strongly attached to his friends. He loved good food, and for relaxation and pleasure, he read history and archaeology and played cards. He also continued to have a strong passion for architecture. Since his death in 1957, the House of Dior has continued under the direction of other designers: YVES SAINT LAURENT until 1960, MARC BOHAN until 1989, then GIANFRANCO FERRÉ, and since 1996 by JOHN GALLIANO. ROGER VIVIER and Christian Dior also collaborated and introduced the first ready-to-wear designer label shoes, Christian Dior created by Roger Vivier, in 1955. Christian Dior, Inc., has become a vast international merchandising operation with the Dior label on jewelry, scarves, men's ties, furs, stockings, gloves, ready-to-wear, and perfume.

Silk and wool suit, 1947.

BORN Domenico Dolce; Polizzi Generosa, Palermo, Italy, September 13, 1958

Stefano Gabbana; Venice, Italy, November 14, 1962

Members of the avant-garde of Italian fashion, Dolce (DOL-chay) and Gabbana (Gab-BAH-nah) came to their craft by disparate routes: Dolce, whose father had a small clothing factory in Sicily, attended fashion school, but Gabbana was totally lacking a fashion background, having studied graphics and working in an advertising agency.

Designers Stefano Gabbana (left) and Domenico Dolce (right).

The two met in Milan in 1980, became assistants to a Milanese designer, and in 1982 joined forces in their own business, working as consultants to other companies while creating their own line.

Their first international recognition came in 1985 when they were chosen by the Milano Collezioni as one of three young Italian talents to be given formal presentations. Their first knitwear collection appeared in 1987; they have since added men's wear and, in 1994, a lower-priced collection called D&G.

Dolce & Gabbana continue to evolve along their own highly individual path. Their look, based on body clothes, seasons the modern with romantic historical references, and the pieces are designed to be worn in different ways. In their men's wear, a Sicilian-influenced combination of strict, structured tailoring with avant-garde shirts and accessories appeals to the man who is not afraid of attention.

Left: Ready-to-wear, fall 2005.

Right: Spring/summer 2009.

Carrie Donovan

Fashion writer and the *New York Times* editor Carrie Donovan.

BORN Carolyn Gertrude Amelia Donovan; Lake Placid, New York, March 22, 1928
DIED November 12, 2001

The last of a line of fashion editors with larger-than-life fashion personalities, including DIANA VREELAND and CARMEL SNOW, Carrie Donovan had a varied career that lasted nearly 50 years. Her first ambition was to be a designer, and she studied dressmaking at Parsons School of Design in New York City, from which she graduated in 1950. She then turned to fashion journalism in 1955, working first at the *New York Times* before going to *Vogue* under Vreeland. In 1972, when Vreeland was fired from the magazine, Donovan moved to *Harper's Bazaar* as fashion editor, leaving in 1976 to become vice president of communications at Bloomingdale's.

She then returned to the *Times* in 1977 as style editor for the *New York Times Magazine*. There she stayed until her retirement in 1995, but her love of fashion remained. She wrote a column for *Allure* magazine, before undertaking a new career in 1997 as spokesperson for Old Navy. For the store she appeared in newspaper ads and television spots wearing her trademark pearls and oversized black-framed glasses. Thus, she became a celebrity in the world beyond the small one of fashion, recognized on the street by people of all ages who sometimes saluted her by singing an Old Navy jingle.

She was actively engaged in promoting new talent, introducing designers such as DONNA KARAN and PALOMA PICASSO to her readers and acting as matchmaker between designer and prospective employer. She was instrumental in bringing ELSA PERETTI's modern jewelry approach to Tiffany, a bastion of tradition.

She never learned to use a typewriter (or a computer) and always wrote her copy by hand. With her enthusiasm and outgoing personality, she had a wide circle of friends in the fashion community, and even those who knew her only slightly would find their world a little less colorful with her passing in 2001.

BORN Paris, 1853
DIED Paris, 1929

With its beginnings in the silk trade around 1820, the House of Doucet (Due-say) is the oldest of the Paris couture houses. Jacques Doucet joined the family business in 1870, and began to focus primarily on custom-made women's apparel. He was just 18 years old when he opened his first boutique. Doucet was known for his love of iridescent silk and abundant use of lace. His tea gowns and tailored suits were among his most popular ensembles. Doucet designed for several of the most popular actresses of the time, including Gabrielle Réjane and Sarah Bernhart. Many designers apprenticed with Doucet, including a young PAUL POIRET. By the 1920's, Doucet's designs had fallen behind the times. In 1929, after his death, the company was merged with Doeuillet, but soon folded in 1932.

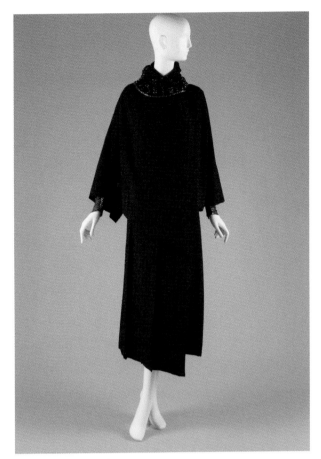

Wool, silk, and glass dress, 1920-1923.

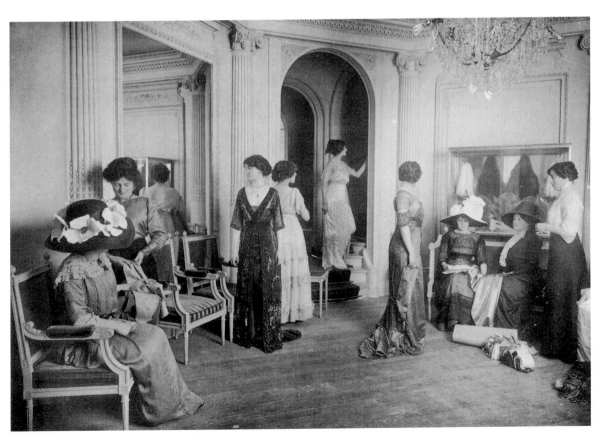

Salon de vente (sale room) at the House of Doucet, 1910.

Drécoll

FOUNDED Paris, France, 1905
CLOSED 1929

The House of Drécoll was established in Vienna by a Belgian, Baron Christopher Drécoll. He bought the name and moved the business to Paris, where it survived through the first World War, but it could not change with the times. Drécoll was never one of the top Paris houses, but in the pre-war period its elaborate clothes fit in and the house prospered. After the war, women had new attitudes and expected new clothes. Unable to change direction, the house was forced to close.

Pink chiffon robe with brown trim, 1909.

Pale blue robe with large white feathered hat, 1908.

BORN Dean and Dan Calen; Ontario, Canada, 1965.

AWARDS *Golden Needle Award, 2006*

Dean and Dan Caten, identical twin brothers born in Willowdale, Ontario, in 1965 are the duo behind Dsquared2. The two brought their rugged American dreams to Milan in 1991 and forged them together with Italian craftsmanship and fine tailoring. Since 1994, their collection has been building a steady audience around the world.

Their influences are clear: cowboys, truckers, military men, motocross riders, matadors, the residents of trailer parks, and "Mad Max" himself. Using reams of leather and denim and black, their creations are witty, steamy, ironic, and not for the faint of heart. Their staples include lean tailored jackets and outerwear, tight tees and low-cut jeans, mixed and matched with a subtext of sex.

In 2007, the Dsquared2 flagship store opened in Milan. In 2008, they signed an eyeglass wear deal with Marcolin, one of the top sunglass and spectacle manufacturers in Italy. The brothers also opened stores in Capri, Kiev, Istanbul, Hong Kong, and Dubai, and in May of 2009, opened a boutique in Cannes. Their celebrity clients include Justin Timberlake, Lenny Kravitz, Ricky Martin, Nicolas Cage, and Madonna.

Designers Dean Calen (left) and Dan Calen (right).

Advertisement, spring/summer 2006.

Gilles Dufour

Designer Gilles Dufour (center) with Karl Lagerfeld and models.

BORN Lyon, France

AWARDS Chevalier des arts et Letters, 2008

Gilles Dufour (DOO-for) established his own prêt-à-porter label in March 2001 after an already extensive career, including collaboration with KARL LAGERFELD at CHLOÉ and FENDI and 15 years as Lagerfeld's number two at CHANEL. He has freelanced in New York and Paris for ready-to-wear, leathers, and furs, and put in three seasons as prêt-à-porter stylist at BALMAIN. He graduated from L'École Supérieure des Arts Décoratifs in Paris and studied in New York at the School of Visual Arts, after which he worked at CARDIN on both ready-to-wear and couture.

Extremely versatile, Dufour has designed just about everything a woman could wear, from accessories to bridal to furs to sportswear, and, in addition, sportswear for men. He has also created sets and costumes for ballet, opera, and film. His assured designs show a light touch—witty trompe-l'oeil knits, sexy sweaters, little black dresses, and trademark T-shirts bearing naughty legends that vary with each collection.

Currently, he is designing for Gripoix. In 2008, he was honored along with AZZEDINE ALAÏA and Lee Radziwell, with the "Chevalier des arts et Letters," an award of merit given to artists who make extraordinary contributions to French culture.

8th Chocolate Fair in Paris, 2002.

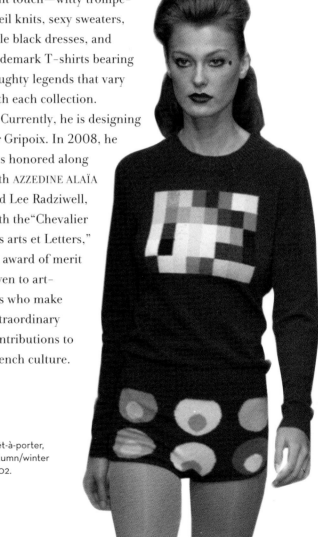

Prêt-à-porter, autumn/winter 2002.

Designer Randolph Duke (center) with models.

BORN Las Vegas, Nevada, January 14, 1958

Randolph Duke studied at the University of Southern California and at the Fashion Institute of Design and Merchandising in Los Angeles, from which he graduated in 1978 with the Bob Mackie and Peacock awards. He began his career immediately as a swimwear designer, working successively for various West Coast companies—Jantzen, Cole of California, the ANNE COLE Collection—and until 1987 for Gottex.

To establish his own label, Duke relocated to New York. For a time he had a shop on the Upper West Side of Manhattan and a wholesale business that closed in 1992. He then joined a private label producing exclusive signature collections for retail stores.

In 1996 he became creative director for the newly-resuscitated HALSTON label, where over several seasons he oversaw its revival with clothes of an American smartness consistent with the Halston name, glamorous and luxurious. Following his stint at Halston, Duke launched RANDOLPH DUKE, a couture evening collection.

He has sold his clothes successfully in personal appearances on the QVC shopping channel and created collections of apparel and accessories for the Home Shopping Network, meanwhile selling his signature collection through select specialty stores such as Neiman Marcus, Saks Fifth Avenue, and Barneys. Duke's attention-getting evening dresses have been chosen for award appearances by numerous actresses, including Jennifer Aniston, Minnie Driver, Angelina Jolie, and Hilary Swank.

Look from Spring 2008.

Angelina Jolie at Golden Globe Awards, 1999.

Stephen Dweck

Designer Stephen Dweck.

BORN Brooklyn, New York, August 10, 1960

Graduating from New York's School of Visual Arts in
1980 with a gold medal in sculpture, Stephen Dweck
went into business as a jewelry designer the same
year in partnership with his brothers. Working with
sterling silver, vermeil, and bronze, he combines the
metals with natural minerals and semiprecious stones
for jewelry that is modern with overtones of fantasy
and hints of ancient cultures. He utilizes natural
forms such as beetles, butterflies, leaves, and vines
for his jewelry and for the collections for the home,
which he creates for others. These have included
china for Sasaki and sterling silver gifts and accessories for Lunt Silversmiths. He has also designed a belt
collection.

Dweck has worked with some of the biggest
designers in the country; including GEOFFREY BEENE,
DONNA KARAN, and OSCAR DE LA RENTA. His designs
can be viewed at the Smithsonian Institute Fashion
Archives in Washington, D.C., the Metropolitan
Museum of Art in New York, and the Dallas Museum
of Art. One can identify his work by the use of
"Adam," a beetle found on all of his pieces.

Free-form pyrite and
bronze ring, 2008.

Lapis and turquoise rings, 2007.

Florence EISEMAN

Alber ELBAZ

Perry ELLIS

Elizabeth EMANUEL

ERIC

ERTÉ

ETRO

Florence Eiseman

BORN Minneapolis, Minnesota, September 27, 1899
DIED Milwaukee, Wisconsin, January 8, 1988

AWARDS Neiman Marcus Award (the first children's designer recipient), 1955 • *Swiss Fabrics Award*, 1956 • *Dallas Fashion Award*, 1980

Two Florence Eiseman sayings are: "Children have bellies, not waists" and "you should see the child, and not the dress first." Ruled by these precepts, and by her belief that children should not be dressed in small versions of adult clothing, Eiseman produced simple styles distinguished by fine fabrics and excellent workmanship, with prices to match. The clothes were so classic and so well made they were frequently handed down from one generation to another.

Eiseman took up sewing as a hobby following the birth of her second son, Robert. As her children grew she turned out quilts and clothing for them and for her neighbors' children. In 1945, when family finances were pinched, her husband Laurence took samples of her organdy pinafores to Marshall Field & Co. in Chicago. The $3,000 order he came away with put them in business with her as designer and him as business manager/salesman.

Eiseman first worked out of her home, enlisting other women to sew for her. Next, with two sewing machines, she took over a corner of her husband's toy factory. Within a few years, Laurence Eiseman gave up his toy business to devote himself to the clothing firm, which in a short time grew into a large operation, with sales across the United States and abroad. Eiseman functioned successively as vice president, president, and chairman.

She became known as the "NORMAN NORELL of children's clothes," making dresses and separates, swimsuits, playclothes, sleepwear, and boys' suits. In 1969 she added less-expensive knits, brother-sister outfits and, for a short time, a limited group of women's clothes. In 1984 the company was asked by Neiman Marcus to do a luxury collection of dress-up clothes at prices beginning where the regular collection left off. The result was Florence Eiseman Couture, not custom-made but using rich fabrics and many hand touches. Its introduction in September

Designer Florence Eiseman, left.

Display at Denver Art Museum's 1984 retrospective of Eiseman's designs.

1984 coincided with Eiseman's 85th birthday, finding her still actively involved in the company she founded. The same year, the Denver Art Museum presented a retrospective of her work. Upon her death, she was praised for her role in raising the standards of fashion and quality in children's clothes and for encouraging manufacturers to trade up.

Designer Alber Elbaz.

BORN Morocco, 1961

Alber Elbaz (El-bahz) grew up in Tel Aviv, where he graduated from the Shenkar College School of Fashion and Textiles. He served three years in the Israeli Army and, when he was 25, left Israel for New York. He immediately started working on Seventh Avenue, designing inexpensive evening dresses, and a few years later was introduced to GEOFFREY BEENE, who hired him on the spot. He worked for Beene for seven years as a design assistant before moving to Paris in 1996 for the top job at GUY LAROCHE.

After successfully invigorating Laroche, he was hired away in 1998 to become head women's designer at YVES SAINT LAURENT Rive Gauche. In 1999, when Saint Laurent was bought by Gucci, he was supplanted by TOM FORD. He then worked briefly for Krizia in Milan before being hired as creative director for LANVIN late in 2001.

The Elbaz style is based on classic shapes, beautiful, womanly clothes without elaborate trimming or silhouettes, flattering colors, and a few feminine turns such as beading or ribbons to give them pizazz. Without losing sight of wearability, he is fascinated with new ways of cutting fabric or placing a seam, visualizing a client who wants something both beautiful and comfortable. For evening he aims at glamour but never extravagance: "When a woman walks into the room, no one will faint, but she will be noticed."

Looks from Alber Elbaz for Lanvin, pre-fall 2009.

Look from Alber Elbaz for Lanvin, spring 2010.

Perry Ellis

BORN Portsmouth, Virginia, March 3, 1940
DIED New York City, May 30, 1986

AWARDS Neiman Marcus Award, 1979 • Coty American Fashion Critics' Award *"Winnie,"* 1979; *Return Award, 1980; Hall of Fame, 1981; Special Award (men's wear), 1981; Hall of Fame Citation (women's wear), 1983; Men's Wear Return Award,* 1983; *Hall of Fame (men's wear), 1984; Hall of Fame Citation (women's wear),* 1984 • Council of Fashion Designers of America (CFDA) *Outstanding Designer in Women's Fashion,* 1981; *Outstanding Designer in Men's Fashion:* 1982, 1983 • Cutty Sark Men's Fashion Award *Outstanding Men's wear Designer:* 1983, 1984 • *Fashion Walk of Fame,* 2002

Perry Ellis came to fashion design relatively late, having previously worked in retailing and merchandising. He took his B.A. at William and Mary College, and his M.A. in retailing from New York University. He was a sportswear buyer for Miller & Rhoads in Richmond, leaving in 1967 to work as a merchandiser for John Meyer of Norwich, a conservative sportswear firm. There he acquired three important design

Designer Perry Ellis.

tools—sketching, patternmaking, and fabric selection. In 1974 he joined the Vera Companies as merchandiser, and the next year became designer for the Portfolio division of Vera.

Perry Ellis Sportswear, Inc., was established in 1978 with Ellis as designer and president; men's wear followed in 1980. Then came furs, shearling coats for both men and women, cloth coats, and for Japan, a complete sportswear line. There were shoes, legwear, scarves, *Vogue* patterns, sheets, towels, and blankets. A fragrance collection was launched in 1985.

From the beginning, the clothes were distinguished by a young, adventurous spirit and the use of natural fibers: cotton, silk, linen, and pure wool. Hand-knitted sweaters of cotton, silk, and cashmere became a trademark. This use of fine fabrics and handwork soon drove the collection up into a higher price bracket. Hence, in 1984, the Portfolio name was revived for a moderately priced collection with much the same relaxed classic look as the original.

Ellis was active in the Council of Fashion Designers of America and served two terms as president—elected to a third term the week before his death in 1986. In his honor, the organization established the Perry Ellis Award, to be given annually "for the greatest impact on an emerging new talent."

The company has continued in business under the direction of a number of designers. MARC JACOBS took over in 1989 and was dropped by the company in February 1993, when the designer and bridge sportswear collections were discontinued. The Perry Ellis name continues to be licensed in both the United States and in Europe.

Design by Perry Ellis.

BORN Elizabeth Florence Weiner; London, England, July 5, 1953

Elizabeth and David Emanuel gained international attention for their wedding dress for Diana, Princess of Wales. They attended Harrow School of Art and together took a postgraduate course in fashion at the Royal College of Art. They opened their own ready-to-wear firm in 1977, switching to custom-made in 1979. In June 1990 they closed their business and announced the end of their marriage.

The Emanuels' fantasy ball gowns and wedding dresses, afloat in lace, taffeta, organza, and tulle, evoked a romantic, bygone, never-never time. Licenses included bed linens, sunglasses, and perfume.

During the 1990s, Elizabeth Emanuel concentrated on costume design for the film industry. She was also successful in designing uniforms for Virgin Airlines and Britannia Airways.

In March 1999, she launched a new venture with backer Richard Thompson. The range consisted of bridal, couture, and ready-to-wear, all displaying the same attention to detail and exquisite fabrics that have become her hallmark.

From 2001–2002 she worked as the designer for The Luxury Brand Group concentrating on the development of their newly acquired Norman Hartness brand. Three years later Emanuel saw the acquisition of her new studio in Little Venice and launch of her label "Art of Being."

Designer Elizabeth Emanuel (left) and model wearing Emanuel's design.

Sketch of design for Princess Diana's wedding dress, 1981.

In 2006, *A Dress for Diana*, cowritten by David Emanuel, was published and relaunched as a limited edition in 2007, with a framed swatch of fabric from the same bolt used to make Princess Diana's wedding dress.

In February 2007, Emanuel completed a multi-feature DVD called *Metamorphosis*, featuring her new fall/winter collection.

Designers David Emanuel (left) and Elizabeth Emanuel (right).

Eric

BORN Carl Erickson; Joliet, Illinois, 1891
DIED 1958

The son of Swedish immigrants, Eric studied at the
Art Institute of Chicago before heading for Paris to
become a painter. After he married a fashion artist
on the staff of French *Vogue*, his seemingly off-hand
fashion sketches began appearing in *Vogue's* pages.
There, during the 1930s and 1940s he influenced
fashionable life with his elegant watercolors of chic,
super-slim women, often shown from the back,
and set against a background of elegant restaurants,
exclusive resorts, and other haunts of the rich and
famous. In her book, *In My Fashion*, the fashion
editor Bettina Ballard wrote, "His drawings over the
years evoked a promise of beauty that photographs
could never equal." The sketches are still coveted by
collectors.

Illustration of Vionnet design in *Vogue*, 1937.

Illustration of Christian Dior design.

Designer Erté.

BORN Romain de Tirtoff; St. Petersburg, Russia, November 23, 1892
DIED Paris, France, April 21, 1990

The son of an admiral in the Russian Imperial Navy, Erté studied painting in Russia then went to Paris in 1912 to study at Académie Julian. He took a new name for himself from the French pronunciation of his initials R.T. (air-tay), got a job sketching for PAUL POIRET, went on to design for opera and theater, creating costumes for such luminaries as the opera soprano Mary Garden.

From 1914 into the 1930s, he produced illustrations and covers for various magazines, including *Harper's Bazaar*. During his 22-year stint with *Harper's Bazaar*, he created more than 250 covers. He designed for the Folies Bergère, came to the United States in the 1920s to work for Ziegfeld and other impresarios, and tried Hollywood briefly in 1925. There he created beautiful and esoteric costumes for several silent films, including *The Mystic*, *Ben Hur*, and King Vidor's *La Boheme*, but impatient with financial restrictions placed on him, returned to Paris after eight months.

In 1967, at the age of 75, he attracted the attention of art dealer Eric Estorich. To celebrate his eightieth birthday, Erté selected more than a hundred of his designs for clothes, jewelry, and accessories, to be shown in London and at the Grosvenor Gallery in New York. The exhibition contained some of the most elegant and individual designs of the art deco period. The New York exhibition was bought in its entirety by the Metropolitan Museum of Art. He also produced three large format books: *Erté at Ninety*, *Erté at Ninety-Five*, and *Erté Sculpture*. Erté died in 1990, when he was hailed as "a mirror of fashion for 75 years."

Designer Erté (left) with actress wearing his costume design.

Etro

FOUNDED Milan, 1968

Established by Gimmo Etro as a family business in 1968, the Italian fashion house Etro made its debut with colorful, luxurious textiles for haute couture and ready-to-wear. In 1981 the paisley collection was introduced, and the brightly patterned designs—combined with impeccable classic tailoring—became the company's signature look. By the time the flagship store opened in Milan in 1983, Etro's accessories included luxe ties and scarves, and was followed by handbags, luggage, home accessories, fragrances, shoes, and eyewear.

In the 1990s, the company made its first foray into ready-to-wear apparel with a runway debut in 1994. Today both the women's wear (designed by Veronica Etro) and men's wear (designed by Kean Etro) collections are known for their sharp tailoring contrasted with printed and bright patterns. Also continuing the family legacy are Jacopo and Ippolito, who are in charge of textiles, accessories, and home divisions. Now available at boutiques in Europe and Asia, as well as in high-end department stores such as Harrods and Bergdorf Goodman, Etro remains a distinctive family business that combines tradition with innovation.

Designer Veronica Etro.

Left: Ready-to-wear, fall 2009.

Right: Men's wear, spring 2010.

John B. FAIRCHILD

Jacques FATH

FENDI

Louis FÉRAUD

Salvatore FERRAGAMO

Gianfranco FERRÉ

Alberta FERRETTI

Patricia FIELD

Eileen FISHER

Anne FOGARTY

FONTANA

Tom FORD

Mariano FORTUNY

Toni FRISSELL

John B. Fairchild

BORN Newark, New Jersey, 1927

John B. Fairchild began his career as a reporter for *Women's Wear Daily* in 1951, two years after graduating from Princeton University. It was only three years later that Fairchild moved to Paris to take over the French bureaus of the newspaper—part of Fairchild Publications, a company founded by his grandfather Edmund Fairchild—in the move that made him famous.

In this position, Fairchild shook up the world of haute couture by mixing gossip in with the newspaper's traditional stories as well as printing sketches of clothes when he wanted, as opposed to when fashion houses approved their release. When Fairchild arrived in Paris, the reporters for his newspaper were often seated in back rows of fashion shows. Feeling slighted by this, Fairchild went about raising the visibility of the paper and turning the once-fusty publication into a must-read, known in the industry as "the Bible of fashion" and ensuring his reporters the access and respect he felt they deserved.

On the heels of his work in Paris, Fairchild was named publisher of *WWD* and returned to New York City in 1960. He brought his innovations with him, and the paper soon began including society and event coverage in addition to trade stories. Five years later, Fairchild was named CEO of Fairchild Publications, steering the company to launch *WWD* offshoots *W* and *M*.

In 1965, Fairchild penned *The Fashionable Savages*, a series of candid looks at the designers who ruled the fashion world at the time and the women who kept them in business. In 1989, Fairchild wrote another book, *Chic Savages*, a biting memoir of life in the fashion world that took on industry giants like OSCAR DE LA RENTA, MARY MCFADDEN, and ANNA WINTOUR, which cemented his reputation as a provocateur, albeit a well-liked one.

Fairchild retired in 1997 at the age of 70, but remained contributing editor at large for *W* and *WWD*. He also authors a column for *W* under the name Louise J. Esterhazy.

Women's Wear Daily editor John B. Fairchild.

Designer Jacques Fath (right) with model.

BORN Lafitte, France, September 6, 1912
DIED Paris, France, November 13, 1954

AWARDS Neiman Marcus Award, 1949

Jacques Fath's clothes were flattering, feminine, and sexy without slipping into vulgarity. They followed the lines of the body with hourglass shapes and swathed hips, and often had full, pleated skirts and plunging necklines. He did not sew or sketch but draped material while his assistants made sketches.

Son of an Alsatian businessman, grandson of a painter, and great-grandson of a dressmaker, Fath attended both business school and drama school, acting briefly in films. He showed his design talent early on in costumes for theater and films, opened his first couture house in Paris in 1937 with a small collection of 20 models. He went into the Army in 1940, was captured, and on his release reopened his house, which he managed to keep open during the war. After liberation, he became enormously successful, eventually expanding his salon from the single wartime workroom with one fitter to an establishment with 600 employees. In 1948 he signed with a U.S. manufacturer to produce two collections a year, one of the first French couturiers to venture into ready-to-

wear. The Fath name also went into perfume, scarves, stockings, and millinery.

Handsome and personable, Fath had a flair for publicity and showmanship and became one of the most popular designers of his time. He loved parties and with his wife, actress Geneviève de Bruyère, gave elaborate entertainments at their Corbeville chateau. He was also an excellent businessman. After his death from leukemia at the age of 42, his wife continued the business for a few years, closing it in 1957.

In early 2002 the name was bought by a newly-formed conglomerate, France Luxury Group, and Lizzy Disney, a young Brit who graduated from Central St. Martins the same year as STELLA MCCARTNEY, was hired as designer. In 2007, Daniel Chocu became CEO of Jacques Fath. With no creative director, the company premiered a well-received 2008 collection with an in-house design team.

Polka dot strapless dress, 1951.

Fendi

FOUNDED 1918

Specializing in furs, handbags, luggage, and sportswear, Fendi was founded in 1918 by Adele Fendi. After her husband's death in 1954, Signora Fendi called on her five daughters for help—Paola, Anna, Franca, Carla, and Alda were at that time aged 14 to 24. Working as a team, the sisters, with their husbands, have built and expanded the Fendi business, continuing to explore new areas. Their daughters, in turn, have also come into the firm. Adele Fendi died March 19, 1978, at the age of 81.

In 1962 the Fendis hired KARL LAGERFELD to design their furs, backing him with a dazzling array of new, unusual, or neglected pelts and the most inventive techniques. Their mother had made coats out of squirrel and had made it fashionable; the Fendis today still use squirrel, as well as badger, Persian lamb, fox, and sundry unpedigreed furs, often several in one garment. They are noted for such innovations as furs woven in strips and coats left unlined for lightness—the furs are always lighthearted and fun. Fendi styles have glamour, but their success is based on an understanding of what women need and want. The Fendi double F initials, designed by Lagerfeld, have become an international status symbol.

Chinchilla and fox coat and belt, 2007.

Designer Silvia Fendi (right) in the family's fashions, 1965.

Designers Silvia Fendi (left) with Karl Lagerfeld (right).

In addition to furs, there are Fendi accessories and ready-to-wear for women and men. Lagerfeld continues to be responsible for the women's ready-to-wear, and the avant-garde men's collection is designed by Silvia Fendi. Previously entirely a family business, the firm is now part of the LVMH empire.

Designer Louis Féraud.

BORN Arles, France, February 13, 1921
DIED Paris, December 28, 1999

Louis Féraud founded a couture house in Cannes, France, in 1950 which was visited by many movie stars coming to the Cannes film festival. By 1957, he established a house in Paris and designed for the Paris elite and his close friend Bridgette Bardot. In the 1960s he moved to Paris and started a ready-to-wear business, hiring Jean-Louis Sherrer. By 1962, his ready-to-wear line was sold at Saks Fifth Avenue and at Harrods and Fortnum in London. Inspired by the colors of South America, he was a known and accomplished painter, and used that art in his designs. Throughout his lifetime, Féraud presented exhibitions of his work in some of the most prestigious venues in the world.

In 1965, Féraud presented his first perfume Justine, and later in the decade, he introduced the first Russian model to Paris, Tamara. In the 1980s, he designed perfume for Avon and founded the Louis Féraud Golf Tournament in Cannes. In the 1990s,

he opened his boutique in New York and was elected "Prince de L'art de Vivre" in 1991. He was decorated by French President François Mitterrand with the Officier de la Legion d'honneur on March 16, 1995.

By the end of the 90s, Féraud's daughter Kiki had presented her first collection, and in 1999, Féraud died of Alzheimer's disease. The company he developed chose Yvan Mispelaere as artistic director in 2000. Two years later the German company, Escada, bought 90 percent of the company and hired Jean-Paul Knot as artistic director. He remained with the company for three years, until Féraud joined Alliance Designers Group. The current artistic director is Jean-Pierre Marty.

Autumn/winter 1997-1998.

Salvatore Ferragamo

BORN Bonito, Italy, June 5, 1898
DIED Fiumetto, Italy, August 7, 1960

AWARDS Neiman Marcus Award, 1947

Salvatore Ferragamo (Fair-a-GAH-moe) began working as a shoemaker in Bonito when he was 13, then emigrated to the United States in 1923. He studied mass shoemaking techniques then opened a shop in Hollywood, designing shoes and making them by hand for such film stars as Dolores Del Rio, Pola Negri, and Gloria Swanson. He also maintained a successful business in ready-made shoes.

He returned to Italy and in 1936 opened a business in Florence. By the time of his death in 1960 he had ten factories in Italy and in Great Britain. After his death, the business was carried on by his wife and daughters Fiamma and Giovanna, and his son Ferruccio. In addition to shoes, the Ferragamo name appears on handbags, scarves, and luxury ready-to-wear sold in freestanding boutiques and in major specialty stores.

Early Ferragamo designs are fantasies of shape, color, and fabric. He is said to have originated the wedge heel and the platform sole, also the Lucite

Designer Salvatore Ferragamo (left).

heel. While still elegant, the emphasis for many years shifted to ladylike, conservative styling and comfortable fit but in the age of the stiletto, the house has shown more extreme styles and proved itself very much in step with the times.

Above: Couture shoe design.

Right: Ankle-strap sandal, 1938.

BORN Legnano, Italy, August 15, 1944
DIED Milan, June 17, 2007

Gianfranco Ferré's (Ferr-ay) day clothes have a strong sculptural quality, yet they are fluid, clean-lined, and comfortable. A fine tailor and leading exponent of architectural design, Ferré originally intended to be an architect and studied in Milan qualifying in 1967. After a period of working for a furniture maker and time off for travel, he began designing jewelry, and by 1970 had made a name for himself as an accessories designer. He sold his shoes, scarves, and handbags to other designers, including KARL LAGERFELD, and designed striped T-shirts for Fiorucci. As a freelancer he began designing sportswear and raincoats, and by 1974 was showing under his own name.

In 1989 he joined CHRISTIAN DIOR, replacing MARC BOHAN as design director. At Dior his clothes were marked by lush extravagance in the traditional couture mode. He was replaced at Dior by JOHN GALLIANO in 1996. Up until his death in 2007, Ferré continued to produce his signature ready-to-wear collection in Italy with what is considered the most accomplished workroom in Milan.

Gianfranco Ferré

Designer Gianfranco Ferré.

Above: Spring 2005.
Left: Spring 2007.

Alberta Ferretti

BORN Gradara (near Riccione), Italy, May 2, 1950

Born into the business, Alberta Ferretti began at an early age to collaborate with her mother who owned an atelier. By the age of eighteen, she had her own boutique, and her first collection appeared in 1974. From 1981, when she presented her first prêt-à-porter collection, her business has grown to include the signature couture collection, diffusion sportswear, and a Japanese operation with boutiques in Tokyo, Osaka, and Yokohama. She is owner and managing director of Aeffe, which produces and distributes her clothes. It also produces MOSCHINO Cheap & Chic, Ultra OZBEK, NARCISO RODRIGUEZ, and JEAN-PAUL GAULTIER.

Ferretti's approach is feminine and elegant—soft, traditional shapes tweaked to make them contemporary and interpreted in the finest Italian fabrics. It's a look that's both witty and sexy. Her other projects have included glassware, ceramics, and a perfume, Femina.

Designer Alberta Ferretti.

Left: Spring 2008.

Right: Polka dot silk dress with fringe skirt, 2009.

Stylist and designer Patricia Field.

Patricia Field

ly got a lot more fun: Field combined pricey designer duds with whimsical accessories (including MANOLO BLAHNIK shoes) and almost single-handedly banished the idea of severe, all-black professional outfits.

Though Field also has her own design collection, House of Field with herself and David Dalrymple as the head designers, it is for her costuming skills—and ability to create entire looks—that she is lauded. She won four Costume Designers Guild Awards and an Emmy for her work on *Sex and the City*, along with BAFTA and Academy Award nominations for her work in the fashion insider's film *The Devil Wears Prada* (2006). She has also worked on the television series *Ugly Betty*.

BORN New York, New York, February 12, 1942

AWARDS Emmy Award for Outstanding Costume Design, 1990, 2002 • Costume Designers Guild Award, 2000, 2001, 2004, 2005

Native New Yorker Patricia Field is a costume designer, stylist, and fashion designer who established her own boutique with downtown style in the Bowery in 1966. Her eclectic sensibility was a hit with cutting-edge urban fashion fans, club kids, and drag queens—and Hollywood. As a stylist, she worked on creating the looks for television such as the 1960s-era mafio show *Crime Story*, *L.A. Takedown*, and *Wiseguy*. It was on the set of the film *Miami Rhapsody* in 1995 that she met actress Sarah Jessica Parker; when Parker was slated to star in HBO's *Sex and the City* (1998–2004), her fashion-obsessed character Carrie Bradshaw became a fashion icon in Field's hands. Being a chic New York woman sudden-

Actress Sarah Jessica Parker wearing flower dress in *Sex and the City*, 2008, styled by Patricia Field.

Eileen Fisher

BORN Des Plaines, Illinois, 1950

Eileen Fisher's fashion ideal—simple, loose, yet flattering outfits—was imprinted upon her at a young age, when she was a student of parochial schools in Chicago. After graduating from the Universtiy of Illinois at Urbana-Champaign, Fisher moved to New York City. The daily routine of getting dressed for work became overwhelming to her, and she longed for the ease and simplicity of her school uniforms.

In 1984, with $350 in startup money, Fisher began designing tops, vests, and pants. She presented four of her designs at the Boutique Show in New York and subsequently received clothing orders worth about $3,000. Eileen Fisher, Inc., now earns more than $254 million in annual revenue and sells in at least 37 stores. The company has been praised by Social Accountability International for its labor and safety standards, and in 2007, it was named one of the 50 best companies to work for by the Society for Human Resource Management.

Fisher is known for using natural fibers like silk crepe and Irish linens to create spare, comfort-

Ready-to-wear, spring 2008.

Designer Eileen Fisher.

able garments—kimono jackets, sleeveless shells, loose tunics, and elastic-waist skirts and slacks. She describes hers as the ideal style for a working woman who doesn't have the time to deal with complex outfits. "What we do is keep what's good about the school uniform, but not that limited," she has said. "It's a simplified system, like a Lego system, where it's simple pieces [are] used in different ways."

Silver sequined dress, 1966.

BORN Pittsburgh, Pennsylvania, February 2, 1919
DIED New York City, January 15, 1981

AWARDS Coty American Fashion Critics' Award *Special Award (dresses)*, 1951 • Neiman Marcus Award, 1952 • International Silk Association Award, 1955 • National Cotton Fashion Award, 1957

Anne Fogarty is best known for her "paper doll" silhouette and crinoline petticoats under full-skirted shirtdresses with tiny waists, a chemise gathered onto a high yoke, and lounging coveralls. In the early 1970s she showed a peasant look with ruffled shirts and hot pants under long quilted skirts. She also designed lingerie, jewelry, shoes, hats, coats, and suits.

After study at Carnegie Tech, Fogarty moved to New York, where she worked as a model and stylist. Between 1948 and 1957 she designed junior-size dresses for the Youth Guild and Margot, Inc., and spent the next five years at Saks Fifth Avenue. She established Anne Fogarty Inc. in 1962 and closed it 12 years later. By the time of her death in 1981 she had completed a collection of spring-summer dresses and sportswear for a Seventh Avenue firm.

Voile dress, 1970.

Fontana

FOUNDED Parma, Italy, 1907

Originally a small dressmaking establishment founded in Parma by Amabile Fontana, the business was taken over by her three daughters, with Micol and Zoe as designers, and Giovanna in charge of sales. In 1936 they moved to Rome and after World War II made a name for themselves in the emerging Italian haute couture as *Sorelle Fontana* (Fontana Sisters). Their designs were marked by asymmetric lines and interesting necklines, and were noteworthy for delicate handwork. They were particularly admired for their evening gowns.

Fontana created Ava Gardner's clothing for *The Barefoot Contessa*, Margaret Truman's wedding gown, and clothes for Jacqueline Kennedy. The house was at its peak in the 1950s, when it contributed largely to Italian fashion. To this day, the company still caters to the Italian elite.

Designers Zoe Fontana (left) and Micol Fontana (right).

Princess di Strongoli of Italy, wearing Fontana design, 1954.

Designer Tom Ford.

BORN Austin, Texas, August 27, 1961

AWARDS Awards CFDA 1996, 2001, 2002, 2004 • VH-1/*Vogue Fashion Award* 1995, 1996, 1999, 2002 • Fashion Editor's Club of Japan, 2000 • U.S. Accessory Council, *ACE Award*, 2001, and *Launch ACE Award*, 2006 • Elle Style Awards, *Style Icon Award* (UK), 1999 • British GQ *International Man of the Year Award*, 2000 • The Fashion Group, *Superstar Award* (U.S.), 2000 • *TIME Magazine, Best Fashion Designer*, 2001 • *GQ Designer of the Year* (U.S.), 2001 • Cooper Hewitt Design Museum's *Fashion Design Achievement Award*, 2003 • *Rodeo Drive Walk of Style Award*, 2004 • *Andre Leon Talley Lifetime Achievement Award*, 2005 • GLAAD's *Vito Russo Award*, 2007

Tom Ford moved from Santa Fe to New York as a teenager. He enrolled at New York University, attending courses in art history. He later redirected his studies to concentrate on architecture at Parsons School of Design in New York and Paris.

In 1990, Ford moved to Milan to join GUCCI as the company's women's wear designer. In 1994, he was appointed creative director and was responsible for the design of all product lines, advertising campaigns, and store design.

In 2000, following the acquisition of YVES SAINT LAURENT and YSL Beaute

by the GUCCI Group, Ford became creative director of Yves Saint Laurent Rive Gauche and YSL Beaute, in addition to his duties at Gucci. He also served as creative director of the Gucci Group and was made vice chairman of the board in 2002. In 2004, Ford resigned from his post at Gucci Group following a buyout by Pinault Printemps Redoute.

In 2005, Ford announced the creation of the TOM FORD brand. He announced his partnership with the Marcolin Group to produce and distribute optical frames and sunglasses under his brand. Tom Ford and Estee Lauder also joined together and launched a stand-alone fragrance and beauty collection under the TOM FORD BEAUTY label in 2006, with a signature fragrance called TOM FORD BLACK ORCHID. It was followed by TOM FORD BLACK ORCHID VOILE DE FLEUR and TOM FORD FOR MEN in 2007.

In 2006, Ford announced a licensing agreement with Ermenegildo Zegna Group for the production and worldwide distribution of luxury men's ready-to-wear and made to measure clothing, footwear, and accessories under the TOM FORD label.

In 2007, his first directly owned flagship store opened in New York, and TOM FORD INTERNATIONAL announced a global expansion. Exclusive, limited distribution of the TOM FORD MEN'S WEAR collection was released in 2008.

Ford also directed and produced his first film, *A Single Man*, which was released in 2009.

Left: Look for Gucci, fall/winter 2004.

Right: Three piece suit from the Tom Ford men's wear collection, fall/winter 2008.

Mariano Fortuny

Natalia Vodianova wearing Fortuny at the MET's 2009 Costume Institute Gala.

BORN Granada, Spain, May 11, 1871
DIED Venice, Italy, May 3, 1949

Mariano Fortuny's father was a well-known painter who died when his son was only three years old. After art studies—painting, drawing, and sculpture—Fortuny became interested in chemistry and dyes, which he studied in Germany. At the turn of the twentieth century he moved to Venice where he experimented with every aspect of design, from dyeing and printing silks by methods and in patterns of his own invention, to shaping clothes to his own aesthetic standards.

His silk tea gowns in rich and subtle colors have been widely collected, both by museums and by women who treasure the rare and beautiful. The most famous design is the *Delphos* gown, which first appeared in 1907 and was patented. This is a simple column of many narrow, irregular, vertical pleats permanently set in silk by a secret process. Slipped over the head and tied at the waist by thin silk cords, it clings to the figure and spills over the feet. It may have sleeves or be sleeveless. There is also a two-piece version called *Peplos*, with a hip-length overblouse or longer, unpleated tunic. These dresses are both beautiful and amazingly practical. For stor-

age, each is simply twisted into a rope and coiled into a figure eight, then slipped into its own small box. Status symbols at the time they were made, the dresses have become so once again, bringing such high prices at auction they are almost too costly to wear. He also designed tunics, capes, scarves, and kimono-shaped wraps to be worn over the *Delphos*.

Fortuny invented a process for printing color and metals on fabric to achieve an effect of brocade or tapestry. Velvets were dyed in many layers and sometimes printed with metallics, gold, or silver. Fortuny fabrics are still used in interior design, and manufactured in Venice.

Painter, photographer, set/lighting designer, and inventor, Fortuny has, in recent years, been recognized again for his originality and wide-ranging creativity. An exhibition showing more than 100 examples of his work—including dresses, robes, textiles, and clocks—opened in Lyon, France, in May 1980. From there it traveled to New York's Fashion Institute of Technology and on to the Art Institute of Chicago. Fortuny designs are regularly included in costume exhibitions at museums and design schools.

Evening cape, early 1930s.

Photographer Toni Frissell (left) with daughter.

BORN Antoinette Frissell Bacon; New York City, March 10, 1907
DIED Saint James, New York, May 17, 1988

Before taking up photography, Toni Frissell worked for a painter and trained as an actress; she also worked in the advertising department of Stern Brothers and in 1929 went to work for *Vogue* as a caption writer. She had dabbled in photography but did not take it seriously until after the death of her brother, a documentary filmmaker, in an accident on location. It was at *Vogue* that she took her first fashion photographs in the informal style described by

the magazine as "sunlit, windblown records of action outdoors." She is also well-known for her work at *Harper's Bazaar*, with outdoor work being her specialty. She would tilt her camera to achieve dramatic diagonals, and would often shoot from below with a short-focus lens to elongate the model's body.

During WWII she volunteered her photographic services to the American Red Cross, Women's Army Corps, and Eighth Army Air Force. On their behalf, she produced thousands of images of nurses, front-line soldiers, WACs, African-American airmen, and orphaned children. This lead her to abandon fashion and focus more on hard news stories and, later, portraits.

In the 1950s, Frissell took photographs of the famous and powerful in the United States and Europe, including Winston Churchill, Eleanor Roosevelt, John F. Kennedy, and Jacqueline Kennedy. As the first woman on staff at *Sports Illustrated* in 1953, she worked there during its first four years, and also undertook assignments for *Life*, *Look*, and some documentary projects. In later work she concentrated on photographing women from all walks of life.

The Duchess of Windsor, photographed by Toni Frissell.

James GALANOS

John GALLIANO

Jean-Paul GAULTIER

Rudi GERNREICH

Nicolas GHESQUIÈRE

Charles DANA GIBSON

Romeo GIGLI

Marithé & François GIRBAUD

Hubert DE GIVENCHY

Robin GIVHAN

Andrew GN

Alix GRÈS

Jacques GRIFFE

GUCCI

James Galanos

BORN Philadelphia, Pennsylvania, September 20, 1925

AWARDS Neiman Marcus Award, 1954 • Coty American Fashion Critics' Award "*Winnie*," 1954; *Return Award*, 1956; *Hall of Fame*, 1959 • National Cotton Fashion Award, 1958 • Council of Fashion Designers of America (CFDA) *Lifetime Achievement Award*, 1984 • *Fashion Walk of Fame*, 2001

One of the greatest, most independent designers working in America during the last half century, James Galanos has been widely considered the equal of the great European couturiers. His ready-to-wear became a symbol of luxury both for its extraordinary quality and for stratospheric prices comparable to those of the couture.

The son of Greek immigrants, Galanos left Philadelphia for New York to study at Traphagen School of Fashion and after only a few months began selling sketches to manufacturers. He worked for HATTIE CARNEGIE in 1944, and went to Paris where he worked with ROBERT PIGUET (1947–1948). He returned to New York and designed for Davidow, moved to Los Angeles, and worked at Columbia Pictures as assistant to JEAN LOUIS. In 1951, with two assistants and a $500 loan from Jean Louis, he started his own business; he gave his first New York showing in 1952 in a private apartment.

Designer James Galanos.

In an age where hems were left unfinished, linings banished, and seams worn inside-out, Galanos still believed that a garment should be as luxurious inside as out and insisted on lining his clothes. Intricate construction, flawless workmanship, and magnificent imported fabrics were his hallmarks, as well as detailing, which was rarely found in ready-to-wear. Impeccably precise matching of plaids and the delicate cross-pleating of his legendary chiffons are just two examples. Long admired by connoisseurs of fashion, he achieved wider recognition as one of Nancy Reagan's favorite designers. She chose a white satin Galanos gown for the first Inaugural Ball in 1981 and, for the second in 1985, a slim, jeweled dress with bolero top.

Because he likes the climate and relaxed living style, Galanos chose to live and work in Los Angeles, where he assembled a workroom of near-miraculous proficiency and skill. He did not give large public showings, preferring to exhibit his clothes to the press and retailers in the more intimate settings of hotel suites. In 1976, New York's Fashion Institute of Technology presented "Galanos—25 Years," a special fashion show and exhibition celebrating his 25th year in business. He retired and closed his business in January 1998.

Printed silk dress, 1965.

BORN Gibraltar, November 28, 1960

AWARDS British Fashion Council *Designer of the Year*, 1987 • Council of Fashion Designers of America (CFDA) *International Award*, 1997

The son of a Spanish mother and an English father, John Galliano (Gall-lee-a-no) was not permitted by his parents to study art until he reached college. At London's prestigious St. Martins College of Art and Design, he studied textiles, learning about fabric, color, and the way cloth drapes, before switching to design. His graduation collection in 1984 was called "Les Incroyables" after the group of young French dandies of the Directoire period who went by that name.

Galliano started his career as part of the wildly uninhibited avant-garde London design scene. His designs were twisted and artfully torn, weird but also beautiful. By the end of the 1980s, his style had evolved and matured into a smoother, more sophisticated

Designer John Galliano (left) with actress Charlize Theron.

manner based on flawless technique and complete command of craft, a synthesis of the original and the salable. In 1990 he joined the Paris ready-to-wear showings and has also shown in New York. His work is worldly and assured, in the forefront of fashion. In 1993 he was introduced to Portuguese socialite and fashion patron Sao Schlumberger and financial backers from investment bank Paine Webber International. It was through this partnership that Galliano received the funds and high-society stamp needed to give him credibility in Paris. This collection was important in the development of John Galliano as a fashion house.

In July 1995 he was named to succeed HUBERT DE GIVENCHY as designer of both Givenchy couture and ready-to-wear, and in 1996 moved to CHRISTIAN DIOR, another LVMH holding. His first couture show for Dior coincided with the label's 50th anniversary, on January 20, 1997. There, in collection after collection, Galliano has proceeded to deconstruct Dior's bourgeois image, sometimes to critical outrage, and in the process has helped return the house to profitability. Currently, between his own label and Dior, Galliano produces six couture and ready-to-wear collections a year and a new mid-season range under his own name "G Galliano."

John Galliano for Christina Dior ready-to-wear, spring 2010.

Jean-Paul Gaultier

BORN Paris, France, April 24, 1952

AWARDS Council of Fashion Designers of America (CFDA) *International Designer of the Year*, 2000

At age 14 Jean-Paul Gaultier (GO-tee-AY) was presenting minicollections of clothes to his mother and grandmother, and at 15 he had invented a coat with bookbag closures, an idea he was to use in a later collection. When he was 17, he sent some design sketches to CARDIN, for whom he worked as a design assistant for two years. Other stints followed at Esterel and PATOU, after which he turned to freelancing in 1976.

Once on his own, Gaultier rejected the attitudes of his couture training, reflecting much more the spirit of London street dressing. He became the bad boy of Parisian fashion, using his considerable dressmaking and tailoring skills to produce irreverent send-ups of the fashion establishment. His juxtapositions of fabrics, scale, and shapes are unexpected and often witty, such as gray lace layered over voluminous gray wool knits, and overscaled coats over tiny vests cropped above the waist. Madonna has worn his designs—the notorious cone bra, for example—and modeled in his showings. His perfume, in a corseted bottle packaged in a beverage can, was introduced in 1994.

Hermès acquired a 35 percent share of the company in 1997, enabling Gaultier to open shops internationally and enter the couture arena. The fashion

Fall 2009.

Designer Jean-Paul Gaultier.

world has since watched, astonished, as its one-time *enfant terrible* uses his creativity and awesome technical ability in the service of French classicism. In May 2003 he was named the replacement for MARTIN MARGIELA at Hermès, with his first collection for fall/winter 2004.

In 2006 he renamed his men's wear line Gaultier 2 and presented his first show for the label.

Jean-Paul Gaultier's men's fragrance, Fleur du Mâle (Flowers of Evil), was launched in April 2007 and shortly thereafter, Eau de Cologne Fleur du Mâle. The newest in the Gaultier family of fragrances is Madame for women.

BORN Vienna, Austria, August 8, 1922
DIED Los Angeles, California, April 21, 1985

AWARDS Coty American Fashion Critics' Award
Special Award (innovative body clothes), 1960;
"*Winnie*," 1963; *Return Award*, 1966; *Hall of Fame*,
1967 • Knitted Textile Association *Crystal Ball Award*,
1975 • Council of Fashion Designers of America
(CFDA) *Special Tribute*, 1985 • *Fashion Walk of
Fame*, 2000

Probably the most original and prophetic American
designers of the 1950s and 1960s, Rudi Gernreich
was the only child of an Austrian hosiery manufacturer who died when he was eight years old. He
was first exposed to fashion in his aunt's couture
salon, where he made sketches and learned about
fabrics and dressmaking. In 1938 he left Austria
with his mother and settled in Los Angeles where he
attended Los Angeles City College and Art Center
School. In 1942 he joined the Lester Horton Modern
Dance Theater as a dancer and costume designer. He
became a U.S. citizen in 1943.

After five years with the Horton company,
Gernreich decided he was not sufficiently talented as
a dancer and left. For the next few years he sold fabrics. When he designed a series of dresses to demon-
strate his wares, the dresses aroused so much interest
that in 1951 he formed a partnership with William
Bass, a young Los Angeles garment manufacturer,

Topless swimsuit, 1964.

and began developing his personal view of fashion.
He established his own firm in 1959, and, during this
time, designed a collection for Harmon Knitwear, a
Wisconsin manufacturer.

Gernreich specialized in dramatic sports clothes
of stark cut, enriched by bold, graphic patterns and
striking color combinations. Always interested in liberating the body, he introduced a knit maillot without
an inner bra in 1954, the era of constructed bathing suits. He favored halter necklines and cut-back
shoulders to allow free movement and designed the
soft "no-bra" bra in skin-toned nylon net. He also
created "Swiss cheese" swimsuits with multiple cut-
outs, see-through blouses, and knee-high hosiery
patterned to match tunic tops and tights. Gernreich's
favorite shifts kept getting shorter until they were
little more than tunics, which he showed over tights
in bright colors or strong patterns.

Designer Rudi Gernreich (left) with models.

Gernreich, continued

His innovations often caused a commotion, the see-through blouse, for example, and the topless bathing suit he showed in 1964. Gernreich was never interested in looking back, disdaining revivals of past eras. In 1968, at the height of his career, he announced he was taking a sabbatical from fashion.

He never again worked at it full time, although he did return in 1971 with predictions for a future of bald heads, bare bosoms with pasties, and unisex caftans. He also freelanced in the fields of furniture, ballet costume, and professional dance and exercise clothes.

Quiet and cultivated in his tastes, Gernreich lived in a Hollywood Hills house furnished with modern classics by Charles Eames and Mies van der Rohe.

High-waisted dress, 1967.

Designer Nicolas Ghesquière.

BORN Comines, France, 1971

AWARDS Council of Fashion Designers of America *International Designer of the Year*, 2001

Unlike many of his designing contemporaries, Nicolas Ghesquière (Guess-Ki-air) never formally studied dress design; instead, he had part-time internships starting at the age of 14 with such working designers as AGNÈS B. and Corinne Cobson. He grew up in Central France, with a Belgian father who managed golf courses and a French mother with a liking for fashion. As a child, he was in love with *Star Wars* and sports, particularly riding, swimming, and fencing.

After completing school, he worked from 1990 to 1992 with JEAN-PAUL GAULTIER, designing knits and working on Gaultier's junior line, a period he considers his true fashion education. He was at BALENCIAGA designing uniforms and funeral clothes for a Japanese licensee when head designer Joseph Thimister left, and in 1997 the young designer was given a chance at the top job. He was so completely unknown that no one came to his first show, but word soon got out and he is now considered one who must be watched, a leader of the avant-garde. The clothes may range from elaborate patchwork minis to rugged leather jackets, and he has developed a devoted following of young fashionables, particularly for his fitted trousers.

Ghesquière has switched the emphasis at Balenciaga Le Dix from evening under Thimister to day clothes, in which some viewers find subtle references to Balenciaga styles of the 1940s and 1950s. In July 2001, when Balenciaga was acquired by GUCCI, Ghesquière was given a 9 percent share in the house, and as creative director, extensive responsibility for "the brand's creative direction and image."

Look from Balenciaga, fall 2007.

Spring 2008

Nicolas Ghesquière

Charles Dana Gibson

BORN Roxbury, Massachusetts, September 14, 1867
DIED Maine, December 23, 1944

Charles Dana Gibson learned to draw at an early age from his father, an amateur artist who nurtured his son's talent. By the time he was a young adult, his family had saved enough money to send him to the Art League in Manhattan, but after two years he was forced to quit due to financial hardships. In 1886 at the age of 19, Gibson sold four of his drawings to *Life* magazine, the publication that would feature his drawings on a weekly basis for the next three decades. In 1889, Gibson studied abroad in London and Paris, working with his idol, the admired English illustrator and intellect George du Maurier, who introduced Gibson to drawing high-society women. By 1890,

Illustrator Charles Dana Gibson.

Gibson was illustrating for *Harper's Monthly, The Century, Harper's Bazaar,* and *Scribner's Magazine.*

Inspired by his wife, Virginia aristocrat Irene Longhorne, Gibson created the "Gibson Girl," a spunky, down-to-earth, turn-of-the-century American society girl. The Gibson Girl would become an iconic figure for more than two decades, arguably setting the first national standard for feminine beauty. Out of this incredible popularity, Gibson capitalized on merchandising opportunities, including Gibson Girl wallpaper, ashtrays, china, souvenir spoons, pillows, and umbrellas; and to compliment the Gibson Girl, he created the handsome, courteous, and witty "Gibson Man." In 1918, after firmly establishing his reputation as an illustrator, and accumulating his wealth (raking in a reported $75,000 yearly in 1910), Gibson took over as editor and owner of *Life.* The Gibson Girl's unparalleled popularity would not fade until after World War I.

In 1932, he sold *Life* and retired as one of the most respected illustrators of the late-nineteenth and early-twentieth centuries. He drew and practiced with oils until his death in 1944.

Illustration of "Gibson Girl," wearing gown with corset, 1890s.

BORN Italy, 1950

Romeo Gigli's father and grandfather were antiquarian booksellers, and he grew up in an aura of antiquity. This background is in some contrast to the simplicity and modernity of his clothing designs, which nevertheless have something about them romantically

Designer Romeo Gigli.

rich and strange. Trained as an architect, he began designing in 1979, launching his own company in 1983.

Since then, his style has become more pronounced—a close, gentle fit, soft draping, and a liking for asymmetry—over all, a sense of fluidity and graceful movement. The pieces mean little on the hanger but take shape on the body. Using rich and luxurious fabrics in sundried colors, he achieves a kind of throwaway chic, and except for the romanticism of his designs could be considered one of the minimalists.

In 1989 Gigli made a controversial move, taking his style presentations from Milan to Paris, where he continued to show under the tents outside the Louvre. In 1991, Gigli separated from his two business partners, restructured his business, and created "Romeo World."

In 1999, IT Holding acquired majority control of his brand, which led to Gigli severing all connections with the house that bore his own name in 2004. In February 2005 his successor, Anna Cuimo, presented the collection "Romeo Gigli" for fall/winter 2005–2006 in Milan. Today the clothes of "Romeo Gigli" are sold in more than 200 boutiques in Europe and in the United States.

Fall 2003.

Marithé & François Girbaud

Designers François Girbaud (left) and Marithé Girbaud (right).

BORN Marithé; Lyon, France, 1942
François; Mazamet, France, 1945

Champions of relaxed sportswear, Marithé & François Girbaud established their business in 1965. The clothes, for both men and women, seem totally unconstructed but are more complex than they appear, and entirely functional. Jackets are often double, with one layer that buttons on for warmth; sweaters may be wool on the outside, cotton inside. This same thinking goes into their clothes for children. In the United States they are best known for their jeans and fatigue pants of soft, stonewashed denim. In April 2001 they were commissioned to design uniforms for Air France.

Autumn/winter 2009-2010.

Above: Designer Hubert de Givenchy.

Below, right: Audrey Hepburn wearing lamé dress, 1966.

BORN Beauvais, France, February 20, 1927

Hubert de Givenchy (Jhee-Von-Shee) studied at L'École des Beaux Arts in Paris, and at age 17 went to work in couture at LELONG. He later worked at PIGUET and FATH, and spent four years at SCHIAPARELLI where he designed for the boutique. In February 1952 he opened his own house near BALENCIAGA, whom he admired greatly and by whom he was much influenced.

His youthful separates brought early recognition, especially the "Bettina" blouse, a peasant shape named for the famous French model who worked with him when he first opened. When Balenciaga closed his house, Givenchy took over many of the workroom people, assuming much of the older designer's reputation for super-refined couture, with clothes noted for masterly cut, exceptional workmanship, and beautiful fabrics. Clothes designed for day remained within a framework of quiet elegance, while the late-day and evening segments of the collection were more exuberantly glamorous to fit the lives of

his conservative clientele. His client list included The Duchess of Windsor, Jacqueline Kennedy, and Mercedes Kellogg. It was his friendship with Audrey Hepburn that would help to bring about some of his most recognizable work. A devoted fan, Hepburn requested Givenchy's designs for the costumes for both *Breakfast at Tiffany's* and *Funny Face*.

In 1988 Givenchy sold his business to LVMH (Moët Hennessy LOUIS VUITTON), with a seven-year contract to remain as designer. He announced his retirement in July 1995, following the presentation of his final haute couture collections. JOHN GALLIANO, the British designer, was named to replace him, followed by ALEXANDER MCQUEEN when Galliano moved to DIOR in 1996. McQueen left in early 2001 and was replaced in March of that year by the Welsh designer, JULIEN MACDONALD. In 2003, British designer OZWALD

Givenchy, continued

BOATENG was hired as creative director for Givenchy Homme, and in 2005, Riccardo Tisci was appointed creative director for Givenchy's femme haute couture and ready-to-wear lines.

In addition to couture, Givenchy's interests include Nouvelle Boutique ready-to-wear, perfumes, and men's toiletries. Licensing commitments have extended from men's and women's sportswear and shirts to small leathers, hosiery, furs, eyeglasses, and home furnishings.

Quilted jacket and printed ballet length skirt, 1953.

Transparent pleated lapel, 1969.

Robin Givhan

AWARDS Pulitzer Prize, 2006 • Council of Fashion Designers of American (CFDA), *Eugenia Sheppard Award*, 2007

Valedictorian of her high-school class and a graduate of Princeton University with a bachelor's degree in English, Robin Givhan earned her master's degree in journalism from the University of Michigan in 1988. Starting out working at the *Detroit Free Press* as a reporter in the entertainment section, Givhan worked her way up to features writer and eventually became the paper's fashion reporter. Seven years later, Givhan departed for a job at the *San Francisco Chronicle*, where she worked briefly as a features writer before decamping to the *Washington Post* in 1995 to cover fashion. In 1995, Givhan left the newspaper to work as an associate editor at *Vogue*, but

lasted only six months on the job before returning to the *Post*.

Givhan developed a devoted following, thanks to her acerbic wit and no-holds-barred writing style, taking on the sartorial choices of celebrities and political figures with uncommon candor. In 2006, Givhan was awarded the Pulitzer Prize for Criticism—the first ever awarded to a fashion critic. The following year she was awarded the *Eugenia Sheppard Award* from the Council of Fashion Designers of America (CFDA). Givhan's unique style landed her as a guest on *The Colbert Report* in 2006 and has made her a closely watched and buzzed about fashion insider.

In 2009 Givhan, who had been a New York-based correspondent for her newspaper, moved to Washington, D.C., to take on a new role at the *Post* covering Michelle Obama and the first family as well as penning a weekly fashion column, Additionally, Givhan has worked as a contributor to *Harper's Bazaar, Vogue Italia, Marie Claire,* and *Essence.* She has contributed to the books *Runway Madness, No Sweat: Fashion, Free Trade and the Rights of Garment Workers,* and *Thirty Ways of Looking at Hillary: Reflections by Women Writers.*

Writer Robin Givhan.

Andrew Gn

BORN 1966, Singapore

Andrew Gn (Gin) grew up amidst rich textiles. Gn's father would bring home exotic fabrics from his travels, and he soon developed a strong interest in learning more and more about different types of fabric. He graduated from Central Saint Martins School of Art in 1989 and received a master's degree from Domus Academy in Italy in 1992. Also in 1992, he took a position as assistant designer to EMANUEL UNGARO. In 1996 Gn started his own line, Andrew Gn, with manufacturing facilities in Italy and France.

In 1997, Gn was given the title of artistic director of BALMAIN's ready-to-wear and accessories collection. But after his debut collection received negative reviews, Gn left Balmain to focus on his solo collection, which in turn has been critically successful. Gn's style is characterized by of lots of bows, floral appliques, and cashmere.

In October, 2008, Gn debuted his made-to-measure atelier line: 18 limited-edition outfits boasting lavish couture-grade handwork.

Designer Andrew Gn.

Left: Accessories, spring 2009.

Right: Spring 2009.

BORN Germaine Emilie Krebs; Paris, France, November 30, 1903

DIED November 24, 1993

AWARDS *Légion d'Honneur*, 1947 • Chambre Syndicale de la couture Parisienne *Golden Thimble Award*, 1976

Designer Alix Grès.
Bottom left: Evening dress, 1958.

Considered one of the most talented, imaginative, and independent designers of couture, Alix Grès (Greh) is ranked by many with VIONNET, although she was very different. Grès first wanted to be a sculptor, but the combination of family disapproval and lack of money turned her to dressmaking. Under the name Germaine Barton, she apprenticed at the House of Premet and in the early 1930s was making and selling muslin toiles, copied from the couture. In 1933, with anonymous financial backing, she opened a salon, Alix, where she was not a principal but a salaried employee, obtaining a half interest in the house in 1938. As Grès refused to take German clients and had a tendency to defy Nazi edicts, the house closed in 1940. A few years later, having lost the right to the name Alix, she reopened briefly as Grès but was forced to close after only six months. After the war, she reopened under the same name.

Her background as a sculptor showed in her mastery of draping, especially in the evening dresses of chiffon or the fine, silk jersey (called Alix after her use of it) she had encouraged the mills to make. Working directly with the fabric on a live model, Grès molded it to the figure, often baring some portion of the midriff; a gown could take two to three months to complete. These dresses, so fluid in feeling, were actually intricate marvels of construction. Other recurring themes were jersey day dresses with cowl necklines, deep-cut or dolman sleeves, kimono-shaped coats, and asymmetric draping. She traveled widely and brought back ideas that inspired her in her own work.

Grès was always shy of publicity and details of her life are scarce. It is known that her husband was a painter and sculptor who left Paris for Tahiti soon after the birth of their one daughter, Anne, in 1939. Professionally, she went her own way; she resisted doing ready-to-wear until 1980, the last of the couture designers to make the move.

Grès was elected chairman of the Chambre Syndicale de la Haute Couture in 1973 and continued as honorary president throughout the 1980s.

Grès sold her house to a French industrialist in 1984; it was resold in 1986, and went bankrupt and closed in 1987. In 1988 the name was sold to a Japanese company and the business continued, primarily in Japan in prêt-à-porter and with numerous licenses in France and overseas.

On December 13, 1994, the fashion world was shocked to learn from a story in the French newspaper *Le Monde* that Grès was dead, and had indeed died more than a year before in a retirement home in the Var region of France.

Jacques Griffe

BORN Carcassonne, France, 1910
DIED 1994

As a young boy Jacques Griffe learned the finer points of tailoring watching his mother repair and make clothes. At 16 he interned with a tailor and apprenticed with a couturier. His family moved to Paris in 1936 and Griffe obtained an internship with the House of VIONNET from 1936 to 1939. At the House of Vionnet he learned how to apply and maneuver fabric on a mannequin and a human body. While serving France in World War II, he was captured and spent 18 months as a POW. Later, in 1951, Griffe started his own line, "Jacques Griffe Revolution." Through his internship at the House of Vionnet, he'd become a master of cut in its relationship to fabric. Griffe could drape with ease and was bold in his use of stiffer fabrics such as taffeta, or dupioni. His designs were innovative and of a high quality. In 1958 he was credited with creating the sack dress. Griffe retired from the fashion business in 1974 and died at the age of 84.

Wedding gown, 1955.

Evening dress, 1955.

Designer Guccio Gucci.

FOUNDED 1921

The son of a struggling Italian merchant, Guccio Gucci (Goo-chee) was the founding father of one of the most successful luxury brands in the world. Gucci, who grew up in Florence, Italy, grew the Gucci clothing company out of his family's leather saddlery shop. Gucci's strong work ethic, along with his appreciation for fine craftsmanship, helped to strengthen his family's ailing business and helped grow it into a powerful leather company. His four sons eventually joined the firm and helped lead the company forward. In 1938 he expanded the business to Rome, and by 1953 the company had opened a shop in New York.

Gucci made his mark by capitalizing on the strength of its equestrian-inspired collection—and the company's logo is endemic of its connection to the world. During the 1940s, materials shortages forced Gucci to explore and innovate with new fabrics. The forced exploration lead to the creation of Gucci's iconic "Bamboo Bag" and helped cement the company as a luxury leader.

After his death in 1953, the Gucci brand continued to grow—thanks in part to a large following of celebrity admirers, including Liz Taylor, Jackie Kennedy, and Peter Sellers, all of whom loved Gucci's unisex "Hobo Bag." But while the company expanded into a world-

Designer Frida Giannini.

Model holding Gucci bag, 1956.

Gucci, continued

wide brand, it remained a family business; Guccio's four sons and his grandson Maurizio all joined the family firm. In the early 1980s, the company also brought in Domenico De Sole to head up Gucci's American division, while Maurizio served as CEO.

Under Maurizio's leadership, however, the company floundered, and the Gucci brand was sold to multinational conglomerate Investcorp in 1993. Two years later, American designer TOM FORD took the helm and helped revitalize the brand while De Sole was brought on as CEO. De Sole pushed the company to expand and become a multibrand conglomerate and under his leadership the company acquired YVES SAINT LAURENT, STELLA MCCARTNEY, and ALEXANDER MCQUEEN. Ford and De Sole left Gucci in 2004, but the company continues to flourish, in part because of Guccio's commitment to and legacy of high-quality luxury goods.

In 2005, Frida Giannini was named creative director of Gucci Women's ready-to-wear, in addition to her responsibility for all accessories. In 2006, she took over men's wear, thus rising to sole creative director of the label.

Look from spring 2010.

Handbag featuring design for Unicef, 2009.

HALSTON
Katharine HAMNETT
Norman HARTNELL
Edith HEAD
Jacques HEIM
Joan HELPERN
Stan HERMAN
Carolina HERRERA
Tommy HILFIGER
Horst P. HORST
Cathy HORYN
George HOYNINGEN-HUENE

Halston

BORN Roy Halston Frowick; Des Moines, Iowa, April 23, 1932

DIED San Francisco, California, March 26, 1990

AWARDS Coty American Fashion Critics' Award *Special Award (millinery)*: 1962, 1969; *"Winnie,"* 1971; *Return Award*, 1972; *Hall of Fame*, 1974 • *Fashion Walk of Fame*, 2000

Halston grew up in Indiana and attended Indiana University and the Chicago Art Institute. While still in school, he designed and sold hats. He moved to New York in 1957, worked for LILLY DACHÉ, and in 1959 joined Bergdorf Goodman as a milliner. There he gained a name and a fashionable clientele. He originated the scarf hat and designed the pillbox hat Jacqueline Kennedy wore for her husband's inaugural.

In 1968 Halston opened his own firm for private clients and immediately established himself with a pure, all-American look. His clothes were elegant and well-made, with the casual appeal of sportswear. His formula of luxurious fabrics in extremely simple, classic shapes made him one of the top designers of the 1970s. Among his successes were the long cash-mere dress with a sweater tied over the shoulders; the combination of wrap skirt and turtleneck; evening

Designer Halston.

caftans; and long, slinky, haltered jerseys, and was a pioneer in Ultrasuede®. Halston worked closely with ELSA PERETTI, and she also designed the containers for his successful signature fragrance, Halston.

He expanded into knitwear and accessories in 1970, then into ready-to-wear. In 1973 Halston sold the business to a conglomerate, becoming the first American to franchise his name. In 1983 when he signed with JC Penney for a cheaper line, a number of his accounts dropped his regular line. He attempted to regain ownership in late 1984 but was unable to do so and went out of business.

After his death in 1990, the label had eight separate owners and six designers, from John David Ridge to Bradley Bayou, including RANDOLPH DUKE in 1997. In 2007 Halston was acquired by Hilco Consumer Capital and The Weinstein Co., and by fall 2008, Harvey Weinstein, JIMMY CHOO's Tamara Mellon, and stylist Rachel Zoe revived the name. The owners then installed former VERSACE designer Marco Zanini as creative chief, who showed his first collec-tion in February 2008. Net-a-Porter signed on to sell pieces immediately, but Zanini was dismissed in July 2008. The subsequent spring 2009 collection was presented and created by an unnamed design team. As of July 1, 2009, Marios Schwab was appointed as the new creative director and resurrected the brand's once-thriving scent business.

Black jumpsuit for Halston Limited, 1971.

BORN Katharine Eleanor Appleton; Kent, England, August 16, 1947

AWARDS *Cotton Designer of the Year,* 1982 • *British Designer of the Year,* 1984

As both a feminist and a supporter of the peace movement, Katharine Hamnett has often carried her political concerns into her work. Her 1983 "Choose Life" T-shirt collection, for example, displayed such slogans as "Worldwide Nuclear Ban Now," "Stop Acid Rain," and "Preserve the Rainforests."

She was born into a diplomatic family, educated at Cheltenham Ladies College, and studied art in Stockholm before enrolling at St. Martins College of Art and Design in London to study fashion. While still in school, she worked as a freelance designer and after graduation in 1969 opened a sportswear firm, Tuttabankem, with a school friend. After its demise, she designed for a number of firms in England, France, Italy, and Hong Kong before establishing Katharine Hamnett Ltd. in 1979.

Her clothes are relaxed and easygoing classics with a witty attitude and are often based on work clothes. Men's wear—with the same feeling as her women's clothes—appeared in 1982. The clothes have been sold through high-end specialty stores and in her own freestanding shops; she has had her own accessory, shoe, tie, and eyewear lines.

True to Hamnett's beliefs, her company emphasizes environmentally sound practices, with a minimum use of packaging and a maximum use of natural fibers such as cotton and wool, plus those like Tencel®, which are considered environmentally friendly. In late 2001, financial problems forced her to shut down part of her business, shrinking it "back to the core." As an indirect result of the war and environmental problems of the time, her political designs regained popularity in 2003. In 2008, she criticized designers at London's Fashion Week for what she deemed an increasing exclusion of women of color on the runway.

Katharine Hamnett

Designer Katharine Hamnett (left) and Naomi Campbell (right).

Norman Hartnell

BORN London, England, June 12, 1901

DIED Windsor, England, June 8, 1979

AWARDS Neiman Marcus Award, 1947

Educated at Cambridge University, where he designed costumes and performed in undergraduate plays, Norman Hartnell was expected to become an architect but instead turned to dress design. After working briefly for a court designer and selling sketches to LUCILE, he opened a business with his sister in 1923. At the time a French name or reputation was indispensable to success in London so in 1927 he took his collection to Paris. In 1930 he again showed in Paris, resulting in many orders, particularly from American and Canadian buyers. The Hartnell couture house became the largest in London. He was dressmaker by appointment to H.M. the Queen, whose coronation gown he designed. He was knighted in 1977.

Hartnell is most identified with elaborate evening gowns, lavishly embroidered and sprinkled with sequins, particularly the bouffant gowns designed

Designer Norman Hartnell (center) with models.

for the Queen Mother and for Queen Elizabeth II. He also made well-tailored suits and coats in British and French woolens and tweeds. By the 1970s, before his death in 1979, he was making clothes in leather, designing furs and men's fashions. In September 1990, the house was revived with MARC BOHAN as fashion director. The first collections were couture; ready-to-wear followed in fall 1991. The firm has since gone out of business.

Queen Elizabeth II wearing Norman Hartnell design, 1957.

BORN San Bernardino, California, October 28, 1897
DIED Los Angeles, California, October 24, 1981

AWARDS Motion Picture Academy Awards: *The Heiress*, 1949; *Samson and Delilah*, 1950; *All About Eve*, 1950; *A Place in the Sun*, 1951; *Roman Holiday*, 1953; *Sabrina*, 1954; *The Facts of Life*, 1969; *The Sting*, 1973

Edith Head had a long and illustrious career of more than 50 years, starting at Paramount Pictures where she was chief designer for 29 years. Hired as a junior designer by Howard Greer sometime in the 1920s, she became the studio's number one designer in 1938 when the then department head, TRAVIS BANTON, left Paramount for Universal Studios.

She graduated from the University of California at Berkeley where she majored in languages, and went on to Stanford for a master's degree in French. She taught French at private schools for girls and studied art at night at Otis and Chouinard, before answering a want ad for an artist, which led to her first job at Paramount. When Greer left Paramount to open his own salon, he was succeeded by Banton, who made Head his assistant.

As Banton's assistant and later as head designer, she designed for stars as diverse as Mae West,

Designer Edith Head (right).

Dorothy Lamour (the sarong), Barbara Stanwyck, and Audrey Hepburn. Head created designs for all types of films, including westerns, drawing room comedies, musical comedies, and monster movies. Given the variety of movies and the sheer quantity of her production, it is not surprising that she did not establish an "Edith Head look." When Paramount was acquired by Gulf+Western in 1966, Head was out of a job but soon moved to Universal to become resident costume designer. Over the years, she won eight Oscars for her work, starting in 1949 with *The Heiress*, and received 33 nominations. She also freelanced at MGM, Warner Brothers, Columbia, and Fox.

In addition to her film work, she did opera costumes, women's uniforms for the Coast Guard and Pan American Airlines, and designed printed fabrics. She also taught a course at UCLA, wrote articles and books, appeared on television and radio talk shows, and lectured to clubs around the country. Unlike many of her colleagues, she did not do custom work and was not interested in dressing women for the world outside of movies.

Actress Marlene Dietrich wearing an Edith Head costume in the film *Desire*, 1936.

Jacques Heim

Designer Jacques Heim (right) with model.

Striped swimsuit, 1956.

BORN Paris, France, May 8, 1899
DIED Paris, France, January 8, 1967

Although now not a household name, Jacques Heim
was an important and influential designer in his time.
Heim's parents, Isadore and Jeanne, were fashionable furriers in the 1920s, and it was in their firm
where he started his design career when he was 26.
He introduced cotton beachwear to the haute couture
in 1937 and was the first to recognize the younger
customer with his Heim Jeunes Filles collection. He
helped popularize the bikini, and beginning in 1946,
opened his own chain of boutiques. He was also president of the Chambre Syndicale de la Couture from
1958 to 1962.

His clothes were elegant and refined, very much
in the haute couture tradition. After his death in
1967, direction of the firm was taken over by his son,
Philippe, but the house closed in 1969.

Joan Helpern

BORN New York, New York

AWARDS Coty American Fashion Critics' Award *Special Award (footwear)*, 1978 • Cutty Sark Men's Fashion Award *Men's Footwear Design*, 1986 • Fairchild Publications and *Footwear News Footwear Designer Award*, 1988; *Hall of Fame*, 1990 • *Golden Slipper*, Florence, 1988 • *Scarpe d'Oro*, "The Golden Shoe Award" in Italy, 1989 • Fashion Footwear Association of New York, *Ffany Award*, 1990 • Silver Trophy, Florence, 1992 • Italian Trade Commission *Michelangelo Award for Design* (first designer award to an American for footwear), 1993

The family firm established in 1967 by Joan and David Helpern, is primarily known for imaginative, fashionable shoes for women and men. The firm has been involved in every aspect of the shoemaking process—designing, manufacturing in Italy, distribution, and retailing. Starting in 1986, other fashion categories were added: bags, belts, socks, scarves, sportswear, knitwear, jewelry, sunglasses, shawls, umbrellas, and hats.

Joan Helpern, the design half of the team, believed that the design of a product should be relevant to its use. In approaching her work she matched a fresh, inventive approach to the desires and needs of her customer, whom she saw as highly intelligent and motivated, with a clear sense of self and personal style.

Helpern has been widely recognized for her accomplishments, both in her own field with citations from industry publications, and by such magazines as *Savvy* and *Working Woman* for her business success. She is a member of the Council of Fashion Designers of America and of the Committee of 200, an international organization of leading businesswomen.

The firm was sold in October 2000. In September 2002, Helpern was appointed adjunct professor and executive-in-residence at Columbia University's School of International and Public Affairs (SIPA).

Designer Joan Helpern.

Designer Stan Herman.

BORN New York, New York, September 17, 1930

AWARDS Coty American Fashion Critics' Award *Special Award (Young Contemporaries Design),* 1965; "*Winnie,*" 1969; *Special Award (Loungewear),* 1975 • Store Awards: Burdine's, 1965; Hess, 1967; Joseph Horne, 1968

Hard working and versatile, Stan Herman has turned his designing hand variously to hats, dresses, sportswear, lingerie and loungewear, and uniforms. He has also done a stint as a nightclub entertainer. After earning a B.A. from the University of Cincinnati, he worked in the New York garment industry while attending Traphagen School of Fashion. By 1954 he was designing hats at John Frederics. He went on to work at a number of firms before arriving at Mr. Mort in 1961, leaving in 1971. He has continued to design for many other companies, often concurrently, including Henri Bendel, Youthcraft-Charmfit, Slumbertogs, and multiple uniform houses. His

designs are always priced in the affordable range, and have appeared with great success on QVC.

Herman believes that fashion is one of life's nourishments, which, like all good food, must be grown each season to remain fresh. That is why he prefers to freelance. He recharges his creative energies through painting, singing, sailing, tennis, opera, and community activism. A member of the Council of Fashion Designers of America since 1967, he served as vice president from 1982–1991, and then as president from 1991–2006. As president, he played a key role in the highly successful fashion fundraiser for AIDS, *Seventh on Sale.* In 2008, the designer celebrated his tenth year on QVC, where he has expanded his collection to include accessories and housewares. Herman has also designed uniforms for FedEx, McDonald's, Amtrak, TWA, United Airlines, and JetBlue Airways.

Amtrak employee uniform, 1999.

Carolina Herrera

BORN Maria Caroline Josefina Pacanias y Niño; Caracas, Venezuela, January 8, 1939

AWARDS Dallas Fashion Awards *Fashion Excellence Award* • Council of Fashion Designers of America (CFDA) *Women's wear Designer of the Year*, 2004 • *Geoffrey Bean Lifetime Achievement Award*, 2008

Carolina Herrera (Hair-era) came to fashion from a background where couture clothes and private dress-makers were the norm—she grew up among women who appreciated and wore beautiful clothes. In 1980 she moved to New York with her husband and family and, encouraged by DIANA VREELAND among others, established her own firm in April 1981 with the backing of a South American publisher. Going into the dress business seemed a natural step, as she had worked closely with couturiers, often designing her clothes herself. She quickly made a name and developed a following.

Best known for her designer ready-to-wear—elegant clothes with a couture feeling and feminine details—she also makes clothes to order for private clients, many of whom are her friends. Estée Lauder, the late Jacqueline Kennedy, and Nancy Reagan have

Bridal, spring 2010.

all worn her designs. She is also known for making Caroline Kennedy's wedding dress. In 2000 she opened her first flagship store on New York City's Madison Avenue. In 2001 she launched CH Carolina Herrera, expanding the brand to accessories, handbags, shoes, and eyewear. She also has had licensing agreements in Japan and designed furs for Revillon. In 2003 she launched the fragrance Carolina and has created numerous perfumes, including 212 Sexy and 212 Sexy Men.

Herrera recognizes BALENCIAGA as her greatest influence. His example can be seen in her emphasis on a clear, dramatic line and her insistence that women can be feminine, chic, elegant, and, at the same time, comfortable.

Above: Designer Carolina Herrera.
Right: Ruffled satin dress, 2008.

Tommy Hilfiger

BORN Elmira, New York, March 24, 1951

AWARDS Council of Fashion Designers of America (CFDA) *Men's Wear Designer of the Year*, 1995 • Parsons School of Design *Designer of the Year Award* 1998

Tommy Hilfiger was something of a fashion boy wonder, starting out by selling hippy chic to New York college kids, and had a string of ten specialty stores named People's Place in upstate New York by the time he was 26. He moved to New York City and into designing in 1979; his first collection under his own label appeared in 1984, preceded by an advertising campaign that pronounced him the new leader in men's fashion.

Designer Tommy Hilfiger.

His first customers were predominantly middle-class, white males, but in the early 1990s when rapper Snoop Doggy Dog wore one of his shirts on Saturday Night Live, sales took off and he immediately moved to exploit this new market. Designs moved toward the street with baggier pants and more casual styles.

Hilfiger has proved himself a gifted marketer and an astute businessman. In addition to his core men's business, he has added sportswear and intimate apparel for women and juniors, clothes for children, and plus sizes. There are also multiple accessories and fragrances for both men and women and home furnishings. As of fall 2008, Tommy Hilfiger is sold exclusively in the United States at Macy's and Tommy Hilfiger boutiques.

Actively involved in a number of charities, Hilfiger serves on the board of directors for The Fresh Air Fund and the Race to Erase MS (Multiple Sclerosis).

Above: Designer Tommy Hilfiger (back center) with a group of models wearing his designs for fall 2009.

Left: Tommy Hilfiger's Macy's line, 2009.

Model Jean Patchett in a bathing suit, photographed by Horst, 1951.

At the time Horst went to work for the magazine, *Vogue* publisher Condé Nast exerted rigid control over photography, demanding that all work be done on large-format studio cameras. Sets were elaborate and each detail was expected to be perfect, resulting in refined, but static images. Despite these limitations, Horst introduced energy into his photographs through dramatic lighting and camera angles, and managed to take risks, giving an edge to the required elegance. With the acceptance of smaller cameras, he moved outdoors and brought action into his shots. His influences include both Hoyningen-Huene and EDWARD STEICHEN, although he considered Steichen better at portraits than at fashion. In addition to fashion, he also photographed interiors for *Vogue*. His last fashion commission for the magazine was in 1992.

BORN Horst Paul Albert Bohrmann; Weissenfels-an-der-Saale, Germany, August 14, 1906
DIED Palm Beach Gardens, Florida, November 18, 1999

Horst P. Horst studied furniture design with Walter Gropius at the School for Applied Arts in Hamburg and went to Paris in 1930 to study architecture with Le Corbusier. In Paris he met and modeled for GEORGE HOYNINGEN-HUENE, who became a lifelong friend, and took up photography himself. He photographed for French *Vogue*, then was brought to New York to work for American *Vogue*. He joined the Army during World War II, working as a photographer. Because his name, Bohrmann, was too close to that of Hitler's close associate, he had it changed legally.

Model wearing an Emme design, photographed by Horst, 1961.

Cathy Horyn

BORN Coshocton, Ohio, September 11, 1956

AWARDS Council of Fashion Designers of America (CFDA) *Eugenia Sheppard Award*, 2001

Best known for her work as the widely-read fashion critic for the *New York Times*, Cathy Horyn is a powerful force in the fashion world. An Ohio native who went into journalism when she found out that a local reporter was sent to New York twice a year to cover the fashion shows, Horyn graduated Barnard College in 1978 and earned a master's degree in journalism from Northwestern University's Medill School of Journalism. Her first job was as a fashion reporter for the *Detroit News*—a post she got by answering a help wanted ad—from 1986 until 1990. She then held a position at *The Washington Post*, also as a fashion reporter, until 1994. She then worked as contributing editor to *Vanity Fair* and in 1988, joined the *New York Times* and was soon promoted to fashion critic. In 2001 Horyn received the Council of Fashion Designers of America's (CFDA) *Eugenia Sheppard Award* for fashion writing.

Horyn has become known for her sharp tongue, finding herself banned from high-profile fashion shows like those of GIORGIO ARMANI—who uninvited her from his fall 2008 show because he disliked her previous coverage. She's taken on the biggest names in fashion, covering its designers, their actual collections, and other media figures with the same intense scrutiny. In addition to her newspaper and magazine writing, Horyn has contributed to a number of books, including biographies of fashion titans BILL BLASS and NARCISO RODRIGUEZ. She also writes the fashion blog, On the Runway, for the *New York Times*.

Journalist Cathy Horyn.

BORN Baron George Hoyningen-Huene; St. Petersburg, Russia, September 4, 1900
DIED Los Angeles, California, 1968

George Hoyningen-Huene was the son of the chief equerry to the Tsar; his mother was the daughter of a former American ambassador to Russia. His family fled the Russian Revolution, ending up in London. During World War I he served with the British; after the war he moved to Paris where he supported himself with odd jobs, including work as an extra in the infant movie industry. It was there that he was able to observe and learn lighting techniques that were the basis for his later photographic work. He worked as a sketch artist in his sister's dressmaking firm, in 1925 was designing and preparing backgrounds in the photo studios of French *Vogue*, and by 1926 was taking photographs. He was discovered by MAINBOCHER, then the magazine's editor, became chief photographer, was brought to New York briefly, then returned

Photographer George Hoyningen-Huene (left).

Divers, 1930.

to Paris. In 1935 he moved to New York and went to work for *Harper's Bazaar.* He lost interest in fashion during the 1940s, moved to Los Angeles in 1946, and taught photography at the Art Center School. He was also color consultant to George Cukor. He traveled widely, taking what he called "archeological photographs" in Greece, Egypt, and Mexico, and subsequently published them in books.

At the start of his career, Hoyningen-Huene was influenced by STEICHEN but rapidly developed his own style. His photographs have an aristocratic assurance and innate, unforced elegance, which seem to come from within rather than be imposed from without. He was quite at home with his sitters, usually society women or other celebrities as there was at that time no corps of professional models. The later, nonfashion photographs have this same quality of confident communication.

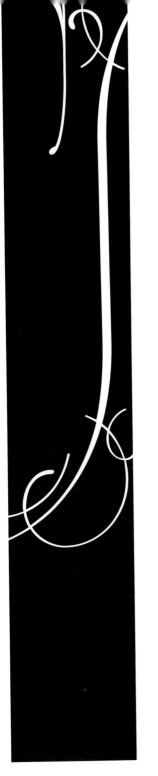

IRENE

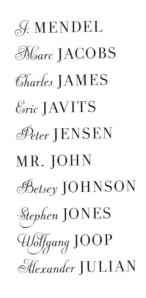

J. MENDEL

Marc JACOBS

Charles JAMES

Eric JAVITS

Peter JENSEN

MR. JOHN

Betsey JOHNSON

Stephen JONES

Wolfgang JOOP

Alexander JULIAN

Irene

BORN Irene Lentz; Brookings, South Dakota, December 8, 1900

DIED Los Angeles, California, November 15, 1962

Irene designed in two worlds, one the world of film and the other of real women. She started by dressing many of Hollywood's brightest stars for their private lives and was more and more often commissioned to design their on-screen wardrobes. Her first screen credit was at RKO in 1932—shared with Howard Greer; in 1942 she became executive designer at MGM when ADRIAN left. Her MGM years were not happy—she had to deal with other executives, producers, directors, cameramen, and publicity people, and was more involved with administrative duties than with design—but she stayed throughout her seven-year contract. After she left, she continued to design personal wardrobes for a number of stars; she rarely designed again for the screen.

Accomplished in custom and ready-to-wear as well as film, Irene came to design after a brief fling with acting. She studied music at the University of California at Los Angeles, then draping, drawing, and fashion design at the Wolfe School of Design. Around

Designer Irene.

1928, at the urging of her new husband and friends, she opened a small dress shop on the UCLA campus. This quickly became a success, attracting affluent students and, eventually, movie stars Lupe Vélez and Dolores del Rio. When her husband died suddenly, she closed her shop and spent some time touring England and the continent, living for several months in Paris. This period, which exposed her to the Paris couture, had a lasting influence on her work.

On her return from Europe, Irene reopened her salon, soon moved to larger quarters, and in 1936 was persuaded to become designer and head of the Custom Salon at Bullocks Wilshire. Her clothes were not only beautiful but very expensive, even more so than comparable Paris creations, marking their wearers as women of means as well as taste. Shortly before her contract with MGM expired, Irene was granted permission to design for a wholesale concern, a venture financed by 25 leading department stores who held exclusive rights to the designs. The project was a success from coast to coast.

Overwhelmed by personal problems, she committed suicide in 1962. Her last project before her death was designing costumes for the Doris Day film *A Gathering of Eagles.*

Actress Lana Turner wearing an Irene design in the movie *The Postman Always Rings Twice*, 1946.

FOUNDED Paris, 1870

Established in 1870 by furrier Joseph Breitman, J. Mendel gained a reputation for luxury by keeping the Russian aristocracy in well-designed sable furs. The company has remained family-owned since its inception and today—five generations later—Gilles Mendel has both maintained and expanded that tradition.

Based in New York City since the 1990s, J. Mendel ventured into women's ready-to-wear more or less accidentally. Facing protests from the animal rights group PETA, Mendel displayed simple yet elegant sheath dresses in the flagship store's windows as a distraction. Mendel officially debuted his women's wear collection at New York's Fashion Week in the fall of 2004. His designs combine skillful, clean tailoring with luxurious details such as fur trims and piping, and have been described as "old world meets the new." The collection has since expanded to include women's suits and jackets. While J. Mendel is aimed undeniably at the high-end customer—the spring 2009 collection included colorful fur vests as thin as fabric over floaty, draped chiffon dresses—it's also clear that Gilles Mendel has reinvented the concept of fur for a new generation.

Fall 2009.

Above: Designer J. Mendel.
Below, right: Fall 2009.

Marc Jacobs

BORN New York City, April 9, 1963

AWARDS Council of Fashion Designers of America (CFDA) *Perry Ellis Award for New Fashion Talent,* 1987; *Women's wear Designer of the Year,* 1992, 1997; *Accessory Designer of the Year,* 1998–1999 • *Fashion Walk of Fame,* 2002

While still a student at Parsons School of Design, Marc Jacobs was designing sweaters and also working as a stock boy at one of New York's Charivari stores. He was hailed as a "hot talent" on his graduation and was building a reputation as an original designer of young fashion with a flair for lighthearted, individualistic clothes when the firm he was working for went out of business in October 1985.

He reopened on his own for fall 1986, and in 1988 moved to PERRY ELLIS International to design their women's collection. While often well-received by retailers and press, the collection was never profitable and was dropped in February 1993, leaving Jacobs without a backer. After freelancing as a design consultant, he showed a small collection under his own name for fall 1994, backed partly by the Perry Ellis organization. The clothes were characteristically spirited and were favorably received.

In 1997 Jacobs sold the company to LVMH and became

Designer Marc Jacobs.

the designer at LOUIS VUITTON for both women and men. He moved to Paris but has continued to show in New York—his men's collection and his two women's lines, Marc Jacobs, and the lower-priced Marc by Marc Jacobs, which launched in 2001. He then launched a full line of children's wear in 2007 named Little Marc Jacobs. As of 2009, Jacobs remains the creative director for Louis Vuitton.

Above: Spring 2009.
Left: Look from Marc by Marc Jacobs, 2008.

Designer Charles James (center).

BORN Sandhurst, England, July 18, 1906
DIED New York City, September 23, 1978

AWARDS Coty American Fashion Critics' Award *"Winnie,"* 1950; *Special Award (innovative cut),* 1954 • Neiman Marcus Award, 1953 • *Fashion Walk of Fame,* 2001

Stormy and unpredictable, fiercely independent, Charles James is considered by many students of fashion to be a genius, one of the greatest designers, ranking with BALENCIAGA. His father was a colonel in the British Army, his mother an American from a prominent Chicago family; Charles was educated in England and in America. After a brief stay at the University of Bordeaux, he moved to Chicago where he began making hats. He moved to New York in 1928, went on to London where he produced a small dress collection, which he brought back to New York. He then traveled back and forth between the two cities before moving to Paris around 1934 to open his own couture business.

In Paris, James formed close friendships with many legendary couture figures, including PAUL POIRET and CHRISTIAN DIOR. His exceptional ability was recognized and acknowledged by his design peers. While he admired ELSA SCHIAPARELLI in her unadorned period, ALIX GRÈS was his favorite designer because she thought as he did in terms of shape and sculptural movement.

He returned to New York around 1939 and established his custom house, Charles James, Inc. He worked exclusively for Elizabeth Arden until 1945, and continued to operate in New York and sometimes London until 1958, when he retired from couture to devote himself to painting and sculpture.

During the 1960s James conducted seminars and lectured at the Rhode Island School of Design and Pratt Institute. He designed a mass-produced line for E.J. Korvette in 1962, invented new techniques for dress patterns, created a dress form, jewelry designs, and even furniture, and occupied himself with preparing his archives. For five years, usually at night, he worked with the illustrator ANTONIO, who made drawings of all his work to be kept as a permanent record.

James was a daring innovator, a sculptor with cloth. Each design began with a certain "shape," and hours were spent on the exact placement of a seam. Bold and imaginative, his designs depended on intricate cut and precise seaming rather than on trim. He was noted for his handling of heavy silks and fine cloths, for his batwing, his oval cape coat, bouffant ball gowns, dolman wraps, and asymmetrical shapes.

Since he considered his designs works of art, it is only appropriate that they are in the costume collections of many museums, including the Metropolitan Museum of Art, the Brooklyn Museum, the Smithsonian Institution, the Fashion Institute of Technology, and London's Victoria and Albert Museum. His ideas are still influential today.

Gowns, 1948.

Eric Javits

BORN New York, New York, May 24, 1956

It could be said that Eric Javits came to hat design through a combination of genes and childhood influences—his grandmother, Lily Javits, was a milliner and painter and he used to watch her at work in her studio. Javits attended a succession of private schools and the Rhode Island School of Design, where he studied painting, sculpture, drawing, and photography, and made hats in his spare time. He graduated in 1978 with a degree in fine arts and with Eliot Whittall founded Whittall and Javits, Inc., producing hats in the bridge and better price ranges. He was bought out in 1985, then founded Eric Javits, Inc., specializing in women's hats, often with coordinated handbags.

His hats are romantic and flattering and have been worn in films, used in advertising promotions,

Designer Eric Javits.

shown in designers' runway presentations, and on the covers of fashion magazines. He also has a large and diverse international clientele. Javits promotes his business with television guest appearances and is active in professional organizations; he is a member of the Council of Fashion Designers of America (CFDA) and the Millinery Institute of America. Outside of business, he pursues his interest in painting and is involved in community service and charitable activities.

Actress Leighton Meister wearing a hat by Eric Javits, 2008.

Designer Peter Jensen.

BORN Logstor, Denmark

After graduating from Central Saint Martins in 1999, Peter Jensen immediately created his first men's wear collection. Two years later he'd already achieved cult-like status for his playful take on conventional clothing. At first look, his collections seem quite traditional; consisting of tailored pants, floral print frocks, and Oxford shirts. A closer viewing, however, may reveal a hemline a bit too high or a trouser fit a bit too tight by mainstream standards. Jensen's subversive style is also reflected in his choice of famous women about which to base the themes of his collections. Inspired by the likes of both Sissy Spacek and disgraced figure skater Tanya Harding, Jensen is celebrated for adding a post-modern twist to somewhat buttoned-up and traditional styles. The London-based designer has many fans, including actress Nicole Kidman and singer Amy Winehouse.

Spring/summer, 2008.

Mr. John

BORN Germany, March 14, 1902

DIED New York City, June 25, 1993

AWARDS Coty Fashion Critics Award *Special Award* (*millinery*), 1943

Gloria Swanson, the Duchess of Windsor, Rosalind Russell, Greta Garbo, Marlene Dietrich, and Marilyn Monroe were just a few who wore Mr. John's hat creations. An original and prolific designer, he made every style from close-fitting cloches to picture hats, relying on shape when other milliners were loading hats with flowers and plumes. Wearable and flattering, his creations included such touches of wit as a face-hugging veil studded with a single rhinestone as a beauty mark.

Dotted dress with wide collar, 1972.

Designer Mr. John (right) with model.

Born in Germany to Rose and Henry Harberger, Mr. John came to the United States with his parents. He worked briefly in his mother's Manhattan millinery shop, then in 1928 formed a partnership with Frederic Hirst to make hats as John-Frederics. He changed his name legally to John-Frederics but in 1948, after breaking up with Hirst, opened the Mr. John salon on East 57th Street and again changed his name, this time to John P. John. He designed accessories, women's clothing, and furs, but hats were his primary claim to fame. The business closed in 1970, although he continued to design for private clients until a year or so before his death.

BORN Wethersfield, Connecticut, August 10, 1942

AWARDS Coty American Fashion Critics' Award *"Winnie,"* 1971 • Council of Fashion Designers of America (CFDA) *Special Award (for her timeless talent),* 1998–1999 • *Fashion Walk of Fame,* 2002

Betsey Johnson attended Pratt Institute for one year, then went to Syracuse University, graduating cum laude and a member of Phi Beta Kappa. In her senior year she was guest editor at *Mademoiselle* magazine where the sweaters she made for editors earned her a job designing at the Paraphernalia boutiques. These collections, original and irreverent, established her at age 22 as a leader of the youth-oriented, anti–Seventh Avenue design movement of the 1960s. At this time, she found herself in the Warhol scene. Edie Sedgwick was her house model, and she designed for the Velvet Underground's John Cale who she married in 1968.

In 1969, Johnson and two friends started the boutique Betsey Bunky Nini; she has designed for Alley Cat, Michael Milea, and Butterick Patterns. In July 1978, with a partner, Chantal Bacon, she formed Betsey Johnson, Inc., to manufacture sportswear, bodywear, and dresses. She also operates a number of Betsey Johnson retail stores. In addition to apparel, her line includes handbags, fragrance, eyewear, watches, jewelry, hosiery, and swimwear.

Johnson has always designed to please herself. Over the years, her ideas have included: "the Basic Betsey," a clinging T-shirt dress in mini, midi, or maxi lengths; a clear vinyl slip-dress complete with a kit of paste-on stars, fishes, and numbers; and "the Noise Dress" with loose grommets at the hem. There have been tutu skirts, bubble minis and microminis, pretty suits that managed to be both cheeky and wearable, and dresses that toe the line between risqué and cute. She has worked in a variety of fabrics, from cotton-and-spandex knits to rayon challis to heavyweight spandex in vibrant colors, designing her own fabrics and knits.

Johnson is unique. Imaginative and uninhibited, she designs for spirited nonconformists like herself, of whom there are enough to have kept her in business for more than 30 years. She has consistently kept her clothes affordable for a younger customer,

Above: Designer Betsey Johnson.
Below, right: Spring 2008.

only adding a more expensive Ultra line in the late 1990s, which she says was necessary to grow the business.

A survivor of breast cancer herself, in 2003, the CFDA invited her to be an honorary chairman of their *Fashion Targets Breast Cancer* initiative. In 2004 she was awarded another honor by the National Breast Cancer Coalition for her continued fight against the disease. Johnson, often viewed as fashion's "wild child," has even gone as far as to use her designers and staff members as models, shocking—and delighting—the fashion world with her rebellious streak. Her most signature quirk is the cartwheel with which she graces audiences at the close of each Betsey Johnson show.

Stephen Jones

Designer Stephen Jones (right) with model.

BORN West Kirby, England, May 31, 1957

In 1984 Stephen Jones became the first British milliner to work in Paris, designing hats for the collections of JEAN-PAUL GAULTIER, THIERRY MUGLER, and REI KAWAKUBO of Comme des Garçons. He has worked with ZANDRA RHODES, JOHN GALLIANO, and VIVIENNE WESTWOOD, among other English designers. Combining fantasy with confident style, his hats have been described as witty, outrageous, and daring; he continues to collaborate with designers around the world.

Educated at Liverpool College, Jones went on to study at St. Martins College of Art and Design, graduating in 1979. He immediately began to make hats for his friends in the pop world, including Steve Strange, Boy George, and Duran Duran. In September 1980 he opened his first salon in a store called PX in Covent Garden, and soon established a burgeoning custom clientele. He has been invited to represent Great Britain in fashion shows in New York, Montreal, Helsinki, and Tokyo, and his hats are in the permanent collections of the Victoria and Albert Museum in London, the Brooklyn Museum, and the Australian National Gallery in Canberra.

Other design projects have run the gamut from scarfs, handkerchiefs, and gloves to interior design and TV commercials.

Left: Flair, autumn/winter 2001.

Right: Iceberg, autumn/winter 2002.

BORN November 18, 1944, Potsdam, Germany

AWARDS Fil d'Or, 1983

Wolfgang Joop is one of Germany's most celebrated designers. Born near the Sanssouci Palace—the palace of Frederick the Great—in the mid-1940s, Joop grew up surrounded by inspiration. In his younger years he studied advertising, psychology, and art education at the University of Braunschweig but dropped out before completing his degree. He then went on to work as an art professor at the University of Fine Arts in Berlin, and as a freelance designer for several design houses in France, Italy, and Germany.

In 1970, with the help of his former wife Karin Benatzky, he entered a fashion design competition, and won the top three prizes. He presented his first in 1979, and by 1981 the JOOP! Label was launched. He showed his first ready-to-wear line in 1982 and began designing a fur collection in 1987. He later added eyewear, knitwear, shoes, accessories, and perfume to Joop's roster. In 1998, after nearly 30 years in the business, he sold 95 percent of his company, keeping only 5 percent, and in 2001 he completely divested of the company.

Three years later he returned with Wunderkind, a line of women's clothing that reflects the contemporary, sophisticated, and independent side of women. The clothes are soft and fluid, but retain structural and masculine elements. In 2004, Wunderkind was shown during New York's Fashion Week, marking

Designer Woolfgang Joop.

the launch of Joop's "personal vision of what a contemporary, sophisticated, and independent woman wants in her wardrobe." Wunderkind made its Paris premiere with the spring/summer 2007 collection in October 2006. Wunderkind is currently being sold in more than 100 stores worldwide.

A well-known illustrator, Joop now draws professionally. His illustrative work was exhibited and has been received in several museums' permanent collections. He has also written editorial pieces for several magazines and newspapers, including *Zurichen* and *Der Spiegel*.

Wolfgang Joop is also known for his charitable works. He is involved in Dunkeziffer e.V., which helps children that are sexually and physically abused. He also worked with Hamburg Leuchtfeuer, which helps to support HIV-positive people.

Spring/summer 2008.

Alexander Julian

BORN Chapel Hill, North Carolina, February 8, 1948

AWARDS Coty America Fashion Critics Award *Men's wear Trophy*, 1977, *Men's wear Return Award*, 1979, *Hall of Fame Award*, 1980, *First Citation*, 1983, *Second Citation*, 1984

In 1942, Alexander Julian's father established the men's clothing store, Julian's, with the intention of serving the uniform needs of attendees at the Officer Training School at the University of North Carolina at Chapel Hill. Soon, the store earned notoriety in the area and grew to accommodate the whole university community. Julian, who grew up learning the family

Designer Alexander Julian.

business, opened a boutique on Franklin Street in Chapel Hill called Alexander's Ambition at the age of 19. In 1975, he moved to New York City to found the successful brand, Alexander Julian Company, N.Y. Since then, he's been celebrated for his use of vivid colors and lively textile patterns of his own making. His suit jackets that double as sports coats are one popular example of his versatile designs. Julian was the youngest designer ever to receive the prestigious Coty Award in 1977 when he was just 29 years old.

In 1994, Julian introduced the furniture line, Alexander Julian Home Colours, a successful venture which has since expanded to include home accents and home improvement items. In fact, he is the first fashion designer to be recognized with the Pinnacle Award from the American Society of Furniture Designers. He and his sister Missy still run the family business, Julian's. His clothes are worn by celebrities such as Harry Connick, Jr., Tim Robbins, and Bill Cosby.

Look from Private Reserve Collection.

Norma KAMALI
Donna KARAN
Rei KAWAKUBO
Elizabeth KECKLEY
Patrick KELLY

KENZO
Emmanuelle KHANH
Barry KIESELSTEIN-CORD
Charles KLEIBACKER
Anne KLEIN
Calvin KLEIN
Lloyd KLEIN
KOOS
Michael KORS
Albert KRIEMLER

Norma Kamali

BORN Norma Arraes, New York City, June 27, 1945

AWARDS Coty American Fashion Critics' Award *"Winnie,"* 1981; *Return Award,* 1982; *Hall of Fame,* 1983 • Council of Fashion Designers of America (CFDA) *Outstanding Women's Fashions,* 1982; *Innovative Use of Video in Presentation and Promotion of Fashion,* 1985 • Fashion Institute of Design & Merchandising (Los Angeles) *FIDM Award,* 1984 • The Fashion Group *"Night of the Stars"* Award, 1986 • *Fashion Walk of Fame,* 2002 • Council of Fashion Designers of America Honoree for the Board of Directors, *Special Tribute Award,* 2005.

Of Basque and Lebanese descent, Norma Kamali grew up on New York's Upper East Side where her stepfather owned a candy store. Her mother made most of her daughter's clothes, as well as costumes for neighborhood plays, dollhouse furniture—"anything and everything." Kamali studied fashion illustration at the Fashion Institute of Technology, graduating in 1964.

Swimsuit, 2008.

Designer Norma Kamali.

Unable to find work in her field, she took an office job with an airline, using the travel opportunities to spend weekends in London.

In 1968 she married Eddie Kamali, an Iranian student. They opened a tiny basement shop in which they sold European imports, largely from England, and also Kamali's own designs in the same funky spirit. In 1974 they moved to a larger, second floor space on Madison Avenue and Kamali moved away from funk, instead making suits, lace dresses, and delicate things. Divorced in 1977, she established a retail boutique and wholesale firm the next year on West 56th Street, naming it OMO (which stands for On My Own) Norma Kamali. In 1983 she moved her thriving business across the street into a multilevel, multiangled environment finished in concrete. Here, with video monitors showing film productions of her collection, she can display everything she designs, from accessories to couture.

Kamali was first recognized for adventurous, body-conscious clothes with giant, removable shoulder pads. Definitely not for the timid, her clothes were collected by such members of the fashion avant-garde as Donna Summer, Diana Ross, and Barbra Streisand.

Dancers at the Metropolitan Opera House perform "Rabbit and Rogue" in costumes by Kamali, 2008.

Tunic-length sweatshirt, 1981.

Subsequent collections have included swimsuits cut daringly high on the hip, children's clothes, lingerie, and, at one time, a moderately-priced line for the Jones Apparel Group. She has since added fragrance and beauty products, as well as eyewear and innovative activewear. In 1978, her draped and shirred jumpsuits, using parachute fabric and drawstrings, were included in the *Vanity Fair* show at the Costume Institute of the Metropolitan Museum of Art, where they are now part of the permanent collection. She has continued to include parachute designs in her work.

Starting with her *Fall Fantasy* video in 1984, she has moved into the use of technologies and direct mail for selling her designs. Her 1996 fall collection was presented on the Internet and since 1998 it has been possible to shop on her Web site for anything Norma Kamali, from shoes to swimwear to wedding gowns.

In 1997 Kamali started working with art students at New York's Washington Irving High School, her alma mater, helping them to form a business so that while in school they might learn the importance of art and commerce in making a living. The same year, the school inducted her into their Hall of Fame, which honors alumni who have contributed to the arts.

By 2006, Norma Kamali was collaborating with several companies. Everlast and Kamali partnered to create a sportswear collection. She also collaborated with Spiegel to create Norma Kamali Timeless. In 2007, she teamed up with Wal-mart and created normakamali for Wal-mart, which was released in the fall of 2008.

Donna Karan

BORN Donna Ivy Faske; Forest Hills, New York, October 4, 1948

AWARDS Coty American Fashion Critics' Award *"Winnie"* (with LOUIS DELL'OLIO), 1977; *Hall of Fame* (with Louis Dell'Olio), 1982; *Special Award (women's wear)* • The Fashion Group *"Night of the Stars" Award*, 1986 • Council of Fashion Designers of America (CFDA) *Special Award*, 1985; *Special Award*, 1986; *Women's wear Designer of the Year*, 1992, 1996; *Lifetime Achievement Award*, 2004 • Parsons *Fashion Critics Award for Influence in Head-to-Toe Dressing*, 1996 • *Fashion Walk of Fame*, 2001 • Fashion Group International "Superstar Award" (first American), 2003

Daughter of a fashion model and a haberdasher, Donna Karan was in fashion from childhood. After her second year at Parsons School of Design, she took a summer job with ANNE KLEIN and never returned to school. She was fired by Klein after nine months and went to work for another sportswear house, returning to Klein in 1968, becoming associate designer in 1971. When Anne Klein became ill in 1973, Karan became head designer and asked LOUIS DELL'OLIO, a school friend, to join her as co-designer. While it is impossible to separate her designs at Anne Klein from Dell'Olio's, their hallmark was always wearability—terrific blazers, well-cut pants, strong coats, sarong

Designer Donna Karan.

Spring 2009.

Karan (center) with models, 1987.

skirts, easy dresses, and classic sportswear looks with a stylish edge and an element of tough chic.

In 1984 Karan and her late husband, the sculptor Stephan Weiss, founded Donna Karan New York with the backing of Takihyo Corporation of Japan, Anne Klein's parent company. Karan's first collection under her own label established her immediately as a new fashion star. It was based on a bodysuit over which went long or short skirts, blouses, or pants, to make a complete, integrated wardrobe. These pieces were combined with well-tailored coats and bold accessories, everything made of luxurious materials. As the clothes followed the body closely without excess detail or overt sexiness, the effect was both spare and sensuous. Her idea was to design only clothes and accessories she would wear herself—the best of everything for a woman who could be a mother, a traveler, perhaps a business owner, someone who doesn't have time to shop. The clothes are definitely in the status category.

Her company has grown into a giant with myriad divisions, including the hugely successful DKNY brand that launched in 1989 and its numerous offshoots. Donna Karan Men was founded in 1991, followed in 1992 by DKNY Men. Home furnishings, eyewear, accessories, and underwear are all part of the mix; fragrances and cosmetics were licensed to Estée

Lauder in 1997. There are also retail stores worldwide, both company-owned and licensed. The firm went public in 1996, and in 2001 Donna was acquired by the LVMH conglomerate Karan International. Karan still has creative control of the company's fashion lines.

Karan is on the board of directors of the CFDA, the Design Industries Foundation Fighting Aids (DIFFA), and the Parsons School of Design, where she also lectures and is a critic. She has also been involved in numerous activities connected with social causes, including her Urban Zen Initiative founded in 2007.

Fall 2007.

Rei Kawakubo

BORN Tokyo, Japan, October 11, 1942

AWARDS The Fashion Group *"Night of the Stars" Award*, 1986 • Mainichi Fashion Awards, 1983 • Veuve Cliquot, Paris, *Business Woman of the Year*, 1991 • French Ministry of Culture *Chevalier de l'Ordre des Arts et des Lettres*, 1993

Designer Rei Kawakubo.

The most avant of the Tokyo avant-garde, Rei Kawakubo was a literature major at Keio University in Tokyo, graduating in 1965. She came to fashion design after two years in the advertising department of a textile firm and three years as a freelance stylist. She started designing women's clothes under the label Comme des Garçons in 1969, establishing Comme des Garçons Co., Ltd., in 1973. Her company, of which she is president, has expanded to include men's wear, knits, fragrance, home furnishings, and freestanding stores worldwide. Her collections are shown in Tokyo and Paris.

Originally, Kawakubo designed almost exclusively in tones of gray and black; she has since softened the severity of her view with subtle touches of color. She plays with asymmetrical shapes, and drapes and wraps the body with cotton, canvas, or linen fabrics, often torn and slashed. In her early Paris showings, she emphasized the violence of her designs by making up her models with an extreme pallor and painted bruises and cuts.

She has been successful in the United States with in-store boutiques and her own freestanding shops. These are so minimalist that there is often nothing at all on display. In spring 1987, the Fashion Institute of Technology included her clothes in an exhibition entitled, "Three Women: Kawakubo, VIONNET, MCCARDELL".

Kawakubo created the 2008 fall guest designer collection at H&M, designing men's, women's, and some children's clothing.

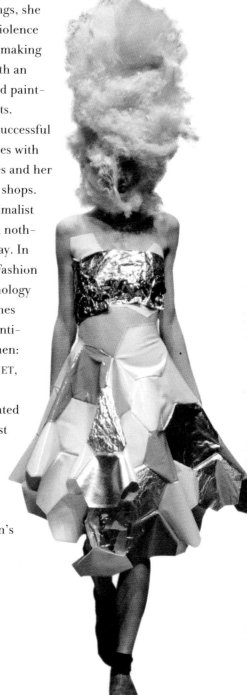

Above: Look from Commes des Garçons collection, fall 2009.
Right: Look from Commes des Garçons collection, spring 2009.

BORN Virginia, c. 1818

DIED Washington, D.C., 1907

Born into slavery, Elizabeth Keckley's perseverance and skills as a seamstress secured her a place in fashion history. Her early life was one of hardship: fathered by a white plantation owner, she was separated from her family in Virginia and sent to work for her master's son in North Carolina, where she endured physical and sexual abuse. At the age of 14 she gave birth to an illegitimate son. She was later sent to St. Louis with her master's daughter and her husband, where Keckley soon, in her words, "acquired something of a reputation as a seamstress and dress-maker." She supported the entire family with her earnings. Eventually one of her St. Louis patrons, impressed with her talents and her integrity, loaned her the necessary funds to secure freedom for herself and her son.

Designer Elizabeth Keckley.

After her emancipation, Keckley moved to Washington, D.C., in 1860 and established her own dressmaking business. Her reputation in the city grew and one of her clients recommended her to First Lady Mary Todd Lincoln. Keckley designed several gowns for Mrs. Lincoln—many of which received glowing praise in newspapers—and her business thrived.

Keckley also became the troubled Mrs. Lincoln's closest confidante—a relationship that later soured when Keckley wrote *Behind the Scenes*, a memoir of her life that included details of her time in the Lincoln White House. In 1892 Keckley joined the faculty of Wilberforce University in Ohio (the first private university for African-Americans), teaching in the Department of Sewing and Domestic Science Arts. She returned to Washington, D.C. six years later and lived the remainder of her life in the Home for Destitute Women and Children.

Mary Todd Lincoln wearing an Elizabeth Keckley dress for the inauguration of Abraham Lincoln, 1861.

Elizabeth Keckley

Patrick Kelly

BORN Vicksburg, Mississippi, September 24, 1954
DIED January 1, 1990

Patrick Kelly was an African-American designer whose work was characterized by an energy, exuberance, and envelope-pushing critique of staid fashion culture.

Kelly studied art history and African-American history at Jackson State University in Mississippi, and after graduation, moved to Atlanta, Georgia, to work as a window dresser for YVES SAINT LAURENT's Rive Gauche boutique. In the early 1980s, an anonymous admirer purchased Kelly a one-way ticket to Paris; he moved there immediately and began selling his flamboyant garments at street fairs and flea markets. In 1984, his designs caught the attention of the Parisian boutique Victoire, who furnished him with a workshop and showroom, and within three years, his work had been purchased by the Warnoac fashion conglomerate for millions. The deal put Kelly's designs into Henri Bendel, Bergdorf Goodman, and Bloomingdale's.

Kelly was known for his attention to detail: he utilized whimsical mismatched buttons, fringe, humorous patterns, and prints. He also gained recognition for his savvy critique of racial politics. Kelly's designs often challenged traditional conceptions of African-Americans by presenting darkly comical interpretations of racial themes. Kelly claimed to be as equally inspired by the works of couture designer MADAME GRÈS and YVES SAINT LAURENT as the fashion in a church on Sunday.

Like many designers, he struggled to fund his elaborate designs, but with the help of high-profile patrons like Grace Jones and Bette Davis, his clothes were known nationally and internationally. He was also recognized for his immense skill by others within his field; in 1988, Kelly became the first American to be accepted into the Chambre Syndicale de la Couture Parisienne, an organization of prestigious French designers. Two years later, in 1990, Kelly died due to complications from AIDS.

Designer Patrick Kelly (front center) and models.

Designer Kenzo.

photographic mannequins rather than regular runway models. These were innovations, and like many other Kenzo ideas were the beginning of a trend.

Kenzo was always a prolific originator of fresh ideas, known for spirited combinations of textures and patterns in young, wearable clothes that were often copied. His designs have been widely distributed in the United States in both his own freestanding shops and in-store boutiques. A renowned party-lover, he celebrated his 1999 retirement with a two-hour extravaganza, presenting his final collection and a retrospective of his 30-year career to 4,000 of his favorite party guests. The Kenzo company has continued with Frenchman Gilles Rosier as designer of the women's clothes and a succession of designers for men. It is now a part of the LVMH fashion empire. In 2005, Kenzo reemerged as a home fashions designer with his Gokan Kobo line of tableware, furniture, and home accessories.

BORN Kyoto, Japan, February 28, 1940

The son of hotel keepers, Kenzo won top prizes in art school, and began his fashion career in Tokyo designing patterns for a magazine. He arrived in Paris in 1964, one of the first of his compatriots to make the move, and found work with a style bureau. He sold sketches to FÉRAUD, and freelanced for several collections, including Rodier.

In 1970 he opened his own boutique, decorating every inch with jungle patterns, and named it Jungle Jap. The clothes were an immediate success with models and other young fashion individualists. Money was scarce for his first ready-to-wear collection, so although designed for fall/winter, it was made entirely of cotton, much of it quilted. He showed it to the sound of rock music, using

Left: Spring 2009.

Right: Spring 2007.

BORN Plain, France, September 7, 1937

AWARDS Chevalier des Arts et des Lettres, 1989

Emmanuelle Khanh started designing in 1959 with a job at Cacherel. Although she began her fashion career as a mannequin for BALENCIAGA and GIVENCHY, she rebelled against the couture in her own work and is credited with starting the young fashion movement in France. She was a revolutionary who is quoted as saying, "This is the century of sex. I want to make the sexiest clothes."

She first became known for "The Droop," a very slim, soft, close-to-the-body dress, contrasting sharply with the structured couture clothes of the time. Her clothes had a lanky 1930s feeling with such signature details as dog's ear collars, droopy lapels on long, fitted jackets, dangling cufflink fastenings, and half-moon moneybag pockets. Altogether, her work reflected an individual approach symbolic of the 1960s. Khanh survived the era and for a number of years continued to produce soft and imaginative fashions. In 2002, the company was acquired by France

Designer Emmanuelle Khanh.

Luxury Group, a new conglomerate that at the same time bought the JACQUES FATH name and that of JEAN-LOUIS SCHERRER.

She is married to Vietnamese engineer and furniture designer, Nyuen Manh (Quasar) Khanh, also prominent in avant-garde fashion circles of the 1960s.

Knit poncho, 1970.

Spring/summer 1976.

Designer Barry Kieselstein-Cord.

Gold filigree bracelet, 2008.

Alligator bag with 18k-gold hardware, 2004.

BORN New York City, November 6, 1943

AWARDS Art Directors Club of New York, 1967 • Society of Illustrators New York, 1969 • Coty American Fashion Critics' Award *Outstanding Jewelry Design*, 1979; *Excellence in Women's wear Design*, 1984 • Council of Fashion Designers of America (CFDA) *Excellence in Design*, 1981

Barry Kieselstein-Cord comes from a family of designers and architects, including his mother, father, and both grandfathers. His formal education included study at Parsons School of Design, New York University, and the American Craft League. He first attracted the attention of the fashion world with his jewelry, which was introduced at Georg Jensen around 1972. By the end of the decade, his designs included handbags and other accessories that were sold around the United States and exported abroad.

Working mainly in gold and platinum, Kieselstein-Cord starts with a sketch, moving from there directly into metal or wax, depending on whether the design will be reproduced by hand or from a mold. Each piece is finished by hand. His jewelry has been praised for elegance, beauty, and superb craftsmanship, which is also true of his handbags and other accessories. While he aims at timeless design not tied to fashion, pieces such as the Winchester buckle and palm cuffs have been collected by fashion designers and celebrities everywhere.

In addition to his designing career, he has worked as art director/producer of commercial films at an advertising agency and as creative director for a helicopter support and maintenance company. He has also served as vice president of the Council of Fashion Designers of America (CFDA).

Charles Kleibacker

Designer Charles Kleibacker.

BORN 1921

Charles Kleibacker was exposed to fashion at an early age, having grown up in the ready-to-wear department of his parent's department store in Cullman, Alabama. After graduating from the University of Notre Dame, he worked as a reporter in his home state and then moved to New York City to work as an advertising copywriter. He later took a job working for the singer Hildegarde, who brought him to Paris and subsequently exposed him to haute couture and all of its intrigue. Kleibacker then worked as an assistant designer to Antonio Castillo of the house of LANVIN in Paris for three years, then returned to New York in 1958 to design for Nettie Rosenstein.

Inspired in part by MADELINE VIONNET's delicate and meticulously made creations, he opened his own studio in Manhattan in 1960. His designs were known for their traditional contour look, and were produced in limited numbers. Diahann Caroll and Irving Berlin are just two of the celebrities who wore his garments.

From 1984 to 1995, he served as director and curator of the Department of Consumer and Textile Sciences at Ohio State University.

In 2001, the Kent State University Museum held an exhibition of Kleibacker's work entitled "Charles Kleibacker: Master of Bias". In 2008, the Ohio Arts Council's Riffe Gallery presented "Kleibecker: New York Designer to Ohio Curator," a retrospective of his work.

White dress.

Design cut on the bias.

Above: Designer Anne Klein.

Below, right: Actress Candice Bergen wearing a look from Anne Klein for Mallory Leathers, 1967.

BORN Brooklyn, New York, August 3, 1923
DIED New York City, March 19, 1974

AWARDS Coty American Fashion Critics' Award "*Winnie*," 1955; *Return Award*, 1969; *Hall of Fame*, 1971 • Neiman Marcus Award: 1959, 1969 • *Fashion Walk of Fame*, 2001

Anne Klein was just 15 when she got her first job on Seventh Avenue as a sketcher; the next year she joined Varden Petites as a designer; and in 1948 she and her first husband, Ben Klein, formed Junior Sophisticates. She designed for Mallory Leathers in 1965; operated Anne Klein Studio on West 57th Street in New York; and in 1968, with Sanford Smith and her second husband, Chip Rubenstein, formed Anne Klein & Co., wholly owned by Takihyo Corporation of Japan.

Early in her career, Klein became known for her pioneering work in taking junior-size clothes out of little-girl cuteness and into adult sophistication. At Junior Sophisticates there was the skimmer dress with its own jacket, long, pleated plaid skirts with blazers, and gray flannel used with white satin. At Anne Klein & Co., the emphasis was on investment sportswear, an interrelated wardrobe of blazers, skirts, pants,

and sweaters, with slinky jersey dresses for evening. Klein was also a pioneer in recognizing the value of sportswear as a way of dressing uniquely suited to the American woman's way of life. In 1973, she was among five American and five French designers invited to show at the *Grand Divertissement* at the Palace of Versailles. The other Americans were BILL BLASS, STEPHEN BURROWS, HALSTON, and OSCAR DE LA RENTA.

After Anne Klein's death, the firm continued with DONNA KARAN and LOUIS DELL'OLIO as codesigners. When Karan left in 1984 to establish her own label, Dell'Olio became sole designer.

Struggling to redefine its identity, Anne Klein ran through a dizzying succession of designers, at least five, including RICHARD TYLER. In 1999 the company was acquired by Kasper ASL, Ltd., which, in February 2001, changed designers once more, naming Charles Nolan. Nolan, formerly with Ellen Tracy, resigned in 2003 to work on a political campaign.

Meanwhile, after many label changes, Anne Klein became Anne Klein New York while Anne Klein 2 was rechristened AK Anne Klein. Furs, swimwear, and sleepwear were added to the existing licenses, as well as coats and accessories. Designer ISABEL TOLEDO was brought on in 2007 to design a top-tier collection but the line was shut down after only two seasons. In 2008, Ted Kim, who previously designed for both Donna Karan and MICHAEL KORS, was named vice president of design.

Calvin Klein

Designer Calvin Klein.

BORN New York City, November 19, 1942

AWARDS Coty American Fashion Critics' Award *"Winnie,"* 1973; *Return Award, 1974; Hall of Fame, 1975; Special Award (fur design for Alixandre), 1975; Special Award (contribution to international status of American fashion),* 1979; *Women's Apparel,* 1981 • Council of Fashion Designers of America (CFDA) *Best American Collection:* 1981, 1983, 1987; *Women's wear Designer of the Year, 1993; Men's wear Designer of the Year,* 1993 • *Fashion Walk of Fame,* 2000

Calvin Klein attended New York's School of Industrial Art (now the High School of Art and Design) and the Fashion Institute of Technology, from which he graduated in 1962. He spent five years at three large firms as apprentice and designer; his first recognition came for his coats.

In 1968, with long-time friend Barry Schwartz, he formed Calvin Klein Ltd., which has developed into an extensive design empire. Besides women's ready-to-wear, sportswear, and men's wear, it has

Spring/Summer 2002.

1992 advertisement featuring Mark Wahlberg and Kate Moss.

also marked his 25th anniversary in his own business. In 2002, Klein hired FRANCISCO COSTA as creative director of his women's wear line. Later that year, the company was sold to Phillips-Van Heusen, at which point Klein retired. The current creative directors for men's wear and the Calvin Klein and Calvin Klein Jeans lines are Italo Zucchelli and Kevin Carrigan, respectively.

Fall 1996.

included everything from blue jeans to furs to shoes to women's undergarments. He has also created bed linens, cosmetics, skin care, and fragrances. Calvin Klein Home, a luxury home furnishings collection was introduced in April 1995. He has promoted his products with provocative, sexy, often controversial advertising, notably for his jeans and for Obsession, the first of his women's fragrances.

Considered the foremost exponent of spare, intrinsically American style, Klein has kept his initial focus and maintained a consistent vision while remaining completely in touch with the times. He has said, "It's important not to confuse simplicity with uninteresting," and executes his simplified, refined, sportswear-based shapes in luxurious natural fibers, such as cashmere, linen, and silk, as well as leather and suede. His color preferences are for earth tones and neutrals—his hallmark is a lean, supple elegance and an offhand, understated luxury.

In June 1993, as part of a benefit in the Hollywood Bowl for AIDS Project Los Angeles, the designer presented a 20-minute showing of his collection, which

Lloyd Klein

BORN Paris, France

Lloyd Klein was a student of architecture; however, his interest turned to fashion after attending a GIVENCHY fashion show during his twenties. Soon after this life changing experience, he began studying the works of YVES SAINT LAURENT, HALSTON, and JACQUES FATH in an effort to educate himself more on the world of couture. In 1994, he presented his first collection in Paris, and by that fall he was appointed head designer at ALIX GRÉS. He was quickly recognized by many critics as a master of drapery, tech-

Designer Lloyd Klein.

Spring 2005.

nical cutting, and fit. Klein remained with Grés for five seasons, then left to establish his own label. He decided to set up headquarters in the United States in 1998 and began showing in Bryant Park in 1999. Klein presented his first official men's wear collection during his fifth consecutive season press show with New York's Fashion Week. He designs in Paris, but his parent company, Groupe Klein Vendome, is based in West Hollywood, California.

Klein has shown collections all over the globe, and his designs can be seen on celebrities including the likes of Jessica Simpson, Halle Berry, and Eva Longoria. Ultimo, Tootsies, Martha's, and Red Velvet have opened their doors for his designs.

BORN Koos van den Akker; Holland, ca. 1932

AWARDS American Printed Fabrics Council *"Tommy" Award* for his unique use of prints, 1983

Koos started making dresses when just 11 years old. He studied at the Netherlands Royal Academy of Art, worked in department stores in The Hague and in Paris, and whizzed through a two-year fashion program at L'École Guerre Lavigne in Paris in seven months. After an apprenticeship at CHRISTIAN DIOR, he returned to The Hague and spent six years there selling custom-made dresses in his own boutique.

In August 1968, with a portable sewing machine and very little money, he came to New York. He first set up his "office" by the fountain at Lincoln Center, taking commissions from passers-by. After this, he designed lingerie for Eve Stillman and eventually opened his own boutique. He has survived the death of his partner and severe financial problems and been reborn with a new partner, a new boutique, and a monthly show on QVC. There he has, with great suc-

Designer Koos.

cess, sold his secondary line—Chinese-made versions of his costly collages translated into printed fabrics. The boutique sells the collage originals and also his one-of-a-kind furniture pieces. Past projects have included men's wear, furs, home furnishings, and theater designs.

For his women's clothes, Koos has always specialized in simple shapes in beautiful fabrics, enriched with his signature "collages" of colorful prints and lace. They are considered collectors' items and have been on display in the Museum of Contemporary Crafts, New York. Customers have included Cher, Madeleine Kahn, Elizabeth Taylor, and Gloria Vanderbilt.

Recently, references to his patchwork collages have showed up in the work of several younger designers, MARC JACOBS and NICOLAS GHESQUIÈRE, to name just two. In 2008, the famous Koos van den Akker sweaters worn by Bill Cosby on the *The Cosby Show* were auctioned off for charity.

Inspiration for designs.

Above: Designer Michael Kors (left) and model.
Below, right: Fall 2009.

BORN Long Island, New York, August 9, 1959

AWARDS Council of Fashion Designers of America
(CFDA) *Women's wear Designer of the Year,*
1998/1999; *Men's wear Designer of the Year,* 2003

Michael Kors attended the Fashion Institute of
Technology for one semester in 1977. He then worked
for three years as designer, buyer, and display director
for a New York boutique before starting his own business in 1981. His first collection of 16 pieces, entirely in
brown and black, sold to eight accounts. By 1986 the
list had grown to over 75 specialty stores. He has also
designed a secondary collection called Kors, approximately half the price of the regular collection, has done
cashmere knits for the Scottish firm of Lyle & Scott,
and had licensing agreements for shoes and swimwear.

In 1977 Kors signed an agreement with Céline,
a division of LVMH, as design director for ready-
to-wear, with his first collection for fall 1998. This
made him part of the group of younger American
and British designers hired to reenergize aging
French houses—think JOHN GALLIANO, TOM FORD,
MARC JACOBS, ALEXANDER MCQUEEN, and JULIEN
MACDONALD. When objections were raised that he was
really an American sportswear designer, he pointed
out that both CHANEL and YVES SAINT LAURENT,
quintessentially French designers, had strong sportswear orientation. He has continued to present his
Michael Kors and Kors by Michael Kors collections in
New York.

Kors designs individual pieces, then combines
them into outfits. His aim is a flexible, versatile way of
dressing by which a woman can put pieces together in
different ways to achieve any desired
effect, from the most casual
to the dressiest. The clothes
are clean and understated in
cut and executed in the most
luxurious fibers and fabrics—
cashmere, silk, leathers, fur.
They fit securely into the deluxe
sportswear category and
are clearly meant for
a sophisticated,
modern woman
of means who
dresses to please
herself.

Since 2004,
Michael Kors has
been a judge on
the Emmy nomi-
nated reality show,
Project Runway.
During the same
year, he launched
the MICHAEL
Michael Kors
line, which
includes ready-
to-wear, swim-
wear, and
accessories.

Designer Albert Kriemler.

has a somewhat less expensive, younger-looking line called Akris Punto. Each of his collections give the impression that time stands still while also moving forward into contemporary fashion. Kriemler continuously strives to combine sophisticated fabrics of the highest quality with his keen eye for trends.

Distribution has grown from around one dozen outlets to 600 worldwide. The brand's flagship stores are on Avenue Montaigne in Paris, on London's Bond Street, and on Madison Avenue. For U.S. department stores such as Neiman Marcus and Bergdorf Goodman, Akris is one of the top-selling luxury labels. His client list includes Princess Caroline of Monaco, Condoleezza Rice, and Diane Sawyer.

In 2008, Kriemler took center stage with the design of sculptural and modern costumes for the Hamburg Ballet's premiere of *The Legend of Joseph* by Richard Strauss. Kriemler was approached by fellow creative John Neumeier, who is in charge of the set and choreography. The duo had worked together previously on the ballet's New Year's 2006 concert.

BORN Speicher, Switzerland, 1960

Albert Kriemler, with the help of his brother Peter who handles the business end of the company, has expanded his grandmother's apron business into a dynasty. The name Akris was inspired by an acronym of his grandmother's name, Alice Kriemler Schoch. Kriemler had planned to attend a fashion school in Paris and intern with GIVENCHY; however, in 1980 when his father's key aide passed away, he joined the family business. Much to the fashion world's surprise, a family company from provincial St. Gallen, Switzerland, has come to be a prêt-à-porter brand of international standing. Founded just over 20 years ago, and equally represented in the Asian, American, and European markets, Akris remains the only Swiss brand to be granted membership to the Chambre du prêt-à-porter in Paris, and to present two collections per year in the city of fashion.

Because the studio is still in its original and remote location, Kriemler relies on the expensive tailors and technicians of the town. Many of the textiles are made specifically for a dress in mind, and all pieces are constructed in the company's own studios. He also

Left: Spring 2009.
Right: Fall 2009.

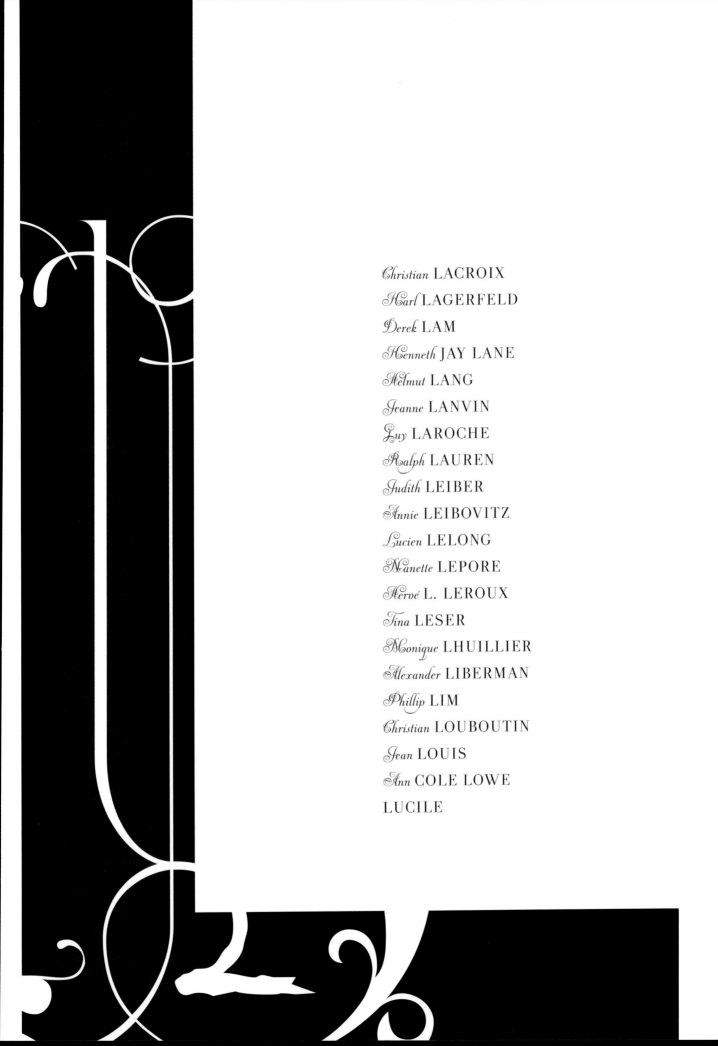

Christian LACROIX
Karl LAGERFELD
Derek LAM
Kenneth JAY LANE
Helmut LANG
Jeanne LANVIN
Guy LAROCHE
Ralph LAUREN
Judith LEIBER
Annie LEIBOVITZ
Lucien LELONG
Nanette LEPORE
Hervé L. LEROUX
Tina LESER
Monique LHUILLIER
Alexander LIBERMAN
Phillip LIM
Christian LOUBOUTIN
Jean LOUIS
Ann COLE LOWE
LUCILE

Christian Lacroix

Designer Christian Lacroix.

BORN Arles, France, May 16, 1951

AWARDS French government *Légion d'Honneur* for services to fashion, 2002

Christian Lacroix (La-cwa) is given credit by some critics for revitalizing Paris couture at a time when it had grown stale, and with his irreverent wit and sense of humor, returning an element of adventure to fashion.

A native of Provence in the South of France, he grew up surrounded by women, developing an early interest in fashion and accessories. After studies in art history and classic Greek and Latin at the University of Montpellier, he went to Paris in 1972 to attend L'École du Louvre. A stint as a museum curator followed, then in 1978 Lacroix turned to fashion, first as a design assistant at Hermès, next for two

years at Guy Paulin. He went to Japan for a year as an assistant to a Japanese designer, returned to Paris and joined JEAN PATOU in 1982 as chief designer of haute couture.

At Patou, he produced collection after idea-filled collection of theatrical, witty clothes and fantastic accessories. Imaginative and elegant, not all were wearable by any but the most daring, but many would appeal to an adventurous woman with flair and confidence in her own style. After five years with Patou, Lacroix left in 1987 to establish his own couture house backed by LVMH, the French conglomerate that also owns DIOR. The arrangement includes ready-to-wear. Under his own name, he has continued to show the same irrepressible instinct for drama, with the ready-to-wear somewhat less extreme than the couture. In 2002 he was also named creative director of PUCCI, another LVMH holding, and stayed with the house until 2005.

In 2004, he signed a five-year contract to create a lingerie line in conjunction with Sociètè Internationale de Lingerie (S.I.L.), and in 2007, he partnered with Avon to market two fragrances: Christian Lacroix Rouge for women and Christian Lacroix Noir for Men. In 2009, Lacroix displayed a twenty-year collection of costumes at an exhibit at the National Museum of Singapore.

Haute couture, winter 2008.

Designer Karl Lagerfeld (center) with models.

BORN Hamburg, Germany, September 10, 1939

AWARDS Neiman Marcus Award, 1980 • Council of Fashion Designers of America (CFDA) *Special Award*, 1982; *Special Award for House of Chanel*, 1988; *Accessory Award for House of Chanel*, 1991

Karl Lagerfeld arrived in Paris in 1953, at 14 already determined to become a clothes designer. That year he won an award for the best coat in the same International Wool Secretariat design competition in which SAINT LAURENT won for the best dress. In 1954 he was working for BALMAIN, and three and a half years later went to work for PATOU.

He left Patou, again tried school, and after two years he began freelancing. In 1963 he went to work for the upscale ready-to-wear house, CHLOÉ, as one of a team of four designers. The team of four became two, Lagerfeld and the Italian GRAZIELLA FONTANA. They continued to design the collection together until 1972 when Lagerfeld became sole designer.

In 1982 he became design director for CHANEL, but continued with Chloé until 1984 when he severed the connection to work solely for Chanel and to inaugurate his first collection under his own label. Enormously hard-working and prolific, he has had a sportswear collection under his own name designed specifically for the United States, designed gloves, and done shoes for Mario Valentino and Charles Jourdan, and created sweaters for Ballantyne. He does both furs and sportswear for FENDI, and resumed designing for Chloé, where he was succeeded in 1997 by STELLA MCCARTNEY. He has a number of successful fragrances for women and men.

In 2004 he designed some outfits for Madonna for her Re-Invention World Tour and recently designed outfits for Kylie Minogue's Showgirl tour. Lagerfeld

Chanel haute couture fall 2009.

Lagerfeld, continued

also collaborated with the H&M, offering a limited range for men and women in chosen outlets.

In 2006, Lagerfeld announced the launch of a new collection for men and women dubbed K Karl Lagerfeld. The collection included fitted T-shirts and a wide range of jeans.

He has also signed an exclusive deal with Dubai Infinity Holdings (DIH); an investments enterprise, to design limited edition homes on Isla Moda, the world's first dedicated fashion island, set in the iconic development, The World.

Lagerfeld is an unpredictable, original designer, highly professional and a master of his craft. At his best, he mixes inventiveness and wearability, spicing the blend with a dash of wit. He likes to remove clothes from their usual contexts—he has used elaborate embroidery on cotton instead of the usual silk, made dresses that could be worn upside down, and shown *crepe de chine* dresses with tennis shoes long before it was a styling cliché. He is credited with bringing Chanel into the present while retaining its distinctive character, although inevitably, the house has become more Lagerfeld than Coco.

Chanel ready-to-wear, fall 2009.

Freida Pinto in Chanel and Karl Lagerfeld, 2009.

Derek Lam

BORN San Francisco, 1966

AWARDS Ecco Domani Fashion Foundation, *Award for New Designers*, 2004 • Council of Fashion Designers in America, *Perry Ellis Swarovski Award for Women's wear*, 2005

When Derek Lam was a child, his Chinese-American parents ran a garment-manufacturing business in San Francisco that specialized in wedding dresses, and he spent a lot of time with the seamstresses in the factory. Seeds having been sewn, an older Lam traveled to New York to attend Parsons School of Design. After graduating, he went to work for MICHAEL KORS, eventually earning himself a promotion to head designer at KORS by Michael Kors. During his 12-year tenure with Kors, Lam briefly left for Hong Kong to work with a major Asian retail brand.

Lam ventured out on his own in 2002, when he debuted his women's clothing line at Olympus Fashion Week. Buyers from Barneys and Bergdorf Goodman were quick to place orders. In 2006, he was appointed creative director of Tod's accesory company.

While formfitting dresses are not anomalous in Lam's collections, he leans toward fabrics that hold their shape rather than mold to the woman's body. "I like to take fabrics and not make costumes, but very modern silhouettes," Lam says.

Concerned with the restrictiveness of genre, Lam has said he deliberately chose to eschew Eastern

Spring 2009.

Spring 2010.

Designer Derek Lam.

influence in his work. His style is said to draw influence from Kors, in that it seeks to reinvent American sportswear in a way that is modest yet highly variable. His collections include fall/winter and spring/summer ready-to-wear outfits as well as a line of colorful, feminine resort wear.

BORN Detroit, Michigan, April 22, 1932

AWARDS Coty American Fashion Critics' Award *Special Award for "Outstanding Contribution to Fashion,"* 1966 • Neiman Marcus Award, 1968

Kenneth Jay Lane attended the University of Michigan for two years, went on to the Rhode Island School of Design, from which he graduated in 1954 with a degree in advertising. He worked on the promotion art staff at *Vogue* and there met French shoe designer ROGER VIVIER. Through him, Lane became an assistant designer for Delman Shoes, then associate designer of CHRISTIAN DIOR Shoes, spending part of each year in Paris working with Vivier.

In 1963, still designing shoes, Lane made a few pieces of jewelry that were photographed by the fashion magazines and bought by a few stores. Working nights and weekends, he continued to design jewelry, using his initials K.J.L. By June 1964 he was able to make jewelry design a full-time career.

Like a designer of precious jewels, Lane first makes his designs in wax or by carving or twisting metal. He

Above: Designer Kenneth Jay Lane (left) and Nan Kempner (right).
Below, right: Couture bangles.

says, "I want to make real jewelry with not-real materials," and he sees plastic as the modern medium—lightweight, available in every color, and perfect for simulating real gems. He likes to see his jewelry intermixed with the real gems worn by his international roster of celebrity customers. This list is long and includes both Jacqueline Onassis and the Duchess of Windsor, and more recently, First Ladies Nancy Reagan, Barbara Bush, Hillary Clinton, and Laura Bush.

His jewelry is sold in fine department and specialty stores throughout the world and he has promoted it with great success on the televised home shopping channel QVC both in the United States and in Japan. Lane has been recognized worldwide with awards from magazines, design schools, and his own industry. His book, *Kenneth Jay Lane: Faking It*, was published in 1996.

Necklace and earrings by Kenneth Jay Lane.

BORN Vienna, Austria, March 10, 1956

AWARDS Council of Fashion Designers of America (CFDA) *International Award*, 1996; *Men's wear Designer of the Year*, 2000

Helmut Lang was raised in the Austrian Alps, and at 18 moved to Vienna to study business. He worked behind a bar, became involved with artists and "night people," and was encouraged by his friends to do something creative. He got into fashion when he met someone who could make up the things he had in his mind, as at that time he had no idea how to put them together himself. His vision of fashion developed gradually until in 1984 he opened a shop in Vienna. By 1987 he had a contract with an Italian textile firm and a licensing agreement with Mitsubishi in Japan, where he now has numerous boutiques. Lang lived in Vienna and showed in Paris until 1999 when he sold 50 percent of his company to PRADA, moved to New York to live, and began showing in the 7th on Sixth shows in New York.

Designer Helmut Lang.

Variously dubbed a deconstructionist, a minimalist, a follower of the Japanese avant-garde, Lang is really none of the above but very much his own man. An anomaly simply by being Austrian, he exhibited his distinctive view of fashion and clothes fully formed with his first Paris showing in 1986, when he sent out waiflike models with scrubbed faces in simple silhouettes and somber colors. His personal stamp—experimentation with fabric technology, including PVC, nylon, Lurex®, stretch synthetics, shiny cellophanelike effects, and his rumpled looks and subtle layerings—was there from the beginning and have been enormously influential. One wing of fashion sees him as a prophet; the other sees him as the antithesis of fashion. He believes that fashion has to do with attitude, appearance, and character, and that it defines the spirit of the time. His clothes express his view of how modern men and women want to dress: without affectation and with the understanding that perfect cut, comfort, and ease of movement are among fashion's great luxuries.

In 2005, Lang resigned from the label, and in 2006 Prada sold the label to Link Theory Holdings. The company then revived the Helmut Lang label with new designers, hiring Michael and Nicole Colovos as the creative team.

Lang began to explore other artistic endeavors and, in 2008, he had his first institutional solo art exhibition in Hanover.

Spring 2005.

Designer Jeanne Lanvin.

BORN Brittany, France, January 1, 1867
DIED Paris, France, July 6, 1946

AWARDS *Légion d'Honneur*

The eldest of a journalist's ten children, Jeanne Lanvin (Lon-Van) was apprenticed to a dressmaker at the age of 13, and became a milliner when she was 23. The dresses she designed for her young daughter, Marie-Blanche, were admired and bought by her hat customers for their children, and this business in children's clothes evolved into the couture house of Lanvin, located on Paris' rue du Faubourg St. Honoré.

Lanvin's designs were noted for a youthful quality, often reflecting the influence of the costumes of her native Brittany. She collected costume books, daguerreotypes, historical plates, and drew inspiration from them, notably for the *robes de style* for which she was famous, and for her wedding gowns. She took plain fabrics and decorated them in her own workrooms, maintaining a department for machine embroidery under the direction of her brother. The house also produced women's sports clothes and furs, children's wear, and lingerie. In 1926 she opened a men's wear boutique, the first in the couture, directed by her nephew, Maurice Lanvin.

She was famous for her use of quilting and stitching, for her embroideries, for the discreet use of sequins. Fantasy evening gowns in metallic embroideries were a signature; she introduced the chemise during World War I. She was also one of the first couturiers to establish a perfume business, with Arpège and My Sin among the most notable fragrances.

Lanvin was an accomplished businesswoman and was elected President of the Haute Couture Committee of the Paris International Exhibition in 1937. She represented France and the couture at the 1939 New York World's Fair. After her death the House of Lanvin continued under the direction of her daughter, the Comtesse de Polignac.

The couture was designed by Antonio del Castillo from 1950 to 1963, and from 1963 until 1984 by JULES-FRANÇOIS CRAHAY. Control of the firm passed from the Lanvin family in 1989. Maryll Lanvin, who had taken over design direction of ready-to-wear, and after Crahay's retirement of the couture, was replaced by CLAUDE MONTANA for couture and ERIC BERGÈRE for ready-to-wear. The couture operation was discontinued in 1992. Since 1989 the women's ready-to-wear has been the province of a succession of designers, including Dominque Morlotti, Ocimar Versolato, and Cristina Ortiz.

The firm, which was owned by L'Oréal, was sold in July 2001 to a Taiwanese investment group. ALBER ELBAZ was named designer for women's fashion in 2001, with his first collection for fall/winter 2002.

In October of 2001, Elbaz was appointed creative director of the couture enterprise. To this day, Lanvin Paris is revered as the oldest of the French couture houses, and has subsidiaries in Japan, Hong Kong, Taiwan, and the Middle East, as well as in the United States and Europe.

Designer Guy Laroche.

Influenced by BALENCIAGA, in the beginning Laroche soon developed a younger, livelier, less formal look. "It was very, very conservative when I started. I gave it color . . . youth, suppleness and informality." His evening pants were worn by the most fashionable women in Paris.

Laroche had his greatest fame during the early 1960s. At the time of his death, he presided over an extensive company producing both Laroche couture and ready-to-wear, and with boutiques around the world. Other licensed ready-to-wear labels in the group included Christian Aujard, Lolita Lempicka, Angelo Tarlazzi, and a lower-priced collection by THIERRY MUGLER. The Laroche name has been on products ranging from intimate apparel, furs, luggage, sportswear, rainwear, dresses, and blouses to sunglasses, accessories, footwear, and fragrances.

BORN La Rochelle (near Bordeaux), France, ca. 1923
DIED February 16, 1990

Guy Laroche (La-roash) arrived in Paris at age 25 with no immediate goals and no interest in clothes. Through a cousin working at JEAN PATOU, he toured several couture houses and fell in love with the business. He got a job as assistant to JEAN DESSÈS and stayed with him five years. From 1950 to 1955 he freelanced in New York, then returned to Paris and opened a couture establishment in his apartment. His first collection was for fall 1957. In 1961 he expanded and moved to the Avenue Montaigne, where the house is still located.

Autumn collections, 1971-1972.

Ralph Lauren

Designer Ralph Lauren.

BORN New York City, October 14, 1939

AWARDS Coty American Fashion Critics' Award *Men's Wear*, 1970; *Return Award (Men's Wear)*, 1973; *"Winnie,"* 1974; *Return Award*, 1976; *Hall of Fame (men's wear)*, 1976; *Hall of Fame (Women's Wear)*, 1977; *Men's Apparel*, 1981; *Special Award (Women's Wear)*, 1984 • Council of Fashion Designers of America (CFDA) *Special Award*, 1981; *Retailer of the Year*, 1986 • *Fashion Walk of Fame*, 2000

A gifted stylist, Ralph Lauren has taken his dream of a mythic American past of athletic grace, and discreet elegance, and transformed it into a fashion empire. He chose the name Polo as a symbol of men who wear expensive, classic clothes, and wear them with style. He extends the same blend of classic silhouettes, superb fabrics, and fine workmanship to his women's apparel. For both women and men, the attitude is well-bred and confident, with an offhand luxury. He has projected his romantic view in his advertis-

Above: Spring/summer 1989.

Right: Fall 2008.

Fall 2009.

ing, featuring a large cast of models in upper-crust situations, and through his flagship New York stores. Definitely investment caliber, the clothes are known for excellent quality and high prices.

The son of an artist, Lauren arrived in the fashion world without formal design training. He took night courses in business while working days as a department store stock boy. After college he sold at Brooks Brothers, was variously an assistant buyer at Allied Stores, a glove company salesman, and New York representative for a Boston necktie manufacturer. He started designing neckties, and in 1967 persuaded Beau Brummel, a men's wear firm, to form the Polo neckwear division. The ties were unique, exceptionally wide, and made by hand of opulent silks. They quickly attracted attention to the designer and brought him a contract to design the Polo line of men's clothing for Norman Hilton, with whom he established Polo in 1968 as a separate company producing a total wardrobe for men. In 1971 Lauren introduced finely tailored shirts for women and the next year a complete ready-to-wear collection.

Lauren has also done film work, designing for the leading men in *The Great Gatsby* in 1973, and in 1977, the clothing for *Annie Hall*. His myriad brands include Polo Ralph Lauren, Polo Sport for active sports, and the Ralph Lauren Collection, as well as products for a total home environment introduced in 1983. There are also fragrances for both men and women. In 2002 he showed his top-of-the-line Purple Label men's collection in Milan, where it was very well received.

Some collections are distributed only outside the United States in countries such as Canada and Japan, and licensing has expanded worldwide. In 1997 he took his company public on the New York Stock Exchange.

Lauren recently launched the Rugby line, which is targeted to the 16- to 25-year-old age group. He also established an international Web site for his brand. The Polo Ralph Lauren label was an official outfitter of the U.S. Open up to 2009, and of Wimbledon through 2010. Ralph Lauren also designed the motifs and uniforms for the U.S. team at the opening of the Olympic Games in Beijing.

Spring/summer 2008.

Judith Leiber

Designer Judith Leiber.

BORN Judith Peto; Budapest, Hungary, January 11, 1921

AWARDS Coty American Fashion Critics' Award *Special Award (Handbags)*, 1973 • Neiman Marcus Award, 1980 • Council of Fashion Designers of America (CFDA) *Lifetime Achievement Award*, 1994 • Dallas Fashion Award *Fashion Excellence Award* • Accessories Council *Hall of Fame Award*, 2001

Renowned for her fantastic jeweled evening bags, Judith Leiber learned her craft in Budapest, starting as an apprentice at 19, the only woman in what was considered a man's trade. It was there she met her future husband, an American, at the end of World War II; they married and she came to the United States as a war bride in 1946. She worked in the handbag industry until 1963 gaining a diversified experience in every type of bag and every price range. Then she and her husband went into business for themselves. The company was sold to a British conglomerate in 1993, resulting in expansion of the business and the addition of a retail presence.

Minaudière clutch purse in the shape of a sitting Buddha, 2009.

Leiber designed everything, from the small animal shapes encrusted with thousands of jewels to daytime bags in rare leathers, softened with pleats, braids, coins, charms, and stones. She listed her influences as the 1920s, 1930s, and oriental art, and wanted her bags to be great to hold, beautiful to look at, and practical. She also made some accessories, such as wallets, key chains, and belts, but is best known for her crystal-adorned minaudieres, which appeared in 1967, each made by hand and taking up to two weeks to complete. The bags have become collector's items for women who wear real jewelry and designer clothes.

She has been much honored with innumerable awards from trade groups, colleges and universities, and charitable organizations. In late 1994, New York's Fashion Institute of Technology marked her 30th year in business with an exhibition of her work. She announced her retirement in January 1998.

In September 2000 the company was again sold, this time to a consortium of investors known as the Pegasus Group, subsequently renamed the Leiber Group for its most productive division.

Handbag, 2008.

Photographer Annie Leibovitz.

BORN Waterbury, Connecticut, 1949

AWARDS Clio Award, 1987 • Barnard College Medal of Distinction • French Minister of Culture's Commandeur dans l'Ordre des Artes et des Lettres • *Infinity Award in Applied Photography* from the International Center of Photography • Smithsonian Magazine *"Innovators of Our Time" Award* • Library of Congress *Living Legend Award* • *Georgia O'Keeffe Museum Women of Distinction Award*, 2009

Known for her close collaboration between photographer and subject, Annie Leibovitz has created some of the most iconographic portraits of the twentieth century—and defined much of our popular culture.

Leibovitz studied painting at the San Francisco Art Institute in the late 1960s, and discovered a passion for photography after visiting Japan and the Philippines. When she returned to the United States in 1970, she was hired as a staff photographer for the fledgling magazine *Rolling Stone*. She was named chief photographer for the magazine in 1973, and in 1975 went on tour with the band Rolling Stones as the official tour photographer. Leibovitz would work for *Rolling Stone* until 1983, and her celebrity portraits shaped the look of the magazine.

In 1980, she took a photo for *Rolling Stone* of the nude John Lennon curled up next to a clothed Yoko Ono in bed. Five hours later Lennon was murdered outside his apartment in New York City, making Leibovitz's photograph the last professional picture taken of the musician.

She published her first book, *Annie Leibovitz: Photographs*, in 1983, and signed on with the magazine *Vanity Fair* that same year. Notable photographs for *Vanity Fair* include cover shots of the actress Demi Moore pregnant and nude (1991); in 2006, she depicted actresses Keira Knightley and Scarlett Johansson nude with fully-clothed designer Tom Ford. Controversy erupted in 2008 when Leibovitz shot the 15-year-old singer Miley Cyrus, clad in a sheet, causing the teen star to apologize for her participation in the photo shoot.

Leibovitz has also taken photographs to support social and political causes. In 1989 she photographed author Susan Sontag for her book *AIDS and Its Metaphors*, beginning a relationship that Leibovitz has said influenced her work profoundly and lasted until Sontag's death in 2004. Encouraged by Sontag, Leibovitz documented her trip to war-town Sarajevo in 1993, and in 1999 she published *Women*, juxtaposing photographs of famous women with those of miners, soldiers, and showgirls.

A major retrospective featuring more than 200 of her photographs opened at the Brooklyn Museum in 2006 and has since traveled to major venues in Washington, D.C., San Francisco, and, in 2009, to Berlin.

"Alice in Wonderland" shoot for *Vogue* featuring Stephen Jones (center) and Christian Lacroix (right), 2003.

Lucien Lelong

BORN Paris, France, October 11, 1889
DIED Anglet (near Biarritz), France, May 1, 1958

Lucien Lelong made his first designs at the age of 14 for his father, a successful dressmaker. Trained for business, he decided on a career in couture and designed his first collection; two days before its presentation in 1914, he was called into the Army. He was wounded in World War I, discharged after a year in the hospital, and received the *Croix de Guerre*.

In 1918 he entered his father's business and took control soon after. By 1926, the year he established Parfums Lelong, the house was flourishing and continued to do so until World War II. A farsighted businessman, he was one of the first to have a ready-to-wear line, established in 1934. Lelong was elected president of the Chambre Syndicale de la Couture Parisienne in 1937. He held the post for ten years, including the Occupation period when the Germans

wanted to move the entire French dressmaking industry to Berlin and Vienna. Lelong managed to frustrate the plan and guided the couture safely through the war years. He reopened his own house in 1941 with DIOR and BALMAIN as designers. A serious illness in 1947 caused him to close his couture house, but he continued to direct his perfume business.

Lelong was considered a director of designers rather than a creator. Pierre Balmain, Christian Dior, and HUBERT DE GIVENCHY all worked for him, and Dior particularly praised him as a good friend and a generous employer. From 1919 to 1948, his house produced distinguished collections of beautiful, ladylike clothes for a conservative clientele. Lelong believed strongly in honest workmanship and good needlework and it was his credo that a Lelong creation would hold together until its fabric wore out. He was also an accomplished painter, sculptor, composer, and sportsman.

Designer Lucien Lelong (left) and Lady Mendl (right).

Designer Nanette Lepore.

BORN Youngstown, Ohio, 1958

Her mother an art professor and her father an abstract painter, Nanette Lepore was born into a family that placed a high value on art. Inspired by the myth and romance of gypsy wanderlust, Lepore's creative spirit blossomed during family road trips across historic U.S. Route 66. Lepore exhibited an early inclination for fashion when she designed her first outfit for the child of a neighbor at age nine. After graduating from Youngstown University with a bachelor's degree, she moved to New York City to attend the Fashion Institute of Technology, earning a degree in design. After graduation she worked for several

shops in New York's Garment District and married painter Robert Savage before opening her own business in 1992.

With her husband Robert serving as president of her corporation, Nanette Lepore markets her collections to stores such as Saks Fifth Avenue, Neiman Marcus, and Macy's. She launched a shoe collection in 2006, adding to her already popular lines of dresses and handbags. She has also produced two perfumes, Shanghai Butterfly and Nanette Lepore, available at her nine boutiques worldwide. Lepore's colorfully patterned clothes are often described as gypsy-like and free-spirited. She enjoys a strong following among editors, stylemakers, and celebrities including Eva Longoria Parker, Kerry Washington, and America Ferrera.

Right: Spring 2008.

Left: Spring 2007.

Hervé L. Leroux

BORN Hervé Léger; Bapaume (Pas de Calais), France, May 30, 1957

In his previous design incarnation as Hervé Léger, Leroux was known for his instantly-recognizable, body-enhancing banded dresses. He was forced from his own design house by investors in 1998, reemerging in 2000 with a small fall/winter collection and a new name suggested by KARL LAGERFELD, which translates as Hervé the Red.

The designer's preparation for a fashion career was an education in art history and theater. In 1975 he began designing hats and accessories for designers such as Tan Giudicelli, and two years later started his serious apprenticeship, first as assistant to Giudicelli, then assisting Karl Lagerfeld at FENDI and CHANEL. He spent two years designing for the Italian firm Cadette, then in 1985 joined LANVIN, working with Maryll Lanvin on the ready-to-wear and couture collections. Lanvin gave him a boutique under his name in the same year. He also collaborated with DIANE VON FURSTENBERG in that year. He has designed furs for CHLOÉ, ready-to-wear for Charles Jourdan, and costumes for theater and advertising campaigns.

Designer Hervé L. Leroux.

His first collection under the Léger label appeared in 1992 with both couture and deluxe ready-to-wear. These were frankly sensuous clothes that wrapped the body closely with bands and tucks, at their best both seductive and beautiful. His new approach replaced bands with draping, and brash, bright colors with subtler, deeper tones—the clothes were beautiful, glamorous, and elegant. He was looking, he said, for a new way to wrap and follow the female form. Leroux acknowledges CHARLES JAMES as his major influence, followed by Lagerfeld.

In 1999, Parisian couture house Hervé Léger was acquired by Los-Angeles-based fashion giant BCBGMAXAZRIA Group.

In 2000, he made a comeback and opened a boutique in Paris under the name of Hervé L. Leroux.

Presentation for Guy Larouche in Paris.

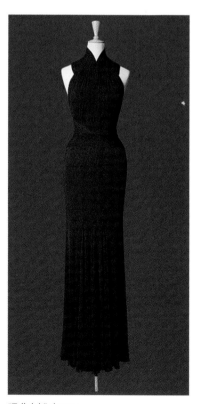

"Tallelah" design.

Designer Tina Leser (left) modeling her clothing at a party.

One of the group of innovative sportswear design-ers that included CLAIRE MCCARDELL and TOM BRIGANCE, Leser always was distinguished by her romanticism and her use of exotic fabrics from the Orient and Hawaii. These she often enriched with embroidery and metallic threads. She used hand-painted prints and was one of the first to design harem pajamas, toreador pants, and dresses from cashmere.

BORN Christine Wetherill Shillard-Smith; Philadelphia, Pennsylvania, December 12, 1910
DIED Sands Point, Long Island, January 24, 1986

AWARDS Neiman Marcus Award, 1945 • Coty American Fashion Critics' Award "*Winnie*," 1945

Tina Leser studied art in Philadelphia and Paris. In 1935 she opened a shop in Honolulu to sell her fash-ion designs; she returned to New York in 1942 after the outbreak of World War II and began to make the glamorous sportswear that became her trademark. For ten years she designed for a sportswear manufacturer, and in 1952 formed her own company, Tina Leser Inc. She retired in 1964, returned to fashion in 1966, and then quit for good in 1982.

Model in yellow silk blouse and blue pants, 1959.

Monique Lhuillier

BORN Cebu City, Philippines, 1971

AWARDS *Glamorous Bridal Designer Award, 2001 • Avant Garde Bridal Designer Award, 2002 • Wedding Dresses Magazine Designer of the Year Award, 2003*

Raised in a prominent society family in the Philippines, Monique Lhuillier (Loo-lee-ay) was interested in fashion at an early age. After attending boarding school in Switzerland, she moved to Los Angeles to enroll at the Fashion Institute of Design and Merchandising (FIDM), where she later received a scholarship to attend the advanced studies program. As a young bride-to-be in the early 1990s, she designed dresses for herself and her wedding party when she couldn't find any that suited her. Thus, the business was born. With her husband, Tom Bugbee, she launched her upscale bridal company in 1996, and success among celebrities and the fashion-savvy quickly followed.

Lhuillier's designs distinguish themselves from much of the bridal market for their glamour and sophistication—designs that are dramatic but soft, often with a textural interplay of fabrics. This sensibility has also translated well to her expansion into eveningwear, launched in 2001, and ready-to-wear, which she introduced in 2003. Her spring 2009 ready-to-wear collection reached even further, by pairing her floaty evening fabrics with sportier skirts for a chic contrast.

Spring/summer 2009.

Designer Monique Lhuillier.

Spring/summer 2009.

Art Director Alexander Liberman.

BORN Kiev, Ukraine, September 12, 1912
DIED Miami, Florida, November 19, 1999

AWARDS *Gold Medal for Design*, Exposition Internazionale, Paris, 1937

As Condé Nast's editorial director for 34 years, Alexander Liberman nurtured a love of painting, sculpture, and photography, all while fulfilling vast professional responsibilities. While he is a legend of the fashion publication business, one cannot overlook his accomplishments in public sculpture, or his influence upon twentieth-century intellectual and artistic culture.

Alexander Liberman

Born to a prosperous timber merchant, Liberman was so disturbed by the 1917 Russian Revolution that his father brought him to London in 1921 at the age of nine. He attended boarding schools, learning the language and manners of the English gentry, then moved again in 1924 with his mother to Paris. There, he studied painting and architecture at the École des Beaux-Arts and worked for graphic designer Adolphe Cassandre.

In 1931, Liberman became art director and later was promoted to managing editor of *Vu* magazine, an early precursor to *Life*. He fled occupied France in 1941 and made his way to New York, where he took a position at *Vogue*, eventually becoming the magazine's artistic director. In 1960 he became art director of all Condé Nast publications and then editorial director in 1962, continuing in that position until his retirement in 1994. Such longevity is regarded as a rare achievement in an industry known for short editorial tenure.

Liberman is responsible for the avant-garde vision of Condé Nast throughout the revolutionary 1960s and 1970s, forever altering the look and philosophy of fashion magazines. His adaptive style and eye for social change kept the publications under his watch—fresh, hip, and attuned to the zeitgeist.

Liberman continued to exhibit and showcase his work while working at Condé Nast. He produced several books including *The Artist in His Studio*, *Marlene: An Intimate Photographic Memoir* (a tribute to Marlene Dietrich), and his last book, *Then*, a black-and-white photographic collection of celebrities ranging from Truman Capote to COCO CHANEL. His highly regarded metal sculptures are found in parks, campuses, and private grounds all over the world.

Phillip Lim

BORN Thailand, 1973

AWARDS First place in the Women's Designer "Rising Star" category by Fashion Group International, 2006 • Council of Fashion Designers of America (CFDA) *Swarovski Award for Emerging Talent in Women's wear*, 2007

A former design assistant to Katayone Adeli, Phillip Lim is one of America's most popular young sportswear designers. After graduating from Cal State Long Beach in 1997, Lim assisted Adeli for a year and a half, leaving to become cofounder and head designer for the L.A.-based label Development. Four years later, in 2005, Lim moved to New York, and, with the help of his friend and business partner Wen Khou, both 31 years of age, established his own label, 3.1 phillip lim.

In 2006, less than a year after launching his company, Lim was a finalist for the prestigious CFDA/*Vogue Fashion Fun Award*, and was a runner-up again in 2007. Also in 2007 he was a finalist for the *Fashion Design Award* of the Cooper-Hewitt Museum of Design. In that year he opened his first store in Soho and, in 2008, he created a limited edition line for The Gap, and opened new boutiques in Tokyo and Los Angeles.

His mission is to design "clothes people wear," and his collections have been described as "pretty but cool," and "super-chic without the sky-high prices." His collections include shoes, belts, handbags, a men's wear line, and a children's line called kid by phillip lim. They have been worn by some of the hottest young talent, including Keira Knightley, Kate Bosworth, and Amanda Peet.

Designer Phillip Lim.

Above: Fall 2009.
Left: Spring 2009.

BORN Paris, France, January 7, 1964

Christian Louboutin (Loo-boo-tin), whose father was an architect-designer of train interiors, fell in love with shoes at an early age when he was taken to a museum with a magnificent parquet floor. At the entrance there was a large sign, like a traffic sign, with the silhouette of a high-heeled pump in a red circle sliced through with a red line, and inside women were walking around shoeless. He then started sketching the design on school books, homework, and notebooks. At 16, he was given a book on the shoe designer ROGER VIVIER, and his dedication to shoes became total.

His education continued backstage at the Folies Bergère, where he learned the importance of function—shoes had to be sturdy enough to take the grind of dancing, jumping, and kicking, and not cause injuries. At 18, an interview at CHRISTIAN DIOR led to a job with Dior's shoe designer, Charles Jourdan, where he learned technique. He freelanced for CHANEL, SAINT LAURENT, Maud Frizon, and then worked with his

idol Roger Vivier on his retrospective at the Louvre. Watching and studying, Louboutin developed his own characteristic silhouette—slim and pointy-toed, reminiscent of the 1950s—and his signature red soles.

The first Louboutin shop opened in Paris in 1992, followed by boutiques in London, New York, and Los Angeles, and in luxury stores from Tokyo to São Paulo. He has continued to collaborate with designers as varied as Saint Laurent, GAULTIER, RODARTE, and SCOTT.

Red-soled peep-toe, 2009.

Designer Christian Louboutin.

Christian Louboutin

Jean Louis

BORN Jean Louis Berthault; Paris, France, October 5, 1907

DIED Palm Springs, California, April 20, 1997

AWARDS *Motion Picture Academy Award* for *The Solid Gold Cadillac*, 1956

First at Columbia, where JAMES GALANOS worked as his assistant, and later at Universal, Jean Louis was head designer for major Hollywood movie studios. His 60 film credits include *Pal Joey*, *Ship of Fools*, *Born Yesterday*, *A Star is Born*, and *From Here to Eternity*. He made costumes for the films and fashions for the closets of many of Hollywood's brightest stars, including Lana Turner, Vivien Leigh, Joan

Designer Jean Louis (left) and Nina Foch (right).

Crawford, Rosalind Russell, Greta Garbo, Katharine Hepburn, and Judy Garland. He also designed the gowns for Loretta Young's entrances on her *Loretta Young Show*, an eight-year fixture on NBC TV.

Louis trained in Paris, came to the United States in 1936, and went to work at HATTIE CARNEGIE, where he designed the prototype of the little Carnegie suit. With its closely-fitted jacket and straight skirt, it became the uniform of ladies who lunch. His tenure there coincided with that of both CLAIRE MCCARDELL and NORMAN NORELL.

In 1943, he left New York and private customers for Hollywood, working for the studios until the early 1960s. He then opened a salon in Beverly Hills, continuing film work on a freelance basis. Louis retired in 1988 and in 1993 married Loretta Young.

Actress Marilyn Monroe wearing dress by Jean Louis.

BORN Clayton, Alabama, 1898
DIED 1981

AWARDS *Couturier of the Year Plaque*, 1961, by New York Fashion Society

Anne Cole Lowe is one of the many talented African-American designers that time forgot. Born at the turn of the nineteenth century in Clayton, Alabama, her mother was a competent seamstress who sewed for some of the state's top figures. When Lowe was still a child, she and her mother moved to New York; shortly after, her mother died, and Lowe diligently took over her mother's seamstress work. At age 14, she married; that same year, she applied and attended S.T. Taylor School, pursuing a degree in fashion design—the first African-American to do so.

After graduating, she moved with her husband to Tampa, Florida, and opened a small salon. A few years later, she and her husband divorced and she returned to New York. In 1951, she had a chance meeting with Jacqueline Bouvier, who requested several dresses from her. After her engagement to then-Massachusetts Senator Jack Kennedy, she asked Lowe to design her wedding dress, as well as ten other dresses for various members of her wedding party. The dress was called "the most photographed wedding dress in American history." While few acknowledged her contribution at the time, her relationship with Jackie Kennedy later led to more high-profile positions designing for New York and Washington D.C.'s elite, such as the Rockefellers.

In 1962 Lowe opened a boutique in Saks Fifth Avenue, where she was known for using the "trapunto"—or whole-cloth quilting technique—in sewing. Unfortunately, in her later years she was stricken with glaucoma and became legally blind in one eye. By her retirement in 1970 she was penniless. Lowe died in 1981 at the age of 83.

Jacqueline Kennedy in her wedding gown designed by Anne Cole Lowe, 1953.

Lucile

BORN Lucy Christiana Sutherland; London, England, 1862

DIED London, England, 1935

Now known mainly for the designers who worked for her, including MOLYNEUX and TRAVIS BANTON, Lucile was the most successful London-based couturiere of her time.

Her fashion career began in the 1890s when she and her mother set up as dressmakers; as they became known and their business grew, she started doing business under the name Lucile. Around the turn of the century she married Sir Cosmo Duff-Gordon and as Lady Duff-Gordon was soon dressing London's grandest ladies. She opened a New York branch for Lucile Ltd. in 1910, and a salon in Paris in 1912. (In 1912 she and her husband also survived the Titanic tragedy.)

Her business declined after World War I, when her floating chiffons were too exotic for the times. Her design viewpoint was romantic and theatrical, and she was a tough and forward-thinking business-woman with the vision to see the potential of the North American market and the ability to succeed there.

Designer Lucile.

Dancer Irene Castle wearing a gown by Lucile.

Julien MACDONALD
Bob MACKIE
Tomas MAIER
MAINBOCHER
Catherine MALANDRINO
Man RAY
Mariuccia MANDELLI
Martin MARGIELA
Vera MAXWELL
Claire MCCARDELL
Patrick MCCARTHY
Stella MCCARTNEY

Jessica MCCLINTOCK
Mary MCFADDEN
Arthur MCGEE
Alexander MCQUEEN
Steven MEISEL
Suzy MENKES
Nicole MILLER
MISSONI
Issey MIYAKE

Isaac MIZRAHI
Anna MOLINARI
Captain Edward MOLYNEUX
Claude MONTANA
Hanae MORI
Franco MOSCHINO
Roland MOURET
Thierry MUGLER
Jean MUIR

Julien Macdonald

BORN Wales, March 19, 1971

When Julien Macdonald was chosen by LVMH to replace ALEXANDER MCQUEEN at GIVENCHY in 2001, he was not well known beyond fashion's inner circles but had a solid background designing knitwear for CHANEL couture. His success at knits would seem natural as he grew up in a family of gifted knitters steeped in an age-old Welsh knitting tradition.

After some dance training, Macdonald enrolled for one year at Cardiff Art College where he discovered a passion for textile design. He moved on to Brighton, began experimenting with knitwear techniques, and earned a B.A. in Fashion Textiles. He then went to London to obtain a M.A. from the Royal College of Art. His 1996 graduate collection of finely-spun knit dresses and cobwebby crochets caught the attention of KARL LAGERFELD, who brought him to Chanel as a knitwear designer.

Macdonald launched his own company in 1997 with a spectacularly experimental collection. Subsequent showings have attracted a considerable celebrity following with his combination of ethereal, gossamer knits and glitzy sequined dresses featuring serious slits. The London fashion press has dubbed him "the Welsh Versace."

He stayed for three years with Givency, and in January 2004 Macdonald announced he was leaving the house— a day after showing his spring 2004 haute couture collection. Since 2003, Macdonald has also designed the lower-priced Star label for Britain's Debenhams department store.

Designer Julien Macdonald (left) and model.

Above: Fall 2005.
Left: Spring 2004.

Designer Bob Mackie.

the fall of 1999. It covered every aspect of his work, from the designs he did for Carol Burnett's TV show and the costumes for Cher, to his own couture and ready-to-wear. There was even a series of costumes for Barbie, in which she appeared as assorted historical characters. What was completely evident was his technical mastery, allied with an ebullient wit and sense of fun. In 2008, Cher was awarded a contract to perform at Casears Palace in Las Vegas, and Bob Mackie designed her costumes for the engagement.

BORN Los Angeles, California, March 24, 1940

AWARDS Council of Fashion Designers of America (CFDA) *Special Award for his Fashion Exuberance*, 2001

Bob Mackie grew up in Los Angeles where he studied art and theater design. While still in art school, he worked as a sketcher for designers JEAN LOUIS and EDITH HEAD, and for Ray Aghayan, whose partner he became. The spectacular costume designs he and Aghayan, together and separately, have designed for nightclub performers and stars of TV and movies have established the two in the top rank of their field. Among the celebrities they have dressed are Marlene Dietrich, Carol Burnett, Mitzi Gaynor, Barbra Streisand, Raquel Welch, Carol Channing, and notably, Cher.

Mackie's talents extend well beyond costumes—he has been successful in both couture and ready-to-wear and has also ventured into swimwear and loungewear. His work was the subject of a major show at New York's Fashion Institute of Technology in

Model wearing design by Bob Mackie.

Designer Tomas Maier.

BORN Phorzheim, Germany, 1957

German-born designer Tomas Maier grew up watching his architect father working at his drafting table, and may have inherited his love of precision, clean lines, and timeless luxury. After training in Paris with SONIA RYKIEL, Revillon, and Hermès (where he spent ten years), he launched his own label in 1997. His line of elegant resort wear and accessories is sold in boutiques in Florida and elsewhere.

Maier went high-profile in 2001, when the GUCCI Group purchased the ailing Italian luxury line Bottega Veneta and hired him as creative director. The company's original advertising slogan from the 1970s, "When Your Own Initials Are Enough," along with the famous woven *intrecciato* pattern, was a perfect fit for Maier's clean concept of luxury. (Maier has claimed that the fashion world will never see a short-lived "It" bag from the company.) Expansion proved to be the key to success: today Maier oversees Bottega Veneta's handbags, luggage, shoes, eyewear, jewelry, fragrance, and a home collection, along with ready-to-wear lines for men and women. His designs are sleek, classic, and super-luxe, both upholding and updating the company's premiere profile.

Bottega Veneta, fall 2009.

Bottega Veneta men's, spring 2010.

Designer Mainbocher.

BORN Main Rousseau Bocher; Chicago, Illinois, October 24, 1890
DIED Munich, Germany, December 26, 1976

Noted for a nearly infallible sense of fashion, Mainbocher created high-priced clothes of quiet good taste, simplicity, and understatement. He was the first American designer to succeed in Paris and before that had a distinguished career as a fashion journalist.

Encouraged by his mother, he studied art at the Chicago Academy of Fine Arts and in New York, Paris, and Munich. In 1917 he went to France with an American ambulance unit and stayed on in Paris after the war to study singing. To support himself he worked as a fashion illustrator for *Harper's Bazaar* and *Vogue*. By 1922 he had abandoned music and become a full-time fashion journalist, first as Paris fashion editor for *Vogue* then as editor of French *Vogue*. During his journalistic career, he invented the "Vogue's Eye View" column and discovered the artist, ERIC, and the photographer, GEORGE HOYNINGEN-HUENE. He resigned from the magazine in 1929 to open his own Paris salon.

With his many influential contacts and sure fashion sense, he had an immediate success. The Duchess of Windsor, whose wedding dress he made, and Lady Mendl were among his clients. It is said that in his first year in business he introduced the strapless evening gown and also persuaded French textile manufacturers to again set up double looms and weave the wide widths not produced since before World War I. Mainbocher left Paris at the outbreak of World

War II and in 1939 opened a couture house in New York. He became the designer with the most snob appeal, designing elegant and expensive clothes for elegant and expensive women, screening his clients according to his own stringent standards. He also designed uniforms for the American Red Cross, the Waves, the Spars, and the Girl Scouts.

In his work he was greatly influenced by VIONNET and used the bias cut with great mastery. Elegant evening clothes were his forte, from long ball gowns of lace or transparent fabrics to short evening dresses and beaded evening sweaters with jeweled buttons. He made dinner suits of tweed, combining them with blouses of delicate fabrics. Pastel gingham was a signature, accessorized with pearl chokers, short white kid gloves, and plain pumps. Mainbocher knew his own worth and insisted that fashion magazines show his designs on two facing pages, never mixed with those of other designers, no matter how great.

A skillful editor of others' work as well as a creator, Mainbocher has been ranked with MOLYNEUX, SCHIAPARELLI, and LELONG. His design philosophy, often quoted: "The responsibility and challenge . . . is to consider the design and the woman at the same time. Women should look beautiful, rather than just trendful."

The Duke and Duchess of Windsor (in Mainbocher) on their wedding day, 1937.

Catherine Malandrino

BORN Grenoble, France

A graduate of L'Ecole Supérieure des Arts et techniques de la Mode (Esmod) in France, Catherine Malandrino began her career with the houses of Dorothée Bis, LOUIS FÉRAUD, EMANUEL UNGARO, and Et Vous. In 1998 she came to the United States to help relaunch the DIANE VON FURSTENBERG label as head designer, and presented her first Collage collection in New York that year. In 2000, her Flag collection debuted to critical acclaim and was worn by several celebrities, including Halle Berry and Madonna. Malandrino also designed a collection for Mary J. Blige in 2001 and a collection worn by Sarah Jessica Parker on the television show *Sex and the City* in 2002.

Malandrino opened her flagship store in 2004 in the Meatpacking District in New York City, and opened a boutique in Paris the following year. The next year saw the debut of her couture line Malandrino, to supplement her contemporary line, Catherine Malandrino. In 2008, she presented her first costume jewelry line and opened a boutique in Akaretler, Istanbul. She has also opened new boutiques in Kuwait and the United Arab Emirates. Two additional boutiques opened in the United States in 2008, including Catherine Malandrino Maison, a new concept store that includes a Catherine Malandrino café, library, and outdoor terrace. Today, she lives in New

Model in flag dress.

Models backstage at Catherine Malandrino's spring 2007 runway show.

York with her husband, Bernard Aidan, and their son, Oscar.

Her overall look employs knitwear, silks, and playful accents to showcase a rock-and-roll attitude. She has said that she wants to "design irresistible clothes that make a woman desirable . . ."

Designer Catherine Malandrino.

BORN Emmanuel Radnitzky; Philadelphia, Pennsylvania, August 27, 1890

DIED Paris, France, November 18, 1976

Man Ray was born as the eldest child to Russian-Jewish immigrants. In early 1912, his family changed their surname from Radnitzky to Ray—a reaction to the ethnic discrimination and anti-Semitism that was prevalent during that time. He also shortened his first name Emmanuel to Man, and gradually began to use Man Ray as his combined single name.

More interested in art than in commercial photography, Man Ray was nevertheless one of the fashion world's most innovative photographers, introducing elements of surrealism into his fashion work. He first worked for PAUL POIRET around 1921 or 1922, using glass plates and operating out of Poiret's darkroom. He photographed the couture section of the 1925 Decorative Arts Exposition in Paris. After working in New York, he returned to Paris with American models, who brought an American accent to his work. He photographed the Paris collections from 1938 to 1940, sometimes during air raid warnings, before returning to the United States. After World War II he abandoned fashion to devote himself to art and experimental photography.

Denise Poiret photographed by Man Ray.

Rose Sélary photographed by Man Ray.

Photographer Man Ray.

Mariuccia Mandelli

Designer Mariuccia Mandelli.

new licensing agreements including Krizia World, Krizia Eyewear, Segreti di Krizia, and Krizia Kids. A year later, she introduced a new fragrance, Easy Krizia, 1999.

A witty, fertile designer, Mandelli filled each collection with ideas, veering between classicism and craziness. Her animal sweaters—a different bird or beast for each collection—were famous and often copied; she is also known for fantastic evening designs, such as the tiered, fan-pleated cellophane dresses that looked like the Chrysler building. Walter Albini was a design collaborator for three years and LAGERFELD has been a consultant.

An accomplished businesswoman with a sure grasp of company affairs, Mandelli has also devoted her considerable energy to various causes of the Milan design community and is considered responsible for moving the ready-to-wear showings from Florence to Milan.

BORN Bergamo, near Milan, Italy, ca. 1933

Krizia, the firm headed by Mariuccia Mandelli and her husband, Aldo Pinto, was founded in Milan in 1954. She took the name of the company from Plato's dialogue on the vanity of women, an example of her sense of humor. Always interested in fashion, Mandelli was teaching school when she became frustrated by the clothes available to her in shops. With a friend, she made up some of her own designs and personally carried them around Italy to sell to retail outlets. The process gave her valuable insights into customer preferences and soon her business had grown from two workers to a premiere and six workers. The clothes were young and original with a sense of fantasy, and her first show in 1957 won favorable response and a fashion press award. As her business blossomed, she persuaded her husband to become her business partner and to supervise her knitwear company, Kriziamaglia, which took off in the early 1970s. In 1997, she signed with Grace Silver to open three Krizia stores in China and in 1998 saw several

Sweater for Krizia.

Spring 2009.

BORN Belgium, April 9, 1957

Martin Margiela first burst onto the Paris scene in the late 1980s, one of a group of fashion iconoclasts from unexpected venues—from Belgium in the case of Margiela and DRIES VAN NOTEN, and HELMUT LANG from Austria. Well-trained in classic techniques, they have used their considerable skills to turn accepted ideas about clothes inside-out and upside-down, dismantling conventional approaches to beauty and fashion.

From 1976 to 1980, Margiela studied at the Academy of Fine Arts in Antwerp, and in 1984 went to work in Paris as assistant to JEAN-PAUL GAULTIER. In 1988 he presented his first collection for spring/ summer 1989. Reflecting his view of the times we live in, he has made clothes of recycled materials: turned used linings into dresses, made subway posters or broken china into waistcoats, and constructed shirts from ripped-apart socks and hosiery. He thinks "it is beautiful to make new things out of rejects or worn

stuff," and when he slashes down old or new clothes, it is not to destroy them but rather to bring them back to life in a different form. For his fifth anniversary in 1993, he recreated his favorite pieces from the previous five years. Unconventional clothes have been matched by off-beat show locations: a children's playground, a parking lot, an abandoned subway station, the Salvation Army's flea market, and the cellar of the Pont Alexandre III—perhaps the most beautiful bridge in Paris. One of fashion's true originals, he became known through his press-attracting ploys but is personally reclusive and refuses to be photographed. He is a master of classic tailoring on which his best work rests.

In addition to his own collection, Margiela has been a consultant to two Italian sportswear houses and, from 1997 to 2003, was head designer for the venerable French house of Hermès, a bastion of tradition. At the end of his contract, he was replaced at Hermès by Jean Paul Gaultier. In 2002, his company was sold to Renzo Rosso, the owner of the Italian company Diesel Group. The company celebrated its twentieth anniversary in October 2008 with a special exhibition at the MoMu Fashion Museum in Antwerp.

Spring 2008.

Martin Margiela

Vera Maxwell

BORN Vera Huppe; New York, New York, April 22, 1901

DIED Rincón, Puerto Rico, January 14, 1995

AWARDS Coty American Fashion Critics' *Special Award (coats and suits)*, 1951 • Neiman Marcus Award, 1955

Vera Maxwell was one of a small group of American craftsmen-designers of the 1930s and 1940s, true originals such as CASHIN and MCCARDELL, who worked independently of Europe. She also represents an even smaller group of women who successfully ran their own businesses.

She was the daughter of Viennese parents with whom she traveled to Europe and whose values provided the core of her early education. She went to high school in Leonia, New Jersey, studied ballet, and danced with the Metropolitan Opera Ballet from 1919 until 1924.

Maxwell specialized in simple, timeless clothes, marked by the effortless good looks and ease of movement particularly valued by active American women. These were largely go-together separates in fine Scottish tweeds, wool jersey, raw silk, Indian embroideries, and Ultrasuede®. Among her numerous innovations were the weekend wardrobe of 1935, consisting of a collarless jacket in tweed and gray flannel, a short pleated flannel tennis skirt, a longer pleated tweed skirt, and cuffed flannel trousers. There was also a cotton coverall for war workers that could be considered the precursor of the jumpsuit, print dresses with coats lined in matching print, and the "Speed Dress" with stretch-nylon top, full skirt of polyester knit, and print stole—no zippers, no buttons, and no hooks.

She was honored in 1970 with a retrospective at the Smithsonian Institution in Washington, D.C. In 1978, a party and show were given at the Museum of the City of New York to celebrate her 75th birthday and 50th year as a designer. She continued to work until early 1985, when she abruptly closed her business. In 1986, at age 83, she went back to work with a fall collection of sportswear, dresses, and coats but soon retired again to spend most of her time working on her memoirs, which were never published.

Designer Vera Maxwell.

Designer Claire McCardell.

BORN Frederick, Maryland, May 24, 1905
DIED New York City, March 23, 1958

AWARDS Coty American Fashion Critics' Award
"*Winnie*," 1944; *Hall of Fame (posthumous)*,
1958 • Neiman Marcus Award, 1948 • National
Women's Press Club, 1950 • Parsons *Medal for
Distinguished Achievement*, 1956 • *Fashion Walk of
Fame*, 2000

Claire McCardell is credited with originating the
"American Look," easy and unforced, and a striking
contrast to structured, European-inspired fashion.
She had complete understanding of the needs of the
American woman with her full schedule of work and
play, and designed specifically for this customer.
Her philosophy was simple: clothes should be clean-
lined, functional, comfortable, and appropriate to the
occasion. They should fit well, flow naturally with the
body and, of course, be attractive to look at. Buttons
had to button, sashes were required to be long
enough not only to tie, but to wrap around.

Her father was a banker and state senator, and
McCardell grew up in comfortable circumstances.

As a child, she showed her interest in clothes with
paper dolls and as a teenager she designed her own
clothes. She attended Hood College for Women in
Maryland and studied fashion illustration at Parsons
School of Design and for a year in Paris. Returning
to New York, she painted lampshades for B. Altman
& Co. and modeled briefly, joining Robert Turk, Inc.
in 1929 as model and assistant designer. When Turk
moved to Townley Frocks, Inc., McCardell moved
with him, taking over as designer after his death. She
stayed with Townley until 1938 when she moved to
HATTIE CARNEGIE, returning to Townley in 1940, first
as designer, then as designer–partner. She remained
there until her death in 1958.

McCardell picked up details from men's clothing
and work clothes, such as large pockets, blue-jeans
topstitching, trouser pleats, rivets, and gripper fas-

Claire McCardell

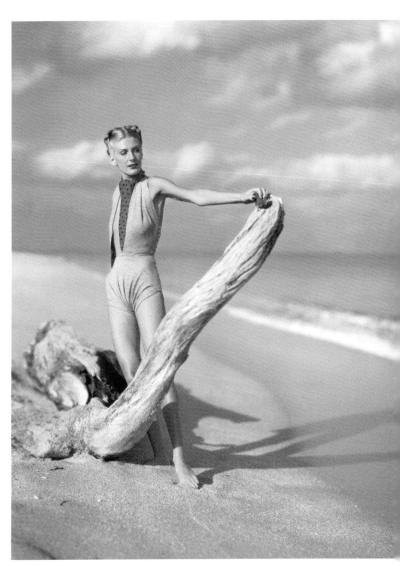

Model wearing Claire McCardell design.

McCardell, continued

tenings. Favorite fabrics were sturdy cotton denim, ticking, gingham, and wool jersey. She used colored zippers in an ornamental way, spaghetti ties, and surprise color juxtapositions. The result was sophisticated, wearable clothes, often with witty touches.

Among her many innovations were the diaper bathing suit, the monastic dress—waistless, bias-cut, dartless—the "Popover," the kitchen dinner dress, and ballet slippers worn with day clothes. She also designed sunglasses, infants' and children's wear, children's shoes, and costume jewelry. Her designs were totally contemporary; the proof of her genius is that they still look contemporary. As evidence, Parsons School of Design honored her in 1994 with an exhibition, "Claire McCardell: Redefining Modernism," one of the events celebrating the school's 100th anniversary. The show also included a selection of clothes from contemporary American designers whose work might be considered in the

Model wearing bare-back sundress.

Model wearing pink dinner shirt tucked into light, full skirt in sheer cotton chambray.

McCardell tradition: DONNA KARAN, ISAAC MIZRAHI, ANNA SUI, ADRI, and MICHAEL KORS.

A big McCardell year was in 1998. Her designs were included in the show *American Ingenuity* at the Costume Institute of the Metropolitan Museum of Art; she was also honored by a show at the Maryland Historical Society in Baltimore, and in November the Fashion Institute of Technology mounted an exhibition, "Claire McCardell and the American Look."

Stanley Marcus spoke of her as ". . . the master of the line, never the slave of the sequin. She is one of the few creative designers this country has ever produced."

BORN June 15, 1951

AWARDS Council of Fashion Designers of America's (CFDA) *Eugenia Sheppard Award for Fashion Journalism*, 1994

Ever since taking a job as a reporter in the Washington, D.C., bureau of Fairchild Publications in 1977, Patrick McCarthy has spent his entire journalism career with the company, and has had many different positions, including London Bureau Chief, Paris Bureau Chief, European editor, and editor and executive editor of *W* and *Women's Wear Daily*. He was also executive vice president of editorial for the company and, since 1997, chairman and editorial director of Fairchild Publications, succeeding John B. Fairchild. In 2006, McCarthy was named chairman and editorial director of *W* and Fairchild Fashion Group, which includes *WWD* and *Footwear News*.

McCarthy studied at Boston and Stanford universities before joining Fairchild Publications where he became known early on for his biting interview technique—he's sat down with famous designers from Karl Lagerfeld to Giorgio Armani—often getting his subjects to divulge more than they'd originally planned.

Perhaps most notably, McCarthy presided over the transformation of *W* in 1993 from a biweekly broadsheet newspaper to a glossy monthly magazine, steering the focus of the magazine away from only the traditional couture houses and including stories on new luxury brands and popular retail operations as well as celebrity, lifestyles, and business.

During his tenure *W* has received 13 National Magazine Award nominations, winning for Photo Portfolio/Photo Essay in 2004 and Photography in 1998 and 2006.

Journalist and editor Patrick McCarthy.

Patrick McCarthy

Stella McCartney

BORN London, England, September 13, 1971

AWARDS VH1/Vogue Fashion and Music, *Designer of the Year Award*, 2000 • *Glamour* Award for *Best Designer of the Year*, 2004 • The Fashion Group International, Star Honoree, 2004; the *Organic Style Woman of the Year Award*, 2005 • *Elle* Style Award for *Best Designer of the Year Award*, 2007; Spanish *Elle* Awards, *Best Designer of The Year*, 2008 • British Style Awards, *Best Designer of The Year*, 2007 • ACE Awards, the *Green Designer of the Year*, 2008 • Honored by Natural Resources Defense Council, Time 100 and *Glamour* Woman of the Year Award, 2009.

Stella McCartney graduated from Central St Martins in 1995. A signature style of sharp tailoring, natural confidence, and sexy femininity was immediately apparent in her first collection. After only two collections, in 1997, she was appointed the creative director of Chloé in Paris and enjoyed great success during her tenure.

Designer Stella McCartney.

In 2001, McCartney launched her own fashion house in a joint venture with GUCCI Group. She understands the needs of those in her own age group and designs clothes to fit their lives, combining sensuality with a contemporary edge. However, she does not use any leather or fur in her designs. McCartney's collections include women's ready-to-wear, accessories, eyewear, fragrance, and organic skincare. Her perfume, Stella, launched successfully in 2003.

In addition to the main line collection, McCartney entered into a long-term partnership with adidas in 2004. The acclaimed sports performance collection, adidas by Stella McCartney, has since successfully grown to include several sports categories.

In 2005, the one-off collection Stella McCartney for H&M sold out worldwide in record time. Her fragrance Stella In Two was introduced in 2006.

She unveiled CARE by Stella McCartney, the first luxury 100 percent organic skincare line in collaboration with YSL Beaute, in 2007, followed by a new lingerie line and a limited edition travel collection with LeSportsac in 2008.

McCartney operates 14 stores worldwide. Her collections are now distributed in more than 50 countries, including specialty shops and department stores.

Spring 2010.

Spring 2010.

Designer Jessica McClintock (center) with models.

BORN June 19, 1930

AWARDS American Printed Fabrics Council "*Tommy*" Award, 1968 • Dallas Fashion Awards: 1987, 1988, 1990, 1993

Jessica McClintock was raised in Maine by her mother, and as a child designed her own clothes and made patterns. Her training came from her grand-mother, who was a patternmaker and seamstress. She married at 19, moved to California, and after her husband's death in 1963, remarried, divorced, and taught school. In 1969, she invested $5,000 in a tiny California company called Gunne Sax. From this small beginning, she has built a multifaceted compa-ny operation internationally and carved a niche in the market with her highly personal blend of prettiness and old-fashioned allure.

A formidable businesswoman, McClintock has, from time to time, added various divisions, extending her romantic viewpoint to bridal fashion and chil-dren's wear, plus licensing for accessories, china, and home furnishings. There are numerous fragrances and company-owned boutiques. She has received awards from a wide range of business, charitable, and educational organizations and is a member of the Council of Fashion Designers of America (CFDA).

Model wearing Jessica McClintock design.

Mary McFadden

Designer Mary McFadden.

BORN New York City, October 1, 1938

AWARDS Coty American Fashion Critics' Award *"Winnie,"* 1976; *Return Award,* 1978; *Hall of Fame,* 1979 • American Printed Fabrics Council *"Tommy"* Award, 1984, 1991

Until she was ten, Mary McFadden lived on a cotton plantation near Memphis, Tennessee, where her father was a cotton broker; after his death, she returned north with her mother. She attended Foxcroft School in Virginia, Traphagen School of Fashion in New York, and École Lubec in Paris; she studied sociology at Columbia University and the New School for Social Research.

From 1962 to 1964, McFadden was director of public relations for CHRISTIAN DIOR—New York. She married an executive of the DeBeers diamond firm and moved to Africa in 1964. There she became editor of *Vogue* South Africa; when it closed, she continued to contribute to both the French and American editions. She also wrote weekly columns on social and political life for *The Rand Daily Mail.* She divorced, remarried in 1968, and moved to Rhodesia, where she founded Vokutu, a sculpture workshop for native artists.

McFadden returned to New York in 1970 with her daughter, Justine, and went to work for *Vogue* as special projects editor. While there she designed three tunics using unusual Chinese and African silks she had collected on her travels; these were shown in the magazine as a new direction and were bought by Henri Bendel, New York. The silks were handpainted using various resist techniques; the colorings were oriental in feeling with a use of calligraphy and negative spacing that became hallmarks of her future style. Mary McFadden Inc. was established in 1976.

Exotic colorings, extensive use of fine pleating and quilting, and ropes wrapping the figure have all been recurring themes. Her poetic evening designs are best known but all her work shares the same original viewpoint refined and sophisticated. In addition to the very high-priced luxury collection, her design projects have ranged from lingerie and at-home wear to furs, bed and bath, and upholstery fabrics. She is a past president of the Council of Fashion Designers of America (CFDA).

Model wearing hand-quilted jacket by Mary McFadden.

Designer Arthur McGee.

BORN Detroit, Michigan, 1933

Arthur McGee grew up in Detroit watching his mother sew for a living. In 1951, he noticed an ad for a design competition at the prestigious Traphagen School of Design. He won the contest and was awarded a scholarship to attend the school but was disappointed with the program and chose instead to pursue an education at the Fashion Institute of Technology.

In 1957, he produced designs for Bobby Brooks, becoming the first African American to design on Seventh Avenue. He later opened his famous shop on St. Mark's Place in New York. His shop produced out-fits for a variety of professional clientele that included many celebrities, such as Cicely Tyson, Mrs. Harry Belefonte, Stevie Wonder, and Arthur Mitchell—

founder of the Dance Theater of Harlem. His designs were influenced by Asian and African culture. He loved ethnic prints and simple shapes.

McGee makes great pains to be acknowledged not as an African–American designer but as an American designer. In a 1992 *Newsweek* interview he said, "We are not 'black' designers but American designers, the way Bill Blass is an American designer. As soon as you categorize us, you can erase us."

Design by Arthur McGee.

Alexander McQueen

Designer Alexander McQueen.

BORN London, March 17, 1969

AWARDS Best British Designer of the Year, 1996, 1997 (shared with JOHN GALLIANO) • Council of Fashion Designers of America (CFDA) *Designer of the Year,* 2007

Alexander McQueen has cultivated his image as a bad boy of fashion with presentations and designs, such as his low-cut "bumsters," which attract headlines and disguise their exquisite craftsmanship with in-your-face outrageousness. He was born in East London, the son of a taxi driver, graduated from Central St. Martins College of Art and Design, and was immediately awarded an apprenticeship with a firm of prestigious Savile Row tailors. He then worked for ROMEO GIGLI and Koji Tatsuo before opening his own East London studio.

In 1996, citing his "creative brilliance and technical mastery," LVMH named him to succeed John Galliano as chief designer at GIVENCHY. He produced four collections at the house before making an arrangement with LVMH rival, GUCCI, to back him in his own business, whereupon he was replaced at Givenchy by JULIEN MACDONALD.

McQueen was among the designers featured in the "London Fashion" exhibit at New York's Fashion Institute of Technology in 2001 and the same year in the "Extreme Fashion" exhibit at the Metropolitan Museum of Art.

In 2005, McQueen collaborated with Puma to create two lines of footwear for men and women. A casual denim ready-to-wear collection called McQ followed in 2006. Then, in 2007 he partnered with luggage giant Samsonite to create the black label line by Alexander McQueen. His line McQ Alexander McQueen for Target launched in March 2009, which was inspired by youth subcultures, music, rebellion, and style revolution.

Left: Spring 2010.
Right: Fall 2008.

BORN New York City, 1954

Steven Meisel studied photography at Parsons School of Design. He was working as a fashion illustrator for *Women's Wear Daily* and as an art teacher at his alma mater when photographs he took of the actress Phoebe Cates caught the attention of the fashion community. He went on to work on advertising campaigns for PRADA, DOLCE & GABBANA, VALENTINO, and VERSACE.

He later moved to the editorial side of publishing, and in 1988, he became the premier photographer for both the Italian and American editions of *Vogue*. In 2005, he designed a controversial issue of Italian *Vogue* called "Makeover Madness," a glossy, glamorous photo-narrative of dramatic plastic surgery operations.

One of Meisel's most famous works is *Sex*, published in 1992. The book was replete with gritty, erotic photographs of Meisel's friend Madonna and her androgynous young playmates. In 2004, Meisel's work was featured in an exhibition titled "Fashioning Fiction in Photography since 1990" at the Museum of Modern Art in New York. He has also exhibited work at the Moderna Museet in Stockholm and at the National Museum of Photography, Film, and Television in Bradford, England. In 2008, Meisel developed a 1,000-piece jigsaw puzzle of the model Meghan Collision, which retailed for $750.

"I hate the technical stuff," Meisel has said. "I'm an artist. The camera and lights get in my way. They distract me. I would like to just blink my eyes and have the picture."

Photographer Steven Meisel.

Suzy Menkes

BORN England, December 24, 1943

AWARDS *Order of the British Empire, French Legion of Honor*

The famed fashion editor of the *International Herald Tribune*, Suzy Menkes is known for both her signature pompadour hairstyle (which has earned her the nickname Samurai Suzy) and for attending hundreds of fashion shows each year—filling nearly two million words on fashion as a result.

After graduating high school in East Sussex, England, Menkes moved to Paris to study dressmaking for a year and was brought to her first fashion show, NINA RICCI, immediately falling in love with couture. She then left to attend Cambridge University on a scholarship, studying history and English literature. It was there she began honing her journalism skills as a fashion columnist for the school paper, *Varsity*, and became its first female editor in her senior year.

Menkes was later hired by the *Times of London* as a junior fashion reporter and in 1978 became its fashion editor. It was 10 years later that the *Tribune* hired Menkes away, making her the third fashion editor in the paper's history, following in the footsteps of Hebe Dorsey and Eugenia Sheppard, for whom the CFDA's annual journalism award is named.

Menkes is known for her detailed reviews of runway shows and evenhanded opinions though she is not afraid to share an occasional, biting put-down.

Editor Suzy Menkes.

Menkes makes it a point of not accepting gifts from fashion houses or often wearing designer clothes, but has been able to set herself apart with her miniature pompadour set loosely above her forehead.

Menkes has contributed to several books on fashion and on the British Royalty, including *The Royal Jewels* and *Queen and Country.*

Designer Nicole Miller.

BORN ca. 1952

Nicole Miller was raised in Lenox, Massachusetts, the child of an American father and French mother. She attended the Rhode Island School of Design, and as a sophomore took a year off to study dress cutting in Paris. She was designing coats at Rain Cheetahs in 1975 when she was hired as head dress designer at P. J. Walsh; in 1982 the company was renamed Nicole Miller.

She first gained attention for the prints she designed for scarves, which when transferred to men's ties, became an immediate hit. Boxer shorts followed and men's wear with the inimitable prints used as linings. The prints—representing everything from comic book characters to magazine covers to wine labels to brand logos—are in bold graphics and brilliant colors.

In addition to the prints, there is also ready-to-wear in the mid-priced range, which is young and sexy. Miller is now also known particularly for her festive special occasion clothes, including a sophisticated bridesmaid collection she says is "for brides who want to keep their friends." She has an extensive list of licenses—handbags, shoes, eyewear, fragrance, cosmetics, and skin care. A collection of fine and costume jewelry was launched on QVC in August 2002.

In 2003, she launched her contemporary sportswear line millergirl, as well as a new line of shoes. Miller also launched a line of cold weather accessories in 2007.

Left: Fall 2007.
Right: Fall 2009.

Missoni

Designers Rosita and Ottavio Missoni.

Designer Margherita Missoni.

FOUNDED Gallarate, Italy, 1953

AWARDS Neiman Marcus Award, 1973 • Fashion Group International *Design Award*, 1991

There's no mistaking a colorful Missoni knit—and this family-owned company has produced their innovative designs for over 50 years. Founded in a small town north of Milan in 1953 by newlyweds Ottavio and Rosita (who had met when traveling abroad from Italy to London), the company first produced knitwear for Italian department stores and for other designers. The Missoni label was introduced five years later. Stripes and zig-zags adorned Missoni's dresses, tunics, sweaters, and pants. Though the line took a few years to catch on, it received its first big boost in 1965 when Italian fashion editor Anna Piaggi praised the collection. In 1966 the line took on a radical shift when French stylist Emmanuelle Khanh was

hired to collaborate on design. At this point Rosita took over designing the clothes, while Ottavio created the knits.

At the Florence fashion shows in 1967, Rosita had the models remove their bras when the lines interfered with those of the light knit dresses they were wearing. The stage lighting turned the clothes transparent—and Missoni made fashion headlines. The controversy resulted in Missoni being disinvited to show at Florence the following year, so the company took its collection to Milan (which contributed to that city's rise as Italy's fashion capital). By this time, Missoni designs were being featured in *Vogue*.

Missoni was at its height as a status symbol in the 1970s. Keeping the clothing shapes simple and production limited, Missoni designs were often considered to be a form of art. This is a philosophy embraced by the company, which believes that fashion should not dictate timeless style.

Missoni branched out from women's clothing to create men's wear and children's designs,
along with fragrance, textiles, and home décor. The
Missoni children joined the company in the 1990s,
and today Vittorio Missoni is the marketing director,
Luca is creative director, and Angela (who originally went into business for herself) at the helm of
design. Licensing deals have been expanded, and a
bridge line, M Missoni, was introduced in 1999. The
third generation is now also involved, with Angela's
daughter Margherita launching the fragrance Missoni
Profumi in 2006. She is also a model and the "face"
of the perfume and officially joined the company to
begin designing in 2009.

Though by now established as a fashion classic,
Missoni continues to draw attention by keeping its
look both classic and energetic. The spring 2010 collection was praised for its light layers, slender silhouettes, and exceptional handiwork.

Missoni designs, 1968.

Missoni sketch.

Issey Miyake

BORN Hiroshima, Japan, April 22, 1938

AWARDS *Mainichi Newspaper Fashion Award*, 1976, 1984 • Council of Fashion Designers of America (CFDA) *Special Award*, 1983 • Neiman Marcus Award, 1984

From his first collection in 1971, Issey Miyake has been one of the most innovative and influential designers of his time; his imagination ranging far beyond the business of fashion to a fascination with the human body, the space that surrounds it, and the movement that reveals it. He has, in fact, preferred to be regarded simply as a designer and a maker of clothes, rather than as a fashion designer per se. His clothes have long been favorites of women with a strong sense of fashion and of their own style.

A 1964 graduate of Tama Art University in Tokyo, Miyake moved to Paris in 1965 to study at L'École de la Chambre Syndicale. Starting in 1966, he spent two years as assistant designer at GUY LAROCHE, went to GIVENCHY in the same capacity, and in 1969 and 1970 was in New York with GEOFFREY BEENE. In 1970 he returned to Tokyo and formed Miyake Design Studio, showing his first collection in 1971 in Tokyo and New York.

One of the earliest Japanese designers to make the move to Europe, Miyake has shown regularly at the Paris prêt-à-porter collections since 1973. Previously the 1968 Paris student revolution shook up his thinking, leading him to question traditional views of

Designer Issey Miyake.

fashion as applied to the modern woman. At that time he began to use wrapping and layering, combining Japanese attitudes toward clothes with exotic fabrics of his own design.

He is known for innovative fabrics, brilliant use of textures, and mastery of proportion. Licenses have ranged from home furnishings and hosiery to bicycles and luggage; a fragrance, Léau d'Issey, appeared in 1994.

"Issey Miyake Making Things," a ten-year retrospective of the designer's work, opened in Paris at the Cartier Foundation for Contemporary Art in October 1998 and was restaged at the Ace Gallery in downtown New York in November 1999. The exhibition, an exhilarating mating of architecture, space, and movement—clothes floated up in the air and descended, appeared as flat abstractions that turned into three dimensional dresses, and generally explored the outer possibilities of clothing the human form—illustrated the designer's radical approach to clothing, combining respect for tradition with the most unfettered technological experimentation. He turned over design of both the men's and women's collections to Naoki Takizawa in October 1999.

He created a garment dubbed the A-POC (A Piece of Cloth), which is a tube-shaped ready-to-wear garment that the consumer could cut into different shapes. He also started the famous apparel line, Pleats Please Issey Miyake.

Since spring 2006, designer Dai Fujiwara has run the House of Issey Miyake.

Spring/summer 1999.

Isaac Mizrahi

BORN New York City, October 14, 1961

AWARDS Council of Fashion Designers of America (CFDA) *Perry Ellis Award for New Fashion Talent*, 1988; *Designer of the Year*: 1989, 1991; *Special Award* (with Douglas Keeve) for *Unzipped*, 1995 • Dallas Fashion Award *Fashion Excellence Award*

When Isaac Mizrahi opened his own company, he was 26 years old, having already worked on Seventh Avenue for six years. He grew up in Brooklyn, the son of a children's wear manufacturer and of a fashionable mother whose clothes came from BALENCIAGA and NORELL. He attended the Yeshiva of Flatbush, the High School of Performing Arts, and Parsons School of Design. At Parsons he received the Chester Weinberg *Golden Thimble Award* and a CLAIRE MCCARDELL scholarship. Starting in 1981, his last year at Parsons, Mizrahi worked at PERRY ELLIS Sportswear, staying there until 1983, when he went to JEFFREY BANKS, and from there to CALVIN KLEIN. In 1987 he left Klein to form his own business. Ten years later he lost his financial backing and closed his company. He has continued with collections of shoes, coats, and fine jewelry, but has moved on to other pursuits.

Mizrahi's chosen category was luxury sportswear, running the gamut from raincoats to eveningwear.

Designer Isaac Mizrahi.

His work was notable for a constant flow of new ideas and for audacity—playing it safe was not his way. The clothes were young and inventive in the CLAIRE MCCARDELL idiom—unexpected colors and fabrics, with their ease and pared-down glamour they appealed to sophisticates with a sense of adventure and an appreciation of quality.

He has designed costumes for movies, theater, dance, and opera in collaboration with Mark Morris, Twyla Tharp, Bill T. Jones, and Mikhail Baryshnikov. The documentary, *Unzipped*, which recorded the travails of producing his 1994 collection, was made with his friend Douglas Keeve for an AIDS benefit, and then shown at the Sundance Film Festival where it won the 1995 *Audience Award for Documentaries*. It was later released commercially. He has also written a series of comic books, *The Adventures of Sandee the Supermodel*.

He's also indulged his theater ambitions with an off-Broadway show and cabaret act, *Les Mizrahi*, plus a TV talk show. His numerous design projects have included sets and costumes for theater and dance, as well as interiors.

During 2004 Mizrahi returned to his fashion-design origins with the launch of two new ventures, appealing to very different members of the buying public: an affordable yet fashionable line for discount retailer Target, and Isaac Mizrahi to Order, a company creating high-end custom clothing for consumers.

Isaac Mizrahi's career is flourishing thanks in part to his new position of creative director at LIZ CLAIBORNE, hosting duties on Bravo's reality competition *The Fashion Show*, and a radio show on Sirius XM called *Tell Me Everything*.

Fall 2009.

Anna Molinari

BORN Capri, Italy

AWARDS *Isimbardi Fashion Award* in 2001 • *La Kore Fashion Oscar* in 2003

In 1977, with the help of her husband, Gianpaolo Tarabini, and urged by designer FRANCO MOSCHINO, Anna Molinari established Blumarine, a line "for that brand of Italian miss for whom no dress is too small nor any diamond too big." In 1981, Molinari debuted her collection in front of an international audience at the Modit in Milan. Less than a decade later, she and Tarabini had expanded the Blumarine brand into a worldwide conglomerate.

Designer Anna Molinari.

Blumarine, fall 2009.

The company currently has more than 700 stores worldwide and now boasts lines for girls and teens. Molinari also succeeded with an eponymous division, aimed at a more high-end customer. In 2004, the company added a men's division, and in 2007, the company further expanded with a denim line, dubbed Blugirl Folies.

Molinari's husband died in 2006 and her son, Gianguido Tarabini, took over as CEO. In 2007 her daughter, Rosella Tarabini, resigned as creative director and chose to be artistic director of the Blufin labels and Blumarine advertising campaigns. The collection is now under the direction of Tarabini's former team and is produced by Italian manufacturer Sinv SpA. In 2008, the company entered into a licensing agreement with Vicini to develop a shoe collection.

BORN Hampstead, England, September 5, 1891
DIED Monte Carlo, March 23, 1974

Captain Edward Molyneux is remembered for fluid, elegant clothes with a pure, uncluttered line—well-bred and timeless. These included printed silk suits with pleated skirts, softly tailored navy-blue suits, coats, and capes with accents of bright Gauguin pink and *bois de rose*. He used zippers in 1937 to mold the figure, and was partial to handkerchief-point skirts and ostrich trims. His distinguished clientele included Princess Marina of Greece, whose wedding dress he made when she married the Duke of Kent; the Duchess of Windsor; and such stage and film personalities as Lynn Fontanne, Gertrude Lawrence, and Merle Oberon.

Of French descent and Anglo-Irish birth, Molyneux got his start in fashion in 1911 when he won a competition sponsored by the London couturiere, LUCILE, and was engaged to sketch for her. When she opened branches in New York and Chicago, he went with her to the United States, remaining until the outbreak of World War I. He joined the British Army in 1914, earned the rank of captain and was wounded three times, resulting in the loss of one eye. He was twice awarded the Military Cross for Bravery.

In 1919 he opened his own couture house in Paris, eventually adding branches in Monte Carlo, Cannes, and London. He enjoyed a flamboyant social life, assembled a fine collection of eighteenth century and impressionist paintings, opened two successful nightclubs, and was a personal friend of many of his clients. At the outbreak of World War II he escaped from France by fishing boat from Bordeaux and during the war worked out of his London house, turning over profits to national defense. He established international canteens in London and was one of the original members of the Incorporated Society of London Fashion Designers.

See-thru jersey evening dress, 1965.

In 1946 he returned to Paris and reopened his couture house, adding furs, lingerie, millinery, and perfumes. Because of ill health and threatened blindness in his remaining eye, he closed his London house in 1949, and in 1950 turned over the Paris operation to JACQUES GRIFFE. He retired to Montego Bay in Jamaica, devoting himself to painting and travel. Persuaded by the financial interests behind his perfumes to reopen in Paris as Studio Molyneux, he brought his first ready-to-wear collection to the United States in 1965. The project was not a success: Molyneux's elegant, ladylike designs were out of step with the youth-obsessed 1960s. He soon retired again, this time to Biot, near Antibes.

Captain Edward Molyneux

Claude Montana

BORN Paris, France, 1949

Claude Montana began designing in 1971 on a trip to London. To make money, he concocted papier-maché jewelry encrusted with rhinestones, which were featured in fashion magazines and earned him enough money to stay for a year. On his return to Paris, he went to work for Mac Douglas, a French leather firm. Montana has also designed knitwear for the Spanish firm Ferrer y Sentis and collections for various Italian companies including Complice. His reputation grew throughout the 1970s and 1980s, and in 1989, he joined LANVIN to design their couture collection, while continuing his own ready-to-wear business. His couture designs were very well received by the press and praised for their elegance and modernity,

Designer Claude Montana (center) and models.

but he and Lanvin parted company in 1992 and the Lanvin couture operation was discontinued.

Beyond the biker's leathers that made his name, Montana developed into one of the more interesting of the contemporary French designers, with an eye for proportion, cut, and detail. He is a perfectionist, with the finesse of a true couturier and a leaning toward operatic fantasy. His clothes feature strong, uncompromising silhouettes and a well-defined sense of drama. They have been sold in fine stores in the United States, Italy, Germany, and England, and under license in Japan.

In 1999, Montana designed Montana Blu, a more affordable collection for women. He also has several perfumes, including Montana en Turquoise, which launched in 2008.

Fall 2002.

Designer Hanae Mori.

BORN Tokyo, Japan, January 8, 1926

AWARDS Neiman Marcus Award, 1973

Actively engaged in fashion for more than 40 years, Hanae Mori was a quiet phenomenon—a Japanese woman, working wife, and mother, who became extraordinary successful. She graduated from Tokyo Christian Women's College with a degree in Japanese literature, and after marrying Ken Mori, heir to a textile firm, went back to school to study sewing, sketching, and design. In 1955 she opened a small boutique in the Shimjuku section of Tokyo where her clothes attracted the attention of the burgeoning Japanese movie industry. After designing costumes for innumerable films, she opened a shop on the Ginza, Tokyo's famous shopping street.

With her husband, Mori developed a multi-million-dollar business with approximately 20 affiliated companies. Her ready-to-wear was sold at fine stores worldwide and in her own boutiques in Japan, Paris, and the United States, along with accessories, sportswear, and children's clothes. Fabric designs were licensed for bed and bath linens. There were

Fall 2004.

hair salons and TV shows; a publishing division, headed by Akira Mori, the elder of her two sons, who edited the Japanese edition of *Women's Wear Daily,* among other titles. The younger son, Kei, directed the firm's European operations. In June 1978 she consolidated her business offices, couture operation, and boutiques in a glass-and-steel headquarters building designed by noted Japanese architect Kenzo Tange.

In January 1977 Mori brought her couture collection to Paris and continued to show there each season. She was the first Japanese designer to be admitted to the Chambre Syndicale de la Haute Couture Parisienne.

While her design approach was the most international of her compatriots, Mori made extensive use of her Japanese background in her fabrics, which were woven, printed, and dyed especially for her. She utilized the vivid colors and bold linear patterns of Hiroshige prints, while butterflies and flowers—the Japanese symbols of femininity—showed up frequently in her prints, which she has used to great advantage in cocktail and evening dresses, meticulously executed in Eastern-flavored patterns with Western styling and fit. Her clients included film celebrities and the wives of affluent Japanese politicians; she designed the ivory satin gown for Masako Owada's 1993 wedding to Japan's Crown Prince Naruhito.

In late December 2001 the company announced the sale of most of its ready-to-wear, licensed apparel business, and directly-owned shops to a Japanese-British investment group. Mori was expected to continue with the couture. A few months later, buffeted by the long-term Japanese recession, the company filed for bankruptcy.

Franco Moschino

BORN Abbiategrasse, Italy, February 27, 1950
DIED Lake Annone, Italy, September 18, 1994

Franco Moschino's father, the owner of an iron foundry, died when his son was four. As a child, Moschino amused himself by drawing; at 18 he went to Milan to study art at the Accademia di Belle Arti, supporting himself by work as a waiter and a model. In the early 1970s, the fashion drawings he was making for various magazines attracted the attention of GIANNI VERSACE, who used his work in a publicity campaign. He worked as a sketcher for GIORGIO ARMANI on collections for Beged-Or and Genny, and for 11 years designed for Cadette. In 1983 he launched his own company.

Moschino became known, if not universally admired, for his irreverent send-ups of conventional fashion thinking. He sent pairs of models out on the runway in the same outfit, one wearing it as it would appear in a serious fashion presentation, the other as it might be worn on the street. He distributed fresh tomatoes to the audience so they could toss them at any styles they disliked. He incorporated statements such as "Ready to Where?" and "Waist of Money" into jackets, shirts, and belts. These pieces and others of the same kind became bestsellers, not only because of the gags but also because the clothes were carefully tailored and of fine quality.

He believed that fashion should be fun and that people should take clothes and wear them with their own particular style. His motto was "*De gustibus non est disputandum*," which translates as "Who's to say what is good taste?" The paradox was that as much as he made fun of the fashion establishment he was so successful that in the end he became part of the very thing that he was ridiculing.

At the time of Moschino's death there was, in addition to the signature collection, a secondary line called Cheap & Chic, men's wear, children's wear, jeans, accessories, perfumes, and two Milan shops. His last collection was shown after he died in 1994 and was well received. Moschino's Creative Director Rossella Jardini took over the company in 1994, and in 1999 the label became part of the Aeffe Fashion Group SpA.

With a design staff of about a dozen and licenses ranging from swimwear and lingerie to perfume and sunglasses, the firm has continued in business, celebrating its 20th year in business in 2003.

Princess Diana in a Moschino suit, 1991.

BORN Lourdes, France, 1962

AWARDS *Elle* Style Awards *British Designer of the Year,* 2002

The London-based French designer Roland Mouret is a former stylist and art director who has little formal training in fashion (a few months at a Paris fashion college in the late 1970s). When he debuted his own designs in 1998, he became known for his draping and folding skills that allowed him to create "cut without pattern." Financial backers purchased his line and Mouret made a move to New York, where he had his first sell-out hit with his Galaxy dress in 2005. Just months later, he split from his backers, citing creative differences, but they retain the rights to the Roland Mouret brand.

For two years Mouret produced in limited quantities: a limited-edition run of dresses for Bergdorf Goodman, each individually signed, and a capsule collection for the Gap. He relaunched his own line in 2007 after securing new financial support. RM by Roland Mouret was a highly anticipated collection, and Mouret didn't disappoint with yet another "It" dress, this time the "Moon" dress, which sold out within days. The rest of the collection was available for sale on the Internet and also sold quickly.

Designer Roland Mouret.

For his 2009 collections he expanded into knitwear and applied his figure-hugging style to a wider range of daytime dresses appropriate for stylish working women who still want to be fashion-forward.

Models on the runway at RM by Roland Mouret, spring 2010.

Thierry Mugler

BORN Strasbourg, France, 1948

The son of a doctor, Thierry Mugler started making his own clothes while in his teens. He was part of a Strasbourg ballet company, dressed windows in a Paris boutique, and moved to London in 1968. After two years, he moved on to Amsterdam, then back to Paris. His first collection appeared in 1971 under the label Café de Paris; by 1973 he was making clothes under his own name.

Inventive and individual, Mugler came into prominence in the late 1970s with high-priced separates and dresses marked by broad-shoul-dered, defined-waistline silhouettes. While he claimed to admire ALIX GRÈS, his cloth-ing appeared to be descended more from the structured chic of JACQUES FATH. His ten-dency toward histrionic, often outrageous pre-sentations tended to obscure what he was trying to say but he cut a sexy, saucy suit as well or better than any-body, and his collections were known for a sunny freshness and gaiety. As shown, the clothes were apt to appear aggressive and tough. Close up, they proved to be simple, well-cut, body-fit-ted, not overly detailed, with the ready-to-wear more acces-sible than the couture.

Mugler retired from fashion in 1999 to concentrate on perfume. His

Spring/summer 1997.

Designer Thierry Mugler.

Actress Naomi Watts for "Angel" perfume.

firm, owned by Clarins, closed in December 2002, with the perfume business continuing; his latest being Angel Sunessence, introduced in 2009. Angel the original perfume that launched in 1992 is still one of his most popular perfumes.

BORN London, England, July 17, 1928
DIED London, England, May 28, 1995

AWARDS Maison Blanche *"Rex"* Award, New Orleans:
1967, 1968, 1974, 1976 • Fellow of the Royal Society
of Arts, 1973 • Neiman Marcus Award, 1973 •
Commander of British Empire, 1983 • British Fashion
Council *Hall of Fame,* 1994

Of Scottish descent, Jean Muir began her career in
1950 in the stockroom at Liberty. She then sold lingerie, became a sketcher in Liberty's made-to-measure department, and in 1956 joined Jaeger and soon
became responsible for designing the major dress and
knitwear collections. Starting in 1961, she designed
under her own label that she established in partnership with her husband, Harry Leuckert, a former
actor, but which they did not own. In 1966 the two
founded their own company, Jean Muir, Inc.

Designer Jean Muir.

Model wearing design by Jean Muir.

Muir was one of the breed of anticouture, anties-
tablishment designers who came on the scene in the
late 1950s and early 1960s. While others have disappeared, she not only survived but also flourished;
her clothes are treasured by women looking for a
low-profile way of dressing and quality of a very high
order. She created a signature look of gentle, pretty
clothes in the luxury investment category, flattering,
and elegant, usually in the finest English and Scottish
wools, cashmeres, and suedes. She was especially
admired for her leathers, which she treated like jersey, and for her jerseys in tailored shapes that are
completely soft and feminine, distinguished by the
most refined details—the slight bell cut of a cuff, the
subtle flare of a jacket.

Hardworking and demanding, Muir believed in
technical training as the only serious foundation for a
designer; she encouraged and worked with British art
students, urging more emphasis on craft, less on art.
Following her death, the company has continued with
a design team that had worked with Muir.

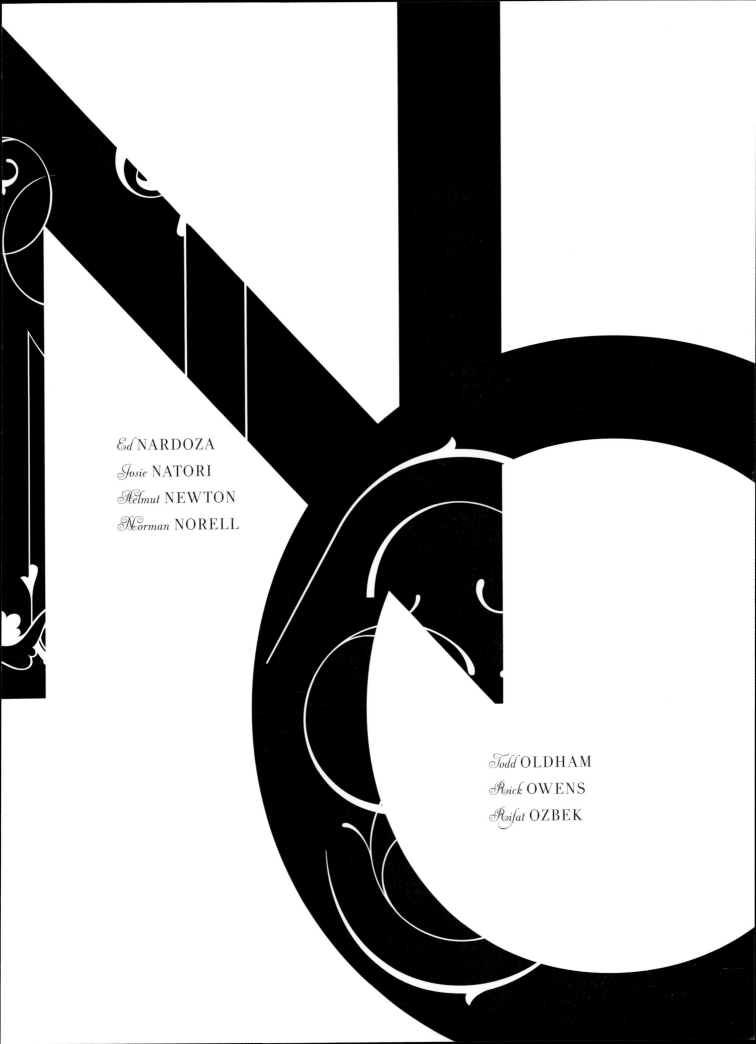

Ed NARDOZA
Josie NATORI
Helmut NEWTON
Norman NORELL

Todd OLDHAM
Rick OWENS
Rifat OZBEK

Ed Nardoza

Editor Ed Nardoza.

BORN Edward Nardoza; New York, October 29, 1953

AWARDS Council of Fashion Designers of America (CFDA) *Eugenia Sheppard Award* (for fashion journalism), 2009

Ed Nardoza is currently editor-in-chief of *Women's Wear Daily*, a position he has held since 1991. He is also associate editorial director of Fairchild Fashion Group, with editorial responsibility for the company's business publications. Prior to *WWD*, he was editor of *Daily News Record*, the former business/fashion publication for the men's wear industry. Nardoza joined the Fairchild team in 1978 as a general assignment reporter for *Footwear News*.

At *WWD*, he expanded the paper's international coverage, marketing, media, financial and technology beats, and steered its reporting into varied distribution channels. During his tenure, the paper has targeted coverage of numerous vertical industries and launched new publications and special editions, including *WWD Collections*, a consumer/business hybrid covering the international collections scene for women's and men's published four times a year; *WWD Scoop*, a magazine covering international fashion and culture; *WWD Accessories*, a biannual trend magazine; *WWD Century* and *WWD Ninety*, histories of the industry and the newspaper, respectively; and *BeautyBiz*, a magazine about strategies in the cosmetic and fragrance businesses.

In 2008, *WWD* relaunched its global Web site, WWD.com, with a paid circulation, 24/7 news model. The site won Media Industry Newsletter's 2009 *Best of the Web Award* for design. His work is considered top notch in no small part because he considers all aspects of a fashion story; covering clothing is not just about trends for Nardoza, but about breaking stories on fascinating people, places, and businesses.

Designer Josie Natori.

niche when a friend back home sent her some hand-embroidered blouses and a Bloomingdale's buyer suggested that she lengthen them into nightshirts.

Natori designs rely on simple, sexy shapes in luxurious fabrics, usually with the signature Philippine embroideries and appliqués, lace, and feminine detailing. In addition to the sleepwear, made in the Philippines in her own factory, there are robes, bras, and panties, and accessories such as shawls of piña fabric, a pineapple derivative, and evening handbags of exotic skins or antique silks. There is also a hipper, more affordable Josie line; Natori Home; and Natorious, a ready-to-wear line launched in 2008.

Natori has received much recognition for her achievements. She is a member of many business groups, including the Council of Fashion Designers of America and the Fashion Group International, and is involved in a number of cultural institutions—the Asia Society, for one. She is also active in the Philippines on behalf of women and fashion.

BORN Josefina Almeda Cruz; Manila, Philippines, May 9, 1947

AWARDS *Galleon* Awards, 1998; *LaKandula Award*, 2007; "Peopling of America" Award, 2007

Before she became known for sophisticated, sensuous lingerie, Josie Natori had already established herself in the world of finance, as the first woman vice-president at Merrill Lynch. As a child she studied music in Manila, but with business genes in her blood (both her mother and grandmother were successful businesswomen), she moved to New York at age 17 to study economics at Manhattanville College. After her marriage and the birth of her son, Natori began casting around for something more creative to do, her own business. "I was really looking for something that would allow me to take advantage of being Filipino and a woman," she said. She found her

Josie Natori's opulent animal-print slip and wrap.

Helmut Newton

BORN Helmut Neustädter; Berlin, Germany, October 31, 1920

DIED Los Angeles, January 23, 2004

AWARDS Grand Prix National de la Photographie, 1990 (France) • Das Grosse Verdienstkeruz, 1992 (Germany)

Helmut Newton achieved enormous fame in the latter portion of the twentieth century as a provocative and controversial photographer. His subject of choice was nude women, and he seemed to never run out of creative ways to capture their images. He grew up in Berlin and attended the American school there, followed by another school in Berlin-Grunewald. Between 1936 and 1938, he apprenticed with fashion photographer Yva (Elsa Neulander Simon). However, the Nazi occupation prompted him to flee the city in 1938. Newton first went to Singapore, where he worked as a reporter and portrait photographer at *The Straits Times*. He subsequently made his way to Australia and became a citizen in 1946.

His photographs gained a reputation for their use of bold color, light, and controversial style. He preferred to shoot out on the streets or, if he did use an interior, he would manipulate the setting to gain every advantage. These methods intrigued *Vogue* magazine, and in 1956, he acquired a contract with the British edition of that fashion publication. Newton quit after less than a year to work for Australian *Vogue*. By 1961, he had advanced to a full time position with French *Vogue*. In addition, he oversaw editorial photography of French *Elle* from 1964–1966. He established a trademark of erotic, stylized scenes, often with sado-masochistic and festishistic touches.

After a severe heart attack in 1970, Newton's wife, actress June Brunell, took over some of the photography. However by 1975, he had recovered, and opened his first one-man show at the Nikon Gallery in Paris. He has published more than 35 books of his work and received numerous awards: In 1992, Newton was appointed "Officer des Arts, Lettres et Sciences" by S.A.S. Princess Caroline of Monaco, and in 1996, he was honored as "Commandeur de l'Ordre des Arts et des Lettres" by the French Minister of Culture. For his 80th birthday in 2000, there was an exhibition in his honor at the New National Gallery in Berlin.

Photographer Helmut Newton (center) and models.

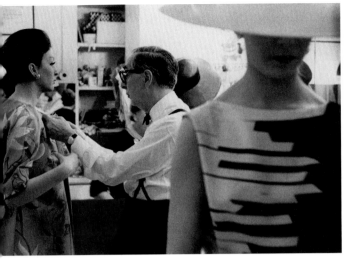

Designer Norman Norell (center) and model.

BORN Norman David Levinson; Noblesville, Indiana, April 20, 1900

DIED New York City, October 25, 1972

AWARDS Coty American Fashion Critics' Award First "*Winnie*," 1943; First *Return Award*, 1951; First to be elected to *Hall of Fame*, 1958 • Neiman Marcus Award, 1942 • Parsons *Medal for Distinguished Achievement*, 1956 • City of New York Bronze Medallion, 1972 • Pratt Institute, Brooklyn, Honorary Degree of Doctor of Fine Arts, 1962, conferred upon him in recognition of his influence on American design and taste, and for his valuable counseling and guidance to students of design, the first designer so honored

Norman Norell and HATTIE CARNEGIE could be said to be the parents of American high fashion, setting standards of taste, knowledge, and talent, and opening the way for the creators of today.

As a young child, Norell moved with his family to Indianapolis, where his father opened a haberdashery. From early boyhood his ambition was to be an artist and in 1919 he moved to New York to study painting at Parsons School of Design. He switched to costume design, and in 1921 graduated from Pratt Institute. His first costume assignment was for *A Sainted Devil*, a Rudolph Valentino film. He created Gloria Swanson's costumes for *Zaza*, and then joined the staff of the Brooks Costume Company.

In 1924, in a move from costume to dress design, he went to work for dress manufacturer Charles Armour, remaining until 1928 when he joined Hattie Carnegie. He stayed with Carnegie until 1940, not only absorbing her knowledge and sense of fashion, but traveling with her to Europe where he was exposed to the best design of the day. In 1941 he teamed with manufacturer Anthony Traina to form Traina-Norell. The association lasted 19 years, at which time Norell left to become president of his own firm, Norman Norell, Inc. The first collection was presented in June 1960.

From his very first collection under the Traina-Norell label, the designer established himself as a major talent, quickly becoming known for a lithe, cleanly proportioned silhouette, an audacious use of rich fabrics, for faultless workmanship, precise tailoring, and purity of line. Over the years he maintained his leadership, setting numerous trends that have become part of the fashion vocabulary and are taken for granted today. He was first to show long evening skirts topped with sweaters, initiated cloth coats lined with fur for day and evening, which were spangled with sequins. He revived

Model in Norell brown dress, 1962.

Norman Norell, continued

the chemise, introduced the smoking robe, and perfected jumpers and pantsuits. His long, shimmering, sequined dresses were so simple they never went out of date, worn as long as their owners could fit into them and treasured even longer. The perfume Norell made in America, was a major success.

He was a founder and president of the Council of Fashion Designers of America (CFDA). On October 15, 1972, the eve of his retrospective show at the Metropolitan Museum of Art, Norell suffered a stroke; he died ten days later. His company continued for a brief period with GUSTAVE TASSELL as designer.

Sketch of Norell design, 1941.

Flamenco dancer wearing a pailletted-jersey top with black organza overskirt, 1964.

A yellow wool jersey double-breasted belted coat, 1967.

Designer Todd Oldham.

BORN Corpus Christi, Texas, October 22, 1961

AWARDS Council of Fashion Designers of America (CFDA) *Perry Ellis Award for New Fashion Talent*, 1991 • Dallas Fashion Award *Rising Star*, 1992; *Fashion Excellence Award*, 1993

Todd Oldham first appeared as "designer-as-showman." His desire to be a film director was an outlet in the bravura of his showings, attended by celebrity friends and with such features as rap music and drag performers on the runway. By his own account, Oldham barely made it through high school, never went to design school, and taught himself pattern-making. His first fashion experience was in the alterations department of a Polo/RALPH LAUREN boutique.

He started his business in Dallas in 1985 and two years later moved to New York. There he started Times Seven, making women's shirts in basic styles fastened with the uninhibited buttons that became a trademark: some were antique, many designed by his brother, Brad. In 1989 he signed with a Japanese company for a designer collection; his first formal presentation was for fall 1990, attracting considerable attention from the press and orders from stores. Oldham has been design consultant for the German firm Escada and worked successfully with MTV. His last runway collection was in fall 1998, and he has since sold his trademark to Jones Apparel group, which produces and markets Todd Oldham Jeans.

Aside from the Times Seven line, sold only in Japan, Oldham has concentrated on other interests, which are varied. He has designed hotel interiors, worked successfully as a photographer, and designed home furnishings for Target. He has also been active in a wide range of social causes, from AIDS to environmental conservation to child abuse to the humane treatment of animals.

Taking simple shapes, Oldham added unconventional prints or beading and embroidery done in India, sometimes quirky and whimsical, sometimes lavish. A mixture of the commercial with the offbeat, the clothes were very well made and sold in such bastions of the establishment as Bergdorf Goodman and Saks Fifth Avenue.

Other projects Oldham has designed for include, La-Z-Boy and FTD Florist. In 2007, he was named creative director of Old Navy. That same year, he became host of the reality television show *Top Design*.

Model wearing silk striped dress by Oldham.

Rick Owens

BORN California, 1962

AWARDS Council of Fashion Designers *Perry Ellis New Talent Award for Emerging Designers*, 2002 • *Cooper-Hewitt National Design* Award for Fashion Design, 2007 • Fashion Group International *Rule Breakers Award*, 2007

Rick Owens, originally from Southern California, where he studied art at Parsons in LA, now works out of Paris. In 1994, after dropping out of school he began his career as an indie designer with inspirations collected from the eccentric, broken world of Hollywood Boulevard. As his den of dissidents grew, so grew the attention of the New York fashion world.

His first runway show in New York was in 2001 and was sponsored by *Vogue* magazine, which led to his winning the CFDA PERRY ELLIS *Award for Emerging Talent* in 2002. Moving to Paris in 2003, he became artistic director of the centuries-old furrier, Revillon.

Inspired by furniture designer Eileen Grey and Romanian sculptor Constantin Brâncusi, in 2005 he introduced a furniture collection using raw plywood, resin, fiberglass, cashmere, and marble.

He opened his own boutique in Paris in 2006 and by 2007 started designing his own fur collection, Jardins du Palais Royal. That same year, he was awarded the *Cooper-Hewitt National Design Award* for Fashion Design, as well as the *Rule Breakers Award*, plus released his photo book titled *L'Ai-Je Bien*

Designer Rick Owens.

Descendu? The Rick Owens store in Tribeca, NYC, opened July 2008.

The embodiment of Rick Owens's style invokes a postapocalyptic, if not simply postadolescent period. He creates from a personal journey, from wreckage to recovery in dusty gray asymmetry. His fitted jackets along with draped knits cater to the rock star set, however, there are many wearable separates for those looking for function over form.

Most recently introduced is Rick Owens Lilies, a collection of simple yet sterling basics, the perfect introduction to Owens's aesthetic. Also, hot on the scene is DRKSHDW, a reinterpretation of his design ideology in denim. In 2009, Rick Owens opened stores in Tokyo and London.

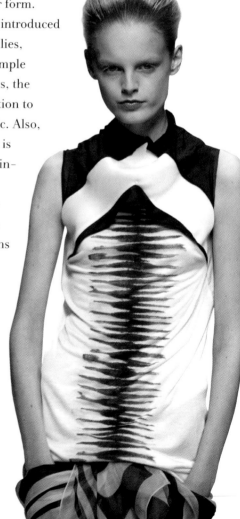

Above: Fall 2009.

Right: Spring 2008.

Designer Rifat Ozbek.

The influence of London street fashion was evident in Ozbek's early work but translated with refinement and understatement. He has also been inspired by the way African natives mix traditional and Western elements in their dress and by the Italian and French movies he saw when growing up. He admires the fashion greats: BALENCIAGA for cut, SCHIAPARELLI for her sense of humor, CHANEL for timelessness, and YVES SAINT LAURENT for classicism. From his first collections and whatever the inspiration, his clothes have been sophisticated and controlled, without the rough-edged wackiness associated with much of London fashion.

BORN Turkey, 1953

AWARD British Fashion Council, *Designer of the Year,* 1988

Rifat Ozbek arrived in England in 1970. He studied architecture for two years at the University of Liverpool then switched to fashion, studying at St. Martins School of Art. After graduation in 1977, he worked in Italy for Walter Albini and an Italian manufacturer before returning to London and a stint designing for Monsoon, a made-in-India line. He presented his first collection under his own label in October 1984, showing out of his apartment; by his third collection he had a stylish new studio off Bond Street. In 1991 he moved his business to Milan, where he showed his collections until 1994 before showing in Paris.

Spring 2007.

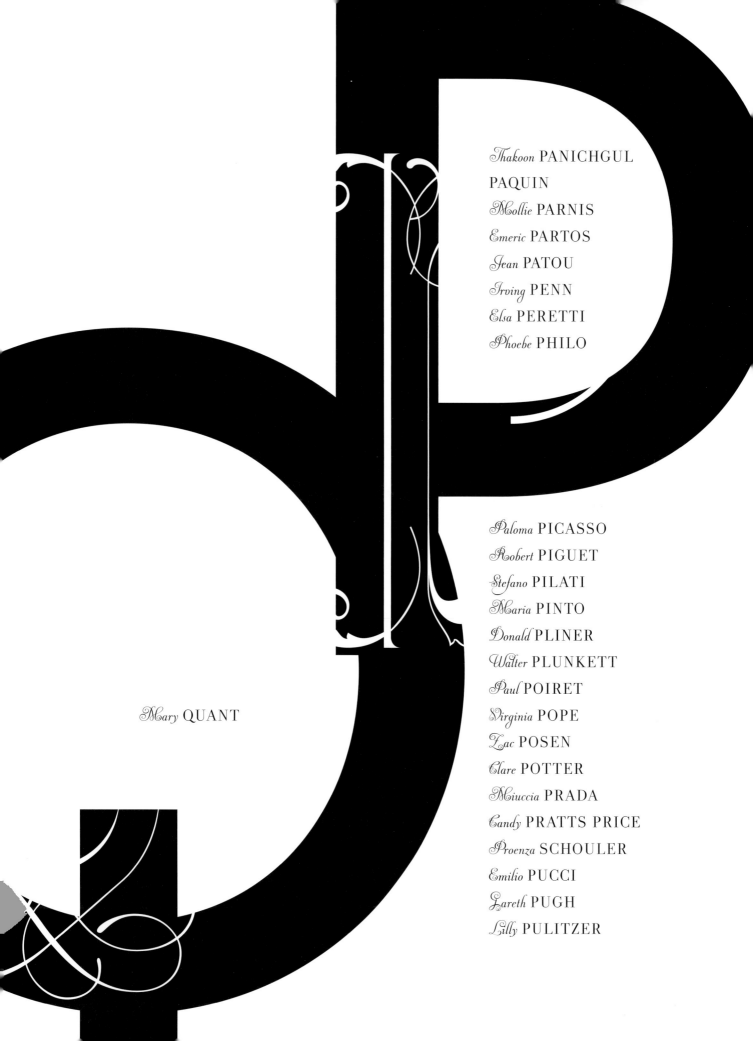

Thakoon PANICHGUL
PAQUIN
Mollie PARNIS
Emeric PARTOS
Jean PATOU
Irving PENN
Elsa PERETTI
Phoebe PHILO

Paloma PICASSO
Robert PIGUET
Stefano PILATI
Maria PINTO
Donald PLINER
Walter PLUNKETT
Paul POIRET
Virginia POPE
Zac POSEN
Clare POTTER
Miuccia PRADA
Candy PRATTS PRICE
Proenza SCHOULER
Emilio PUCCI
Gareth PUGH
Lilly PULITZER

Mary QUANT

Thakoon Panichgul

BORN Chiang Rai, Thailand, September 25, 1974

AWARDS Ecco Domani Fashion Foundation Award for New Talent, 2005

Thakoon Panichgul came to the U.S. from Thailand when he was only eleven-years-old, but didn't begin his fashion career until almost 20 years later. After pursuing a degree in business from Boston University, Panichgul took a position as a merchandiser for J. Crew. He then moved on to an editorial position with *Harper's Bazaar*, and while there, took tailoring classes at Parsons School of Design in his spare time. In 2004—at the age of 29—he started his eponymous label Thakoon, characterized by a sophisticated and minimal style. His designs are at once ethereal and urban—and heavily influenced by his Eastern heritage.

In 2006, he was asked to create a capsule collection for Nine West, and a year later he collaborated with the Gap to develop a limited-edition line of T-shirts. That same year he was a runner-up for the CDFA/ *Vogue* Fashion Award. In 2008, he debuted his collection for the Hogan brand—an accessory and shoe brand owned by Tod's—and was catapulted into the spotlight when First Lady Michelle Obama wore his floral print dress on the final day of the 2008 Democratic National Convention.

His chic, simple, and restrained designs are a favorite of celebrities such as Natalie Portman, Demi Moore, and America Ferrera.

Designer Thakoon Panichgul.

Above: Fall 2009.
Left: Spring 2009.

Light coat with a Lynx fur trim over a sleeveless, two-piece crêpe dress, 1928.

FOUNDED Paris, France, 1891
CLOSED 1956

One of the couture's great artists, Jeanne Paquin (Pack-an) trained at Maison Rouff and opened her couture house with backing from her husband Isidore, a banker and businessman. The House of Paquin developed into a major couture force, becoming synonymous with elegance during the first decade of the twentieth century.

The Paquin reputation for beautiful designs was enhanced by the decor of the establishment and the lavishness of its showings, as well as by the Paquins' extensive social life. Management of the house and its relations with its employees were excellent, some workers remaining for more than 40 years, and department heads were women. The Paquin standards were so high that there was always a demand from other couture houses for any employees deciding to leave.

Jeanne Paquin was the first woman to achieve importance in haute couture. She was chairman of the fashion section of the 1900 Paris Exposition and President of the Chambre Syndicale from 1917 to 1919. Hers was the first couture house to open foreign branches—in London, Madrid, and Buenos Aires. She was the first to take mannequins to the opera and the races, as many as ten in the same costume. The house is credited with being the first to make fur garments that were soft and supple.

She was a gifted colorist, a talent especially evident in her glamorous and romantic evening dresses. Other specialties were fur-trimmed tailored suits and coats, furs, lingerie, and blue serge suits with gold braid and buttons; accessories were made in-house. She claimed not to make any two dresses exactly alike, individualizing each model to the woman for whom it was made. Customers included queens of Belgium, Portugal, and Spain, as well as the actresses and courtesans of the era. Paquin retired and sold the house to an English firm in 1920. She died in 1936.

The House of Paquin witnessed a number of successors and merged with the House of Worth in 1953. The company closed shortly after in 1956.

Robe featuring high-waisted, polonaise style tunic and narrow-trained skirt, 1913.

Mollie Parnis

BORN New York City, March 18, 1905
DIED New York City, July 18, 1992

Mollie Parnis produced flattering, feminine dresses and ensembles for well-to-do woman over 30, emphasizing becomingness in beautiful fabrics, a conservative interpretation of current trends. She felt that good design did not mean dresses that had to be thrown away each year or that went out of date. The boutique collection followed the same principles but with a moderate price tag and the Studio collection, started in 1979, aimed at a younger woman.

The eldest of five children of Austrian immigrants, Parnis always knew she'd have to work for whatever she got. After leaving high school, she went to work in a blouse showroom as an assistant saleswoman and was soon designing.

In 1933 she and her husband Leon Livingston, a textile designer, opened a ready-to-wear firm, Parnis-Livingston. From there she went on to become one of the most successful businesswomen on Seventh Avenue, heading a firm which grew into a

Designer Mollie Parnis (right) with models.

Model wearing a design by Mollie Parnis.

multimillion dollar enterprise, Mollie Parnis Inc. She closed her business briefly in 1962 when her husband died, but reopened it again three months later. She shut down again in 1984 but became bored and went back to work full time at Chevette Lingerie, owned by her nephew, Neal Hochman. Her first loungewear collection was for fall 1985.

A formidable organizer, Parnis routinely managed to administer her business, plan and edit collections with her design staff; supervise selling, advertising, and promotion; and follow through on her civic interests—all in a day that began at 10 a.m. and seldom went beyond 5 p.m. She collected art and was also a noted hostess with a special affinity for journalists and politicians.

Parnis was well known as a philanthropist. She contributed scholarships to fashion schools and gave vest-pocket parks to New York City and Jerusalem, both of which honored her for her outstanding contributions. She was a founder of the Council of Fashion Designers of America and served on the Board of Directors.

BORN Budapest, Hungary, March 18, 1905
DIED New York City, December 2, 1975

AWARDS Coty American Fashion Critics' Award
Special Award (furs), 1957

Emeric Partos studied art in Budapest and Paris, and jewelry design in Switzerland. He served in the French Army during World War II and in the underground movement, where he met Alex Maguy, a couturier who also designed for the theater. After the war, Partos joined Maguy, designing coats and also ballet costumes.

In 1947 he went to work for his friend CHRISTIAN DIOR, whom he considered the greatest living design-er. He stayed with Dior for three years creating coats and suits, but was wooed away in 1950 to be design consultant for Maximilian Furs. He designed furs for Maximilian for five years before moving to Bergdorf Goodman to head its fur department, remaining there until his death twenty years later.

At Bergdorf's, Partos was given a free hand with the most expensive pelts available. He showed a sense of fantasy and fun with intarsia furs such as a white mink jacket inlaid with colored mink flowers, and mink worked in two-tone stripes or box shapes. He designed coats that could be shortened or lengthened by zipping sections off or on, further innovated with silk or cotton raincoats used as slipcovers for mink coats. In addition, he was noted for subtle, beautifully cut classics in fine minks, sables, and broadtail. One of the first to treat furs as ready-to-wear, Partos was a prolific source of ideas, noted for his theatrics but also as a master of construction and detail. He was a favorite with conservative customers as well as with personalities such as Barbra Streisand.

Model wearing design by Emeric Partos.

Jean Patou

Designer Jean Patou.

BORN Normandy, France, 1887
DIED Paris, France, March 8, 1936

Known as the father of sportswear, Jean Patou's first couture venture was a small house called Parry. It opened in 1914, just in time for World War I, which forced him to cancel his first major showing. After four years in the Army as a captain of Zouaves, he reopened under his own name in 1919. The house was an immediate success with private clients; the clothes had simplicity and elegance and looked as if they were intended to be worn by real women, not just by mannequins.

An admirer of American business methods, Patou introduced daily staff meetings, a profit-sharing plan for executives, and a bonus system for mannequins. He was also an excellent showman: he brought six American models to Paris in 1925, using them alongside his French mannequins; he instituted gala champagne evening openings, had a cocktail bar in his shop, and chose exquisite bottles for his per-

fumes. These included Moment Suprême and Joy, promoted as the world's most expensive perfume. He was among the first couturiers to have colors and fabrics produced especially for him, and is given credit for being the first in 1929 to return the waistline to its normal position and to lengthen skirts, which he dropped dramatically to the ankle, and the first to put his initials on clothing.

After Patou's death, the house remained open under the direction of his brother-in-law, Raymond Barbas, with a series of resident designers including: MARC BOHAN (1953–1957), KARL LAGERFELD (1958–1963), Michel Goma (1963–1974), Angelo Tarlazzi (1973–1976), Roy Gonzalez (1976–1981), and CHRISTIAN LACROIX (1981–1987).

Evening dress, 1925.

Photographer Irving Penn.

BORN Plainfield, New Jersey, June 16, 1917
DIED New York, New York, October 7, 2009

A major figure in the field of fashion photography, Irving Penn attended the Philadelphia Museum School of Industrial Art and studied design from 1934 to 1938 with *Harper's Bazaar's* renowned artistic director and developer of talent, Alexey Brodovitch. Penn also freelanced as an artist for *Harper's Bazaar*

from 1937–1939. In 1941 he spent a year painting in Mexico. His first *Vogue* photographs appeared in 1943, the beginning of a long and fruitful relationship with more that 150 *Vogue* covers over 50 years. After war service in the American Field Service in Italy and India, his career blossomed, resulting in a wide variety of photographs of fashion, personalities, and travel. In addition to Condé Nast publications, his client roster included international advertising agencies. In 1950, he married model Lisa Fonssagrives, with whom he first collaborated in 1947 for photographs of the Paris collections; these were unadorned but rich in feeling. Their later location trip to Morocco foreshadowed his future interests and so-called anthropological pictures.

At a time when fashion photography was marked by elaborately artificial lighting, Penn used his lights to simulate daylight, an important and influential move. Posing his models against the plainest backgrounds, he achieved a monumental simplicity and clarity, an elegant femininity. On his location trips, he employed the same economy of means for portraits of native people. In the manner of nineteenth-century photographers he used a portable studio he built to ensure the desired working conditions in the Cameroons, Peru, and other areas where no studios existed.

His work has been exhibited in one-man shows at the Museum of Modern Art in New York and the Metropolitan Museum of Art, and is in the permanent collections of both. His works were also shown in 2005 at the National Gallery of Art in Washington, D.C., at an exhibition entitled "Irving Penn: Platinum Prints"; the Morgan Library in 2007; and at the J. Paul Getty Museum in September 2009. He is also the author of numerous photographic books, from 1960 with *Moments Preserved* through 1991 with *Passage*.

Elsa Peretti

BORN Florence, Italy, May 1, 1940

AWARDS Coty American Fashion Critics' Award *Special Award (jewelry)*, 1971 • Award for Outstanding Contribution to the Cultured Pearl Industry of America and Japan, 1978 • The Fashion Group *Night of the Stars Award*, 1986 • Council of Fashion Designer's of America, *Accessories Designer of the Year*, 1966

The daughter of a well-to-do Roman family, Elsa Peretti earned a diploma in interior design and worked briefly for a Milanese architect. In 1961 she went to Switzerland, then moved on to London and started modeling. She was seen by models' agent Wilhelmina, who suggested that Peretti come to New York. It was there that she worked for a handful of top houses, including HALSTON and OSCAR DE LA RENTA.

In 1969 Peretti designed a few pieces of silver jewelry, which Halston and GIORGIO SANT'ANGELO showed with their collections. These witty objects—a heart-shaped buckle, pendants in the form of small vases, a silver urn pendant that holds a fresh flower—were soon joined by a horseshoe-shaped silver buckle on a long leather belt and other designs in horn, ebony, and ivory. She also designed the bottles for Halston's fragrance and cosmetic lines. In 1974 she began working with Tiffany & Co., the first time in 25 years the company had carried silver jewelry. Among her much-copied designs are necklaces with small, open, slightly lopsided heart pendants and Diamonds by the Yard—diamonds spaced at intervals on a fine gold chain. She has also designed desk and table accessories for the firm.

Peretti is influenced in her work by a love of nature and inspired by Japanese designs. She works in Spain and New York, and has traveled to the Orient to study semiprecious stones. Prototypes for the silver and ivory designs are made by artisans in Barcelona, the crystal pieces are produced in Germany. As a celebration of her 50th birthday and 15-year association with Tiffany, Peretti was honored by the Fashion Institute of Technology in April 1990 with a retrospective exhibit of her work. It was called "Fifteen of My Fifty with Tiffany."

Celebrities Jodie Foster, Gwyneth Paltrow, and Jennifer Aniston are just a few of her devoted fans.

Designer Elsa Peretti.

Designer Phoebe Philo.

Spring 2005.

BORN Paris, France, 1973

Phoebe Philo grew up in England in a London suburb and entered Central St. Martins College of Art and Design in 1993, graduating three years later. In 1997 she joined the French ready-to-wear firm CHLOÉ, as assistant to her friend STELLA MCMARTNEY who had just been made creative director. When McCartney left Chloé in 2001 to form her own business, Philo moved into her position.

In her first collection she immediately established her own style—cool and sexy, yet romantic and luxurious, with a modern edge appealing to the new, younger customer, attracted to the label under McCartney's tenure.

Philo was named creative director of Céline in 2008, replacing Ivana Omazic, and returning to her fashion roots after a sabbatical from the industry, beginning in 2005. Her first collection under the Céline label was presented in March for the fall/winter 2009 season. Céline is owned by the fashion division of LVHM.

Céline, spring 2010.

Paloma Picasso

Designer Paloma Picasso.

BORN Paris, France, April 19, 1949

Not only is Paloma Picasso the daughter of two artists, one of them a monumental figure in twentieth-century art, but she is also a successful designer in her own right. She is at the center of a burgeoning business, involved in everything from jewelry to perfume and cosmetics to home design. Her first jewelry collection was in 1971 for the Greek firm, Zolotas. In 1972 she met Rafael Lopez-Cambil, an Argentine-born playwright who she married in 1978. She designed sets and costumes for him and, after their marriage, Picasso's husband devised a strategy aimed at establishing her name and work in the world of design. They later divorced. In 1980, Paloma Picasso joined Tiffany & Co. with a collection of gold jewelry set with precious and semiprecious stones. She continues designing for them today; her style is marked by bold, sensuous shapes, sometimes inspired by urban graffiti, sometimes of a Renaissance opulence. In addition to cosmetics and perfume, her other U.S. design projects have included top-of-the-line handbags and a less expensive, more casual accessories collection, as well as eyewear, tablewear, fabrics, and wall coverings.

Designer Robert Piguet (right) fitting a model.

BORN Yverdon, Switzerland, 1901
DIED Lausanne, Switzerland, February 22, 1953

Robert Piguet was the son of a Swiss banker and was expected to follow his father's profession. Instead, he went to Paris in 1918 to study design. He trained with the conservative REDFERN and the brilliant POIRET, then opened his own house on the rue du Cirque. In 1933 he moved his salon to the Rond Point where he designed little himself, relying largely on the work of freelance designers. A number of designers, including DIOR and GIVENCHY, worked for him at the outset of their careers; JAMES GALANOS spent three months there working without salary. Dior said, "Robert Piguet taught me the virtues of simplicity . . . how to suppress!" Piguet's clothes appealed to a younger customer: perfectly cut, tailored suits with vests, black-and-white dresses of refined simplicity, after-noon dresses, fur-trimmed coats especially styled

for petite women. He had a flair for dramatic effects, which he used in his extensive work for the theater. In the United States his influence was greater on manufacturers than on custom design.

An aristocratic, solitary man, Piguet was super-sensitive and changeable, with a love of intrigue. Elegant and charming, he was a connoisseur of paint-ing, literature, and music. He suffered from ill health throughout his life, retiring to seclusion after each showing to recuperate from the strain of his profes-sion. He closed his house in 1951.

Rayon and crêpe dress with black wool cape, 1935.

Stefano Pilati

BORN 1955 Milan, Italy

Stefano Pilati took over creative control of the YVES SAINT LAURENT couture (along with the ready-to-wear line Rive Gauche) in 2004 from GUCCI group's marketing head, TOM FORD. The latter was viewed by French fashion pundits as a cultural vandal; indeed Ford moved the brand far into the accessory market—focusing on his YSL emblazoned chunky handbag.

Not yet 40, Pilati had joined YSL in 2000, when he landed there from Miu Miu. He was charged with restoring Yves Saint Laurent to its former chic glory for a new "bohemian's jet set." The latter aesthetic was epitomized by the "Le Smoking" pantsuit—created by the handsome, intelligent, and artistic Saint-Laurent in the 1960s. The look was popularized with the help of Nouvelle Vague, which had embraced it. In June of 2008 Saint Laurent died, giving the brand a window for publicity that the company capitalized on.

By that time, Pilati—who had a rocky first two years as creative director—was finding his footing and the resulting designs were influencing popular high-end prêt-a-porter lines like Max Mara. His first YSL show was an infamous flop, mostly remembered for flowing tulip-shaped skirts that were dismissed by critics. Since that show Pilati has

Left: Spring/summer 2009.
Right: Autumn/winter 2008.

Designer Stefano Pilati.

retrenched, with an eye toward Saint Laurent's comprehensive archive. Pilati is seen as a steady hand guiding the brand back to its cosmopolitan roots. His spring 2009 collection look received notions of androgyny a bit further. The line featured geometric shapes and soft, luxuriant fabrics.

Designer Maria Pinto.

In 2008, her profile suddenly went national when future First Lady Michelle Obama wore a Pinto-designed purple sheath dress the night her husband won the Democratic presidential nomination. Since then, Pinto has seen demand for her designs increase dramatically. Known for strong yet feminine lines—her love of sculpture influences the way she handles seams and draping—Pinto often works with exotic fabrics and unusual materials such as rope, shaped into lacework. Classic with a unique flair, her graceful and modern design sensibility seems poised for a larger stage.

BORN Chicago, Illinois, 1957

AWARDS Gold Coast Fashion Award, 1998; *Chicago Magazine Best of Fashion Award*, 2000

Maria Pinto had an early interest in fashion and art. She graduated from the School of the Art Institute of Chicago with a degree in fine arts, and also studied at Parsons School of Design and the Fashion Institute of Technology in New York. After working for two years as an assistant to GEOFFREY BEENE, where she studied the way his garments were constructed, she designed samples of her own that were noticed by buyers at Bergdorf Goodman. Her women's accessories collection debuted there in 1991. Pinto based her business in her hometown and built up a discerning clientele over the next several years, creating custom designs for prominent local women such as Oprah Winfrey.

Spring 2010.

Donald Pliner

BORN 1943, Chicago Illinois

Donald Pliner was destined to make shoes. His family owned a shoe business, and after learning how the family business was run, he opened his own store in Pappagallo, Beverly Hills, in 1967. The company was so successful that he turned a profit of $1 million in the first year. In 1971, he opened The Right Bank Clothing Company, which was renamed The Right Bank Shoe Company three years later. His was the first American store that sold European designer brands. The brand offered clothing, shoes, and accessories.

Designer Donald Pliner.

Shoes designed by Donald Pliner.

In 1984, Pliner became head of a new line of Spanish footwear called Glacé, and within two years the line was sold internationally. He then reintroduced his own line of footwear and accessories in 1989 in Adventure Mall in Florida.

In 1994, he created an all-elastic shoe, which was so successful that he introduced a men's shoe line in 1998. Pliner's shoes are known for their comfortable fit. The Donald Pliner motto is to "live the luxury of comfortable fashion."

In 2002, he re-launched his handbag collections. The Couture handbag line is produced in Italy, and the Donald Pliner handbag line is produced in China. By 2007, he launched a line called Friends of Babydoll Pliner, not for kids, but for dogs. It offers accessories, outerwear, collars, and carriers.

Donald Pliner and his wife Lisa are cofounders of The Peace for the Children Foundation, which was "created to channel funds to deserving projects and initiatives that advance peace, care, and welfare to children in need."

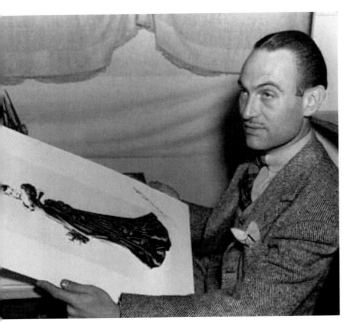

Designer Walter Plunkett.

In addition to his design duties, Plunkett was manager of the RKO wardrobe department, and was in charge of payroll, budget, hiring, and firing. Underpaid and overworked, he quit RKO in 1935, returning the next year at Katharine Hepburn's request to do her costumes for *Mary of Scotland*. From then until his retirement in 1966, he worked on his own terms as a freelance designer, dressing some of the greatest stars in some of Hollywood's most ambitious productions, sometimes sharing design duties with other designers such as TRAVIS BANTON and IRENE SHARAFF.

BORN Oakland, California, June 2, 1902
DIED Santa Monica, California, March 8, 1982

Walter Plunkett was best known for period costumes, and particularly for *Gone With the Wind*. In the mid-1920s, after law studies and an attempt at an acting career, he took a job in the wardrobe department at FBO Studios, then specializing in westerns. Within a few months, the studio changed its name to RKO and Plunkett, without formal training, became its costume designer. He was soon put in charge of setting up a design department. In 1931, after designing for a series of potboilers, he got his first important assignment, *Cimarron*, starring Irene Dunne. In 1933, he did *Flying Down to Rio*, the first film in which Fred Astaire danced with Ginger Rogers, and in 1935 costumed Katharine Hepburn in *Alice Adams*, the beginning of a long collaboration with the actress.

Vivian Leigh in *Gone with the Wind*, wearing a Walter Plunkett design, 1939.

Paul Poiret

BORN Paris, France, April 20, 1879
DIED Paris, France, April 28, 1944

Fascinated by the theater and the arts, Paul Poiret was a flamboyant and theatrical figure, spending fortunes on fetes, pageants, and costume balls, and on decorating his homes. He designed costumes for actresses such as Réjane and Sarah Bernhardt; his friends included Diaghilev, Leon Bakst, Raoul Dufy, ERTÉ, and Iribe.

As a youth, while apprenticed to an umbrella maker, Poiret taught himself costume sketching. He sold his first sketches to MADELEINE CHERUIT at Raudnitz Soeurs, joined JACQUES DOUCET in 1896, and spent four years working for WORTH before opening his own house in 1904.

Considered by many to be one of the greatest originators of feminine fashion, Poiret was extravagantly talented, with a penchant for the bizarre and dramatic. While his forte was costume, the modern silhouette was to a great extent his invention. He freed women from corsets and petticoats, and introduced the first, modern, straight-line dress. Yet, he also invented the harem and hobble skirts, so narrow at the hem that walking was almost impossible. His minaret skirt, inspired by and

Designer Paul Poiret.

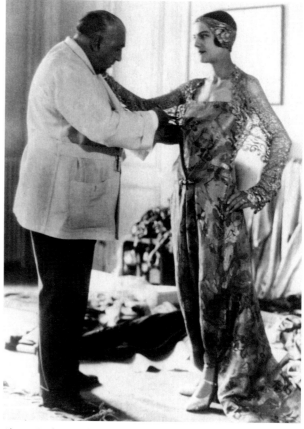

Above: Paul Poiret fitting a model.
Left: Metal, silk, and cotton dress, 1911.

bit parts in movies, wrote his autobiography, and moved to the south of France. He spent his last years in poverty and died of Parkinson's disease in a charity hospital in 1944. Poiret's extraordinary imagination and achievements flowered in the brilliant epoch of Diaghilev and Bakst. It influenced the taste of two decades.

Above: Turban designed by Poiret, 1911. Illustrated by Georges Lepape.

Right: An overskirt wired to give a "lampshade effect" also known as a "sorbet," 1912.

named after a play he costumed, spread worldwide. Influenced by Diaghilev's Ballets Russes, he designed a Russian tunic coat, straight in line and belted, made from sumptuous materials. His taste for orientalism showed up in little turbans and tall aigrettes with which he adorned his models, and he scandalized society in 1911 by taking mannequins to the Auteuil races dressed in *jupes culottes*, also called Turkish trousers.

He established a crafts school where Dufy for a while designed textiles, and was the first couturier to present a perfume. In 1912 he was the first to travel to other countries to present his collection, taking along 12 mannequins. In 1914, along with Worth, PAQUIN, Cheruit, CALLOT SOEURS, he founded the Protective Association of French dressmakers and became its first president.

Unable to adjust his style to changes brought about by World War I, Poiret went out of business in 1924. Bankrupt and penniless, he was divorced by his wife in 1929. Four years later he was offered a job designing ready-to-wear, but his attitude toward money was so irresponsible that the venture failed. He took

Virginia Pope

BORN Chicago, Illinois, June 29, 1885
DIED New York City, January 16, 1978

As fashion editor at the *New York Times* from 1933 to 1955, Virginia Pope is credited with practically inventing fashion reportage. One of the first to look for news in the wholesale market, she reported on the people who made clothes at a time when only Paris fashion was considered newsworthy. She encouraged the American fashion industry in its early years, originating the Fashions of The Times fashion show in 1942 as a showcase for American designers and staging the show each fall for the next nine years. In 1952 the show became a twice-yearly fashion supplement of the same name still published by the *Times*.

Following her father's death, the five-year-old Virginia was taken to Europe by her mother; together they toured the continent for the next 15 years. She became fluent in French, German, and Italian, and familiar with the best of European art and music. They returned to Chicago in 1905. Pope served in the Red Cross during World War I, and then tried various careers in Chicago and New York, including social work, the theater, book translations, and writing.

A late starter in journalism, Pope had a long run. Her first published pieces, which ran in the *New York Times*, were interviews with a visiting German theater group and articles about an Italian neighborhood, results of her facility in languages. She joined the *Times* as a member of the Sunday staff in 1925 and 8 years later became fashion editor, a position she held and developed for 22 years. Following her retirement, Pope joined the staff of *Parade* magazine as fashion editor; her name remained on the masthead until her death.

In addition, she held the Edwin Goodman chair established by Bergdorf Goodman at the Fashion Institute of Technology, giving a course on "Fashion in Contemporary Living." She could often be seen on Seventh Avenue with her students, escorting them to fashion shows and behind the scenes to see how a business worked. She also believed that exposure to culture was essential to a designer's development and regularly took students to performances at the Metropolitan Opera. While her personal style was of the establishment, she understood innovation and could look at clothes objectively. Referring to her conservative appearance and "grande dame" reputation, a fellow editor once said, "she could play the Queen of England without rehearsal."

he was one of ten students chosen to submit designs to the "Curvaceous" exhibit of Victorian underwear at the Victoria and Albert Museum (2001–2002). His contribution was a fitted, six-foot column constructed from vertical strips of glossy brown leather held together by hundreds of hooks and eyes that could be unhooked at any point. It won the V & A prize and became part of the permanent collection.

Posen's designs—dresses, blouses, coats—rely to a great extent on his favored bias cut and possess both disciplined construction and refined workmanship. They have a very modern feminin-ity, sexy without vulgarity, and have been worn by actresses and models such as Natalie Portman and Coco Rocha. They have also been sold at Henri Bendel in New York. In 2004, SEAN JOHN owner Sean Combs acquired half of Posen's company, laying down a business partnership and plans to expand the Posen brand. August 2005 marked the debut of Posen's denim line for 7 For All Mankind.

Above: Designer Zac Posen.

Right: Fall 2009

BORN Zachary Posen; New York City, October 24, 1980

AWARDS Ecco Domani Fashion Foundation Award (one of five young designers), 2002 • Council of Fashion Designers of America (CFDA) *Swarovski-Perry Ellis Award for Women's wear*, 2004

A precocious talent whose designs first showed up on the backs of celebrities who just happened to be friends or schoolmates, Zac Posen was born into the art world, his father a successful painter. From 1996 to 1998—after school, on weekends, and holidays—he interned with Richard Martin at the Costume Institute of the Metropolitan Museum of Art. There he developed a passion for the work of MADELEINE VIONNET and was able to study her bias-cut designs up close. While at London's Central St. Martins College of Art and Design,

Clare Potter

BORN Jersey City, New Jersey, 1903
DIED Fort Ann, New York, January 5, 1999

AWARDS First Lord & Taylor Award (for distinguished designing in the field of sports clothes for women), 1938 • Neiman Marcus Award, 1939 • Coty Fashion Critics' Award, 1946

Clare Potter belonged to the small, influential group of women designers generally considered the inventors of American sportswear—a group that included CLAIRE MCCARDELL and TINA LESER. In the 1930s they were among the first to be recognized by name.

She developed an interest in art during high school and went on to The Art Students League of New York,

Designer Clare Potter.

where she took a draping course though she didn't know how to sew. She then switched to Pratt Institute in Brooklyn and after graduation found work with a dress manufacturer. In 1948 she formed a company in partnership with a former magazine editor and by the mid-1950s was in business for herself.

Potter loved sports and designed for an active woman like herself who preferred casual clothes that were also sophisticated and discreet. Even for eveningwear she stayed casual with a skirt and shirt or pants and a tunic; her evening sweaters were especially noteworthy. She simplified, got rid of ornamentation, and was admired for her use of color and uncomplicated textures. While not as adventurous as McCardell, she was equally immune to European influences and shared her understanding of how the modern American woman lived.

Mink coat draped over a platinum-beige jumper dress, 1943.

Miuccia Prada

Designer Miuccia Prada.

Above: Pre-fall, 2009.

Right: Pre-fall, 2009.

BORN Maria Bianchi, Italy, May 10, 1949

AWARDS Council of Fashion Designers of America (CFDA) *International Award*, 1993

Miuccia Prada (Pra-dah) came into design through her connection with her family's firm, Fratelli Prada, maker of leather goods of the highest quality since 1915. A committed member of the Communist Party during and immediately after her university years, she resisted joining the family business until 1978 when she took over direction from her mother. Her first success was a black nylon backpack; later ones were handheld bags of the same fabric—washable, flexible, tough, and soft.

Her first ready-to-wear collection was for fall 1989, and in 1994 Prada took part in the New York showings. Her clothes, much coveted by the more advanced fashion press, are described as supremely comfortable—nothing on the hanger but coming to life on the body. There is a younger, less expensive Miu-Miu collection, and also men's clothes and accessories.

Under the leadership of Prada's husband, Patrizio Bertelli, the Prada firm has become one of fashion's foremost conglomerates. Its interests include leading international design houses, fine shoemakers, and major Italian production facilities. Prada also operates about 250 stores worldwide.

Candy Pratts Price

BORN Candida Rosa Theresa Pratts; New York City, February 18, 1950

AWARDS Council of Fashion Designers of America (CFDA) *Eugenia Sheppard Award*, 2008

Executive fashion director at Style.com, the online home of *Vogue* and *W*, Candy Pratts Price credits the site's success to her experience working for *Vogue*. She has said that the site functions as a magazine for the Web, breaking stories, and running original content and photos instead of acting as an aggregator.

Under Pratts Price's watch, the Web site has become a go-to spot for fashion insiders, featuring news from *Vogue* and *W* as well as original Web content and highly trafficked slideshows of collections during fashion weeks. The site has been lauded for its strong coverage of major designers as well as the attention it pays to those still up-and-coming.

Pratts Price joined *Vogue* as accessories editor in the 1980s and was soon promoted to fashion director of accessories. A graduate of the Fashion Institute of Technology, she has a sturdy fashion resume, having worked under famed merchandiser Marvin Traub as a designer of store windows and displays for Bloomingdales; as fashion director at *Harpers Bazaar*; and creative director for RALPH LAUREN. Additionally, Pratts Price worked as an executive producer on an E! Networks documentary about the Metropolitan Museum of Arts Jacqueline Kennedy exhibit and as creative director of the VH1/*Vogue* Fashion Awards. She also appears as a trend and fashion expert on television programs, including *Today* and *Good Morning America*. Pratts Price has credited her return to the Condé Nast fold to *Vogue* editor ANNA WINTOUR, who has acted as her mentor. She also published her first book in the fall of 2008, titled *American Fashion Accessories*.

Known for her sharp eye and keen fashion instinct, Pratts Price has credited her success to journalistic curiosity and a zeal for fashion.

Fashion director Candy Pratts Price.

BORN Lazaro Hernandez; Miami, Florida, 1979
Jack McCollough; New Jersey, 1979

AWARDS Council of Fashion Designers of America
(CFDA) *Perry Ellis Award for New Talent*, 2003

The two men met in 1999 at Parsons School of Design,
where they arrived after starting out on other career
paths—Hernandez in medicine, McCollough in glass
blowing. During his sophomore year at Parsons,
Hernandez interned at MICHAEL KORS, a spot he
obtained in storybook fashion through *Vogue* editor,
ANNA WINTOUR. After discovering she was on his plane
from Miami, he sent her a note mid-flight, describing
himself, his love of fashion, and his admiration for her;
she informed Kors that Hernandez should work for
him. Meanwhile, McCollough interned at MARC JACOBS.
They freelanced together at another company during
their senior year and were allowed to do their senior
thesis as a collaboration, producing a 15-piece collection with fabric donated by Kors. The collection was so

Above: Proenza Schouler designers Lazaro Hernandez
(left) and Jack McCollough (right).

Below, left: Fall 2008.

impressive that the judges recommended the designers to Barneys' vice president for merchandising, who
then bought the collection for the store.

Hernandez and McCollough shun the street-
fashion aesthetic to concentrate on grown-up clothes
"for women, not kids," giving a sophisticated twist
to classics. Their emphasis is on spare silhouettes in
fresh proportions and subdued colors, mostly black
and gray, in deluxe fabrics such as cashmere, angora,
and silk. The clothes have received an enthusiastic
response from celebrities and have been embraced by
both the press and retailers.

The duo founded Proenza Schouler (Pro-enza
Skool-er)—the name is a pairing of the designers'
mother's maiden names—in 2002. For spring 2007,
the design duo created an affordable collection of
clothing and accessories for Target. In 2008, Proenza
Schouler collaborated with Giuseppi Zanotti for a line
of shoes, which expanded to 100 styles in the spring
of 2009. Available in the New York, Milan, and Paris
showrooms, the styles include ballet slippers, loafers,
lace-up sandals, and heels.

Emilio Pucci

BORN Marchese di Barsento; Naples, Italy, 1914
DIED Florence, Italy, November 29, 1992

AWARDS Neiman Marcus Award, 1954 • Council of Fashion Designers of America (CFDA) *Special Award*, 1990

Descendant of Russian nobility and member of the Italian aristocracy, Emilio Pucci was educated in Italy and the United States. He was a member of his country's Olympic Ski Team from 1933–1934, and officer of the Italian Air Force during World War II, remaining in the service after the war. Even after he became involved with fashion, he retained his interest in politics and in the 1950s served two terms in the Italian Chamber of Deputies.

Pucci got into fashion by accident when the ski clothes he was wearing in Switzerland caught the attention of photographer TONI FRISSELL. Snug and close-fitting, they were among the first made of stretch fabrics; when the Frissel photographs appeared and attracted attention, he decided to market the

Designer Emilio Pucci.

clothes. However, it was his simple chemises of thin silk jersey that made him a favorite of the international jet set in the 1960s. These dresses, wrinkle-resistant and packable in no space at all, were beloved by fashion professionals everywhere, and the brilliant signature prints in designs inspired by heraldic banners were copied in every price range. In 1990 there was a worldwide revival of interest in the prints. Design projects have included accessories, sportswear, underwear, fragrances for women and men, porcelain, sheets, bath linens, rugs, and airline uniforms. Since his death in 1992, the business has continued.

In the 1990s, Pucci's's daughter, Laudomia Pucci, took over the family business, and in 2000 the Pucci family created an alliance with the LVMH luxury brand, which now controls 67 percent of the company. Laudomia Pucci serves as image director. In October 2006, MATTHEW WILLIAMSON, an English designer, was appointed creative director, taking over for CHRISTIAN LACROIX, who was appointed in 2003. The 60th anniversary of Emilio Pucci was celebrated in 2007. In September 2008 Peter Dundas was named the new creative director.

Slit-prints skirt and thin-strapped top, 1966.

Designer Gareth Pugh.

BORN August 31, 1981

Last November, at the MTV Europe Awards, Beyonce Knowles' stylists jettisoned the pop-star's usual glittery frock and draped her in an edgy, black and white, Gareth Pugh (PYOO) minidress. The strikingly architectural silhouette cut created a media buzz for Pugh in the United States. But the designer had been the darling of the London catwalks since 2003, his final year at St. Martins School of Design, when his balloon-inflected collection caught the eye of the senior fashion editor of *Dazed & Confused* magazine. Since then Pugh has been cast as the *enfant terrible* of the British fashion industry, in the vein of ALEXANDER MCQUEEN. Pugh's couture collections—which rely heavily on fetishist-favored fabrics like latex and chain mail—make almost no concessions to established modes of dress. In 2007, after editor-in-chief of *Vogue* ANNA WINTOUR hailed him as a genius, Pugh told *Icon*

magazine that he had yet to sell a single dress. Pugh's wearable sculptures are frequently menacing or distorting, refiguring the model's body beyond even the most stylized human shape.

A clear line runs from VIVIENNE WESTWOOD's do-it-yourself, groundbreaking Sex collection—which influenced punk rock through the fashion-as-art of the New Romantic London club—scene to Pugh's creations. He shares more than just an aesthetic with those youth cultures; his posture is avowedly working class. When Pugh was asked in an interview why he appeared on the BBC reality show *The Fashion House* (which raised his profile considerably), he replied, "My only other option was the dole."

Left: Fall 2009.

Right: Spring 2009.

Lilly Pulitzer

BORN Lilly McKim; Roslyn, NY, 1931

Lilly Pulitzer started out as a New York socialite, and attended the Chapin School in Manhattan with the Bouvier sisters Jacqueline and Lee, in addition to other private academies. In 1950, she married Peter Pulitzer, grandson of the legendary publisher Joseph Pulitzer. In addition to being known for their bohemian lifestyle, the couple ran several citrus groves that Peter had inherited. Young Lilly decided to open a juice stand right off the trendy Worth Avenue, partly because she thought it would be fun, and partly because she wanted to make use of all the fruit from their groves. She soon discovered that working at the juice stand put vibrant juice stains all over her clothing. As a result, she asked her dressmaker to create a cotton shift in a bright, flowered pattern that would hide the discoloration. The patterned dresses were quite striking, and within a short period of time, Pulitzer's clothing became more famous than her juice. She wore summery shift dresses, capri pants, and simple sheaths, all made from brightly patterned fabrics that would become her signature. Her outfits gained acclaim early on, when First Lady Jackie Kennedy was photographed wearing one for a feature in *Life* magazine.

The bright colors of Pulitzer came to signify the authentic Palm Beach lifestyle, and her signature shades of bright pink and green were considered the color scheme of the affluent at play. Pulitzer designs were frequently spotted on vacationers in the Hamptons, Cape Cod, and at toney resorts. Popular patterns included turtle prints, flowers, and sea life, all in bright summer colors. In a 1980 paperback, *The Preppy Handbook*, author Lisa Birnbach called the Lilly Pulitzer dress one of the essential pieces for "preppy" women. The label thrived well into the 1970s. Pulitzer decided to retire, and shuttered the company in 1984.

The Lilly Pulitzer label experienced a revival in January 1993, and expanded to a network of over 75 stores. The brand is also distributed in leading department stores, and in addition to women's apparel, produces bedding, men's wear, a maternity line, children's clothing, shoes, and accessories.

In 2008, Pulitzer celebrated 50 years in the business, and Parsons School of Design in New York, launched a retrospective to honor the occasion. The show featured Lilly Pulitzer dresses from 1959 to the present. James Bradbeer, Jr., the president of Lilly Pulitzer, stated that it was hard to date some of the pieces because Pulitzer had thrown out many of the archives when she retired. Some dressed were dated by identifying whether they had metal, painted metal, or plastic zippers, as well as by the various prints of the fabrics.

Models wearing Lilly Pulitzer designs, 2002.

Designer Mary Quant.

BORN Blackheath, Kent, England, February 11, 1934

AWARDS O.B.E. (Order of the British Empire)

Mary Quant was a leading figure in the youth revolution of the 1950s and 1960s—her awareness of
social changes and understanding of the young customer made her a celebrity and helped put London
on the fashion map. She studied at Goldsmiths
College of Art in London where she met Alexander
Plunket-Greene, whom she later married. In 1955,
with a partner, she and her husband opened a small
boutique called Bazaar, the first on King's Road
in London's Chelsea district. At the start they sold
clothes from outside designers, but soon became
frustrated by the difficulty of getting the kind of
clothes they wanted from manufacturers. Mary Quant
then began to make her own designs, spirited, unconventional, and instant hits with the young, probably
because they were totally unlike anything their moth-
ers had worn, or ever would wear.

She began on a small scale, running up her designs
in her own flat, but her fame grew along with that of
"swinging London." By 1963 she had opened a second Bazaar, had moved into mass production with her
less expensive Ginger Group, and was exporting to
the United States. With her husband as business partner she had become a full-scale designer and manufacturer. She designed for JC Penney in the United
States and for Puritan's Youthquake promotion. Her
autobiography, *Quant by Quant*, was published in
1966. In the 1970s, while no longer a fashion innovator, she added to her business with licenses for jewelry, carpets, household linens, men's ties, and eyeglasses. In 1973–1974, an exhibition, "Mary Quant's
London," was presented at the London Museum.

In approximately 1964 she became interested in
makeup, and in 1966 launched a cosmetics line with
the colors presented in a paint box and crayon kit.
With Japanese partners she developed a complete
body and skin-care collection as well as makeup, sold
in freestanding shops in Japan. There is a showcase
shop in London and shops in New York and the Far
East, Australia, and New Zealand.

Quant is given credit for starting the Chelsea or
Mod look of the mid 1950s and the miniskirts of the
late 1960s. Whether or not she actually originated the
mini, she certainly popularized it in England and the
United States. She initiated ideas that are now commonplace, using denim, colored flannel, and vinyl in
clothes that only the young could wear, showing them
with colored tights. For her innovative showings she
used photographic mannequins rather than regular
runway models and had them dance down the runway. Whatever her final stature as a designer, she was
a pivotal figure in a fashion upheaval that reflected
major social changes taking place around the world.
The Mod look has since made return appearances in
the work of designers in both Europe and the United
States. Her mini slipdresses in bold prints reappeared
under her own label in 2003.

In October 2001, New York's Fashion Institute
of Technology mounted an exhibition, "London
Fashion," tracing the history of the city's style contributions, from Mary Quant's mini-skirt to designs
by more recent movers and shakers. These included,
among others, JOHN GALLIANO, ALEXANDER MCQUEEN,
HUSSEIN CHALAYAN, and VIVIENNE WESTWOOD.

Paco RABANNE
John RAWLINGS
John REDFERN
Tracy REESE
Zandra RHODES
Nina RICCI
Herb RITTS
Marcel ROCHAS
RODARTE
Narciso RODRIGUEZ
Lela ROSE
Renzo ROSSO
Maggy ROUFF
Cynthia ROWLEY
Ralph RUCCI
Sonia RYKIEL

Paco Rabanne

Designer Paco Rabanne.

BORN Fransisco Rabaneda Cuervo; San Sebastian, Spain, February 18, 1934

Paco Rabanne's family fled to France in 1939 to escape the Spanish Civil War—at the time, his mother was head seamstress at BALENCIAGA in San Sebastian. In Paris, Rabanne studied architecture at the École Supérieure des Beaux-Arts and began designing on a freelance basis—handbags, shoes, plastic accessories, and embroideries.

In his first show in 1966, called "12 Unwearable Dresses," the dresses in question were made of plastic discs linked with metal chains, accessorized with plastic jewelry and sun goggles in primary colors. He continued the linked-disc theme in coats of fur patches and dresses of leather patches, and also used buttons and strips of aluminum laced with wire. In 1970 he was one of the first to use fake suede for dresses. He combines unlikely materials, and has designed coats of knit and fur as well as dresses made of ribbons, feathers, or tassels, linked for suppleness. His experiments have had considerable influence on other designers. Rabanne also has a wide range of fragrances for men and women.

A mystic by nature, Rabanne lives monastically, unencumbered by possessions, and gives the bulk of his money to charity. Although still actively engaged in his firm, he turned over creative direction to Rosemary Rodriguez in 2000. Patrick Robinson replaced Rodriguez in 2005. His company is owned by the Spanish firm, Puig, which also owns NINA RICCI.

Model wearing mini dress made of lacquered-aluminum discs, designed by Paco Rabanne, 1968.

Three models wearing brightly patterned dresses by Rabanne, 1966.

Photographer John Rawlings.

John Rawlings

Always criticizing the master photographers, he was one of the first to craft a truly "all-American" look, a look designer CHRISTIAN DIOR would call the "look sportif." Rawlings consciously chose to move away from dark imagery and metaphors and focused instead on literal portrayals of the clothes.

Rawlings was also one of the first fashion photographers to associate couture dressing with Hollywood celebrities. His photographs graced the covers of over 200 issues of *Vogue* and *Glamour*, and he left an archive of more than 30,000 photos. In addition to his editorial work, he produced two books of nudes, and was considered one of the few photographers who could shoot strong images in both black and white and color.

BORN Ohio, 1912
DIED 1970

Photographer John Rawlings's illustrious career began in 1936 when at the age of 24 he was chosen to apprentice at *Vogue* Studios. Rawlings helped to transform the world of editorial fashion photography. Rawlngs worked closely with *Vogue* editor EDNA WOOLMAN CHASE to create photos that, as she put it, had more information in them and less art—photos that truly celebrated the clothes.

After attending Weslyan University in the early 1930s, Rawlings moved to New York and got a job as a window dresser. Soon after, he purchased a camera to take pictures of his work and discovered a passion for photography. He soon began shooting photographs of his clients with their animals, and one landed on the desk of legendary publisher Condé Montrose Nast. Hired at *Vogue* by Nast, he served as a prop builder and studio hand to several well-known photographers, including CECIL BEATON and HORST P. HORST. He was soon promoted to first assistant and eventually was sent to British *Vogue*, where he worked until the 1940s.

Photograph by John Rawlings, 1943.

John Redfern

BORN England, 1851
DIED England, 1929

English tailor John Redfern is credited with being the first to transform women's dresses from tress-laden masses of froufrou into sleek, tailor-made garments, often with coordinating top and bottom. Thanks to his talent—and trimming—the dress took a cue from the man's suit, and began its march to the twentieth century. Redfern lived and worked in 1860s Cowes, Isle of Wright, a popular destination for yachting. The sport was steadily attracting more women, and as female passengers started showing up at the docks, Redfern designed the apparel for their excursions. His popularity culminated in 1879, when actress Lillie Langtree wore one of Redfern's trainless "tailor-mades" to the Cowes Regatta. The dressmaker became an overnight fashion sensation, and by 1881, he was putting out a full line for women. The sharply tailored ladies' suits attracted an elite clientele, and Redfern was quick to open shops in both Paris and London. Queen Victoria took notice of his work, and in 1888, appointed him royal dressmaker. By the turn of the century, Redfern's popularity soared even further. He proved a master at cutting clothes to complement the S-bend corset, which gave the figure an 'S' shape. When the S-bend faded from style in 1908, Redfern reinvented himself with a high-waisted style known as the Grecian. At the onset of World War I, Redfern designed the first women's Red Cross Uniforms. Both his fashion houses prospered well into the 1920s, but then closed.

Illustration of a design by John Redfern.

Tracy Reese

BORN Detroit, Michigan, February 12, 1964

Tracy Reese specializes in young designer sports-wear—knits, separates, and dresses for women with careers and busy, varied lives. The clothes combine a playful spirit with shape and structure.

After childhood weekends spent in art classes, Reese took a fashion design class at Cass Technical High School in Detroit. She attended New York's Parsons School of Design on scholarship, graduating in 1984, and in the same year went to work as design assistant to MARTINE SITBON. In 1987, she opened her own company, which two years later fell victim to the recession, then worked at PERRY ELLIS as designer for the Portfolio division until it closed the following year. She freelanced briefly with Gordon Henderson, and from 1990 to 1995 was design director at Magaschoni for a bridge collection, Tracy Reese for Magaschoni. Reese then designed an exclusive line for The Limited and in the same year started her

Designer Tracy Reese.

own company, Tracy Reese Meridian. Her designs are sold at upscale stores in the United States, Europe, and Asia. The company comprises two lines: the ultra feminine Tracy Reese and its free-spirited sibling, Plenty by Tracy Reese. The collections are inspired by vintage apparel and bohemian style as well as Reese's many travels. Her trademarks include a vibrant, playful use of color and a curvy cut that emphasizes the beauty of the female figure. Reese also oversees a home collection and accessory line. In 2006, she opened a 2,200-square-foot flagship boutique in New York City's trendy West Village.

Left: Spring 2008.
Right: Fall 2008.

Zandra Rhodes

BORN Chatham, England, 1942

AWARDS British Clothing Institute *Designer of the Year*, 1972

Zandra Rhodes came into view in the late 1960s when she established her dress firm. She had planned to be a textile designer and set up her own print works and a shop to sell dresses made of her fabrics, then decided she was better able to interpret them than anyone else. She was undoubtedly right—her designs and her fabrics are of a piece, unmistakably hers, as eccentric and original as she is.

Rhodes's father was a truck driver; her mother was head fitter at WORTH in Paris before her marriage and afterward a senior lecturer in fashion at Medway College of Art. Zandra studied textile design and lithography at Medway, and then went to the Royal College of Art, graduating in 1966. By 1969 she was producing imaginative clothing, for the most part working in very soft fabrics that float and drift—chiffon, tulle, silk—handscreened in her own prints. These have included art deco motifs, lipsticks, squiggles, teddy bears, stars, teardrops, and big splashy patterns.

She always made news, alternately criticized and applauded. She finished edges with pinking shears and made glamorized punk designs with torn holes or edges fastened with jeweled safety pins, sleeves held on by pins or chains. Her champagne bubble dresses drawn in at the knee with elastic were acclaimed, and flounced hems finished with uneven scallops and

Designer Zandra Rhodes.

adorned with pearls, pompoms, or braids became a signature. The clothes were beautiful and romantic, a fantasy of dressing entirely distinctive and personal. She designed for Princess Diana, and in 1997, was ordained the Commander of the British Empire by the Queen.

Rhodes created her own appearance as imaginatively as her clothing: hair dyed in a rainbow of colors—magenta and bright green, for example—and such makeup effects as eyebrows drawn in one continuous arc. She is considered by many to be one of the creative geniuses of "Swinging London" and has continued to thrive and take risks long after many of her contemporaries have faded from the scene. Her designs were included in the 2001 "London Fashion" exhibition at the Fashion Institute of Technology.

In May 2003, there was a resurgnace of her career: she opened a small Fashion and Textile Museum of her own, dedicated entirely to modern fashion and textiles. It is housed in a brilliant orange-and-pink building in South London reconstructed from a derelict warehouse.

Spring/summer 2007.

Anne Larsen wearing a Nina Ricci design, 1962.

BORN Marie Nielli; Turin, Italy, 1883
DIED Paris, France, November 29, 1970

Nina Ricci moved to Paris with her family when she was twelve. As a child she made hats and dresses for her dolls, and at the age of 13 was apprenticed to a couturier. At 18 she was the head of an atelier, and at 21 a premier stylist. In 1932, encouraged by her jeweler husband, Louis, she opened her own couture house.

Ricci was a skilled technician who usually designed by draping the cloth onto the mannequin, but she was not an originator of fashion ideas. The house specialized in graceful clothes for elegant women who preferred to be in fashion rather than in advance of it; trousseaux were a specialty. Typical of her attention to elegance and detail is the Ricci perfume, L'air du

Temps, presented in a Lalique flacon with a frosted glass bird on the stopper. She was one of the first in the couture business to show lower-priced models in a boutique. After 1945 the house was managed by her son Robert. In 1951 JULES-FRANCOIS CRAHAY became Ricci's collaborator on the collections; he took over complete design responsibility in 1959. He was succeeded in 1963 by Gérard Pipart.

Since 1998, when it was sold to the Barcelona-based beauty and fashion conglomerate Puig Group, the house has had a changing cast of designers, including Olivier Theysken who departed in 2009.

Enid Boulting wearing a 1960s design by Nina Ricci.

Herb Ritts

BORN Los Angeles, California, August 13, 1952
DIED Los Angeles, California, December 26, 2002

AWARDS MTV Music Video Awards: *Best Female Video*, 1991, and *Best Male Video*, 1991

Herb Ritts, internationally acclaimed fashion and celebrity photographer and filmmaker, became legendary in the 1980s and 1990s for his striking, clean lines and black-and-white editorial fashion portraits for *Vogue, Vanity Fair, Interview,* and *Rolling Stone.* Ritts is also renowned for his successful advertising campaigns for fashion brands CALVIN KLEIN, CHANEL, DONNA KARAN, Gap, GIANNI VERSACE, GIORGIO ARMANI, LEVI'S, Polo RALPH LAUREN, and VALENTINO.

Ritts's first passions were economics and art history, which he pursued at Bard College. Following his

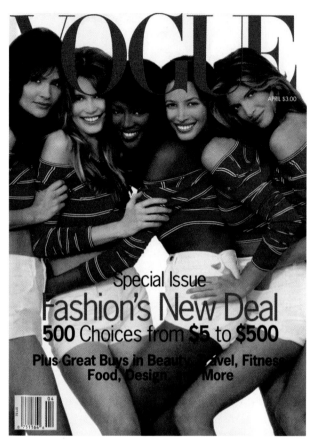

Vogue cover shot by Herb Ritts.

graduation, he took pictures of Rick Schroeder and Jon Voight in *The Champ*, which were selected to be featured in *Newsweek*. Soon thereafter, Ritts photographed aspiring actor Richard Gere, in an impromptu photo session in a desert gas station.

Ritts was credited with capturing with his camera what the Greek masters carved into marble—the human form as a classical study. His images not only captured human beauty but also challenged notions of race and gender. Ritts's striking and memorable portraits feature noted individuals in film, fashion, music, politics, and society.

Ritts also directed two music videos, for Janet Jackson and Chris Isaak, that were recipients of MTV Music Video Awards.

On a personal and philanthropic level, Ritts was strongly committed to HIV/AIDS advocacy and related causes, and contributed to many charities including the Elton John AIDS Foundation and Focus on AIDS. At the age of 50, Ritts died in his native town of Los Angeles due to complications from pneumonia.

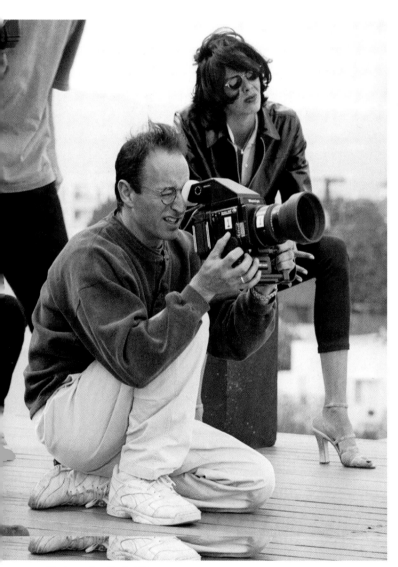

Photographer Herb Ritts.

Designer Marcel Rochas.

Except for a licensed Japanese line, the firm went out of the apparel business with the death of Rochas.

In March 1990, Parfums Rochas announced a new luxury ready-to-wear collection designed by Peter O'Brien. In 2002 OLIVER THEYSKINS was chosen as creative director of Rochas. His creative and well-made lines won the praise of fashion critics and picked up celebrity clients such as Nicole Kidman, Jennifer Lopez, Jennifer Aniston, and Sarah Jessica Parker. In July 2006 owners, Procter & Gamble, closed the Rochas fashion division, which shocked the industry.

In 2008 the fashion side of the Rochas fragrance house was revived with the appointment of Marco Zanini as the new creative director. Italian company Gibò Co. SpA manufactures and distributes Rochas.

BORN Paris, France, 1902
DIED Paris, France, March 14, 1955

Marcel Rochas (Ro-sha), who was known for young, daring designs, opened his couture house in 1924 in the Faubourg Saint-Honoré, and moved to the avenue Matignon in 1931. According to legend, his reputation was made by the scandal that ensued when eight women wore the identical dress from his house to the same party, each having thought she had the exclusive.

Rochas generated an abundance of fantastic, original ideas, using as many as ten colors in combination and lavish quantities of lace, ribbon, and tulle. He showed a broad-shouldered military look before ELSA SCHIAPARELLI, long skirts and an hourglass silhouette several years before the New Look, and invented a waist-cincher. His classic perfume, Femme, was packaged with black lace from his guêpière corset. He maintained a boutique for separates and accessories, and also designed for films. In 1951 he published *Twenty-five Years of Parisian Elegance, 1925–50.*

Tamara de Lempicka wearing a design by Marcel Rochas, 1931.

Rodarte

Rodarte fashion designers Kate and Laura Mulleavy.

BORN Kate Mulleavy, 1979; Laura Mulleavy, 1980, both Pasadena, California

AWARDS Ecco Domani Fashion Foundation Award, 2005 • Council of Fashion Designers of America (CFDA) *Swarovski Emerging Women's wear Designer*, 2008 • Swiss Textiles Award, 2008

Sisters Kate and Laura Mulleavy were fashion out-siders when they graduated from the University of California at Berkeley in 2001 (neither majored in fashion or design). But in 2005, they took the fashion world by storm when

Left: Fall 2007.
Right: Spring 2009.

they made the cover of *Women's Wear Daily* within days of their arrival. The magazine showed designs from their 10-piece, hand-sewn sample collection, and the debut of Rodarte (Ro-dart-tay) (named after their mother's maiden name) was a smash hit. The line was soon picked up by exclusive retailers such as Barneys, Neiman Marcus, and Bergdorf Goodman.

Rodarte is known for its meticulously detailed romantic dresses—hand-crafted pleats, netting, cob-webbing, stripes, draping, and other trim lend an almost otherworldly look to the designs. They have become a favorite with fashion editors and devotees who crave a singular statement look that is also intensely feminine. For some, the Mulleavys' creations are almost too ethereal and delicate to wear, but they have proved them-selves capable of more down-to-earth looks, such as their collection of white shirts and dresses produced for Gap. For fall 2009 Rodarte showed experimental knits and leathers, with more of the innovative detailing they're known for—prov-ing that wearable art may just have staying power for a wider audience.

Narciso Rodriguez

Above: Designer Narciso Rodriguez.

Right: Spring 2009.

BORN New Jersey, January 27, 1961

AWARDS Council of Fashion Designers of America (CFDA) *Perry Ellis Award* 1997 • CFDA *Women's wear Designer of the Year* 2002, 2003

Narciso Rodriguez, the son of Cuban-American parents, studied in New York at Parsons School of Design and first became widely known in 1996 for the bias-cut wedding dress he designed for the late Carolyn Bessette Kennedy. He was, however, hardly a beginner, having worked under DONNA KARAN at ANNE KLEIN immediately after his graduation from Parsons. He later worked at CALVIN KLEIN.

He was soon recognized for his excellent tailoring and feminine, wearable designs and was hired by CERRUTI to update the label; he then moved on to Madrid-based Loewe (owned by LVMH). Rodriguez turned Loewe, previously a little-known leather firm, into a major luxury goods label.

In contrast to the eccentricity of his British design peers, Rodriguez has preferred to concentrate on a less assertive look that emphasizes the woman rather than the clothes. His skillful tailoring, simple and elegant shapes in beautiful fabrics, and merchandising savvy have built his considerable reputation. His own collection, established in 1998 and shown in Milan and New York, has been an outlet for the more extreme elements of his creative imagination. In 2001, he left Loewe to concentrate on his own company, which includes shoes and handbags.

Rodriguez claims his "Latin roots" give his designs "distinctive curve and flair." Today his label is known worldwide.

In November 2008, Michelle Obama wore a dress from the spring 2009 collection when she joined her husband, Barack Obama, in their first TV appearance when he was president-elect. The dress received mixed reviews from the fashion press and public. It had originally fared well at New York City's fall 2008 Fashion Week, and came from the Rodriguez Stress-Relief design collection.

Lela Rose

BORN Texas

Native Texan Lela Rose moved to New York to study fashion at the Parsons School of Design, graduating in 1993. She then worked with designer Christian Francis Roth, and then for three years with RICHARD TYLER, before debuting her own line in 1998. Her profile expanded considerably when she designed gowns for Jenna and Barbara Bush to wear to their father's presidential inauguration in 2001.

"Casual luxury" is Rose's signature style: classic silhouettes with embellished fabric and trim, often with a light, whimsical touch. After securing a following for her dresses, separates, and jackets, Rose launched a bridal collection in 2006; her gowns paired clean, elegant lines with hand-crafted details and sometimes unusual fabrics. She brought a glamorous touch to the discount shoe chain Payless in 2007, launching a line of shoes and accessories.

Designer Lela Rose.

Left: Spring 2009.
Right: Fall 2009.

Renzo Rosso

Designer Renzo Rosso.

BORN Padua, Italy, September 15, 1955

AWARDS Bocconi Institute of Milan and Bain & Company, *Premio Risultati Award*, 1996 • Ernst & Young, *Entrepreneur of the Year*, 1997

Renzo Rosso and his partners at the Genius manufacturing group launched Diesel as a designer jeans label in 1978. Rosso had graduated from textile manufacturing school just a few years prior and was determined to carve a niche for himself in a still malleable high-end denim industry. In 1985, Rosso took full creative control of Diesel after buying out his remaining partners. The company experienced a period of remarkable growth and expansion in the late 1980s and 1990s due to Rosso's vision for dynamic, cosmopolitan ready-to-wear clothing combined with an innovative marketing campaign rivaling that of mega-players CALVIN KLEIN and United Colors of Benetton.

Under Rosso's leadership, Diesel partnered with Fossil to produce watches, and in 2008, Rosso's holding company, Only the Brave, acquired majority interest in VIKTOR & ROLF, thus expanding Rosso's collection of inventive labels attracting younger, edgier consumers. In 2008, Rosso entered into a business arrangement with MARC JACOBS to produce his men's wear collection beginning in 2010. Rosso continues to expand today as a major power in the fashion industry, and Diesel with its trademarked faded and distressed denim has been established as one of the most profitable brands in the clothing business.

Above: Fall 2007.

Right: Fall 2009.

Designer Maggy Rouff.

BORN Maggie Besançon de Wagner; Paris, France, 1896

DIED August 7, 1971, Paris

Maggy Rouff's fate as a fashion designer was decided almost from birth. She had the fortune of having parents who were directors of the great couture house DRÈCOLL in Paris, and though she initially pursued medicine, Rouff eventually followed her parents into fashion design. In 1928 she took over as director of Drècoll and when the house merged with Beer, she created her own line, Maggy Rouff. As the head designer of Maggy Rouff, she created sporty, highly-tailored outfits with collars made of scarves and shawls. During the 1920s, 1930s, and 1940s, she was as known for her refined casual coats, jersey plus-fours, and beach skirts.

Rouff had a knack for not only designing sports-wear, but eveningwear, as well. Rouff's line of evening dresses often included girlish flourishes like ruffles, puffed sleeves, and bow motifs. She employed a variety of fabrics in her work, including organdy, crepe, jersey, and silks. Her designs were known for their feminine style and light, airy feel.

In addition to her design work, Rouff was an accomplished author. She published *America Seen*

through a Microscope, a book about her study trip of the United States, and also wrote *Philosophy of Elegance*, a polemic on the need for style and grace. She retired in 1948, and her daughter Anne-Marie Besançon de Wagner took over the business. The Drècoll house remained open until 1965 and closed after failing to capture the interest of young, modern customers.

Model wearing a Maggy Rouff belted coat, 1953.

Floral print dress with a matching mink fur-trimmed coat, 1954.

Designer Cynthia Rowley.

BORN Highland Park, Illinois, July 29, 1958

AWARDS Council of Fashion Designers of America (CFDA) *Perry Ellis Award for New Fashion Talent* (a tie with Victor Alfaro), 1994

Cynthia Rowley was just seven when she made her first dress. She was also precocious in business, selling her first eight-piece collection, a senior design project, while still at the Art Institute of Chicago. After a few seasons in Chicago,

she moved to New York in 1983; five years later she incorporated her business with herself as sole owner. While truly interested in the money side of the business, she retains a creative insouciance that shows in fresh and fanciful ready-to-wear, where her greatest strength lies in dresses.

Rowley has enlarged her scope in many directions: shoes, men's wear, handbags and myriad accessories, intimate apparel, and tableware. She introduced cosmetics in 2002 and has her own boutiques in the United States and Japan. In 1999, Rowley collaborated with the *New York Times* editor Ilene Rosenzweig on a book, *Swell: A Girl's Guide to the Good Life*. The book created a sensation among smart, stylish women. The duo continued in what became the Swellco partnership, with sequels *Home Swell Home* in 2002, *Swell-Dressed Party* in 2005, and *Slim: A Fantasy Memoir* in 2007. The two friends also created a line of home accessories called Swell, which made its debut at Target stores in 2003.

Left: Spring 2007.
Right: Fall 2007.

Ralph Rucci

Designer Ralph Rucci.

BORN Philadelphia, Pennsylvania, 1957

AWARDS Smithsonian Copper-Hewitt National *Design Award for Fashion*, 2008

Philadelphia native Ralph Rucci's fashion career began when he moved to New York to attend the Fashion Institute of Technology in the late 1970s. After graduating, he began his own line and opened a showroom on New York's famed Seventh Avenue. In 1994 he launched Chado; named for the Japanese tea ceremony symbolizing respect, grace, and tranquility, Chado embraces an Eastern sensibility. Elements of this sensibility can be seen in every drape, cut, and seam of his collection.

Using the finest European mills, Rucci creates gowns in the spirit of master couturiers VALENTINO and BALENCIAGA. His garments are one-of-a-kind artistic designs—architecturally clean, innovative in construction and cut,

Left: Fall 2009.
Right: Spring 2009.

and made from the most luxurious fabrics available. Much of his inspiration is drawn from fine art. In 2002, he became the first American designer since MAINBOCHER to be invited by the Paris Chambre Syndicale to show his collection.

Rucci's work has been showcased at several exhibitions, including The Cooper-Hewitt National Design Museum, The Museum of the Fashion Institute of Technology, The Costume Institute of Kent State University, and The Phoenix Art Museum.

Designer Sonia Rykiel.

BORN Paris, France, May 25, 1930

AWARDS The Fashion Group *Night of the Stars Award*, 1986

Sonia Rykiel (Ree-kee-eel) began in fashion by making her own maternity dresses, continued to design for friends after her child was born, and then for her husband's firm, Laura. The first Sonia Rykiel boutique opened in 1968 in the Paris department store Galeries Lafayette, followed by her own shop on the Left Bank.

Referred to as the "Queen of Knitwear" by *Women's Wear Daily* in 1970, she has made her name with sweaters and sweater looks in apparently endless variations, usually cut seductively close to the body, softened with detail near the face. Rykiel is known for creating the poor-boy sweater, inventing the inside-out stitch, placing seams on the exterior of garments, and occasionally doing away with both hems and lining. When her daughter, Nathalie, became pregnant, Rykiel showed pregnant-looking mannequins in oversized sweaters, and later added a new line of children's wear. She has continued to design for women at her own exalted fashion level and has added a men's line notable for color, joie de vivre, and wit. Rykiel's daughter currently designs for the collection, which now encompasses lingerie as well as the fitness-minded Sonia Rykiel Karma: Body and Soul. In 2008, the redesigned flagship boutique reopened on the Boulevard St. Germain in Paris.

Above: Spring 2009.

Right: Fall 2007.

Elie SAAB
Yves SAINT LAURENT
Fernando SANCHEZ
Jil SANDER
Giorgio SANT'ANGELO
Behnaz SARAFPOUR

Arnold SCAASI
Jean-Louis SCHERRER
Elsa SCHIAPARELLI
Jeremy SCOTT
SEAN JOHN
Ronaldus SHAMASK

Irene SHARAFF
Adele SIMPSON
Martine SITBON
Hedi SLIMANE
Paul SMITH
Willi SMITH
Carmel SNOW

Peter SOM
Kate SPADE
Lawrence STEELE
Cynthia STEFFE
Edward STEICHEN
Jill STUART
Anna SUI

Elie Saab

Above: Designer Elie Saab.
Right: Spring 2007.

BORN Damour, Lebanon, July 4, 1964

In the Middle East, Elie Saab's florid, conspicuous dresses decorate a parade of lady royalty. The American cadre of royalty—red-carpet celebrities—caught on to his distinctive style when it saw Halle Berry accept her 2002 Oscar. She wore a Saab purple taffeta skirt and burgundy tulle top, liberally embroidered with silk flowers and vines.

Saab grew up in a suburb of Beirut, once considered the Paris of the East. A self-taught designer, the young Saab was perpetually cutting up dress designs and decorating his little sister with odds and ends he found in his mother's bedroom. When civil war broke out in Lebanon, Saab's family began to shuttle back and forth between Paris, Cyprus, and their homeland. After a brief stint at a Paris design school, Saab returned to Lebanon to open his first atelier at the age of 18. A year later, he showed his first collection at the Casino du Liban in Beirut.

In 1997, Saab became the first non-Italian invited to show at the Camera Nazionale della Moda Italiana. This success sparked the launch of his ready-to-wear

collection the following year. He opened a salon and showroom in Paris in 2000. In 2003, Saab was invited by the Chambre Syndicale to show his first haute couture collection in Paris. He currently operates boutiques in Paris, Beirut, and, as of 2008, at Harrods in London.

Saab managed to capture the imaginations of western fashionistas by applying the adornments of the Orient to the design cuts of the West. His unabashedly sexy dresses cut close to the body and accent their wearer with elaborate handiwork—beads and sequins, embroidery and jewels. One such dress, slinky and glittering with fat emeralds and diamonds, was purchased by a Persian Gulf princess for $2.4 million.

"There is a certain kind of look—big minks, big hair, big lips—that migrates to certain kinds of shows," the *Times of London* wrote in reference to a Saab fashion show. "When you see it, you know you're about to witness a collection where the glamour is turned on full beam."

Designer Yves Saint Laurent.

BORN Oran, Algeria, August 1, 1936
DIED Paris, June, 2008

AWARDS Neiman Marcus Award, 1958 • Council of Fashion Designers of America (CFDA) *Special Award*, 1981

When Yves Saint Laurent announced his retirement in January 2002, the story made headlines on the front pages of the world's leading newspapers—an acknowledgment of his position as a fashion giant. In an extraordinary career spanning more than 40 years, he changed the way women dressed as profoundly as CHANEL had done before him. Like her, he seemed to sense a woman's needs almost before she herself was aware of them, introducing looks that are now so accepted it's hard to remember they were once considered revolutionary or even scandalous.

The son of a well-to-do French-colonial family, Saint Laurent left Oran when he was 17 to study art in Paris. In 1954 he shared first prize with KARL LAGERFELD in an International Wool Secretariat design competition, and a year later he was hired by CHRISTIAN DIOR as a design assistant. When Dior died suddenly in 1957, Saint Laurent succeeded him as head designer for the house, remaining until 1960 when he was called up for military service. In the Army he suffered a nervous breakdown and was discharged after just three months.

In 1961, with Pierre Bergé, his then lover and subsequent long-time partner, Saint Laurent opened his own couture house, showing the first collection in January 1962. Rive Gauche prêt-à-porter appeared in 1966 and men's wear in 1974. He also designed for film, notably for Catherine Deneuve in *Belle de Jour*, and for opera and ballet. Over the years the YSL initials were licensed for up to 167 products—everything from bed and bath linens to eyeglasses to children's clothes—and there were numerous fragrances, including Y, Rive Gauche, Opium, and Paris.

Within 20 years Saint Laurent reached the peak of his profession and established himself as the king of fashion, alternately taking inspiration from the street and exerting influence on it. Above all, he understood

Model wearing suit designed by YSL, 1967.

Looks from 1967 at YSL haute couture retrospective show, 2002.

Yves Saint Laurent, continued

the life of the modern woman, designing simple, wearable day clothes with a slightly masculine quality in beautiful fabrics, and for evening, clothes of unabashed luxury and sensuousness, enriched with fantasy and drama.

In 1983 the Costume Institute of the Metropolitan Museum of Art mounted a 25-year retrospective of his work, the first time a living designer had been so honored. In it could be seen many of the highlights of his career, from the 1958 Trapeze dress from his first Dior collection, to such classics as the pea coat, the Safari jacket, and the Smoking jacket, and the fantasy of the rich peasants. It was possible to track his increasing mastery and polish, and the blending of vision and rigorous dedication that led to his preeminence.

In 1993 YSL was sold for $650 million to Sanofi, which in 1999 was acquired by GUCCI. The American TOM FORD—already in charge of the Gucci fashion operation—was made creative director for both the women's and men's YSL Rive Gauche collections.

Saint Laurent continued to create the couture line until he retired, remaining dedicated to the ideal of haute couture and the art of dressing women sensibly, yet with a feeling of poetry. In his parting statement he said, "In many ways I feel that I have created the wardrobe of the modern woman. . . . I am extremely proud that women [all over] the world today wear pantsuits, smoking suits, pea coats, and trench coats."

In 2008, the world was shocked when Yves Saint Laurent died of brain cancer.

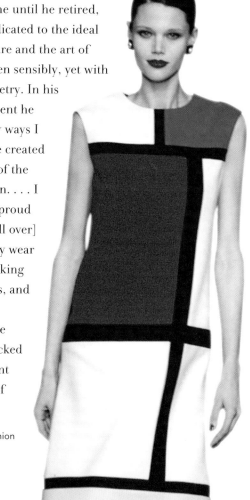

Haute couture fashion show, 2002.

Model wearing a silk camisole and shorts etched in ecru lace, 1976.

BORN Spain, 1936

DIED New York, June 28, 2006

AWARDS Coty American Fashion Critics' Award *Special Award* (lingerie): 1974, 1977, 1981; *Special Award (fur design for Revillon)*, 1975 • Council of Fashion Designers of America (CFDA) *Special Award*, 1981

Fernando Sanchez received his design education in France. As a designer he has been at home in both Europe and America, in fields as disparate as lingerie and furs. Sanchez studied at L'École de la Chambre Syndicale de la Couture Parisienne in Paris and was a prize winner in the same International Wool Secretariat competition in which YVES SAINT LAURENT won an award. He interned at NINA RICCI before joining Saint Laurent at CHRISTIAN DIOR, where Sanchez designed lingerie, accessories, and sweaters for the Dior European boutiques.

He first came to New York to do the Dior American lingerie line, and for several years commuted between Paris and New York. At the same time he began designing furs for Revillon, working for them for 12 years and becoming known for such unconventional treatments as his hide-out mink coats with the fur on the inside. He opened his own lingerie company in 1973, resigned with Revillon in 1984 to produce a collection for the United States.

Sanchez's first successes for his own firm were glamorous lace-trimmed silk gowns, followed by camisole tops, boxer shorts, and bikini pants. He went on to develop lingerie on the separates principle, mixing colors, lengths, and fabrics to make a modern look. In 1983 he extended the same ideas into the men's market. Seductive, luxurious, trendsetting, and expensive, his lingerie has been given credit for reviving interest in extravagant undergarments.

Fernando Sanchez

Red camisole with black trim and matching jacket, 1977.

Jil Sander

Designer Jil Sander.

BORN Wesselburen, Germany, November 27, 1943

Before becoming a major international fashion force, Jil Sander studied textile design, spent two years in the United States, and worked as a fashion journalist. She started designing in 1968, opened a boutique in Hamburg–Poseldorf, and worked as a fashion designer for a major fabric manufacturer. Her first collection under her own label appeared in 1973. Cosmetics were added in 1979, leathers and eyewear in 1984; the flagship store opened in Paris in 1993. Boutiques were also established in Europe, Japan, Hong Kong, and the United States.

When she began, the only German with an international design reputation was KARL LAGERFELD, and he was working in Paris. From the start, her objective was clear—design without decoration, proportions refined to perfection, with lines and cuts that were out of the ordinary. Sander brought a subtle fluidity to the most severe tailoring, her suits were extraordinary for their combination of authority and sensuality, and her dresses had a purity and sexy austerity. Her demands for the highest quality in materials and craftsmanship were matched by her prices.

In 1999 the business was acquired by PRADA; less than a year later Sander left abruptly, following a disagreement with Patrizio Bertelli, Prada's head.

Design of the collection was taken over by Milan Virkmirovic—formerly buyer for Colette, the Paris boutique. Due to the terms of the sale, Sander was precluded from designing for anyone else until 2003. In May 2003 she and Bertelli made their peace and she rejoined the company she founded, then left in 2005. In 2006, Change Capital Partners bought the company from Prada, only to sell it to Onward Holdings Co., Ltd., in 2008. Currently, Belgian designer Raf Simons creates and runs the line.

Spring/summer 2004.

BORN Count Giorgio Impiriale di Sant'Angelo;
Florence, Italy, May 5, 1936
DIED New York City, August 29, 1989

AWARDS Coty American Fashion Critics' Award
Special Award (fantasy accessories and ethnic fash-
ions), 1968; "*Winnie*," 1970 • Council of Fashion
Designers of America (CFDA) *Special Award (con-*
tribution to evolution of stretch clothing), 1987 •
Fashion Walk of Fame, 2001

Giorgio Sant'Angelo spent much of his childhood in
Argentina and Brazil where his family owned proper-
ty. He trained as an architect and industrial designer
before going to France to study art. He came to the
United States in 1962. His art influences ran the
gamut from studies with Picasso to work with Walt
Disney. Moving to New York in 1963, he freelanced
as a textile designer and stylist, and served as design
consultant on various environmental projects. For the
DuPont Company, his experiments with Lucite® as a
material for fashion accessories were a sensation and
received extensive press coverage.

Designs by Sant' Angelo suspended in the Metropolitan Museum of Art, 2009.

Designer Giorgio Sant' Angelo.

While Sant'Angelo's initial success was with accessories, his first clothing collection of gypsy dresses
and modern patchwork clothes was extremely influential. He went on to break more ground with ethnic-
inspired clothing, especially a collection dedicated to
the American Indian. Always very much an individu-
alist, he was interested in new uses for materials such
as stretch fabrics incorporating Spandex. His designs
were for those who liked their clothes a bit out of the
ordinary, and he maintained a couture operation for a
roster of celebrity customers. He also did costumes for
films. The black exploitation vehicle *Cleopatra Jones*
is among the many projects on which he's worked.

His many businesses included ready-to-wear and
separates, as well as extensive licenses—from swimwear and active sportswear to furs to men's wear to
environmental fragrances and home furnishings.
After his death, the business went on for several
years; the licensing operation continues.

Behnaz Sarafpour

Designer Behnaz Sarafpour.

BORN Philadelphia

AWARDS Parsons School of Design *Golden Thimble Award*

Behnaz Sarafpour came to New York to study at Parsons School of Design in 1989. Her design career began even before she graduated, interning at ANNE KLEIN under the guidance of NARCISO RODRIGUEZ and RICHARD TYLER. Soon after Parsons she worked for the designer she has referred to as her mentor, ISAAC MIZRAHI. While working with Mizrahi, she began to develop her signature look with meticulous design and an appreciation for fabrics not often employed in the fashion world. Consequently, she was championed by Barneys New York fashion director Julie Gilhart, and became head designer of its private collection. Finally in 2002, she ventured out on

her own and produced her first runway show, sponsored by Style.com. That same year she received her first of three nominations for the *Perry Ellis Award for Women's Ready-to-Wear*. Since then collections have been sponsored by Style.com, as well as Moët & Chandon, Hewlett-Packard, Van Cleef & Arpels, and Tiffany & Co.

Her aesthetic varies from the elegant to the playful. Her colors: classic black and white, cool and warm grays, an array of tertiaries, and the occasional use of bold metallics. In 2004 *Vogue* editor ANNA WINTOUR recognized her achievements, and she became a member of the CFDA. Sarafpour then created limited-edition lines for Earnest Sewn with Behnaz Sarafpour Jeans, and for Lancôme with her dramatic red lipstick titled simply, Behnaz. In 2006 she was the first American designer to be featured in Target's *Go International* campaign. Her work was shown in New York Fashion Now at the Victoria and Albert Museum in London in 2007. Committed to the environment, she created a line of organic high-end sportswear in 2008, the success of which has inspired her to continue using sustainable fabrics in collections going forward.

Left: Spring 2007.
Right: Fall 2008.

BORN Arnold Isaacs; Montreal, Canada, May 8, 1931

AWARDS Coty American Fashion Critics' Award "*Winnie*," 1958 • Neiman Marcus Award, 1959 • Council of Fashion Designers of America (CFDA) *Special Award (extravagant evening dress)*, 1987 • Dallas Fashion Award *Fashion Excellence Award*

Best known for spectacular eveningwear in luxurious fabrics, Arnold Scaasi is one of the last of the true custom designers in the United States. The son of a furrier, he finished high school in his native Canada then took off for Melbourne, Australia, to live with his stylish aunt who dressed in CHANEL and SCHIAPARELLI. With her disciplined approach to dress and living, she was an important influence on Scaasi. He began art studies in Australia and then returned to Montreal to study couture. There he designed clothes for private clients and saved enough money to go to Paris to continue his fashion studies at L'École de la Chambre Syndicale de la Couture Parisienne. He then traveled in Europe for a year, returning to Paris as an apprentice to PAQUIN.

Designer Arnold Scaasi.

Arriving in New York in 1955, Scaasi worked as a sketcher for CHARLES JAMES, designed coats and suits for a Seventh Avenue manufacturer, and in 1957 opened his own wholesale business on a shoestring budget. In 1960, he bought and renovated a Manhattan town house for his ready-to-wear presentations, but changed his focus to couture in 1963. Another 20 years elapsed before he returned to ready-to-wear with the Arnold Scaasi Boutique, for cocktail and evening dresses.

With the mood of fashion moving away from flamboyance and toward minimalism, he closed the ready-to-wear business in 1994, choosing to concentrate on a handful of licenses and on made-to-order dresses for those women who still cherished his entrance-making designs. Licenses have included costume jewelry, furs, men's ties, loungewear, bridal apparel, sportswear, and knits.

The Scaasi clients have included both socialites and celebrities such as Barbara Walters and Elizabeth Taylor. He also designed for Barbara Bush and her daughter-in-law Laura Bush.

Model Veruschka in striped evening pajamas, 1966.

Jean-Louis Scherrer

Above: Designer Jean-Louis Scherrer.
Below: Spring/summer 1985.

BORN Paris, France, 1936

Jean-Louis Scherrer trained as a dancer at the Paris Conservatory but turned to fashion when he injured his back at the age of 20. The sketches he made during his recuperation were shown to DIOR and he became Dior's assistant at the same time as SAINT LAURENT. It was at Dior that he learned the intricacies of cutting and draping, which are the basis of his craft. After Dior's death and the choice of Saint Laurent as his successor, Scherrer left the house, found a backer, and in 1962 opened his own business. Since then he has had considerable success in both couture and ready-to-wear, with elegant clothes in the more elaborate couture tradition.

In April 1990, majority control of the company was acquired by a holding company, which in December 1992, citing heavy losses, dismissed Scherrer and replaced him as couturier and artistic director. Scherrer sued and negotiated a cash settlement and permission to resume designing, but did not recover the use of his name.

In late 2001 the house was bought by the newly-formed conglomerate France Luxury Group, with the first prêt-à-porter collection presented in March 2002. Currently, designer Stéphane Rolland heads the label.

Elsa Schiaparelli

Designer Elsa Schiaparelli.

BORN Rome, Italy, September 10, 1890
DIED Paris, France, November 13, 1973

AWARDS Neiman Marcus Award, 1940

The daughter of a language professor, Elsa Schiaparelli studied philosophy, and also wrote poetry and articles on music. She married and moved to the United States, where she lived until the end of World War I. When her husband left her in 1920, she returned to Paris with her daughter Marisa with no money.

Her involvement in fashion began when a sweater she designed for herself was seen and ordered by a store buyer. By 1929 Schiaparelli had established Pour le Sport on the Rue de la Paix; by 1930 she was doing business from 26 workrooms and employing

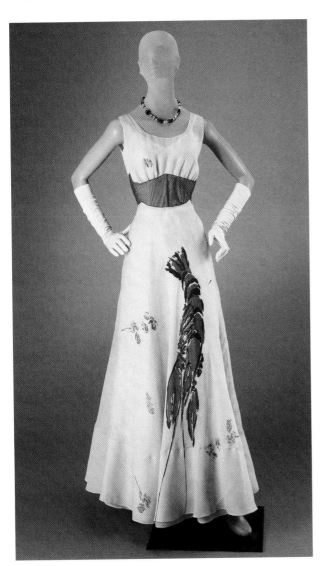

Silk organza "lobster" dress, 1937.

Rayon tulle and glass bead veil, 1938.

Elsa Schiaparelli, continued

2,000 people. In 1935, she opened a boutique on the Place Vendôme for sportswear, later adding dresses and evening clothes.

Like her great rival, CHANEL, Schiaparelli was not only a dressmaker but was also a part of the brilliant artistic life of Paris in the 1920s and 1930s. She had close friendships with artists, among them Jean Schlumberger, who also designed jewelry for her; Salvador Dalí, with whom she worked on designs for prints and embroideries; Jean Cocteau; Kees van Dongen; and MAN RAY. Highly creative and unconventional she shocked the couture establishment by using rough "working class" materials for evening, colored plastic zippers as decorative features, huge ceramic buttons in the shape of hands or butterflies—or whatever caught her fancy—and wildly imaginative accessories.

She showed little "doll hats" shaped like a lamb chop or a pink-heeled shoe, gloves that extended to the shoulders and turned into puffed sleeves. She fastened clothing with colored zippers, padlocks, clips, and dog leashes. She showed witty lapel ornaments in the shape of hands, teaspoons, hearts, or angels, and amusing novelties such as glowing phosphorescent brooches and handbags that lit up or played tunes when opened. She was spectacularly successful with avant-garde sweaters and worked with tattoo or skeleton motifs.

Schiaparelli changed the shape of the figure with broad, padded shoulders inspired by the London guardsman's uniform, a silhouette that lasted until the advent of the New Look. Both a genius at publicity and a trailblazer, she commissioned a fabric patterned with her press clippings then used the material in scarves, blouses, and

"Shocking pink" organza dress, with embroidery and velvet applique, 1953.

beachwear, and she pioneered in the use of synthetic fabrics. Her signature color was the brilliant pink she called "shocking," the name she also gave to her famous fragrance in its dressmaker dummy bottle.

Following the fall of France, she came to the United States, where she waited out the war. She returned to Paris after the Liberation and reopened her house in 1945. While she continued her business until 1954, she never regained her prewar position.

She continued as a consultant to companies licensed to produce hosiery, perfume, and scarves in her name, and lived out her retirement in Tunisia and Paris. Schiaparelli's irreverence and energy could result in vulgarity, but she produced clothes of great elegance that were extremely chic. Her major contribution was her vitality, and her sense of mischief was a reminder not to take it all too seriously.

BORN Kansas City, Missouri, 1976

AWARDS *Venus de la Mode*, 1996, 1997

A fashion nonconformist, Jeremy Scott studied at New York's Pratt Institute and departed for Paris in 1995 "because in Paris you can show whatever you want." After a visit to California, he moved to Paris in 2001.

In Paris he earned both headlines and fashion awards, starting in 1996 with a collection inspired by car crash victims, Band-Aids, and hospital gowns. Successive showings featured dresses made from trash bags, cloven-toed stilettos, one-legged trousers, and white dresses with pleated angel wings. Other shows dazzled with everything gold—leather dresses, ruched lamé skirts, asymmetrical mink boleros. Scott spent the 1998–1999 season as artistic director at Trussardi on their secondary lines, at the same time moving away from trash bag couture and closer to the mainstream. While showing both imagination and skill, his work can veer wildly between the cute-and-wearable and the kitschy. Scott teamed up with Kazuki and Alyasha Owerka-Moore to create a new fashion line for Adidas called Originals by Originals, which launched in 2009. The apparel range features materials such as leathers, cashmere, and silk, while the footwear builds on iconic Adidas styles.

Fashion designer Jeremy Scott.

Left: Fall 2007.
Right: Spring 2008.

Designer Sean John.

FOUNDED 1998

AWARDS Council of Fashion Designers (CFDA) *Men's Designer of the Year*, 2004

Sean John was founded by rap artist Sean John "Puffy" Combs. Combs felt there was a void in men's wear, a lack of well-made, sophisticated, and fashion forward clothing that still maintained an urban sensibility. Beginning as an eponymous urban sportswear label, the Sean John line expanded into an international brand, including Sean John, Bad Boy Sportswear, Sean John Tailored, and Sean John accessories. Product categories have expanded to include leather accessories, eyewear, fragrances, and hats. Beginning in 2000, Sean John has been nominated

Left: Sean John 10-year anniversary at Macy's, September 2004.

Right: Sean John 10-year anniversary at Macy's, September 2004.

five times for excellence in design, sharing that distinction with designers including MARC JACOBS and HELMUT LANG. In February 2001, Sean John produced the first nationally televised runway show on E! Television and The Style Network; in February 2002 the *New York Times* ran a front page story about the success of the company, and in 2004 Sean John was awarded the CFDA's *Men's Designer of the Year* award, the same year the first Sean John boutique opened on Fifth Avenue and 41st Street in New York.

Sean John has been credited with bringing the men's suit back into popularity and bringing excitement back into fashion. Combs states his goal is to be the "future of fashion." He is also an advocate of young people taking part in the political system, and through his nonprofit organization, Citizen Change, launched a "Vote or Die" registration campaign to increase the youth vote during the 2004 election season and again in 2008. Sean John also is an advocate for increasing the number of African-American models on the runways.

BORN Amsterdam, Holland, November 24, 1945

AWARDS Coty American Fashion Critics' Award "*Winnie*," 1981 • Council of Fashion Designers of America (CFDA) *Men's wear Designer of the Year*, 1988

One of a small group of designers with a strong architectural bent, Ronaldus Shamask arrived in New York City in 1971 by a circuitous route—Australia, London, and Buffalo, New York. Essentially self-taught, he moved with his family to Australia when he was 14, worked in the display department of a large Melbourne department store, and in 1967 moved to London where he worked as a fashion illustrator and began to paint. He then went to Buffalo and spent three years designing sets and costumes for ballet, theater, and opera. Next, he moved to New York City and worked on commissioned designs from private clients for interiors and clothing.

Shamask next undertook a 20-piece collection in muslin, cut from patterns that were actually life-sized blueprints. In 1978, he and a friend, Murray Moss, formed a company called Moss and opened a pristine, all-white shop and "laboratory" on Madison Avenue. The first presentation in 1979 consisted of the original muslin collection executed in three weights of linen. The clothes, which combined strong architectural shapes with beautiful fabrics, were cut with the utmost precision and exquisitely made. They were praised for their purity of design and exceptional workmanship.

Since 1986 Shamask has been in and out of women's and men's wear, designed costumes for the modern dancer Lucinda Childs, and returned to women's wear. The clothes, primarily high end sportswear, have been sold through a select group of fine stores, including Bergdorf Goodman and Neiman Marcus.

Model wearing design by Ronaldus Shamask.

Irene Sharaff

BORN Boston, Massachusetts, January 23, 1910
DIED New York City, August 16, 1993

AWARDS Academy Awards for Best Costume Design (Color): *An American in Paris*, 1952; Color, *The King and I*, 1957; *West Side Story*, 1962; *Cleopatra*, 1964; Best Costume Design (black-and-white) *Who's Afraid of Virginia Woolf?*, 1967; Tony Award for Best Costumes, *The King and I*, 1952; TDF Irene Sharoff *Lifetime Achievement Award*, 1993

In a remarkable career that spanned more than 60 years, Irene Sharaff designed costumes for 60 stage productions and 40 films, in addition to work for ballet and television, and even fashion illustration. Her first work, in 1928 while she was still in art school, was for Eva Le Gallienne's Civic Repertory Theatre in New York; her last film costumes were for *Mommie Dearest* in 1981; the last for the stage were for *Jerome Robbins' Broadway* in 1989. Sometimes she designed sets as well as costumes. Over the years, she earned a variety of awards, including five oscars, and nominations for her work in costume and stage work. The TDF Irene Sharaff Awards were also founded in 1993 to pay tribute to the art of costume design.

Sharaff studied at the New York School of Fine and Applied Arts and the Art Students League, while working part time. By 1931, she had enough money saved to spend a year in Paris where she attended the

Costume designer Irene Sharaff with Elizabeth Taylor, 1963.

Grande Chaumière. But even more important than school was her exposure to the theatrical designs of painters CHRISTIAN BÉRARD, Pavel Tchelitchew, and André Derain, and her discovery of the French couture with its emphasis on perfection in both design and execution. All of this had a great influence on her subsequent work. For ten years after her return she worked with great success on the New York stage, moving to Hollywood in 1942 to work on musicals at MGM. Her design work ranged from *Meet Me in St. Louis* to *Who's Afraid of Virginia Woolf*, from *Madame Curie* to *Hello Dolly* and *The Taming of the Shrew*. Most of her work was at MGM, although she designed for a number of movies at other studios.

With rare versatility, Sharaff understood theater, dance, and film, and was at home in both modern and period settings, in realism and fantasy. Her meticulous research translated into a combination of authenticity and function; the costumes were never overpowering and were exquisitely made.

West Side Story, 1961.

BORN Adele Smithline; New York City, December 28, 1904

DIED Greenwich, Connecticut, August 25, 1995

AWARDS *Neiman Marcus Award*, 1946 • Coty American Fashion Critics' Award *"Winnie,"* 1947 • *National Cotton Fashion Award*, 1953

The youngest of five daughters of an immigrant tailor, Adele Simpson began designing at 17 while attending Pratt Institute at night. When she was just 21 she replaced her older sister, Anna, as head designer for an important Seventh Avenue manufacturer and was soon earning the then staggering sum of $30,000 annually and traveling to Paris regularly for her firm. She married Wesley Simpson, a textile executive, in 1927, and then worked for the Mary Lee firm until 1949, when she took over the company and named it Adele Simpson Inc.

Simpson always saw her purpose as dressing women, not just selling dresses—her clothes were pretty, feminine, and wearable and could be coordinated into complete wardrobes. They were known for excellent design and impeccable quality; intended for women of discerning taste, they were conservative but

Cotton chiffon dress, 1955.

Beverly Johnson wearing a slip dress with a rhinestone belt and cardigan sweater, 1974.

not old fashioned. When Donald Hopson took over design of the collection, a younger, more fluid look developed. The family sold the firm in 1991 and it has since gone out of business. An exhibition, "1001 Treasures of Design," included items collected by Adele and Wesley Simpson and was presented by the Fashion Institute of Technology in 1978.

Designer Adele Simpson.

Martine Sitbon

BORN Casablanca, Morocco, ca, 1952

After graduating from the Studio Berçot, Paris, in 1974, Martine Sitbon was a freelancer and a fashion consultant before starting her own line in 1984. Her first show for the 1985 season was in Paris, and this was followed by shows at the Louvre in 1986, as well as the Palladium in New York. Within three years after starting her line, she was appointed creative director of CHLOÉ. She stayed for nine seasons before opening her first boutique in Paris in 1995. In 1998, a licensing deal was signed with Giba, launching Martine Sitbon Tricot.

In 1998, she surprised her audience by launching her men's wear designs during her women's wear fashion show. In 2001, she became director for women's wear, Byblos, and began MS Martine Sitbon handbags. Before her show in 2003, she was a major force in Paris and Tokyo, but she wanted to create a new company that could be a platform to showcase her independent spirit and Parisian elegance. In 2004, she launched Rue de Mail, named after the street that houses her showroom. The first show was held at the Couvent des Cordeliers in 2007 for the fall/winter 2008 ready-to-wear collection.

Sitbon rocks the Rue de Mail with her 1970s inspired rock and roll designs, and at the same time has a mastery of luxurious fabric and exotic textiles. Urban hues are predominant in her winter collec-

Above: Spring 2009.
Below, right: Spring 2004.

tions, but touches of red accentuate. Her spring collections celebrate the rebirth of color; a field of psychedelics. She is known for her collaborations with photographer Javier Vallhonrat, art director Marc Ascoli, and graphic designers Michael Amzalag and Mathias Augustyniak who help market her clothing.

Designer Martine Sitbon.

Hedi Slimane

BORN July 5, 1968

With his international heritage—Tunisian father, Italian mother, and Brazilian grandmother—Hedi Slimane could be considered the epitome of the modern, multicultural man. He studied at L'École du Louvre and worked for José Levy before going to work at YVES SAINT LAURENT.

When the house was sold to GUCCI in 1999, and TOM FORD became creative director for the company, Slimane left as creative director for men's wear, moving to CHRISTIAN DIOR as designer for Dior Homme. His first showing in January 2001 was a highly successful blend of classic French taste with a younger, edgier attitude. The silhouette was narrow and precisely cut, epitomizing his own blend of classicism and modernism. Subsequent collections have confirmed his reputation as an assured tailor whose proportions are just right, mean and lean, and with no allowance for extra pounds. The clothes have also been much admired and worn by fashionable young women.

Designer Hedi Slimane.

Above: Dior Homme, spring 2010.

Right: Dior Homme, fall 2009.

Paul Smith

BORN Nottingham, England, July 5, 1946

AWARDS CBE (for services to the fashion industry), 1994 • Queen's Award for Export, 1995 • Knighthood, 2000 • Queens Award for Enterprise, 2009

Designer Paul Smith.

Paul Smith worked his way up in fashion from the bottom, starting out at age 18 as a lowly gofer in a clothing warehouse. He opened his first tiny shop for men in 1970, using his own savings, staying open only on Friday and Saturday, and carrying designers such as KENZO, not then available outside London. He studied tailoring at night and gradually added his own designs so successfully that by 1974 the shop had moved to larger quarters and was open full time. Developing his own cool, smart style, he had his first Paris showing by 1976 and was consultant to an Italian shirt manufacturer and to the International Wool Secretariat.

The clothes, now for both men and women, rely on simplicity of style with a twist of wit and humor. They are notable for unusual, luxurious fabrics, and attention to detail—hand stitching, embroidery, vivid linings—and include tailored suits, separates, and knits, plus luggage, accessories, and swimwear. He has even designed a Gibson guitar for *Stiletto* Magazine for Auction during the 2005 Music Rising Charity Campaign. While the Paul Smith enterprise has grown into a worldwide chain, Smith still manages

Above: Spring 2007.
Left: Spring 2007.

to advise and steer each division, maintaining the personal character of both merchandise and presentation. In 1995, London's Design Museum celebrated his 25th anniversary in fashion with an exhibit called "Paul Smith True Brit." His book, *You Can Find Inspiration in Everything*, was published in 2002. The Paul Smith brand now encompasses 12 different collections and is sold in more than 35 countries.

Designer Willi Smith and model, 1987.

BORN Philadelphia, Pennsylvania, February 29, 1948
DIED New York City, April 17, 1987

AWARDS Coty American Fashion Critics' Award
Special Award, 1983 • Fashion Walk of Fame, 2002

One of a number of African American designers
who came to the fore in the late 1960s, Willi Smith
was the son of an iron-worker and a housewife. He
originally intended to be a painter, studied fashion
illustration at the Philadelphia Museum College of
Art, and in 1965, at the age of 17, arrived in New York
with two scholarships to Parsons School of Design.
He got a summer job with ARNOLD SCAASI, then spent
two years at Parsons, during which he freelanced as a
sketcher. He then worked for several manufacturers,
including Bobbie Brooks, Talbott, and Digits.

After several failed start-up attempts, WilliWear
Ltd. was established in 1976 with Laurie Mallet as

president, and Smith as designer and vice president.
His innovative, spirited clothes—described as classics with a sense of humor—were fun to wear as
well as functional, and brought fashion verve to the
moderate price range. Collections were consistent in
feeling from one year to another so that new pieces
mixed comfortably with those from previous years.
Preferring natural fibers for their comfort and utility,
he designed his own textiles and went to India several
times a year to supervise production of the collections.
His sister, Toukie, was his primary model. Men's wear
was introduced in 1978 "to bridge the gap between
jeans and suits." Smith also designed for Butterick
Patterns, did lingerie and loungewear, textiles for
Bedford Stuyvesant Design Works, and furniture for
Knoll International. In 1986, Smith caused a notable
stir when he dressed Caroline Kennedy's groomsmen
in blue linen suits with silver ties.

Fall 1987.

BORN Carmel Whilte; Dublin, Ireland, August 27, 1887

DIED New York City, May 9, 1961

Carmel Snow was raised in the fashion business—her mother came to the United States to promote Irish industries at the 1893 Chicago World's Fair and stayed, founding a dressmaking business, Fox & Co. One of the exhibitors at *Vogue*'s first "Fashion Fête" in 1914, the firm made the dress worn on that occasion by *Vogue*'s editor, EDNA WOOLMAN CHASE. A friendship developed and in 1921 Chase offered Snow a job in the magazine's fashion department. In 1929 she became editor of American *Vogue*.

In 1932, in a move that sent shock waves through the fashion world, Snow left to become fashion editor at *Harper's Bazaar*. She remained with *Harper's Bazaar*, first as fashion editor then as editor, until 1957, when she became chairman of the editorial board. Her successor was Nancy White, her niece and godchild.

Tiny in stature but a major fashion presence and forceful personality, Snow was a woman of wit and intelligence, of strong views expressed frankly and with passion. She dressed in great style in clothes from the Paris couture and like a high priestess of fashion, championed each change as it appeared. She recognized BALENCIAGA'S genius and promoted him indefatigably well before the majority of the fashion press; CHRISTIAN DIOR spoke of her "marvelous feeling for what is fashion today and what will be fashion tomorrow." A loyal and powerful champion of the talented, she demanded their best and received their finest efforts. After World War II, she took a leading role in helping the French and Italian textile and fashion industries get back on their feet. She was considered legendary. It is said that Christian Dior would delay openings until she arrived. Even after she no longer had official connections and despite precarious health, she continued to go to Paris twice yearly for the collections.

She married George Palen Snow in 1926 and had three children. Snow worked on her memoirs, published in 1962 in Ireland and in New York. Mary Louise, a fiction editor at *Harper's Bazaar*, collaborated on the life stories as well.

Editor Carmel Snow (center) with Diana Vreeland (left), 1952.

Designer Peter Som.

for their clean lines, luxurious fabrics, and comfortable fit. Som has found fans among a new generation of celebrities; his designs have been worn by the likes of Scarlett Johansson, Maggie Gyllenhaal, and Natalie Portman.

In 2007, he was appointed creative director of BILL BLASS Limited, overseeing the company's women's collection and serving in this capacity until 2008. He is widely credited with bringing the Bill Blass brand back to the forefront of the fashion world. In 2003 Cathy Horyn of the *New York Times* identified Som as "one of the best young designers working today."

BORN San Francisco, California, 1970

The son of architect parents, Chinese-American designer Peter Som grew up in San Francisco and attended Connecticut College, where he majored in art. He continued his studies at the Parsons School of Design in New York, where he did internships with MICHAEL KORS and CALVIN KLEIN. In 1997 Som received recognition from the Council of Fashion Designers of America (CFDA) as a rising young talent. He was also one of ten semi-finalists in the *Vogue*/CFDA Fashion Fund initiative in 2004, and was nominated for the CFDA *Swarovski Emerging Talent Award* in both 2002 and 2005.

Som showcased his collection in Bryant Park in 2001. Described by critics as a new leader in the tradition of American sportswear, his clothes are noted

Left: Spring 2008.

Right: Fall 2008.

Kate Spade

BORN Katherine Noel Brosnahan; Kansas City, Missouri, December 24, 1962

AWARDS Council of Fashion Designers of America (CFDA) *Perry Ellis Award for Accessories*, 1995; *Accessory Designer of the Year*, 1997

Kate Spade has spent most of her professional life with accessories. After graduation in 1986 from Arizona State University, where she majored in journalism, she moved to New York for a job at *Mademoiselle* magazine. When she left the magazine in 1991, she was senior fashion editor/head of accessories.

Feeling that the market lacked stylish, practical handbags, she decided to create her own. In January 1993, with her husband, Andy Spade, she launched kate spade new york—handbags with six designs, simple shapes in satin-finished nylon, emphasizing utility, color, and fabric. These continue to be signature styles. Spade believes that accessories should bring color and texture to a wardrobe, expressing the

Resort 2010.

Fall 2009.

Designer Kate Spade.

wearer's own sense of style and adding personality to her dress. The criterion for new additions is always the same—if it will be out of style tomorrow, it won't be in the line today.

In 2007, Liz Claiborne, Inc. acquired the brand and Deborah Lloyd took the helm as creative director.

The Kate Spade design universe has expanded to include leather bags and accessories, evening bags, luggage, eyewear, shoes, home accessories, paper, and beauty products.

Designer Lawrence Steele.

BORN Hampton, Virginia, July 7, 1963

Lawrence Steele grew up with his father in the Air Force, following him from one air base to another. They traveled from Germany to Spain and eventually back to Illinois, where the family still lives. He majored in fine arts at the Art Institute of Chicago, found a job in Tokyo after graduation, then moved on to Milan where he worked for FRANCO MOSCHINO. In 1990 he went to PRADA, and in 1994 began his own business.

He has gained a reputation for sensuous, sexy, very feminine clothes for late in the day, sophisticated clothes for svelte women unafraid of attracting attention. When his wedding dress for Jennifer Aniston appeared on the cover of *People* magazine, it made his name known to an audience beyond the fashion editors, models, and film stars who were already his devoted clients. His designs have been sold in Europe, North and South America, the Far East, Australia, Russia, and the Ukraine.

Spring 2002.

Cynthia Steffe

BORN Molville, Iowa, June 30, 1957

AWARDS Donna Karan *Gold Thimble Award*, 1981
• Parsons School of Design *Designer of the Year Award*, 1982

Cynthia Steffe grew up in small-town Boyden, Iowa, came to New York and studied at Parsons School of Design (1978–1982). She won many awards during her four-year stay, including the CLAIRE MCCARDELL Scholarship her sophomore year, an award for the most original children's wear design. While still in school, she started working as a design assistant to Donna Karan at ANNE KLEIN & Co. In 1983 she moved to Spitalnick with her name on the label as Cynthia Steffe for Spitalnick, but left in 1988 to form her own company with her husband Richard Roberts. In late 2000, in a move to expand the brand, the company was sold to the Leslie Fay Co.

Designer Cynthia Steffe.

There are now two labels: Cynthia by Cynthia Steffe—essentially sleek, luxury sportswear—and the smaller deluxe Cynthia Steffe black label—ready-to-wear and sportswear in leather, cashmere, suede, and fur. The difference lies mainly in the fabrics, the customer could be the same—a confident woman, young, or with a young attitude, who chooses crisp elegance for day and sexy sophistication for evening and might very well take pieces from both lines to make a look that is modern, innovative, and completely personal.

In addition to her business, Steffe is active in a number of charities and in many industry-related activities. She has served on the Board of Governors at Parsons and as a design critic there, as guest lecturer at the Fashion Institute of Technology, on the Board of Directors of the Council of Fashion Designers of America (CFDA), and as a member of the CFDA Awards Benefits Committee. She is also on the board of the Fashion Group International.

Left: Spring 2007.
Right: Fall 2004.

Photographer Edward Steichen.

BORN Luxembourg, March 27, 1879
DIED West Redding, Connecticut, May 25, 1973

Brought to the United States as an infant, Edward Steichen grew up in the Midwest and studied art at the Milwaukee Art Students League (1894–1898), during which time he was a lithography apprentice and began to teach himself photography. He became a U.S. citizen in 1900, lived in Paris, painting and doing photography from 1900 until 1902, and again from 1906 to 1914. During World War I he served in the U.S. Army Expeditionary Forces (1917–1919) as commander of a photo division. Around 1922, he committed himself entirely to photography.

His first fashion photographs were made in 1911 for PAUL POIRET; it was not until after he was hired by Condé Nast in 1923 as photographic editor-in-chief that he developed his mature style, deeply influenced by his involvement with modern art. He replaced the pictorialism of his predecessor, ADOLFO, with a modernism based on strong, clean lines, plain backgrounds, and an all-new model, the "flapper." He also worked for the advertising agency, J. Walter Thompson.

Steichen essentially abandoned his own photography in 1947 when he became director of the Department of Photography at New York's Museum of Modern Art, a post he held until his retirement in 1962. His best-known show from that era was "The Family of Man," which traveled to a number of other museums around the country. During his long and distinguished career, he accumulated a staggering list of honors and affiliations.

Edward Steichen

Photograph of Gloria Swanson by Edward Steichen, 1924.

Jill Stuart

BORN New York City, January 5, 1965

Jill Stuart, a New York-based designer known for her youthful, vintage-inspired clothing line, grew up in the Garment District (her parents owned the popular Seventh Avenue Boutique Mister Pants) and entered the fashion industry while still attending high school. At the age of 15 her collection of handbags and jewelry was displayed in Bloomingdale's windows.

After studying art and design at the Rhode Island School of Design, she returned to New York, where she met and married Ron Curtis, now CEO of her company. She opened her first boutique in 1988, and in 1993 launched her first full women's collection Skinclothes, a sexy line of leather slip dresses, skirts, jackets, and jeans. Her designs were worn by Alicia Silverstone in the Paramount movie *Clueless* (1995), resulting in nationwide recognition. Recent collections have featured romantic tiered and layered frocks highlighting the use of silk and organza—sensual clothing with a modern edge and a soft color palette.

Today, in addition to clothing, Jill Stuart offers watches, handbags, eyewear, perfume, and makeup. In spring 2007, she surprised the fashion community by launching her first men's wear line called Stuart Curtis, created in conjunction with her husband. Her lines are enormously successful in Japan, where she has flagship stores in Tokyo, Osaka, and Kobe.

Designer Jill Stuart.

Above: Fall 2007.

Left: Resort 2008.

Designer Anna Sui.

Above: Spring/summer 2007.

Right: Spring/summer 2008.

BORN Dearborn Heights, Michigan, August 4, 1964

AWARDS Council of Fashion Designers of America (CFDA) *Perry Ellis Award for New Fashion Talent*, 1992, Geoffrey Beene *Lifetime Achievement Award*, 2009

Anna Sui's restless curiosity and eclectic, unconventional approach to dress made its appearance early in her work. While still in junior high, she sewed many of her own clothes, even appliquéing some of the dress fabrics onto her shoes. In her teens she began to save clippings from fashion magazines in what she calls her "Genius Files" (she still refers to them). After high school she enrolled at Parsons School of Design in New York where she became close friends with STEVEN MEISEL, who was soon to be a top fashion photographer. Sui left Parsons in her second year to work for a junior sportswear company, designing everything from swimsuits to knits and moonlighting as a stylist for Meisel's fashion shoots. Torn between styling and designing, she continued to design, and after selling six of her pieces to Macy's, opened her own business. Her first runway show was in April 1991. By September 1993 Sui had moved her business out of her apartment into quarters on Seventh Avenue and opened two boutiques, one in New York's SoHo and the second in Los Angeles.

In addition to her clothing lines, the Anna Sui label is responsible for creating five fragrances as well as designing a mobile Samsung phone and a limited edition Anna Sui Boho Barbie doll. The designer's products are sold in more than 300 stores in 30 different countries. In 2009 Sui came out with a line of Gossip Girl-inspired looks for Target.

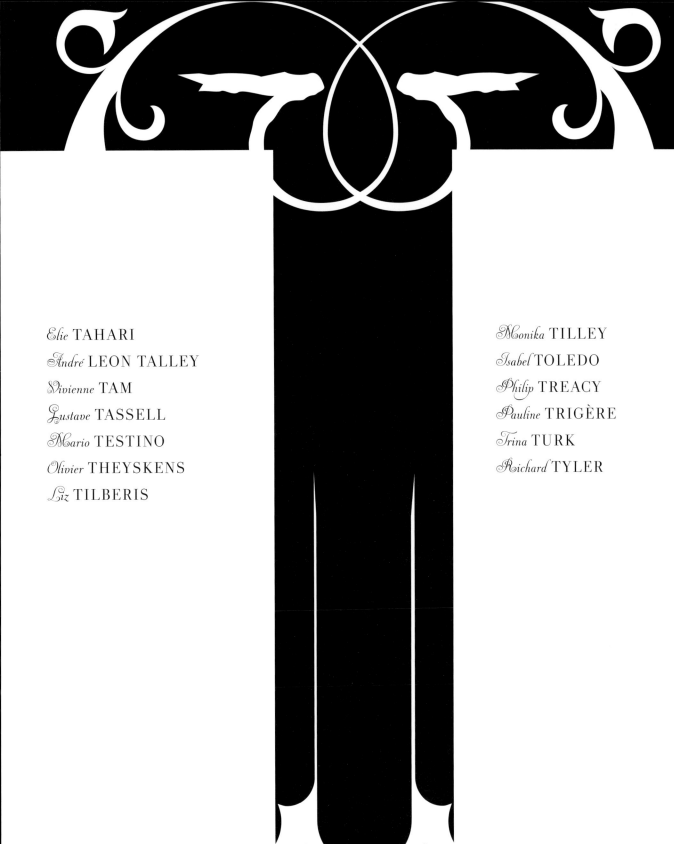

Elie TAHARI

André LEON TALLEY

Vivienne TAM

Gustave TASSELL

Mario TESTINO

Olivier THEYSKENS

Liz TILBERIS

Monika TILLEY

Isabel TOLEDO

Philip TREACY

Pauline TRIGÈRE

Trina TURK

Richard TYLER

Elie Tahari

BORN Israel, 1952

Elie Tahari's reputation for the fine lines and subtly embellished luxury women's apparel—of his eponymous brand—seem to belie his famously tough talking persona; but his style is actually a perfect extension of a maven's expertise. Because of the glacially moving silhouettes of Tahari's women's business suit—a well-known item in the United States—he is usually not considered in the designer class. He has stuck to his guns on not doing runway shows and after three decades in the industry has only met *Vogue* editor ANNA WINTOUR once.

These facts can only be seen in the proper light when one considers that Elie Tahari takes in an estimated $500 million a year. The majority of the revenue comes from his robust profile in the international lower-price-point luxury good market.

Tahari—an Israeli of Iranian Jewish descent—had no formal training in fashion and started out cutting fabric for disco-themed apparel in the 1970s. In 1997 he cofounded Icon with Andrew Rosen, but the former partner has since been bought out. Last year Tahari told *Portfolio* about his aesthetic. "I think it's in the gut. It's street smarts," he said, reaffirming his image. The creative director of the Elie Tahari brand is his wife Rory, whom he married in 2000.

Designer Elie Tahari with model.

Above: Fall 2009.
Left: Fall 2009.

Editor André Leon Talley (left) and Lord Snowden in Fendi, 1987.

André Leon Talley

BORN Durham, North Carolina, October 16, 1949

AWARDS Council of Fashion Designers of America (CFDA), *Eugene Sheppard Award for Outstanding Fashion Journalism*, 2003

An icon in the fashion world, editor and writer André Leon Talley is considered one of the most prominent African-American voices in the industry. As an editor-at-large of *Vogue*, Talley is usually found in the front row of the top fashion shows in New York, Milan, Paris, and London.

In 1977, after graduating from Brown University with a M.A. in French literature, Talley moved to New York where he landed a job as a reporter for *Women's Wear Daily*. Talley stood out—thanks in part to his imposing six-foot-seven-inch frame—and quickly ingratiated himself in the New York social scene, developing friendships with Andy Warhol, KARL LAGERFELD, and Bianca Jagger. His position with *WWD* lead to jobs at *Interview* and the *New York Times*, and in 1983 landed a position as fashion news director of *Vogue*. By 1989, he had worked his way up to creative director of the magazine. While there, he used his personality, knowledge, and position to elevate new and upcoming designers; he was especially committed to helping African-American designers and models.

In 1995, he left *Vogue* to become editor-in-chief of high-end fashion magazine *W*. Three years later he returned to *Vogue* in the capacity of editor-at-large. Through his work at *Vogue* he has helped propel the careers of several African-American luminaries, including Mariah Carey, Beyoncé, and Jennifer Hudson and raised the profile of several designers, including Byron Lars and TRACY REESE.

Vivienne Tam

BORN Guanzhou, China, November 28, 1957

Vivienne Tam grew up in Hong Kong when it was a British crown colony, a bicultural background fundamental to her subsequent East-meets-West design philosophy. After graduating from Hong Kong Polytechnic University, she moved to New York City, where her first collection appeared in 1982 under the East Wind Code label. She showed under her own name for the first time in 1993. Her collection for spring 1995 caused considerable controversy, with prints on T-shirts, jackets, and dresses of Chairman Mao Tse-tung wearing a pigtail or looking cross-eyed at a bee on the end of his nose.

Her stretch mesh prints—dragons, peonies, Buddhas—are especially well known, but Tam is com-

Designer Vivienne Tam.

mitted to providing fashionable clothing for modern women, clothes that are well designed, of superior quality, and affordable. Since she herself is a dedicated traveler, they must also be wearable and good travelers. Her list of celebrity clients includes Julia Roberts, Drew Barrymore, and Reese Witherspoon; the clothes are sold in fine stores in the United States and internationally. They are included in the collections of the Metropolitan Museum of Art, the Fashion Institute of Technology, and the Andy Warhol Museum. A book, *China Chic*, written by Tam, was published in late 2000.

Tam ventured into evening and special occasion dresses in 2003, and launched a secondary sportswear and denim line called Red Dragon. Her flagship store on New York's Mercer Street opened in 2007, and, she was asked by computer giant Hewlett Packard to design the first-ever "virtual digital clutch" in 2008.

Left: Spring 2009.
Right: Dress designed by Vivienne Tam for spring/summer, 1995.

BORN Philadelphia, Pennsylvania, February 4, 1926

AWARDS International Silk Association Award, 1959 • Coty American Fashion Critics' Award "*Winnie*," 1961

Gustave Tassell studied painting at the Pennsylvania Academy of Fine Arts. After serving in the Army, he did window displays for HATTIE CARNEGIE, where he was exposed to the designs of NORELL and was inspired to become a dress designer. He had his own small couture business in Philadelphia then returned to Carnegie as a designer, leaving in 1952 to spend two years in Paris. While there, he supported himself by selling sketches to visiting Americans, including GALANOS. He returned to the United States, and in 1956, aided by Galanos, opened his own ready-to-wear business in Los Angeles. After Norell's death in 1972, Tassell took over as designer, remaining until the firm closed four years later. He then reopened his own business.

Tassell was a friend of Norell, sharing with him a sure sense of proportion, an insistence on simplicity of line and refined detail. He was known for clothes of near-couture sophistication and perfect finish. His work was included in the "Passion for Perfection" exhibit at the Joan Spain Gallery of the Philadelphia Museum of Art from September 2007 through March 2008.

Black-striped Staron brocade fabric coat, 1967.

Mario Testino

BORN Lima, Peru, October 30, 1954

World-renowned fashion photographer Mario Testino began his career by selling portfolios to models who were attempting to jump-start their careers. It was his work with models, after all, that would propel him to the international stage and make him one of the most sought after photographers in the fashion industry.

Considered by many to be a "luxury photographer," the Peruvian-born Testino has showcased his glamorous work for dozens of companies and on the editorial pages of nearly every high-profile fashion magazine. He's become a major editorial voice in *Vogue*, and produced ad campaigns for TOM FORD, Burberry, and MICHAEL KORS, to name a few. One of the highest paid photographers in the industry, he is hailed by critiques for his ability to take photographs that sell clothes. He is also credited with helping bring an end to the reign of the supermodel. Because

Testino refused to pay the fees required of many high profile models, he was able to introduce new faces onto the scene, including Kate Moss—whom he calls "his favorite"—and Stella Tennant.

In the 1990s he became famous for his portraits of Madonna, Gwyneth Paltrow, and Angelina Jolie. And in 1997, he photographed Princess Diana for *Vanity Fair*. His photographs have been featured in a number of magazines and books, including *Let Me In!*.

Testino published his first book of photography entitled *Any Objections?* in 1999. In 2002 The National Portrait Gallery in London staged the landmark exhibition "Portraits" by Mario Testino and, over the four years following, was brought to Milan, Amsterdam, Edinburgh, Tokyo, and Mexico City.

In 2003, he published *Portraits* to accompany his exhibition at The National Portrait Gallery. Later, in 2005, his exhibition of Diana photos, *Diana: Princess of Wales*, opened at Kensington Palace.

Photographer Mario Testino, center, with models.

In what he calls "semicouture," Theyskens creates brilliant, grown-up dresses, coats, and suits notable for assured cut, adventurous, experimental shapes, and a sophisticated color palette. Definitely not for little girls, these are clothes for confident women with a sense of drama. His customer list includes Madonna, Nicole Kidman, and Queen Rania of Jordan. In November 2002 he joined MARCEL ROCHAS as creative director, but in 2006, Proctor and Gamble discontinued the company's fashion division. Theyskens was appointed artistic director of NINA RICCI on November 1, 2006. He left the company in 2009.

Above: Designer Olivier Theyskens.

Right: Nina Ricci, spring/summer 2008.

BORN Brussels, Belgium, January 4, 1977

AWARDS Council of Fashion Designers of America (CFDA) *International Designer of the Year*, 2006

The son of a Belgian father and French mother, Olivier Theyskens is one of the fresh talents that have come out of Belgium to show in Paris and shine on the international fashion scene. He entered Brussels' l'École Nationale Supérieure des Arts Visuels de La Cambre in October 1995 at 18, leaving school in January 1997 (two years into a five-year curriculum) to start work on his own first collection. This was shown in August 1997 in Amsterdam and Knokke, Belgium. His first Paris showing was the following March.

Olivier Theyskens

Liz Tilberis

BORN Elizabeth Jane Kelly; Shirehampton, England, 1949

DIED New York, April 21, 1999

AWARDS Society of Publication Designers' 28th annual competition, *Gold Medal for Overall Redesign*, 1993; Council of Fashion Designers of America (CFDA), *Special Award*, 1993, *Humanitarian Award*, 1998

Liz Tilberis, formerly of British *Vogue*, achieved celebrity status in the United States when she was hired as the new editor-in-chief at the U.S. edition of *Harper's Bazaar*. She began her career in 1970, at British *Vogue*, when she was hired there as an intern. Rising through the ranks, Tilberis eventually became executive fashion editor and then editor in chief. By 1991, she was director of Condé Nast Publications in the U.K. In 1992, during the *Harper's Bazaar* 125th anniversary, Tilberis was offered a position as the publication's new editor-in-chief. She accepted and moved her family to New York. While she was at *Harper's Bazaar*, the magazine received a National Magazine Award twice for photography and for design, respectively. One year into her new position, she was diagnosed with ovarian cancer.

Despite her illness, Tilberis instituted many changes in an effort to turn the 125-year old publication around. She experimented with fresh design talent, innovative layouts, and playful typography. She also broke ground with new photographers; in particular the well-established PATRICK DEMARCHELIER and Peter Limbergh both came to work for her. While Tilberis underwent extensive chemotherapy and surgery, the magazine underwent a makeover. Hearst President and CEO Frank Bennack, Jr., noted that her vision was "for *Harper's Bazaar* to set the agenda for modern elegance." In fact, the cover story of the

Editor Liz Tilberis.

September 1992 issue, her very first, was an invitation to "enter the age of elegance."

Tilberis made no effort to hide her personal story from the public. In fact, she publicly spoke out against cancer, and in 1997 became a President of the Ovarian Cancer Research Fund. She also penned a book of memoirs entitled, *No Time to Die*. During the course of her work, Tilberis befriended Diana, Princess of Wales, who graced the cover of the U.S. edition of *Harper's Bazaar* twice under Tilberis's mantle.

BORN Vienna, Austria, July 25, 1934

AWARDS Coty American Fashion Critics' Award Special *Award* (swimsuits), 1975 • American Printed Fabrics Council "*Tommy*" Award, 1976 (twice in one year: once for beach clothes and sportswear, once for loungewear and lingerie "for her original designs and use of prints")

Monika Tilley made her name with swimwear. She had always been involved in sports so that her sportswear designs, while fashionable and often seductive, were thoroughly functional. She has used bias cuts, cotton madras shirred with elastic, a technique of angling the weave of a fabric so it shapes the body. While she explained her reputation as a top swimwear designer as a matter of longevity—"I've stuck to swimwear longer than anyone else has"—her success was based on fit. She was very product oriented and also worked hard at promoting new lines with trunk shows and personal appearances.

Born into a family of conservative government officials and diplomats, Tilley grew up in Austria and England. After graduation in 1956 from the Academy of Applied Arts in her native Vienna, she studied in Stockholm and Paris before leaving Europe for the United States. She worked briefly as an assistant to JOHN WEITZ, then as a freelance designer of skiwear and children's clothes. Her career began in earnest at White Stag and the Cole of California. She has also held design positions at ANNE KLEIN Studio, Mallory Leathers, and in 1968, at Elon of California. In 1970 she incorporated as Monika Tilley Ltd., a full-service studio covering color and fiber consulting, textile and print design, and designing/marketing, specializing in men's and women's sportswear, women's lingerie, and loungewear. Her list of clients included the Color Association of America, Monsanto, Malden Mills, Levi Straus, Munsingwear, Vassarette, Miss Elaine, and Elon.

In 2007, the Austrian Consul General Brigitta Blaha honored her with The Decoration of Honor in Silver for her cultural contributions to the Republic of Austria.

Designer Monika Tilley (left) and friend.

Models posing in swimsuits designed by Monika Tilley.

Isabel Toledo

BORN Cuba, April 9, 1961

AWARDS Coty American Fashion Critics' Award, *"Winnie,"* 2005; Museum at FIT *Couture Council Award for Artistry*, 2008

Isabel Toledo is one of the designers working in a very personal way somewhat out of the mainstream. She learned to sew as a child in Cuba and started making her own clothes because everything ready made was too big for her. Arriving in the United States with her family, she attended the Fashion Institute of Technology and Parsons School of Design, and studied painting and ceramics before switching to design. She worked with DIANA VREELAND at the Costume Department of the Metropolitan Museum of Art, restoring clothes from the Museum's collection. Her fashion career began in December 1985, when at the urging of her artist husband, Ruben Toledo, she made up a few pieces, which he then took around to the stores. PATRICIA FIELD and Henri Bendel were

Designer Isabel Toledo (right).

her first customers, followed by Bergdorf Goodman, which gave her the 57th Street windows for clothes from her first full collection.

Line and shape are paramount with Toledo, who starts with a shape such as the circle and experiments to see how far she can take it. She believes in arriving at simplicity through innovation, and insists that the design must not be contrived but evolve naturally. Her clothes, which she calls classic, range from sportswear to evening, from simple to flamboyant; they derive their uniqueness from the strength of their shapes and from her eye for details. The designs transcend age categories and appeal to women with a liking for the different.

FIT unveiled an exhibition entitled, *Holy Toledo! Isabel Toledo and the Art of Fashion*, in addition to presenting Toledo with an award. On January 20, 2009, First Lady Michelle Obama chose a green wool lace three-piece coat, dress, and cardigan set designed by Toledo to wear to the Inauguration of her husband President Barack Obama. It was not the first time she had worn a Toledo design, however, the Inaugural outfit gave Toledo the huge international recognition she so richly deserved.

President Obama, and First Lady Michelle in Isabel Toledo, 2009.

BORN County Galway, Ireland, May 26, 1967

AWARDS British Fashion Awards *Accessory Designer of the Year*, 1991, 1992, 1996, 1997

After studies at Dublin's National College of Art and Design, Philip Treacy moved to London in 1988 on a scholarship to the Royal College of Art. While still in school he worked for RIFAT OZBECK and JOHN GALLIANO, among others, and soon after graduating was house milliner at HARTNELL. An interview at CHANEL led to collaboration with KARL LAGERFELD on the spring/summer 1991 couture show, and since that breakthrough he has provided hats to Chanel for both the couture and ready-to-wear collections. His

Designer Philip Treacy.

creations have also appeared regularly in the collections of VALENTINO and THIERRY MUGLER. They are sold in some of the world's finest stores—Bergdorf Goodman and Saks Fifth Avenue in the United States, Harrods and Harvey Nichols in England, and in his own London boutique.

Treacy is fascinated by surrealist themes—animal forms, insects, hands, a crown of thorns—which take shape out of stripped feathers and distressed materials in unlikely juxtapositions. GIANNI VERSACE is reputed to have said of him, "Give him a pin, he makes a sculpture; give him a rose, he makes a poem." In January 2000 he took his creations to Paris for the first showing of haute couture hats there in 70 years.

In 2005, he created hats for the wedding of the Prince of Wales and Camila Parker Bowles. Treacy was appointed honorary office of the Most Excellent Order of the British Empire by the Prince of Wales and the Duchess of Cornwall in 2007. The honor was conferred by her highness the Queen for recognition of his services to the British fashion industry.

Sarah Jessica Parker wearing a hat designed by Philip Treacy.

Pauline Trigère

Designer Pauline Trigère.

BORN Paris, France, November 4, 1908
DIED New York, February 13, 2002

AWARDS Neiman Marcus Award, 1950 • Coty American Fashion Critics' Award "*Winnie*," 1949; *Return Award*, 1951; *Hall of Fame*, 1959 • *Medaille de Vermeil* of the City of Paris: 1972, 1982 • Council of Fashion Designers of America (CFDA) *Lifetime Achievement Award*, 1993 • *Fashion Walk of Fame*, 2001 • French *Légion d'honneur*, December 2001

The daughter of Russian émigrés, her father a tailor, her mother a dressmaker, Pauline Trigère's first career choice was to be a surgeon. When her father opposed the idea, she got a job making muslins at a Paris couture house. In 1929 she married Lazar Radley, another Russian-Jewish tailor. Her husband became alarmed at the rising Nazi tide and in 1936, two years after her father's death, the family—Trigère, her husband, and their two sons, as well as her brother and mother—left France for Chile. Their first stop was New York, and there they stayed.

After a business partnership with her brother and husband fell apart, her husband disappeared and Trigère found work, first with manufacturer Ben Gershel then at HATTIE CARNEGIE as an assistant to TRAVIS BANTON. Fired by Carnegie at the outbreak of World War II, Trigère, with her brother's help, scraped together enough fabric for her first collection—just 11 dresses—ready in March 1942. Her brother took the samples in a suitcase and, traveling around the country by bus, sold them to fine specialty shops from Los Angeles to Minneapolis to Chicago to Philadelphia, with such success that the company was able not only to survive but also to grow.

Trigère cut and draped directly from the bolt—coats, capes, suits, and dresses of near-couture quality in luxurious fabrics, unusual tweeds, and prints. The deceptive simplicity of the clothes was based on artistic, intricate cut, especially flattering to the mature figure. She took care of the designing for her firm while her elder son, Jean-Pierre Radley, as president of Trigère Inc., was in charge of the business end. The Trigère name has appeared on scarves, jewelry, furs, men's ties, sunglasses, bedroom fashions, paperworks, servingware, and a fragrance.

Trigère closed her business in August of 1993. In 2001, she was inducted into the Fashion Walk of Fame, where large, white-bronze plaques honoring American designers—both living and dead—are set into the Seventh Avenue sidewalk between 35th and 41st Streets. Trigère, whose tailoring and draping skills were legendary, chose tailoring shears as her symbol rather than a sketch. In her acceptance speech she quipped that it was the first time she'd ever allowed anyone to walk on her.

Designer Trina Turk.

AWARDS LA Fashion Awards *Fashion Achievement Award*, 2005 • California Designer of the Year Award, 1998

Above: Trina Turk designs.

Right: Model wearing a design by Trina Turk.

Trina Turk always knew she wanted to go into fashion, but didn't expect to be so successful at it. A California native, her Japanese mother taught her how to sew at age 11 and her love of designing clothes was born. After attending the University of Washington, she landed her first job with the Seattle-based sportswear manufacturer Britannia Jeans. She then returned to California to design prints for Ocean Pacific. Tired of working for others, in 1995, with the help of her husband, photographer Jonathan Skow, she opened Trina Turk Company. The collection was so successful that it sold at Barneys, Saks Fifth Avenue, and Fred Segal that same year. Over the next 13 years, Turk built Trina Turk Company into a $40 million-a-year business.

Turk's vision for the company is shaped by her memories of growing up in California in the late 1960s and 1970s. She is also inspired by the multi-cultural mix and architecture of Los Angeles. Her philosophy is to create wearable, optimistic fashion that incorporates the best aspects of classic American sportswear. In 2002 she opened her first free standing boutique in Palm Springs, and four years later followed up with a boutique in New York's meatpacking district. In the spring of 2009, she launched a hosiery "guest designer" line with Hue, and printed fabrics for home furnishings manufacturer Schumacher. Her simple and modern designs are popular with many celebrities, including Eva Longoria, Natalie Portman, Gwen Stefani, and model Kate Moss.

Richard Tyler

AWARDS Council of Fashion Designers of America (CFDA) *Perry Ellis Award for New Fashion Talent,* 1993; *Best Designer,* 1994; *Women's wear Designer of the Year,* 1994; *Perry Ellis Award for Men's wear* (a tie with Edward Pavlick and Richard Bengtsson for Richard Edwards), 1995 • Dallas Fashion Award *Fashion Excellence Award* (for Anne Klein)

When Richard Tyler succeeded LOUIS DELL'OLIO as designer for ANNE KLEIN, he was already a highly regarded fashion name in Los Angeles, producing beautiful clothes of near-custom quality for women and men and selling them from his own boutique. His jackets are particularly admired, not only for their inventive, graceful cut, but also for their perfection-ist tailoring and finish, so flawless they could be worn inside out. Their high quality places the clothes firmly in the deluxe category.

When he was eight years old, Tyler was taught to sew by his mother, who designed costumes for the

Designer Richard Tyler.

Fall 2005.

ballet. Her credo, "Don't send it out unless it's per-fect," has guided him ever since. In his teen years, Tyler apprenticed with the tailor who made suits for the Australian Prime Minister; at 18 he opened his first boutique, Zippity-doo-dah, attracting a clien-tele from the music industry. After touring with Rod Stewart and designing for his tour, he landed in Los Angeles in 1978, and afterward spent time designing in Europe. He continued to design for performers over the next few years. In 1987, he established Tyler/ Trafficante, a partnership with his second wife, Lisa, and her sister Michelle to design, manufacture, and wholesale the clothes. The first New York showing of the women's collection was in April 1993.

In May 1993 Tyler was named as designer for Anne Klein. While the collections were well received by his peers and the press, the traditional Anne Klein customer evidently found them too advanced, and in December 1994 the company announced the end of the arrangement. Tyler continues to produce his sig-nature line and show it in New York, with his opera-tions based in his downtown Manhattan home studio. A more moderately-priced collection called Tyler was announced in March 2002.

In 2006 he designed uniforms for the airline industry called The Richard Tyler Collection for Delta.

Patricia UNDERWOOD
Emanuel UNGARO

VALENTINO

Giambattista VALLI

Dries VAN NOTEN

John VARVATOS

Joan VASS

Donatella VERSACE

Gianni VERSACE

VIKTOR & ROLF

Madeleine VIONNET

Roger VIVIER

Michael VOLLBRACHT

Diane von

FURSTENBERG

Diana VREELAND

LOUIS VUITTON

Patricia Underwood

BORN Patricia Gilbert; Maidenhead, England, October 11, 1947

AWARDS Council of Fashion Designers of America (CFDA), (for American Accessories), 1983 • Coty American Fashion Critics' Awards, 1982

Patricia Underwood worked in Paris as an *au pair* and at Buckingham Palace as a secretary before moving to New York in 1968. She took an evening class at the Fashion Institute of Technology and then, with a friend, decided to go into business making hats. Underwood added scarves, shawls, and gloves that coordinated her collection in the mid-1990s. Her work is mostly ready-to-wear, available through department and specialty stores such as Saks Fifth Avenue and Bergdorf Goodman. Her strength is in elegantly updating classic, simple shapes from the

Designer Patricia Underwood.

past, such as boaters, milkmaids' hats, and nuns' coifs. Her signature hats are made of straw, felt, leather, and cashmere. Underwood's designs have frequently been chosen by designers to complement their collections. The designers she's worked with include RALPH LAUREN, MICHAEL KORS, Band of Outsiders, Abaete and Temperley, NICOLE MILLER, and OSCAR DE LA RENTA. Her hats have also been worn in films such as *Down with Love*, *Cinderella*, *Sabrina*, *Six Days-Seven Nights*, *Four Weddings and a Funeral*, *Austin Powers*, *The Imposters*, *The Pallbearers*, and *Return to Paradise*.

Hat designed by Patricia Underwood, 2005.

Emanuel Ungaro

BORN Aix-en-Provence, France, February 13, 1933

AWARDS Neiman Marcus Award, 1969

Emanuel Ungaro's (OON-Gar-o) parents were Italian immigrants who fled from the Italian government to the south of France. He gained his initial training working with his father, a tailor, from whom he learned to cut, sew, and fit men's clothes. In 1955, at 22, he left Provence for Paris and a job in a small tailoring firm. Three years later he went to work for BALENCIAGA, where he stayed until 1963, then spent two seasons with COURRÈGES.

He opened his own business in 1965. His first collections were reminiscent of Courrèges—tailored coats and suits with diagonal seaming, little girl A-line dresses, and blazers with shorts. The clothes were widely copied in the youth market. Many of his special fabrics and prints were designed by Sonja Knapp, a Swiss graphic artist.

Above: Designer Emanuel Ungaro.
Below, left: Spring/summer haute couture, 1992.

In the 1970s he turned to softer fabrics and more flowing lines, mingling several different prints in a single outfit and piling on layers. His designs became increasingly seductive, evolving into a body-conscious, sensuous look, strategically draped and shirred. As it was immediately and extensively copied, Ungaro himself moved on, retaining his penchant for mixing patterns and prints. His excellent tailoring has always remained in evidence in creations as diverse as a men's wear striped jacket tossed over a slinky flowered evening dress, or daytime suits with soft trousers cut on the bias. He has added ready-to-wear; a perfume, Diva; and also Ungaro boutiques in Europe and the United States. Other projects have included furs and men's wear, sheets, wallcoverings, curtains, and knitwear.

Ungaro celebrated his 35th year in business with a New York party in September 2001; the next month he named his creative director GIAMBATTISTA VALLI as designer of ready-to-wear. Responsibility for the haute couture remained with Ungaro. Since then, the line has gone through three design directors, including ESTEBAN CORTAZAR, who debuted his designs in February of 2008 at the age of 23. Lindsay Lohan was named artistic adviser in 2009 along with head designer Estrella Archs.

Valentino

BORN Valentino Garavani; Voghera, Italy, ca. 1932

AWARDS Neiman Marcus Award, 1967 • Council of Fashion Designers of America (CFDA) *Lifetime Achievement Award*, 2000

Above: Designer Valentino.
Left: Fall 2006.

Valentino left Italy for Paris at age 17 to study at L'École de la Chambre Syndicale de la Couture Parisienne, having prepared himself by studying both fashion and the French language in Milan. In 1950 he went to work for JEAN DESSÈS, stayed five years, then worked as design assistant at GUY LAROCHE until 1958.

In 1959, he opened his own couture house with a tiny atelier in Rome's Via Condotti; within a few years, he was successful enough to move to his present headquarters. His first major recognition came in 1962 when he showed for the first time in Florence. In 1975 he began showing his ready-to-wear collections in Paris, and has continued to do so, with couture showings still held in Rome. His first boutique for ready-to-wear opened in Milan in 1969, followed by one in Rome and then others around the world, including Japan. Other interests include men's wear, Valentino Più for gifts and interiors, bed linens, and drapery fabrics.

Valentino's clothes are noted for refined simplicity, elegance, and all-out glamour—precisely tailored coats and suits, sophisticated sportswear, entrance-making evening dresses—always feminine and flattering. They are notable for beautiful fabrics and exquisite workmanship and have been worn by a diverse international clientele ranging from the late Jacqueline Onassis to Elizabeth Taylor to Jennifer Lopez.

With Giancarlo Giammetti, his partner and business manager, Valentino understands the grand gesture. In 1978 he introduced his signature fragrance in France, sponsoring a ballet performance in Paris with after-theater parties at Maxim's and the Palace. In 1984, he celebrated his 25th year in business and 50th couture collection with an enormous outdoor fashion show in Rome's Piazza d'Espagna. His 30th

anniversary celebration was a week of lavish lunches, dinners, a ball, and two exhibitions, attended by an international assemblage of friends and clients. A Valentino retrospective was part of an Italian promotion at the Park Avenue Armory in 1992.

In 2008, after 45 years in fashion, Valentino retired from the business, with an eye toward pursuing "new interests and challenges."

Above: Spring 2008.
Right: Spring 2008.

Giambattista Valli

BORN Rome, Italy 1966

Giambattista Valli was born into a conservative Italian family, and first attended one of the schools of the Vatican. However, an early interest in design, partly brought on by the urge to recreate drawings by YVES SAINT LAURENT, inspired the young Valli to attend the European School of Design in Germany as well as Central Saint Martins University of the Arts in London. In 1988, he went to work for the public relations department of Italian couturier ROBERTO CAPUCCI, where he was eventually invited to become a designer. Subsequently, he moved on to FENDI, where as a senior designer he created pieces for the young and trendy Fendissime apparel line.

In 1995, Valli became a senior designer for the Italian designer Krizia, and then proceeded to join EMMANUEL UNGARO in 1997. Valli was promoted to art director of Ungaro ready-to-wear and the younger Ungaro Fever line, and remained at that fashion house until 2001.

Designer Giambattista Valli (right).

After a variety of fashion design stints, in 2005 Valli partnered with the Italian licensee Gilmar to create his own label, Giambattista. The designs were opulent, innovative, and fluid in line. Bold colors and revealing cuts helped to establish his signature. Today, Valli is one of the designers most sought after by celebrities. His star clientele includes Queen Rania of Jordan, Victoria Beckham, Penelope Cruz, Naomi Campbell, and Mischa Barton. In November of 2008, Valli premiered his spring 2009 collection at the Royal Ontario Museum in Canada. He also collaborates with ski apparel legend Moncler and creates select bridal pieces and furs.

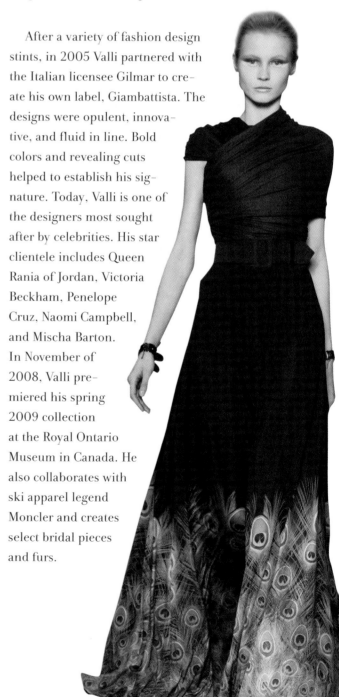

Above: Fall 2008.
Right: Fall 2009.

Designer Dries Van Noten.

Above: Fall 2008.

Right: Spring 2010.

Dries Van Noten

BORN Antwerp, Belgium, May 1958

AWARDS Council of Fashion Designers *International Designer of the Year Award*, 2008 • FIT's *Couture Council Award for the Artistry of Fashion*, 2009

Coming from three generations of tailors, Dries Van Noten (van-note-ahn) took up the family trade while still a student at the Royal Academy of Beaux Arts in Antwerp, working for Belgian and Italian men's wear labels as a freelance designer. His first collection under his own name was in 1985; the next year he went to London as part of the Antwerp Six—a group of influential avantgarde fashion designers who graduated from Antwerp's Royal Academy of Fine Arts between 1980–1981—for a presentation. This brought him press recognition and orders from adventurous retailers internationally, including Barneys in New York. His Antwerp boutique opened in 1989, and his first Paris men's wear showing was in 1991. He has also added women's wear and accessories, showrooms in Milan and Tokyo, and shops in the Far East.

The Van Noten style is a marriage of opposites—simple with sophisticated, classic with modern—both the women's and men's collections reflecting his passion for fabrics, which are usually made exclusively for him. Although he shows in Paris and his clothes are sold around the world, he continues to live and work in Antwerp.

John Varvatos

BORN Dearborn, Michigan, August 8, 1954

AWARDS Council of Fashion Designers of America (CFDA) *Perry Ellis Award for New Men's wear Designer, 2000; Men's wear Designer of the Year, 2001, 2005 • GQ Designer of the Year, 2007*

When John Varvatos (var-VAY-toes) presented his first collection under his own label in 1999 he was hardly a beginner, having already put in 16 years in the men's fashion industry. He attended Eastern Michigan University, studied fashion illustration and

Designer John Varvatos.

Fall 2006 collection.

patternmaking at the Fashion Institute of Technology, and started with RALPH LAUREN in 1983. In 1990 he was wooed away by CALVIN KLEIN to head his men's wear division and establish the cK label. Then in 1994 he went back to Polo RALPH LAUREN as senior vice president and head designer of men's wear, gaining further experience in marketing, production, and financing before embarking on his own in 1998. He has designed a limited edition of athletic shoes for Converse, and opened boutiques in Los Angeles, Las Vegas, San Francisco, and New York City. In 2006 he launched his first eyewear collection.

Varvatos combines the relaxed ease of sportswear with a refined elegance of cut, luxurious materials, and meticulous craftsmanship. He believes in presenting a total wardrobe—tailored clothing, sportswear, leather accessories, and footwear.

In 2008, Varvatos opened a store in New York City in the space that once housed the underground club CBGB.

Joan Vass

BORN New York, New York, May 19, 1925

AWARDS Smithsonian Institution, Washington, D.C., *"Extraordinary Women in Fashion,"* 1978 • Coty American Fashion Critics' Award *Special Award* (crafted knit fashions), 1979 • National Cotton Council *U.S. Cotton Champion Award*, 2001

Joan Vass has built her reputation on crochets and handmade or hand-loomed knits, and imaginative, functional clothes in simplified shapes and subtle colorings, usually in her preferred natural fibers. She is recognized by retailers and the press as a highly creative, original designer.

A graduate of the University of Wisconsin, she majored in philosophy, did graduate work in aesthetics, worked as a curator at the Museum of Modern Art, and as an editor at art book publisher Harry N. Abrams. With no formal fashion training, she got into designing in the early 1970s when two of her concerns intersected. First, she was bothered by the plight of women with salable skills but no outlet for them—specifically, women who either could not work away from home or did not want to be closed up in an office or factory; second, she was convinced there was a market for handmade articles of good quality.

Vass, who had always knitted and crocheted, found a number of women with superior craft skills and in 1973 began designing things for them to knit and crochet, selling the articles privately. This new enterprise took so much time that she wanted to give it up but was dissuaded by her workers. Then came her first large order from Henri Bendel; other stores followed and she was in business. Her firm was incorporated in 1977. In 1988, Joan Vass USA for Men was introduced and in 1992 she introduced a jewelry line called Joan Vass Spa.

In addition to Joan Vass New York—better-priced clothes for men and women—there are Joan Vass boutiques, the moderately priced Joan Vass USA collection, and franchises in Los Angeles, Houston, and New Orleans.

Above: Designer Joan Vass.
Left: Spring 1996.

Donatella Versace

BORN Calabria, Italy, 1955

Donatella Versace (Verr-sa-chay) was ten years younger than her brother, GIANNI VERSACE, but from early on served as his inspiration, even as a child wearing the clothes he designed for her. When he moved to Florence in the mid-1970s to work in knitwear design, she followed, studying Italian literature at the University of Florence and visiting him in his studio on weekends. After graduation she joined him in Milan where they shared an apartment, and when he founded his own company in 1978, she continued to function as both muse and critic. He eventually gave her responsibility for her own diffusion collection, Versus.

Designer Donatella Versace.

Following Gianni's 1997 murder, Donatella managed in three months to produce a creditable ready-to-wear collection—as creative director of the house she has continued to grow, each successive ready-to-wear and couture collection showing increased confidence and a firmer grasp of her craft. Her work is very much in the Versace mode of bold prints and forthright sexiness, not for the timid but appealing strongly to entertainment figures and others for whom understatement is a foreign word.

The Versace business has always been and continues to be a family affair, with oldest brother Santo as president; Donatella's husband, Paul Beck, as director of men's wear; and Gianni's one-time companion, Antonio D'Amico, in charge of Versace Sport. The company has continued to expand into other areas—skin care, perfume, tabletop accessories, even hotels.

In 2008 Donatella Versace was made the honorary chairman for London's Fashion Fringe, judging upcoming designer talent.

Above: Gisele Bundchen wearing a Donatella Versace design.
Left: Fall 2009.

Gianni Versace

He also designed for the theater, including ballet costumes for La Scala and for Béjart's *Ballet of the 20th Century*. "Signatures," a retrospective exhibit celebrating 15 years of his work was mounted at the Fashion Institute of Technology in November 1992.

Versace's 1997 murder snatched a vital force from the fashion world. His business empire, however, has survived and flourished through the efforts of the family team he had formed, under the creative direction of his sister DONATELLA VERSACE. Versace boutiques around the world sell women's and men's clothing, accessories, knits, leathers, and furs; there are also fragrances for both men and women.

Designer Gianni Versace.

BORN Calabria, Italy, December 2, 1946
DIED Miami, Florida, July 15, 1997

As his mother was a dressmaker, Versace's exposure to fashion began very early, but before embarking on a fashion career he first studied architecture. He then began designing knitwear in Florence, and from there moved to Milan where he designed for several prêt-à-porter firms, including Genny and Callaghan. In 1979 he showed for the first time under his own name, a collection of men's wear.

Versace became one of Europe's most popular designers, offering women many options, always sensuous and sexy. His vivid and far-reaching imagination was fueled by an insatiable curiosity and appetite for knowledge, resulting in bold prints inspired by antiquities, Byzantine mosaics, and in the early 1980s, a fabric of metal mesh so soft and pliable it could be sewn by machine. This he used in beautiful, slithery evening dresses worn from California to the Riviera. As a designer he was fearless, using his mistakes to improve and grow. Like ELSA SCHIAPARELLI, he could not only go over the top into vulgarity, but also produced clothes of great sophistication and elegance.

Spring/summer haute couture, 1993.

Viktor & Rolf

BORN Viktor Horsting, May 27, 1969;
Rolf Snoeren, December 12, 1969

AWARDS Festival of Hyères *Young Designers Award*, 1993

Graduates of the Academy of the Arts in Arnhem, The Netherlands, where they studied in the Fashion Department from 1988 to 1992, Viktor & Rolf gained their first attention in 1993 as winners of the prestigious Festival of Hyères *Young Designers Award* (Salon Européen des Jeunes Stylistes).

In the Paris couture showings of January 1998, the first Viktor & Rolf showing featured an "atomic bomb" evening dress collection inspired by mushroom clouds and heralded the arrival of two young designers of abundant talent and a gift for attracting press attention. While equally pressworthy, subsequent showings have earned them a solid reputation for clothes that are not only imaginative but also

Designers Viktor Horsting (right) and Rolf Snoeren (left) with model.

wearable. After five couture collections, the designers decided to concentrate on ready-to-wear, which they began showing in March 2000.

Viktor & Rolf designs are sold in avant garde stores, including Barneys in New York, and have been featured in museum and gallery exhibitions in cities such as New York, Tokyo, Groningen, The Netherlands, Yokohama, and Paris. In April 2002 the pair, who once created a "virtual" perfume in a flacon without an opening, has created two hit fragrances: Anxidote and Flowerbomb. The duo's signature pieces were also featured in an exhibition at the Barbican Art Gallery in London in 2008.

Above: Spring 2010.
Right: Fall/winter 2008.

BORN Aubervilliers, France, June 22, 1876
DIED Paris, France, March 2, 1975

AWARDS Légion d'honneur, 1929

One of the towering figures of twentieth-century couture, Madeleine Vionnet (Vee-OH-nay) still influences us. Her bias technique, her cowl and halter necklines, and her use of pleating are part of the designer's vocabulary.

The daughter of a gendarme, she began her apprenticeship when she was 12, and at 16 was working with a successful dressmaker called Vincent. By the age of 19 she had married, had a child who died, and was divorced. At 20 she went to London, where she stayed five years, working first in a tailor's workroom and then for CALLOT SOEURS. She worked closely with one of the sisters at Callot Soeurs, Mme. Gerber, for whom she made *toiles* and considered even greater

Designer Madeleine Vionnet.

than POIRET. In 1907 she moved to JACQUES DOUCET and in 1912 opened her own house, which closed during World War I. She reopened in 1918 on the Avenue Montaigne, and closed for good in 1940.

Even while working for others, Vionnet had advanced ideas not always acceptable to conservative clients. She eliminated high, boned collars from dresses and blouses, and claimed to have eliminated corsets before Poiret. One of couture's greatest technicians, she invented the modern use of the bias cut, producing dresses so supple they eliminated the need for fastenings of any kind. Without the aid of placket openings, they could be slipped on over the head to fall back into shape on the body. For even more suppleness, seams were often stitched with fagoting.

She did not sketch, but instead draped, cut, and pinned directly on the figure. For this purpose she used a small-scaled wooden mannequin with articulated joints. Designs were later translated into full-size toiles, then into the final material. Most probably she chose this method for convenience. It is doubtful she could have achieved her effects as economically or with as little physical effort by any other means.

Vionnet introduced crêpe de Chine, previously confined to linings, as a fabric suitable for fashion; she transformed Greek and medieval inspirations into

Evening dresses, 1938.

Pale crêpe pajamas, 1931.

The Duchess of Windsor in Vionnet dress, 1937.

completely modern clothes, graceful and sensuous. She did not allow herself to become set in her fashion ways, and it is said that in 1934 she scrapped her nearly finished collection when she realized it was out of step with the new romantic mood, completing an entirely new one in two weeks to show on the scheduled date.

Many designers trained with her. Her assistant for years was Marcelle Chaumont, who later opened her own house. Others included Mad Maltezos of the house of Mad Carpentier, and JACQUES GRIFFE. A person of complete integrity, Vionnet was the implacable enemy of copyists and style pirates. Her motto was, "to copy is to steal."

Madeleine Vionnet presented her last collection in 1939. In 2007, with Sophia Kokosalaki as head designer, the House of Vionnet experienced a revival. Though her first collection with the House was distributed at Barneys New York stores throughout the United States, she ended up leaving to start her own line the same year. In 2008, the House of Vionnet hired designer Marc Audibet, whom many say has succeeded in capturing the mood and art form of the original designer.

Bright green wool coat and purple belted sheath, 1937.

BORN Paris, France, November 13, 1907

DIED Toulouse, France, October 2, 1998

AWARDS Neiman Marcus Award, 1961

Roger Vivier worked at his craft for over 60 years, from the 1930s when he opened a little workshop in Paris in the Place Vendôme, until his death at age 90. To prepare for his métier, he studied drawing and sculpture at L'École des Beaux-Arts and apprenticed at a shoe factory owned by a relative. His shoes—lighthearted and with a spirited sense of fantasy—had a strong structural foundation traceable to his training in sculpture.

Vivier's talent was first recognized by ELSA SCHIAPARELLI in 1937, when she commissioned him to design shoes for a collection. It was at that time that he opened his first boutique, developing a devoted celebrity following that ranged from Princess Margaret and Princess Grace to Elizabeth Taylor, Josephine Baker, and the Rothschilds. He came to the United States in the late 1930s and became associated with American shoe designer Herman Delman, working with him until 1955 and again from 1992 to 1994. The shoes were sold at fine U.S. retailers such as Bergdorf Goodman and Neiman Marcus.

Designer Roger Vivier.

From 1953 through 1963, Vivier was associated with CHRISTIAN DIOR, with whom he developed the first ready-to-wear designer label shoes, Christian Dior created by Roger Vivier. During his time with Dior, he produced a myriad of exquisite evening shoes—always with refined, streamlined silhouettes, frequently exuberantly, extravagantly, jeweled and embroidered. After Dior's death in 1957, he collaborated for many years with YVES SAINT LAURENT and also worked with a number of other top couturiers, including BALENCIAGA, COURRÈGES, UNGARO, GRÈS, and NINA RICCI.

In 1963 he again opened a salon, this time across from Dior, where Marlene Dietrich reportedly visited nearly every day, and it was not unusual for a shoe fitting to take two hours. In 1974 he left Paris for a castle in the Dordogne region of France, where he continued to design shoes, this time for the Japanese market.

Vivier shoes are included in collections at the Metropolitan Museum of Art in New York and in Paris, at both the Musée de la Mode et du Costume and the Musée des Arts de la Mode.

An evening stilletto from the Christian Dior created by Roger Vivier line, 1958.

Above: Designer Michael Vollbracht.

Below, right: Fall 2007.

BORN Quincy, Illinois, November 17, 1947

AWARDS Parsons School of Design *Norman Norell Award*, 1969 • Coty American Fashion Critics' Award *Designer of the Year*, 1980

Michael Vollbracht, former creative director for BILL BLASS, had one of the hottest labels in the 1970s and 1980s. Vollbracht's fashion career started in the early 1960s, when he attended Parsons School of Design. In 1969 he was hired by GEOFFREY BEENE, and two years later, he moved to DONALD BROOKS, where he served as head designer for two years.

In 1978 he began his own label, Michael Vollbracht Collection, and was hailed as one of "Seventh Avenue's bright stars" by *Women's Wear Daily*. His collections were sold at stores such as Bergdorf Goodman and Neiman Marcus, and worn by Farrah Fawcett and Elizabeth Taylor. But in 1985, after a lucrative licensing deal fell through, he closed the doors of his fashion house to pursue his passion for fashion illustration and art.

He worked on illustrations for various stores and excelled in visual arts; in 1989 he was named one of the *New Yorker*'s top illustrators. In 1985 he pub-

lished *Nothing Sacred*, a visual memoir about his life in the fashion industry, which featured an introduction by his friend and mentor Bill Blass. In 1999 Blass retired and asked Vollbracht to help him on a retrospective of his work at Indiana University; Vollbracht authored the book that accompanied the exhibition.

In 2002, shortly after the project was completed, Blass passed away. Spurred on by the death of his friend, Vollbracht returned to the fashion world, and was appointed creative director of Bill Blass. Many believe the appointment was given to him because of his close relationship with Blass, and his knowledge of the Bill Blass identity.

During his five-year stint at Bill Blass, Vollbracht's decisions were closely scrutinized. He had some success with a new scent and managed to maintain the designer's identity. However, some critics and fashion editors claimed that his clothes lacked sex appeal and appeared too matronly. He retired in 2007, pursuing his art career full time.

Michael Vollbracht

Diane von Furstenberg

Designer Diane von Furstenberg.

Above: Fall 2009.

Right: Spring/summer 2009.

BORN Diane Simone Michelle Halfin; Brussels, Belgium, December 31, 1946

AWARD Council of Fashion Designers (CFDA) *Lifetime Achievement Award* 2005

Diane von Furstenberg has had at least three, perhaps four separate fashion careers. She started in 1971 with moderately priced dresses of lightweight jersey, had her own custom shop for a few years on Fifth Avenue, continued with the Diane von Furstenberg Studio and direct TV selling on QVC, and in 1997 was back in the mid-range dress business with an updated version of her wrap dress.

Educated in Spain, England, and Switzerland, Furstenberg took a degree in economics from the University of Geneva, and moved to the United States in 1969. When she saw a need for dresses that were affordable, comfortable, and fashionable, she decided to try design- ing. Her first patterns were cut on her dining table, and shipped to a

Diane von Furstenberg, continued

friend in Italy to be made up. In 1971, she packed her first samples in a suitcase and started showing them to store buyers. The jersey wrap dress with surplice top and long sleeves was an immediate success and made her name. In 1976, *Newsweek* named her the most marketable designer since COCO CHANEL. This is the dress Furstenberg says taught her three essential F's in designing for women. "It's flattering, feminine and, above all, functional." A perfume followed, as well as a cosmetics line and shop, home furnishings, and licenses from eyewear to luggage.

She left the moderate-price dress market in 1977, reentered it briefly in 1985 with a collection based

Designer Diane von Furstenberg, 1972.

on her signature wrap dress. This was followed by her retailing venture and her design-and-marketing studio, and involvement with televised home shopping. In 1994 she was appointed creative planning director for Q^2, QVC's weekend channel. Her 1997 reincarnation was in collaboration with her daughter-in-law, Alexandra Miller von Furstenberg, resulting in a redesign of the famous wrap dress in silk jersey with a new body, shorter length, and subtler details. It was part of a complete collection of modern, wearable, affordable clothes that appeal to active, vital women of any age. She continues to take on new and exciting projects. In fact, in 2003, she teamed up with tennis player Venus Williams and Reebok to create a tenniswear line. The Council of Fashion Designers of America, an organization of which she is currently president, awarded Furstenberg the *Lifetime Achievement Award* in 2005. The designer also penned a limited edition comic book with the message "Be the Wonder Woman You Can Be," which features her life story.

Spring 2008.

BORN Diana Dalziel, Paris France, July 29, 1903
DIED New York, August 22, 1989

AWARDS *Chevalier of the National Order of Merit of France*, 1970 • Légion d'Honneur, 1976 • Lord & Taylor *Dorothy Shaver "Rose" Award*, 1976 • Parsons School of *Design Honorary Doctor of Fine Arts Degree*, 1977

For nearly five decades, Diana Vreeland was a powerful influence on the American fashion consciousness, first as fashion editor and last as museum consultant. Born in Paris to an American mother and English father, raised in a milieu saturated with fashion and the arts, she was by both nature and nurture ideally fitted for her eventual vocation. As a child, she was exposed to extraordinary people and events—Diaghilev, Nijinsky, Ida Rubinstein, and Vernon and Irene Castle were all guests in her parents' apartment—and she remembers being sent to London in 1911 for the coronation of George V. Her family moved to America at the outbreak of World War I. Married in 1924 to Thomas Reed Vreeland, she accompanied her husband as his job took him to Albany, New York, on to London, then back to New York City in 1937. The same year, at the invitation of CARMEL SNOW, she went to work for *Harper's Bazaar*.

At *Harper's Bazaar*, she first wrote "Why Don't You?", a column that quickly became a byword for such suggestions as "Why Don't You. . . . Turn your child into an Infanta for a fancy-dress party?" After six months she became fashion editor, working closely with Snow and art director Alexey Brodovitch to make *Harper's Bazaar* the exciting, influential publication it was. In 1962 she left the magazine to go to *Vogue* as associate editor, then editor-in-chief, a post she held until 1971. After 1971 she was a consulting editor at *Vogue* and began a new career as con-

Editor Diana Vreeland.

sultant to the Costume Institute of the Metropolitan Museum of Art. There she mounted a series of outstanding exhibitions on such subjects as "Balenciaga," "American Women of Style," "The Glory of Russian Costume," "Vanity Fair," and "Man and the Horse."

Vreeland, who as a child felt like an ugly duckling, re-created herself as an elegant, completely individual woman with a strong personal style: jet black hair, heavily rouged cheeks, and bright red lips. For day and small dinners she dressed in simple uniforms—sweaters and skirts or sweaters and pants—appearing for big evenings in dramatic gowns.

Louis Vuitton

FOUNDED 1853

Louis Vuitton was a carpenter's son who at the age of 16 apprenticed for luggage designer Monsieur Marechal in Paris. In 1854, he decided to start his own business making luxury luggage for wealthy traveling Parisians. He made luggage for aristocratic families of the court of Empress Eugenie of Paris.

In 1858, the company created the first flat trunk luggage, with his first signature grey "Trianon" canvas. Trunks were usually round and difficult to stack on railroad cars. People found these new flat trunks very convenient and elegant for travel. At the same time, Vuitton was making trunks for the Empress Eugenie of France. This solidified his status as a luxury company. In 1867 he won the bronze medal at the Universalle Expedition and the Gold in 1889. In 1888, Vuitton introduced the "Damier Canvas" which was branded with the first Vuitton trademark logo, "Marque L. Vuitton Epose." Louis Vuitton died in 1892.

After his death, George Vuitton, Louis's son, took the company to worldwide status. The years spanning 1893 to 1936 are considered the "Golden Age of Louis Vuitton." In 1893, Vuitton displayed products to the United States at the World's Fair in Chicago. The bags were widely copied, so George Vuitton created the famous Monogram Canvas with the trademark LV logo, and prints inspired by the Victorian Period and Japonisme, a Japanese art and craft movement that was very popular in Paris.

By the 1930s, Vuitton began producing ladies handbags. In 1936, upon George's death, his son Gaston-Louis, took Vuitton into the new age. In 1959 the company brought back the monogram canvas, however they were able to perfect a new method of coating. This coating allowed the fabric to breathe while keeping the fabric hard and strong. It is still used on bags to this day.

Designs by Louis Vuitton.

By the 1970's Louis Vuitton was a staple of luxury and refinement. A store was opened in Tokyo, and by 1980, Asian involvement in the company accounted for almost half of its revenues. In 1983, Vuitton became involved in the America's Cup, creating challengers with the "Louis Vuitton Cup." The world of Vuitton would dramatically change when in 1987 they merged with Möet Hennessy to create the LVHM Conglomerate. MARC JACOBS was appointed creative director in 1997 and currently still holds this position.

Karen WALKER
Alexander WANG
Vera WANG
Bruce WEBER

Anna WINTOUR
Charles FREDERICK
WORTH
Jason WU

Chester WEINBERG
John WEITZ
Stuart WEITZMAN
Vivienne WESTWOOD
Edward WILKERSON
Matthew WILLIAMSON

Karen Walker

BORN New Zealand

AWARDS *Prix de Marie Claire* for Best Creative Talent, 2007

New Zealand's premiere fashion designer Karen Walker presented her first collection in Sydney, Australia, in 1998, but it took nearly a decade before her stateside debut, which she presented at New York Fashion Week in 2006.

Walker's collections can be found at present in 250 stores worldwide, including three flagship boutiques in New Zealand and a fourth in Taipei. Walker's designs have been featured regularly in *i-D*, *Vogue*, *Teen Vogue*, *Elle*, *W*, and *Nylon* magazine, and she is well-known for her mixing of seemingly disparate styles—notably Victorian tailoring and ruffles mixed with streetwear that plays on preconceived notions of masculinity and femininity. Walker describes her work as a "celebration of the anti-It girl" and cites Ally Sheedy in *The Breakfast Club*, Diane Keaton in Woody Allen's *Annie Hall*, 1930s comic book heroines leading double lives, and Amelia Earhart among her inspirations.

Walker was recently included in the book *Sample*, which curates the 100 most influential designers to emerge in the last six years, and Taschen selected her for their recent book *Fashion Now 2*, which highlights the world's 160 most important designers as designated by *i-D*. Her recent collaborations include T-shirts with Britain's

Designer Karen Walker.

House of Holland, makeup with Boots 17, and a pop-up concept store in New York called The Den.

Because of her hybrid and eclectic designs that radiate youthful exuberance, Walker has attracted a large Hollywood following, and her designs are worn by Kelly Osborne, Björk, Claire Danes, and Jennifer Lopez.

In addition to her main women's wear collections she also designs Karen Walker men's wear, Karen Walker Jewellery, eyewear, and paint colors.

Left: Fall 2007.
Right: Fall 2005.

Designer Alexander Wang.

BORN San Francisco, California, 1984

AWARDS Ecco Domani Fashion Foundation, *Emerging Designer*, 2008; Council of Fashion Designers of America, *Fashion Fund Prize*, 2008

By his sophomore year at Parsons School of Design in New York, Alexander Wang was already designing out of his dormitory for the first collection of women's wear—primarily knits—on his eponymous label. He used to carry suitcases full of clothing samples door to door, building his client base. In 2007, he launched his first full women's collection, which he sold to more than 150 boutiques and retail stores internationally. As the recipient of the Council of Fashion Designers of America's 2008 *Fashion Fund Prize*, Wang received $200,000 in capital for his next project, topping off his quick ascension from dorm-room designing.

Wang's milieu has always been what is known as the "model off duty" look—comfortable outfits that

not only appear classic and chic but also betray a thrown-together sort of irreverence. A typical Wang outfit might comprise an oversized gray blazer, with sleeves rammed up to the elbows over a wife-beater and shredded cutoffs. "It's that sense of ease and being confident," Wang has said, "like you just rolled out of bed and threw something on."

In 2008, he opened his shoe collection and a lower-priced diffusion line, T, that features languid tees and tanks with stretched arm and neck holes. His footwear line marks a sharp diversion from his trademark style, offering rough leather booties, a heel topped with a fringe, and hints of fetishista fashion supplied by metal piercing rings.

Left: Spring 2009.
Right: Spring 2009.

Vera Wang

BORN New York City, June 27, 1949

AWARDS Council of Fashion Designers of America (CFDA) *Women's wear Designer of the Year*, 2005

After a lifetime focused on fashion—childhood dancer, teenage ice-skating star who designed her own competition costumes, *Vogue* editor for sixteen years, and design director for accessories at RALPH LAUREN—Vera Wang discovered her vocation. She was getting married and could find nothing to wear. So in 1990 she moved into this fashion dead spot and established her own bridal business. Today her name is synonymous with the words "wedding dress."

The Wang style is sleek, modern, sophisticated—the opposite of the sugar-puff dress that makes a bride look like the figure on top of the wedding cake. She has definite ideas about what works: weightless clothes, armholes that add grace, and enough internal support to allow a woman to feel secure while being totally comfortable. Evening clothes were a logical extension of her design philosophy and her garments won a following with stylish celebrities including Sharon Stone, Holly Hunter, Meg Ryan, and Jane Fonda.

In October 2001, *Vera Wang on Weddings* appeared, a coffee-table book containing all you'd ever need to know on the practicalities of getting married. Her business has expanded into ready-to-wear, furs, and shoes, as well as china and

Designer Vera Wang.

glassware, sheets and towels, eyewear, and fragrance.

Vera Wang launched a playful line of clothing and accessories called the Lavender Label in 2005, and in 2008 she entered a three-year shoe license with Brown Shoe to expand this collection.

In 2007 she also launched a lower-priced collection called Simply Vera sold exclusively at Kohl's stores throughout the United States.

Left: Spring 2009 bridal show.

Right: Fall 2009.

Bruce Weber

BORN Greensburg, Pennsylvania, March 29, 1946

AWARDS ICP Infinity Award, 2005 • Clio Award for Recognition in Apparel, 1986

Bruce Weber participated in his first group photo show in 1973, and has been working steadily ever since. Scoring his first solo show just a year later he has gone on to become an award-winning shutterbug for some of the biggest names in fashion, most notably Abercrombie & Fitch, CALVIN KLEIN, and RALPH LAUREN.

Weber attended a number of schools, including Denison University, New York University, and The New School for Social Research, where he studied with famed Austrian photographer Lisette Model. He is credited with giving modern commercial photography a previously unseen artistic bent, often photographing nude or semi-nude chiseled young men. His work has greatly influenced the tone of modern fashion photography, setting a precedent by which photographers are allowed the power to interpret a designer's work and portray it in their own way. The photographer began shooting ads and commercials in the late 1970s for clients like Lauren and Klein, immediately causing controversy with the racy nature of his work. Weber is known for photographing models (often in couples or groups) in various stages of undress—one of his most famous shots is of Brazilian Olympic pole vaulter Tom Hintnaus in white Calvin Klein briefs. Most often Weber's work is shot in black and white or sepia tones, though he has used color in certain projects. Today, nearly two dozen books of Weber's work have been published and his photographs are included in the permanent collections of both the photography division of the City of Paris as well as the Victoria and Albert Museum, London. Additionally, Weber has directed a number of music videos and has produced ten films; shot album covers for musicians looking to trade on his signature style; and his work has appeared in *Vogue, Teen Vogue, Harper's Bazaar, Vanity Fair, Rolling Stone*, and *Elle*.

In 2003, Weber put his years of fashion experience to work with Weberbilt—a line of T-shirts—board shorts, windbreakers, and other casual wear sold exclusively in London and Miami.

Photographer Bruce Weber.

Chester Weinberg

BORN New York City, September 23, 1930
DIED New York City, April 24, 1985

AWARDS Coty American Fashion Critics' Award
"*Winnie*," 1970 • Maison Blanche "*Rex*" Award, 1972

Chester Weinberg built his reputation on simple, elegant designs, sophisticated and classic, never exaggerated or overpowering. They were always marked by beautiful fabrics, which were his passion. "Fabrics set the whole mood of my collection. I cannot design a dress until I know what the fabric will be."

A 1951 graduate of Parsons School of Design, Weinberg went on to earn a B.S. degree in art education from New York University, studying at night while working as a sketcher during the day. After graduation, he worked for a number of Seventh Avenue clothing manufacturers in New York before opening his own business in 1966. From 1977 until 1981 his company was a division of Jones Apparel Group, and when it closed he went to work for CALVIN KLEIN Jeans as design director. He began teaching at Parsons in 1954 and continued to do so until the year before his death.

Designer Chester Weinberg (center) with models.

Model wearing Chester Weinberg design.

John Weitz

Designer John Weitz.

A man of many interests, Weitz was also a licensed racing driver and designed a two-seater aluminum sports car, the X600. His portrait photographs have been shown at the Museum of the City of New York.

BORN Berlin, Germany, May 25, 1923

DIED Bridgehampton, New York, October 3, 2002

AWARDS Coty American Fashion Critics' Award
Special Award for Men's Wear, 1974

John Weitz is considered a pioneer of practical, modern clothes for sports and informal living. He introduced women's sports clothes with a men's wear look in the 1950s, showed pants for town wear, and in the 1960s presented "ready-to-wear couture," where the design could be chosen from sketches and swatches and made to order. For men, he produced Contour Clothes inspired by jeans, cowboy jackets, and fatigue coveralls. He was one of the first U.S. designers to show both men's and women's wear, and one of the first to license his work worldwide.

Educated in England, Weitz apprenticed in Paris at MOLYNEUX. He arrived in the United States shortly before Pearl Harbor, and served in the U.S. Army Intelligence. After the war he showed his designs—women's sportswear based on men's clothes—to Dorothy Shaver, President of Lord & Taylor, who helped him get started in business. He began licensing in 1954 and his men's wear business in 1964. He has also designed accessories, among them watches, scarves, and jewelry.

A woman modeling a zebra outfit by John Weitz, 1960.

Stuart Weitzman

BORN Long Island, New York, July 29, 1941

AWARDS Ernst and Young *Entrepreneur of the Year* • *Footwear News Hall of Fame* • Footwear Plus *Designer of the Year* (for ladies' dress shoes)

While he graduated from Wharton School of Finance, Stuart Weitzman had shoes in his blood—his father was a shoe manufacturer—and following graduation he went into the family business. As an apprentice working beside traditional craftsmen, he learned every step of production and became a skilled patternmaker with a broad understanding of footwear engineering.

Weitzman designs range from the highest-heeled stilettos in exotic materials—lace, silk, brocade, even platinum or 24 karat gold—to shoes made of cork or bamboo, and calfskin. Boots, moccasins, and even sneakers are part of his design vocabulary, in an unusually wide range of over 50 sizes. He can also boast that each pair of shoes goes through 80 craftsmen during the production process, which takes six to seven weeks. His shoes are the choice of celebrities from Calista Flockhart to Laura Bush—perhaps because he believes so strongly that "a beautiful shoe is useless unless it feels as wonderful as it looks." He has opened retail shops in selected cities across the country and in Switzerland.

Designer Stuart Weitzman.

Above: Weitzman's "retro rose" shoe.

Right: Iridescent shoe by Stuart Weitzman.

Designer Vivienne Westwood.

Above: Fall 2009.
Below, right: Spring 2007.

Vivienne Westwood

BORN Tintwhistle, England, April 8, 1941

AWARDS British Fashion Council, *British Designer of the Year*, 1990, 1991; *Order of the British Empire for Outstanding Contribution in Fashion*, 1992

Vivienne Westwood became involved in fashion around 1970 through her association with Malcolm McLaren, manager of The Sex Pistols. At the time she was earning her living as a teacher, having left Harrow Art School after only one term. She went into business with McLaren and together they owned a London shop on King's Road and another in London's West End.

Westwood belongs to the anti-fashion branch of design exemplified by Comme des Garçons, although her approach is totally different. Sometimes beautiful, sometimes ridiculous, never dull, her clothes show a fierce rejection of polite standards of dress. They are often inspired by London street life with wild swings in influences—from the leather and rubber fetishism, punk rock, and S & M of the 1970s, to the New Romanticism and pirate looks of the early 1980s. For fall 1994, she showed bustles, placing fanny pillows under just about everything and proclaiming the rear to be the new erogenous zone. Despite poor finances, she has regularly shown in Paris, and her anarchic view of dressing has had a considerable influence on other designers, both in England and around the world.

She has also had a professorship in design at the University of Berlin, and in June 2001 took an exhibition of her students' work to be shown in Paris. Her designs, both the earliest and the most recent, were shown in the "London Fashion" exhibition at the Fashion Institute of Technology in 2001–2002. In 2004, the National Gallery of Australia exhibited a major retrospective of her career.

Edward Wilkerson

BORN New York

Edward Wilkerson, the design director behind the bridge line Lafayette 148, became interested in fabrics and how they fit the body when he was ten years old. As a teenager, he attended the Art and Design High School in Manhattan, and in the summer of 1984 found a job at ANNE KLEIN, and worked under DONNA KARAN and LOUIS DELL'OLIO. He went on to study fashion at Parsons School of Design, and after graduation he landed a three-year stint at CALVIN KLEIN. Wilkerson then accepted a position as a designer for DONNA KARAN, where he stayed for 15 years. In 1998 Wilkerson joined Lafayette 148, which had been established only two years before by company president, Deirdre Quinn.

Bridge design had never before been considered fashionable. With Wilkerson at the helm, he brought Lafayette 148 solidly into fashion's middle ground. The company's goal was to design clothing for the working woman, but Wilkerson's vision was to enhance and celebrate the woman's body, not hide it and apologize for it. With women

Resort 2008.

Designer Edward Wilkerson.

in sizes from 0 to 16, he designs for the petite and plus size customer with equal attention. Lafayette 148 is the most popular plus size brand in Salon Z at Saks.

Some of his more extravagant designs and his foray into the high-end fashion world have been inspired by his travels to Africa, Bali, and Indonesia. Inspired by costumes from around the world, Wilkerson developed a love of exotic textiles. Much of his palette is also defined by landscapes, and range from amber to the rich blues of the sea and sky.

Wilkerson's vision of fashion has attracted a celebrity clientele, including Oprah Winfrey, Diane Sawyer, Queen Latifah, and Meryl Streep.

pieces, colorful and intricately detailed, appealing to an adventurous customer confident of her taste, Madonna and Sarah Jessica Parker, for example. For spring 2002 Williamson introduced a small group of separates for men in the same spirit as his women's clothes, and a range of scented candles. His clothes and the candles can be found at specialty stores such as Henri Bendel, Barneys, and Kirna Zabête in New York.

Williamson opened his first flagship store in London in 2004. In 2005 he was appointed creative director at the esteemed House of PUCCI. He remained there for three years, leaving in 2008 to focus on his own label's ventures.

Designer Matthew Williamson.

BORN Manchester, England, October 23, 1971

AWARDS *Elle* magazine *Young Designer of the Year*, 2004 • Moet and Chandon *Fashion Tribute Award*, 2005

After college in Manchester, Matthew Williamson attended London's Central St. Martins College of Art and Design, graduating in 1996. Between then and 1998, he worked briefly for ZANDRA RHODES and Monsoon and traveled to India to set up his business. He showed his first collection under his own label in September 1997.

In a small, focused collection he presents modern, easy

Left: Fall 2008.
Right: Fall 2009.

Anna Wintour

Editor Anna Wintour.

BORN London, England, November 3, 1949

One of the most well-known voices in media, Anna Wintour began her fashion career at the age of 15 as a shop girl at a Biba boutique in London. She never attended college, and instead went into a training program at Harrods. After toiling in retail for several years, she began her career in fashion journalism in 1970, when she took an editorial assistant position at *Harper's Bazaar* and *Queen*. She moved up the editorial ladder, and in 1975 was named junior fashion editor of *Harper's Bazaar* but left less than a year later.

Wintour then moved on to a position as fashion editor of the short-lived women's magazine *Viva*. She was there for two years before it folded, and in 1980 succeeded Elsa Klensch as the fashion editor at the women's magazine *Savvy*. Wintour then had a brief stint at *New York* magazine before taking the position of creative director at *Vogue* in 1983. In 1986 she returned to her native London to head up *Vogue*'s British version.

After two years in London, Wintour was named the editor-in-chief of American *Vogue*. Under her tenure, she has raised the profile of the magazine and brought in cutting edge photographers like ANNIE LEIBOVITZ, STEVEN MEISEL, and IRVING PENN.

A perfectionist in even her signature bob and clothing, many have called her icy, rigid, and difficult to work with. In 2003, Wintour's former assistant Lauren Weisberger wrote the scathing roman à clef *The Devil Wears Prada*. Weisberger denied the book—which was later made into a film—was about her former boss, but nevertheless, the novel cemented Wintour's difficult reputation.

Throughout her tenure at *Vogue*, Wintour has helped foster the careers of several major talents, including MARC JACOBS, ALEXANDER MCQUEEN, and THOM BROWNE. Committed to discovering new talent, in 2003 she partnered with the Council of Fashion Designers of America (CFDA) to create the CFDA/*Vogue* Fashion Fund, an annual celebration of up-and-coming designers. Past honorees include ALEXANDER WANG, Trovata, and PROENZA SCHOULER.

In January, 2009, *The September Issue* debuted at the Sundance Film Festival. The feature-length documentary, collaborated by A&E Indie Films and Director R.J. Cutler, chronicles the making of *Vogue*'s September 2007 issue. The film is not a straightforward profile of Wintour, but rather a behind-the-scenes look at the magazine and the world of haute couture.

Above: Designer Charles Frederick Worth.

Right: Evening dress, House of Worth, 1925.

BORN Lincolnshire, England October 13, 1825
DIED Paris, France, March 10, 1895

The founder of the house that became the world's longest-running fashion dynasty got his first job when he was just 11 and worked for a number of London drapers (a dealer in cloth or clothing) before leaving for Paris in 1845. Charles Frederick Worth took a job with a shop selling fabrics, shawls, and mantles, and persuaded the firm to open a department of made-up dress models, which he designed. He was the first to present clothes on live mannequins, using his young French wife as a model. His fashions were showcased at the 1851 Great Exhibition in London, and once more in 1855 at the Exposition Universelle in Paris. In 1858 Worth opened his own couture house on the Rue de la Paix, which closed in 1870 at the outset of the Franco-Prussian War. In 1871 Worth formally established his own couture business, Maison Worth (The House of Worth).

Reestablished in 1874, Worth maintained its fashion leadership for another 80 years.

Worth was court dressmaker to Empress Eugénie of France and to Empress Elizabeth of Austria. He also dressed the ladies of European courts and society women of Europe and America. A virtual fashion dictator, he required his customers, except for Eugénie and her court, to come to him instead of attending

Charles Frederick Worth, continued

them in their homes as had been the custom. He was an excellent businessman, was the first couturier to sell models to be copied in England and America, and was also widely copied by others without his permission. He enjoyed his success and lived in the grand manner.

Worth designs were known for their opulence and lavish use of fabrics, elaborate ornamentation of frills, ribbons, lace, braid, and tassels, as well as a meticulous fit.

Charles Worth, dubbed the "Father of Haute Couture," was not only the first professional designer of women's apparel, but also the first to achieve international fame as such. Worth was a vehement promoter of French-made textiles, and he is credited with having invented designs that utilized them, including the crinoline (a petticoat made of horsehair fabric) and the bustle. He also instigated a unique take on the décolleté neckline, in which a courtly mantle hung from the shoulders. He is credited with innovating what we now know as the princess gown, a waistless dress that hung straight in the front while draping in full pleats in the back, and with offering the first tailored suits for women. As a craftsman, he had a formidable ability to combine different pattern pieces at whim. Worth's designs were influenced by high art, most notably the paintings of Van Dyke, Gainsborough, and Velasquez.

After his death in 1895, the House of Worth continued under the leadership of his sons, Jean-Philippe and Gaston, then of his grandson, Jean-Charles, and finally of his great-grandsons, Roger and Maurice. When Roger retired in

1952, Maurice took over and in 1954 sold the house to PAQUIN. A London wholesale house continued under the Worth name until the 1970s. Parfums Worth was established in 1900, and continues today with Je Reviens, the best-known fragrance.

In 2001, a Worth court gown with train sold at auction in New York for $101,500, a world auction record. It had been worn by Elizabeth Washington Lewis, the great-great-granddaughter of George Washington's sister.

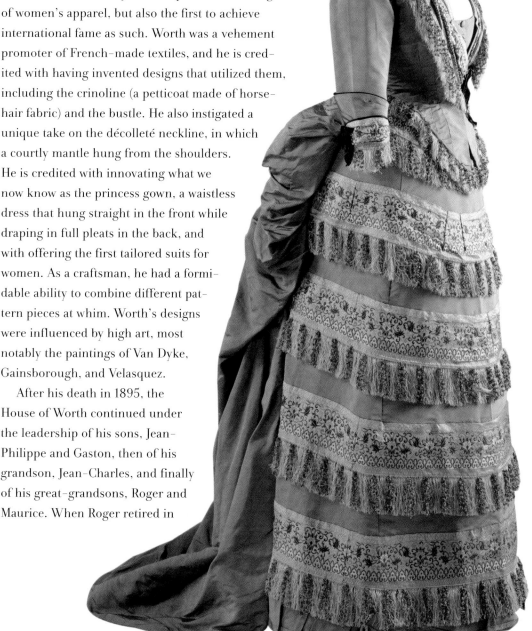

Silk dress, 1872.

President Obama and First Lady, Michelle Obama, in Jason Wu, 2009.

Designer Jason Wu.

BORN Taipei, Taiwan, 1983

AWARDS Fashion Group International's *Rising Star Award for Ready-to-Wear*, 2008 • Finalist CFDA/*Vogue Fashion Fund*, 2008

One of the youngest successful designers in the industry, Jason Wu is considered by many to be a prodigy. Always backed by his parents who ran an import-export business, his family moved Wu to Vancouver, Canada, at the age of nine to receive a better education. In a year, Wu had learned to sew, pattern, and sketch, and by the time he was 14, he was studying sculpture in Tokyo. He spent his senior year of high school studying in Paris, and after that he attended Parsons School of Design for three and a half years, but quit to intern with NARCISO RODRIGUEZ.

Fall 2009.

In 2006, with the financial help of his parents, and money he had saved since becoming a freelance designer at 16, he started his own label. His line of clothing has been called "ladylike." His fashions display hourglass figures with nipped-in waist, and floral prints. Influenced by photographer RICHARD AVEDON, and couturiers JACQUES FATH and CHARLES JAMES, his clothing sells at stores such as Bergdorf Goodman, Neiman Marcus, Saks Fifth Avenue, Jeffrey in Atlanta, and Ikran in Chicago. He is also creative director of Fashion Royalty, a line of high-end designer fashion dolls which sells at FAO Schwartz.

In November of 2008, at the request of Ikram, Wu was asked to design a "sparkly" evening gown for Michelle Obama, the first African-American First Lady of the United States. He was told that he was in contention and that if chosen it would appear in the Smithsonian. On January 20, 2009, to the surprise of Wu, Mrs. Obama came out with the President of the United States wearing his creation. It put Wu on the map. The white one-strap gown was decorated with tiny flowers and Swarovski crystals, and represented youth and change. It received rave reviews.

Yohji YAMAMOTO
YEOHLEE

Zang TOI
ZORAN

Yohji Yamamoto

Designer Yohji Yamamoto.

A graduate of Keio University, he studied fashion at Tokyo's Bunka Fashion Institute under Chie Kolke, who had attended L'École de la Chambre Syndicale de la Couture Parisienne in Paris with YVES SAINT LAURENT. From 1966 to 1968 he followed the standard course, studying all aspects of the clothing industry; by 1972 he had his own company. He showed his first collection in Tokyo in 1976. In 1981 he established himself in France with a boutique in Paris, and his Y-3 line debuted in 2003. Since then, he has shown his designs for both men and women at the Paris prêt-à-porter collections.

In 2008, the Yohji Yamamoto Fund for Peace (YYFP) was established in conjunction with the China Friendship Foundation for Peace and Development (CFFPD), which awards an emerging Chinese designer with a two-year scholarship to a fashion college in Japan or Europe.

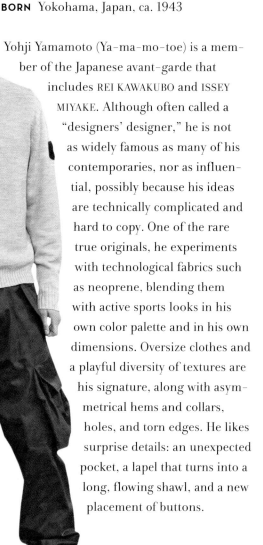

BORN Yokohama, Japan, ca. 1943

Yohji Yamamoto (Ya-ma-mo-toe) is a member of the Japanese avant-garde that includes REI KAWAKUBO and ISSEY MIYAKE. Although often called a "designers' designer," he is not as widely famous as many of his contemporaries, nor as influential, possibly because his ideas are technically complicated and hard to copy. One of the rare true originals, he experiments with technological fabrics such as neoprene, blending them with active sports looks in his own color palette and in his own dimensions. Oversize clothes and a playful diversity of textures are his signature, along with asymmetrical hems and collars, holes, and torn edges. He likes surprise details: an unexpected pocket, a lapel that turns into a long, flowing shawl, and a new placement of buttons.

Above: Spring 2005.
Left: Fall 2009.

Above: Designer Yeohlee.
Right: Fall 2006.

BORN Yeohlee Teng; Penang, Malaysia, ca. 1955

AWARDS Smithsonian Cooper-Hewitt National Design Museum, *Fashion Designer of the Year*, 2004

At the ripe old age of nine, Yeohlee talked her mother into letting her enroll in a patternmaking class. There was no ready-to-wear in Malaysia—clothes were made at home or by seamstresses and tailors—and she was dissatisfied with what her mother produced from English patterns. At 18, she went to New York to study at Parsons School of Design and two years later sold her first five-piece collection to Henri Bendel. She founded her own company in 1981.

Her work is sparse, often dramatic in impact, characterized by clear lines and geometric forms. The clothes are also comfortable and flattering, cut to allow the wearer to move with easy elegance. Yeohlee designs a complete collection but is most admired for her coats, both long and short. Working in the better

price range, she feels that the timeless quality of the design, combined with superior fabrics and workmanship, makes her clothes long-term investments. They have attracted a loyal following.

With their purity of form and distinct vision, Yeohlee's designs have been chosen for numerous exhibits, including shows at the Museum of the City of New York and the Massachusetts Institute of Technology, where they were featured with such designers as ARMANI, FERRÉ, MONTANA, and MIYAKE. They have also been shown at the Victoria and Albert in London and at the Museum of Fashion in Paris, and are in the permanent costume collection of the Metropolitan Museum of Art.

In 2001 she was working on a book exploring the parallels between architecture and clothing design, and in October of that year was honored by a one-woman show at New York's Fashion Institute of Technology entitled "Yeohlee: Supermodern Style". She published *Yeohlee: Work*, a book exploring the parallels between architecture and clothing design in 2003.

In October 2005, her work was included in the Kennedy Center for the Performing Arts' "New China Chic" exhibition. The Museum at the Fashion Institute of Technology featured Yeohlee's work again in their "Love and War" exhibition in 2006.

Zang Toi

BORN Kelantan, Malaysia, June 11, 1961

Zang Toi (TOY) left Malaysia for Canada in 1980, moved on to New York City a year later intending to study painting or interior design. Instead, he switched to fashion, and while at Parsons School of Design went to work for Mary Jane Marcasiano. He graduated from Parsons in 1983 and stayed on with Marcasiano for five years, concentrating on production. Following freelance work at SHAMASK, he opened his own business in 1989.

Designing with a light touch, Toi combines Asian colors and a taste for exotic details with the forthright flair of American sportswear. The result is a fresh twist for classic looks. The clothes are young and spirited, with a sophisticated attitude, while his preference for fabrics such as cashmere and silk and his innate sense of fantasy also means they are fashion of unabashed luxury.

He has also entered the ranks of celebrity designers, and creates apparel for headline names such as Madonna and Sharon Stone. Toi's two signature lines, Zang Toi and House of Toi, are sold at Nordstrom, Neiman Marcus, and specialty boutiques in the United States and around the world.

Designer Zang Toi.

Above: Fall 2007.
Left: Spring 2007.

Above: Designer Zoran Ladicorbic (left).

Right: Model wearing design by Zoran.

BORN Zoran Ladicorbic; Belgrade, Yugoslavia, 1947

Zoran belongs to the fashion minimalists, confining himself to a few pure shapes, always in the most expensive, luxurious fabrics. He studied architecture in Belgrade and moved to New York in 1971. His first fashion recognition came in 1977, when his designs were bought by Henri Bendel.

The early collections were based on squares and rectangles in silk crêpe de Chine, cashmere, and other luxurious fabrics. The designs have evolved from there, retaining their purity and luxury. Zoran works in a limited color range, usually black, gray, white, ivory, and red. It is a relaxed look, sophisticated and utterly simple, a perfection of understatement by a master of proportion and balance. He prefers not to use buttons and zippers and avoids any extraneous detail. Because his customers lead a highly mobile life, he has produced a collection of ten pieces that fit into a small bag so that a woman can look casual and glamorous wherever her travels take her. At a less-costly level, Zoran has made daytime clothes in cotton knit, although evenings are still devoted to satin, velvet, and cashmere. Inevitably, his creations are for women of sophisticated tastes and well-filled bank accounts. With a devoted clientele and an independent attitude, Zoran does not hew to a rigid schedule of twice-yearly showings but shows his collections at such times as the spirit moves him.

Council of Fashion Designers of America (CFDA) Awards

2009

Womenswear Designer of the Year, Kate & Laura Mulleavy for Rodarte

Menswear Designer of the Year, Scott Sternberg for Band of Outsiders and Italo Zucchelli for Calvin Klein (tie)

Accessory Designer of the Year, Jack McCollough & Lazaro Hernandez for Proenza Schouler

Swarovski Award for Womenswear, Alexander Wang

Swarovski Award for Menswear, Tim Hamilton

Swarovski Award for Accessory Design, Justin Giunta for Subversive Jewelry

Eugenia Sheppard Award, Edward Nardoza

Geoffrey Beene Lifetime Achievement Award, Anna Sui

International Award, Marc Jacobs for Louis Vuitton

Board of Directors' Special Tribute, First Lady Michelle Obama

Eleanor Lambert Award, Jim Moore

2008

Womenswear Designer of the Year, Francisco Costa for Calvin Klein

Menswear Designer of the Year, Tom Ford

Accessory Designer of the Year, Tory Burch

Swarovski Award for Womenswear, Kate & Laura Mulleavy for Rodarte

Swarovski Award for Menswear, Scott Sternberg for Band of Outsiders

Swarovski Award for Accessory Design, Philip Crangi

Eugenia Sheppard Award, Candy Pratts Price

Geoffrey Beene Lifetime Achievement Award, Carolina Herrera

International Award, Dries Van Noten

Board of Directors' Special Tribute, Mayor Michael R. Bloomberg

2007

Womenswear Designer of the Year, Oscar de la Renta and Lazaro Hernandez & Jack McCollough for Proenza Schouler

Menswear Designer of the Year, Ralph Lauren

Accessory Designer of the Year, Derek Lam

Swarovski Award for Womenswear, Phillip Lim

Swarovski Award for Menswear, David Neville & Marcus Wainwright for Rag & Bone

Swarovski Award for Accessory Design, Jessie Randall for Loeffler Randall

Eugenia Sheppard Award, Robin Givhan

Geoffrey Beene Lifetime Achievement Award, Robert Lee Morris

International Award, Pierre Cardin

American Fashion Legend Award, Ralph Lauren

Eleanor Lambert Award, Patrick Demarchelier

Board of Directors' Special Tribute, Bono & Ali Hewson

2006

Womenswear Designer of the Year, Francisco Costa for Calvin Klein

Menswear Designer of the Year, Thom Browne

Accessory Designer of the Year, Tom Binns

Swarovski's Perry Ellis Award for Womenswear, Doo-Ri Chung

Swarovski's Perry Ellis Award for Menswear, Jeff Halmos, Josia Lamberto-Egan, Sam Shipley & John Whitledge for Trovata

Swarovski's Perry Ellis Award for Accessory Design, Devi Kroell

Eugenia Sheppard Award, Bruce Weber

International Award, Olivier Theyskens for Rochas

Lifetime Achievement Award, Stan Herman

Eleanor Lambert Award, Joan Kaner

Board of Directors' Special Tribute, Stephen Burrows

2005

Womenswear Designer of the Year, Vera Wang

Menswear Designer of the Year, John Varvatos

Accessory Designer of the Year, Marc Jacobs for Marc Jacobs

Swarovski's Perry Ellis Award for Womenswear, Derek Lam

Swarovski's Perry Ellis Award for Menswear, Alexandre Plokhov for Cloak

Swarovski's Perry Ellis Award for Accessory Design, Nak Armstrong & Anthony Camargo for Anthony Nak

Eugenia Sheppard Award, Gilles Bensimon

International Award, Alber Elbaz for Lanvin

Lifetime Achievement Award, Diane von Furstenberg
Fashion Icon Award, Kate Moss
Board of Directors' Special Tribute, Norma Kamali

2004

Womenswear Designer of the Year, Carolina Herrera
Menswear Designer of the Year, Sean Combs for Sean John
Accessory Designer of the Year, Reed Krakoff for Coach
Swarovski's Perry Ellis Award for Womenswear, Zac Posen
Swarovski's Perry Ellis Award for Accessory Design, Eugenia Kim
Eugenia Sheppard Award, Teri Agins
International Award, Miuccia Prada
Lifetime Achievement Award, Donna Karan
Fashion Icon Award, Sarah Jessica Parker
Eleanor Lambert Award, Irving Penn
Board of Directors' Special Tribute, Tom Ford

2003

Womenswear Designer of the Year, Narciso Rodriguez
Menswear Designer of the Year, Michael Kors
Accessory Designer of the Year, Marc Jacobs
Swarovski's Perry Ellis Award for Ready-to-Wear, Lazaro Hernandez & Jack McCollough for Proenza Schouler
Swarovski's Perry Ellis Award for Accessory Design, Brian Atwood
Eugenia Sheppard Award, André Leon Talley
International Award, Alexander McQueen
Lifetime Achievement Award, Anna Wintour
Fashion Icon Award, Nicole Kidman
Eleanor Lambert Award, Rose Marie Bravo
Board of Directors' Special Tribute, Oleg Cassini

2002

Womenswear Designer of the Year, Narciso Rodriguez
Menswear Designer of the Year, Marc Jacobs
Accessory Designer of the Year, Tom Ford for Yves Saint Laurent
Perry Ellis Award for Womenswear, Rick Owens
Eugenia Sheppard Award, Cathy Horyn
International Award, Hedi Slimane for Dior Homme
Lifetime Achievement Award, Grace Coddington / Karl Lagerfeld
Fashion Icon Award, C.Z. Guest
Creative Visionary, Stephen Gan
Eleanor Lambert Award, Kal Ruttentstein

2001

Womenswear Designer of the Year, Tom Ford
Menswear Designer of the Year, John Varvatos
Accessory Designer of the Year, Reed Krakoff for Coach

Swarovski's Perry Ellis Award for Womenswear, Daphne Gutierrez & Nicole Noselli for Bruce
Swarovski's Perry Ellis Award for Menswear, William Reid
Swarovski's Perry Ellis Award for Accessory Design, Edmundo Castillo
International Award, Nicolas Ghesquière for Balenciaga
Lifetime Achievement Award, Calvin Klein
Eugenia Sheppard Award, Bridget Foley
Humanitarian Award, Evelyn Lauder
Eleanor Lambert Award, Dawn Mello
Special Award, Bernard Arnault
Special Award, Bob Mackie
Special Award, Saks Fifth Avenue

2000

Womenswear Designer of the Year, Oscar de la Renta
Menswear Designer of the Year, Helmut Lang
Accessory Designer of the Year, Richard Lambertson & John Truex for Lambertson Truex
Perry Ellis Award for Womenswear, Miguel Adrover
Perry Ellis Award for Menswear, John Varvatos
Perry Ellis Award for Accessory Design, Dean Harris
International Award, Jean-Paul Gaultier
Lifetime Achievement Award, Valentino
Humanitarian Award, Liz Claiborne
Most Stylish Dot.com Award, PleatsPlease.com
Special Award, The Dean of American Fashion Bill Blass
Special Award, The American Regional Press
Special Award, The Academy of Motion Picture Arts & Sciences

1999/1998

Womenswear Designer of the Year, Michael Kors
Menswear Designer of the Year, Calvin Klein
Accessory Designer of the Year, Marc Jacobs
Perry Ellis Award for Womenswear, Bryan Bradley & Josh Patner for Tuleh
Perry Ellis Award for Menswear, Matt Nye
Perry Ellis Award for Accessory Design, Tony Valentine
International Award, Yohji Yamamoto
Lifetime Achievement Award, Yves Saint Laurent
Eugenia Sheppard Award, Elsa Klensch
Humanitarian Award, Liz Tilberis
Special Award, Betsey Johnson
Special Award, Simon Doonan
Special Award, *InStyle* Magazine
Special Award, Sophia Lauren / Cher

1997

Womenswear Designer of the Year, Marc Jacobs
Menswear Designer of the Year, John Bartlett
Accessory Designer of the Year, Kate Spade

Perry Ellis Award for Womenswear, Narciso Rodriguez
Perry Ellis Award for Menswear, Sandy Dalal
International Award, John Galliano for Christian Dior
Lifetime Achievement Award, Geoffrey Beene
The Stilleto, Manolo Blahnik
Special Award, Anna Wintour
Dom Perignon Award, Ralph Lauren
Special Award, Elizabeth Taylor
Special Tributes, Gianni Versace & Princess Diana

1996
Womenswear Designer of the Year, Donna Karan
Menswear Designer of the Year, Ralph Lauren
Accessory Designer of the Year, Elsa Peretti for Tiffany & Co.
Perry Ellis Award for Womenswear, Daryl Kerrigan for Daryl K.
Perry Ellis Award for Menswear, Gene Meyer
Perry Ellis Award for Accessory Design, Miranda Morrison & Keri Sigerson for Sigerson Morrison
International Award, Helmut Lang
Lifetime Achievement Award, Arnold Scaasi
Eugenia Sheppard Award, Amy Spindler
Dom Perignon Award, Kenneth Cole
Special Award, Richard Martin & Harold Koda

1995
Womenswear Designer of the Year, Ralph Lauren
Menswear Designer of the Year, Tommy Hilfiger
Accessory Designer of the Year, Hush Puppies
Perry Ellis Award for Womenswear, Marie-Anne Oudejans
Perry Ellis Award for Menswear, Richard Tyler / Richard Bengtsson & Edward Pavlick for Richard Edwards
Perry Ellis Award for Accessory Design, Kate Spade
International Award, Tom Ford for Gucci
Lifetime Achievement Award, Hubert de Givenchy
Eugenia Sheppard Award, Suzy Menkes
Special Award, Isaac Mizrahi & Douglas Keeve for "Unzipped" / Robert Isabell / Lauren Bacall
Dom Perignon Award, Bill Blass

1994
Womenswear Designer of the Year, Richard Tyler
Accessory Designer of the Year, Robert Lee Morris, Women's / Gene Meyer, Men's
Perry Ellis Award for Womenswear, Cynthia Rowley / Victor Alfaro
Perry Ellis Award for Menswear, Robert Freda
Lifetime Achievement Award, Carrie Donovon / Nonnie Moore / Bernadine Morris
Eugenia Sheppard Award, Kevyn Aucoin / Patrick McCarthy

Special Award, Elizabeth Tilberis / The Wonderbra / Kevyn Aucoin
Special Tribute, Jacqueline Kennedy Onassis

1993
Womenswear Designer of the Year, Calvin Klein
Menswear Designer of the Year, Calvin Klein
Perry Ellis Award for Womenswear, Richard Tyler
Perry Ellis Award for Menswear, John Bartlett
Lifetime Achievement Award, Judith Leiber / Polly Allen Mellen
International Award, Prada
Eugenia Sheppard Award, Fabien Baron / Bill Cunningham
Special Awards, Fabien Baron / Adidas / Converse / Keds / Nike / Reebok
Industry Tribute, Eleanor Lambert

1992
Womenswear Designer of the Year, Marc Jacobs
Menswear Designer of the Year, Donna Karan
Accessory Designer of the Year, Chrome Hearts
Perry Ellis Award, Anna Sui
Eugenia Sheppard Award, Steven Meisel
International Award, Gianni Versace
Lifetime Achievement Award, Pauline Trigère
Special Award, Steven Meisel / Audrey Hepburn / The Ribbon Project / Visual AIDS

1991
Womenswear Designer of the Year, Isaac Mizrahi
Menswear Designer of the Year, Roger Forsythe
Accessory Designer of the Year, Karl Lagerfeld for Chanel
Perry Ellis Award, Todd Oldham
Lifetime Achievement Award, Ralph Lauren
Eugenia Sheppard Award, Marylou Luther
International Award, Karl Lagerfeld for Chanel
Special Award, Marvin Traub / Harley Davidson / Jessye Norman / Anjelica Huston / Judith Jamison

1990
Womenswear Designer of the Year, Donna Karan
Menswear Designer of the Year, Joseph Abboud
Accessory Designer of the Year, Manolo Blahnik
Perry Ellis Award, Christian Francis Roth
Lifetime Achievement Award, Martha Graham
Eugenia Sheppard Award, Genevieve Buck
Special Awards, Emilio Pucci / Anna Wintour
Special Tribute, Halston

1989
Womenswear Designer of the Year, Isaac Mizrahi
Menswear Designer of the Year, Joseph Abboud

Accessory Designer of the Year, Paloma Picasso
Perry Ellis Award, Gordon Henderson
Lifetime Achievement Award, Oscar de la Renta
Eugenia Sheppard Award, Carrie Donovon
Special Award, The Gap
Special Tribute, Giorgio Sant'Angelo / Diana Vreeland

1988

Menswear Designer of the Year, Bill Robinson
Perry Ellis Award, Isaac Mizrahi
Lifetime Achievement Award, Richard Avedon / Nancy
    Reagan
Eugenia Sheppard Award, Nina Hyde
Special Award, Geoffrey Beene / Karl Lagerfeld for
    House of Chanel / Grace Mirabella / Judith Peabody /
    The Wool Bureau Inc.

1987

Best American Collection, Calvin Klein
Menswear Designer of the Year, Ronaldus Shamask
Perry Ellis Award, Marc Jacobs
Eugenia Sheppard Award, Bernadine Morris
Lifetime Achievement, Giorgio Armani / Horst / Eleanor
    Lambert
Special Awards, Arnell / Bickford Associates and Donna
    Karan / Manolo Blahnik / Hebe Dorsey / FIT / Giorgio
    Sant'Angelo / Arnold Scaasi / *Vanity Fair*
Special Tribute, Mrs. Vincent Astor

1986

Perry Ellis Award, David Cameron
Lifetime Achievement Award, Bill Blass / Marlene Dietrich
Special Awards, Geoffrey Beene / Dalma Callado / Elle

Magazine / Etta Froio / Donna Karan / Elsa Klench /
    Christian Lacroix / Ralph Lauren

1985

Lifetime Achievement Award, Katherine Hepburn /
    Alexander Liberman
Special Tribute, Rudy Gernreich
Special Awards, Geoffrey Beene / Liz Claiborne /
    Norma Kamali / Donna Karan / *Miami Vice* /
    Robert Lee Morris / Ray-Ban Sunglasses /
    "Tango Argentino"

1984

Lifetime Achievement Award, James Galanos
Special Awards, Astor Pale Hair Design / Bergdorf
    Goodman / Kitty D'Alessio / John Fairchild / Annie
    Flanders / Peter Moore NIKE / Robert Pittman MTV /
    Stephen Sprouse / Diana Vreeland / Bruce Weber

1983

Bill Cunningham / Perry Ellis / Norma Kamali / Karl
Lagerfeld / Antonio Lopez / Issey Miyake / Patricia
Underwood / Bruce Weber

1982

Bill Cunningham / Perry Ellis / Norma Kamali / Karl
Lagerfeld / Antonio Lopez

1981

Jhane Barnes / Perry Ellis / Andrew Fezza / Alexander
Julian / Barry Kieselstein-Cord / Calvin Klein / Nancy
Knox / Ralph Lauren / Robert Lighton / Alex Mate & Lee
Brooks / Yves Saint Laurent / Fernando Sanchez

Source: http://www.cfda.com/index.php?option=com_cfda_content&task=fashion_awards_display&category_id=31

Coty American Fashion Critics' Awards

Designer	Award	Year
Robin Kahn	*Special Award (belt and buckle designs for men's wear)*	1984
Donna Karan	*First Citation (women's wear with Louis Dell'Olio)*	1984
Louis Dell'Olio	*First Citation (women's wear with Donna Karan)*	1984
Jhane Barnes	*Men's Wear Return Award*	1984
Perry Ellis	*Hall of Fame (men's wear)*	1984
Perry Ellis	*Hall of Fame (women's wear)*	1984
Alexander Julian	*Second Citation*	1984
Barry Kieselstein-Cord	*Special Award (belts and jewelry)*	1984
Ralph Lauren	*Second Citation*	1984
Adrienne Vittadini	*"Winnie"*	1984
Bill Blass	*Hall of Fame Citation*	1983

Designer	Award	Year
Perry Ellis	*Hall of Fame Citation (women's wear)*	1983
Perry Ellis	*Men's Wear Return Award*	1983
Alexander Julian	*First Citation*	1983
Norma Kamali	*Hall of Fame*	1983
Willi Smith	*"Winnie"*	1983
Adri	*"Winnie"*	1982
Geoffrey Beene	*Hall of Fame Citation*	1982
Bill Blass	*Hall of Fame Citation*	1982
Sal Cesarani	*Men's Wear Return Award*	1982
Louis Dell'Olio	*Hall of Fame (with Donna Karan)*	1982
Norma Kamali	*Return Award*	1982
Donna Karan	*Hall of Fame (with Louis, Dell'Olio)*	1982
Geoffrey Beene	*Hall of Fame Citation*	1981
Perry Ellis	*Hall of Fame*	1981
Perry Ellis	*Men's Wear Award*	1981
Norma Kamali	*"Winnie"*	1981
Ralph Lauren	*First Citation (men's wear)*	1981
Robert Lee Morris	*Special Award (jewelry for Calvin Klein)*	1981
Ronaldus Shamask	*"Winnie"*	1981
Jhane Barnes	*Men's Wear*	1980
Perry Ellis	*Return Award*	1980
Alexander Julian	*Hall of Fame Award*	1980
Calvin Klein	*Special Award (contribution to international status of American fashion)*	1979
Geoffrey Beene	*Hall of Fame Citation*	1979
Perry Ellis	*"Winnie"*	1979
Alexander Julian	*Men's Wear Return Award*	1979
Barry Kieselstein–Cord	*Outstanding. Jewelry Design*	1979
Mary McFadden	*Hall of Fame*	1979
Joan Vass	*Special Award (crafted knit fashions)*	1979
Joan Helpern	*Special Award (footwear)*	1978
Mary McFadden	*Return Award*	1978
Geoffrey Beene	*Hall of Fame Citation*	1977
Stephen Burrows	*"Winnie"*	1977
Louis Dell'Olio	*"Winnie" (with Donna Karan for Anne Klein)*	1977
Alexander Julian	*Men's Wear Trophy*	1977
Donna Karan	*"Winnie" (with Louis, Dell'Olio for Anne Klein)*	1977
Ralph Lauren	*Hall of Fame (women's wear)*	1977
John Anthony	*Return Award*	1976
Sal Cesarani	*Special Men's Wear Award*	1976
Herbert Kasper	*Hall of Fame*	1976
Ralph Lauren	*Return Award*	1976
Ralph Lauren	*Hall of Fame (men's wear)*	1976
Mary McFadden	*"Winnie"*	1976
Geoffrey Beene	*Hall of Fame Citation*	1975
Bill Blass	*Special Award (furs for Revillon America)*	1975
Carol Horn	*"Winnie"*	1975
Calvin Klein	*Hall of Fame*	1975
Calvin Klein	*Special Award (fur design for Alixandre)*	1975
Fernando Sanchez	*Special Award (fur for Revillon)*	1975
Viola Sylbert	*Special Award (fur design)*	1975
Monika Tilley	*Special Award (swimsuits)*	1975
Fernando Sanchez	*Special Award (lingerie)*	1974, 1977
Geoffrey Beene	*Hall of Fame*	1974

Designer	Award	Year
Stephen Burrows	*Special Award (lingerie)*	1974
Sal Cesarani	*Special Men's Wear Award*	1974
Aldo Cipullo	*Special Men's Wear Award (male jewelry)*	1974
Halston	*Hall of Fame*	1974
Calvin Klein	*Return Award*	1974
Ralph Lauren	*"Winnie"*	1974
Bill Tice	*Special Award (loungewear)*	1974
John Weitz	*Special Men's Wear Award*	1974
Oscar de la Renta	*Hall of Fame*	1973
Calvin Klein	*"Winnie"*	1973
Ralph Lauren	*Return Award*	1973
Judith Leiber	*Special Award (handbags)*	1973
John Anthony	*"Winnie"*	1972
Bonnie Cashin	*Hall of Fame*	1972
Halston	*Return Award*	1972
Bill Blass	*Hall of Fame Citation*	1971
Halston	*"Winnie"*	1971
Betsey Johnson	*"Winnie"*	1971
Anne Klein	*Hall of Fame*	1971
Elsa Peretti	*Special Award (jewelry)*	1971
Bill Blass	*Hall of Fame*	1970
Herbert Kasper	*Return Award*	1970
Ralph Lauren	*Men's Wear*	1970
Giorgio Sant'Angelo	*"Winnie"*	1970
Chester Weinberg	*"Winnie"*	1970
Anne Klein	*Return Award*	1969
Giorgio Sant'Angelo	*Special Award (fantasy accessories and ethnic fashions)*	1968
Bill Blass	*First Coty Award for Men's Wear*	1968
Bonnie Cashin	*Return Award*	1968
Oscar de la Renta	*Return Award*	1968
Oscar de la Renta	*"Winnie"*	1967
Rudi Gernreich	*Hall of Fame*	1967
Geoffrey Beene	*Return Award*	1966
Rudi Gernreich	*Return Award*	1966
Kenneth Jay Lane	*Special Award (jewelry)*	1966
Geoffrey Beene	*"Winnie"*	1964
Sylvia Pedlar	*Return Special Award (lingerie)*	1964
Bill Blass	*Return Award*	1963
Rudi Gernreich	*"Winnie"*	1963
Halston	*Special Award (millinery)*	1962, 1969
Bill Blass	*"Winnie"*	1961
Bonnie Cashin	*Special Award (leather and fabric design)*	1961
Gustave Tassell	*"Winnie"*	1961
Rudi Gernreich	*Special Award (innovative body clothes)*	1960
James Galanos	*Hall of Fame*	1959
Pauline Trigère	*Hall of Fame*	1959
Jean Schlumberger	*Special Award (the first given for jewelry)*	1958
Claire McCardell	*Hall of Fame (posthumous)*	1958
Arnold Scaasi	*"Winnie"*	1958
Emeric Partos	*Special Award (furs)*	1957
James Galanos	*Return Award*	1956
Norman Norell	*First designer elected to Hall of Fame*	1956
Adolfo	*Special Award (millinery)*	1955, 1969

Designer	Award	Year
Herbert Kasper	*"Winnie"*	1955
Anne Klein	*"Winnie"*	1955
James Galanos	*"Winnie"*	1954
Charles James	*Special Award (innovative cut)*	1954
Anne Fogarty	*Special Award (dresses)*	1951
Vera Maxwell	*Special Award (coats and suits)*	1951
Norman Norell	*First Return Award*	1951
Sylvia Pedlar	*Special Award (lingerie)*	1951
Pauline Trigère	*Return Award*	1951
Bonnie Cashin	*"Winnie"*	1950
Charles James	*"Winnie"*	1950
Pauline Trigère	*"Winnie"*	1949
Adele Simpson	*"Winnie"*	1947
Tina Leser	*"Winnie"*	1945
Claire McCardell	*"Winnie"*	1944
Lilly Daché	*Special Award (millinery)*	1943
Mr. John	*Special Award*	1943
Norman Norell	*First "Winnie"*	1943

Neiman Marcus Awards

Designer	Year	Designer	Year
Miuccia Prada	1995	Giuliana Camerino	1956
Emilio Pucci	1990	Pierre Balmain	1955
Arnold Scaasi	1987	Florence Eiseman	1955
Issey Miyake	1984	Vera Maxwell	1955
Karl Lagerfeld	1980	James Galanos	1954
Judith Leiber	1980	Charles James	1953
Giorgio Armani	1979	Anne Fogarty	1952
Perry Ellis	1979	Bonnie Cashin	1950
Mary McFadden	1979	Pauline Trigère	1950
Ralph Lauren	1973	Claire McCardell	1948
Rosita & Ottavio Missoni	1973	Christian Dior	1947
Hanae Mori	1973	Salvatore Ferragamo	1947
Jean Muir	1973	Norman Hartnell	1947
Bill Blass	1969	Irene	1947
Emanuel Ungaro	1969	Adele Simpson	1946
Oscar de la Renta	1968	Tina Leser	1945
Kenneth Jay Lane	1968	Adrian	1943
Valentino	1967	Norman Norell	1942
Geoffrey Beene	1964, 1965	Omar Kiam	1941
Jules-François Crahay	1962	Carmel Snow	1941
Roger Vivier	1961	Edna Woolman Chase	1940
Sylvia Pedlar	1960	Lilly Daché	1940
Anne Klein	1959, 1969	Elsa Schiaparelli	1940
Yves Saint Laurent	1958	Hattie Carnegie	1939
Gabrielle "Coco" Chanel	1957	Clare Potter	1939
Cecil Beaton	1956	Mr. John	1938

Fashion Walk of Fame

The Fashion Walk of Fame, established in 1999 by leaders of the fashion industry, is the only permanent landmark paying tribute to the creative talents of American fashion. White bronze plaques, $2^{1}/_{2}$ feet in diameter have been embedded in granite in the sidewalk from 35th to 41st Street, on the east side of Seventh "Fashion" Avenue. Each plaque bears an original fashion sketch and the signature of the designer, with text describing his or her contribution to fashion.

Designer	Year
Liz Claiborne	2008
Diane von Furstenberg	2008
Stephen Burrows	2002
Lilly Daché	2002
Perry Ellis	2002
Marc Jacobs	2002
Betsey Johnson	2002
Norma Kamali	2002
Mainbocher	2002
Willi Smith	2002
Bonnie Cashin	2001
Oscar de la Renta	2001
Giorgio Sant'Angelo	2001
James Galanos	2001
Charles James	2001
Donna Karan	2001
Anne Klein	2001
Pauline Trigère	2001
Geoffrey Beene	2000
Bill Blass	2000
Rudi Gernreich	2000
Halston	2000
Calvin Klein	2000
Ralph Lauren	2000
Claire McCardell	2000
Norman Norell	2000

References

A to Z Blue Jeans. http://atozbluejeans.com. (Accessed March 27, 2009.)

The Age of Worth. Brooklyn Museum of Arts, New York, 1982.

Albo, M. 2008. *New York Times.* "One Size Fits Small." September 2, 2008. (Accessed November 5, 2008.)

Aleksander, I. *New York Observer.* "Marie Claire Jumps on the Reality Show Train." September 9, 2008. (Accessed November 6, 2008.)

Alexander, H. *Daily Telegraph.* "Jigsaw chic by Steven Meisel." http:// telegraph.co.uk/fashion/3441013/ Jigsaw-chic-by-Steven-Meisel.html. (Accessed November 11, 2008.)

Alexander Julian. "Alexander Julian." http:// alexanderjulian.com/flash_content.html. (Accessed November 8, 2008.)

Amies, H. *Just So Far.* St. James Place, London: Collins, 1984.

————. *ABC of Men's Fashion.* London: Newnes, 1964.

————. *Still Here.* London: Weidenfeld and Nicolson, 1984.

Anna Molonari. "Blufin History." http://blufin.it/. (Accessed November 11, 2008.)

Anne Cole. "About." http://annecole.com/index2.html. (Accessed November 17, 2008.)

Anscombe, Isabelle. *A Woman's Touch: Women in Design from 1860 to the Present Day.* London: Virago, 1984.

Answers.com. "Katherine Hamnett."

http://answers.com/topic/katharine-hamnett. (Accessed November 17, 2008.)

Artbook.com. "Juergen Teller: Marc Jacobs Advertising 1997–2008, Volume I."

http:// artbook.com/9783865217158.html. (Accessed November 14, 2008.)

Artdaily.org. "Le Petit Palais in Paris Shows Images and Fashion by Patrick Demarchelier." http://artdaily. com/section/news/index.asp?int._sec=11&int_ new=264488int_modo=1. (Accessed November 6, 2008.)

Ash, J. and Elizabeth Wilson, eds. *Chic Thrills.* Berkeley, CA: University of California Press, 1993.

Bag Snob. "The Grace of Derek Lam." April 23, 2008. http://bagsnob.com/2008/04/the_grace_of_derek_lam. html.(Accessed November 10, 2008.)

Bailey, M.J. *Those Glorious, Glamour Years: The Great Hollywood Costume Designs of the 1930s.* Secaucus, NJ: Citadel Press, Reissue, 1988.

Bailey, S. *Harper's Bazaar.* "Costa's Calvin Klein." http:// harpersbazaar.com/fashion/fashion-articles/ francisco-costa-calvin-klein-0508. (Accessed November 6, 2008.)

Baillen, C. *Chanel: Solitaire.* Translated by Barbara Bray. New York: Quadrangle/The New York Times Book Co., 1974

Baldwin, N. *Man Ray: American Artist.* Cambridge: Da Capo Press, 2000.

Ballard, B. *In My Fashion.* New York: David McKay Co., Inc., 1960.

Balmain, P. *My Years and Seasons* (autobiography). Translated by E. Lanchbery and G.Young. London: Cassell & Co. Ltd., 1964. New York: Doubleday & Company, Inc., 1965.

Barnett, L. *Vogue.com.* "A Valli Happy Occasion." June 27, 2008. http:// vogue.co.uk/news/daily/080627- giambattista-valli-launches-bridal.aspx. (Accessed November 15, 2008.)

Baudot, F. 1999. *Fashion: The Twentieth Century.* New York: Universe Publishing.

BBC News. "Photographer Herb Ritts dies." December 27, 2002. http://news.bbc.co.uk/1/hi/entertainment/ showbiz/2608665.stm. (Accessed November 14, 2008.)

Beaton, C. *The Glass of Fashion.* London: Casssell, 1989.

————. *Fair Lady.* New York: Holt, Rinehart & Winston, 1964.

————. *Cecil Beaton: Memoirs of the 40s.* New York: McGraw-Hill Book Co., 1977.

————. *The Book of Beauty.* London: Duckworth, 1930.

———. *Cecil's Beaton's New York*. London: Batsford, 1938.

———. *Persona Grata* (with Kenneth Tynan). London: G. P. Putnam's Sons, 1954.

———. *The Glass of Fashion*. London: Weidenfeld & Nicolson, 1954.

———. *Cecil Beaton's Diaries—1922–1929, The Wandering Years*, 1961; *1939–1944, The Years Between*, 1965; *1948–1955, The Strenuous Years*, 1973. London; Weinfeld & Nicolson.

———. *The Gainsborough Girls*, 1951.

Bellafante, G. *New York Times*. "Herb Ritts, Photographer Of Celebrities, Is Dead at 50." December 27, 2002.

Ben Silver Classic Style. "All About Suits and Jackets." http://www.bensilver.com/style04/about_SuitsJackets.htm. (Accessed March 27, 2009.)

Bender, M. *Beautiful People*. New York: Coward, McCann & Geoghegan, Inc., 1967

Bennett, L. *St. Petersburg Times*. "Back to the drawing board." April 4, 2003. http:// sptimes.com/2003/04/04/Floridian/Back_to_the_drawing_b.shtml. (Accessed November 15, 2008.)

Bently Lessona, L. *Made-in-Italy.com*. "Fashion Houses: Missoni." http://www.made-in-italy.com/fashion/fashion_houses/missoni/intro.htm. (Accessed October 6, 2009.)

Bercovici, J. *Media Life*. "Alexander Liberman: Major figure in the look of magazines." http://medialifemagazine.com/news1999/nov99/news31122.html. (Accessed November 11, 2008.)

Bernhard, Barbara. *Fashion in the '60s*. New York: St. Martin's Press, 1978.

Bertin, Celia. *Paris à la Mode*. London: Gollancz, 1956.

Between a Rock and a Hard Place: A History of American Sweatshops 1820 – Present. http://americanhistory.si.edu/sweatshops/. (Accessed March 27, 2009.)

Bianchino, G., Grazietta Butazzi, Alessandra Mottola Molfino, and Arturo Carlo Quintavalle.

Italian Fashion. New York: Rizzoli International Publications, 1988.

Biography.com. "Anna Wintour Biography (1949–)."

http:// biography.com/articles/Anna-Wintour-214147. (Accessed November 15, 2008.)

Bissonnette, A. (Curator). *Charles Kleibacker: Master of the Bias*. http://dept.kent.edu/museum/exhibit/kleibacker/kleibacker2.htm. (Accessed November 10, 2008.)

Black, J.A. and Madge Garland. *A History of Fashion*. New York: Morrow, 1980.

Blum, S. *Designs by Erté: Fashion Drawings & Illustrations from Harper's Bazaar*. New York: Harry N. Abrams, 1987.

BookRags. "Encyclopedia of World Biography on Annie Leibovitz." http://www.bookrags.com/biography/annie-leibovitz. (Accessed October 6, 2009.)

Bond, D. *The Guinness Guide to Twentieth Century Fashion*. Middlesex, England: Guinness Superlatives Ltd., 1989

Borrelli, L. *Stylishly Drawn: Contemporary Fashion Illustration*. New York: Harry N. Abrams, Inc., 2001.

Bottega Veneta. http://www.bottegaveneta.com. (Accessed October 6, 2009.)

Boucher, F. with Yvonne Deslandres. *20,000 Years of Fashion: The History of Costume and Personal Adornment*, Expanded Edition. New York: Harry N. Abrams, 1987.

Brady, J. *Super Chic*. Boston: Little, Brown & Co., 1974.

Brogden, J. *Fashion Design*. London: Studio Vista, 1971.

Brooks Brothers. 2007. "Our Heritage." http://brooksbrothers.com/aboutus/heritage.tem. (October 30, 2007.)

Brown, J. *Salon.com*. "Liz Tilberis Harper's Bazaar editor in chief, a legend in the world of fashion, dies of cancer at 51." April 22, 1999. http:// salon.com/people/obit/1999/04/22/tilberis/print.html. (Accessed November 14, 2008.)

Burberry. "About Burberry." http:// burberry.com/AboutBurberry/History.aspx. (Accessed October 13, 2007.)

Burris-Meyer, E. *This is Fashion*. New York: Harper, 1943.

Bustler. "Cooper-Hewitt Announces Winners of the Ninth Annual National Design Awards." May 12, 2008. http://bustler.net/index.php/article/cooper_hewitt_announces_winners_of_the_ninth_annual_national_design_awards/. (Accessed November 14, 2008.)

Butterick. http://butterick.com. (Accessed March 27, 2009.)

Byers, M. *Designing Women*. New York: Simon & Schuster, 1938.

Calasibetta, C.M. and Phyllis G. Tortora. *Fairchild's Dictionary of Fashion*, 3rd ed. New York: Fairchild Publications, 2003.

Carman, R. (2008, January 11). House of Creed. Message posted to http://www.allthebestblog.com/2008/01/house-of-creed.html.

Carmody, D. *New York Times*. "Alexander Liberman, Conde Nast's Driving Creative Force, Is Dead at 87." November 20, 1999.

Carter, E. *Magic Names of Fashion*. New Jersey: Prentice-Hall, Inc., 1980.

———. *Twentieth Century Fashion, a Scrapbook: 1900 to Today*. London: Eyre Methuen, 1975.

———. *The Changing World of Fashion*. New York: G.P. Putnam's Sons, 1977.

Cary, C. "Historic Dressmakers." http://www.whitebow. com/Historic_Dressmakers.html. (Accessed October 6, 2009.)

Cawthorne, N. *Key Moments in Fashion: The Evolution of Style.* London: Octopus Publishing Group, 1998.

CBC News. "Leibovitz gets O'Keeffe accolade." http://www.cbc.ca/arts/artdesign/story/2009/10/03/ leibovitz-okeeffe-honour.html. (Accessed October 6, 2009.)

Chapkis, W. and Cynthia Enloe. *Of Common Cloth: Women in the Global Textile Industry.* Amsterdam: Transnational Institute, 1983.

Charles-Roux, E. *Chanel: Her Life, Her World, and the Woman Behind the Legend She Herself Created.* New York: Random House, 1975.

———. *Chanel and Her World.* London: Weidenfeld & Nicolson, 1981.

Chase, E.W. and Ilka Chase. *Always in Vogue.* New York: Doubleday & Company, Inc., 1954.

Chase, J. and Jennifer Goodkind. *New York Social Diary.* "Teri Agins." http:// newyorksocialdiary.com/ node/2282. (Accessed November 3, 2008.)

Chloe. "History." http://chloe.com/version_en/. (Accessed November 11, 2008.)

Chrisp, P. *A History of Fashion and Costume Vol. 6: The Victorian Age.* New York: Facts on File, 2005.

Coleman, E.A. *The Genius of Charles James.* Published for the exhibition at the Brooklyn Museum. New York: Holt, Rinehart and Winston, 1982.

———. *Changing Fashions, 1800–1970.* New York: Brooklyn Museum, 1972.

———. *The Opulent Era: Fashions of Worth, Doucet and Pingat.* London: Thames and Hudson, 1992.

Collins, A.F. "Toujours Couture." (2009, September) *Vanity Fair.*

Condé Nast Portfolio.com. "Who Is Ungaro's New Designer Esteban Cortazar." November 30, 2007. http:// portfolio.com/views/blogs/fashion- inc/2007/11/30/who-is-ungaros-new-designer- esteban-cortazar. (Accessed November 6, 2008.)

Condra, J. *The Greenwood Encyclopedia of Clothing through World History.* Westport, CT: Greenwood Publishing, 2007.

Corbett, R. *New York Magazine.* "Profile: 55DSL." http://nymag.com/listings/stores/55dsl/. (Accessed November 14, 2008.)

Corrigan, J.C. *Marie Claire.* "Designer Dossier: Anna Molinari." http:// marieclaire.com/hair/fashion/latest/anna- molinari-blumarine-fashion-designer. (Accessed November 11, 2008.)

Cosgrave, B. *The Complete History of Costume & Fashion: From Ancient Egypt to the Present Day.* London: Octopus Publishing Group, 2000.

The Costume Gallery. http://costumegallery.com. (Accessed March 27, 2009.)

Council of Fashion Designers of America. "Tom Ford: CFDA Member Profile." *http://www.cfda.com/index. php?option=com_cfda_content&task=members_ display&user_name=TomFord.* (Accessed October 5, 2009.)

———. "CFDA Fashion Awards: Past Winners, 2009." http://www.cfda.com/index.php?option=com_cfda_ content&task=fashion_awards_display&category_ id=31. (Accessed October 5, 2009.)

Craven, J. *Vogue.com (UK).* "Mario Testino." April 20, 2008. http:// vogue.co.uk/biographies/080420- mario-testino-biography.aspx. (Accessed November 14, 2008.)

Creed, C. *Made to Measure.* London: Jarrolds, 1961.

Creed Fragrances. "Official UK Website." http://www. creedfragrances.co.uk/site. (Accessed October 6, 2009.)

———. "Winner by a Nose." http://www. creedfragrances.co.uk/site/press_coverage/ios_ mar_2003. March 23, 2003.

Creed Perfume. "Official US website." http://www. creedperfumes.us. (Accessed October 6, 2009.)

Daché, L. *Talking through My Hats.* Edited by Dorothy Roe Lewis. New York: Coward-McCann, Inc., 1946.

———. *Lilly Dache's Glamour Book.* Philadelphia: J.B. Lippincott, 1956.

Dars, C. *A Fashion Parade: The Seeberger Collection.* London: Blond & Briggs, 1979.

Davenport, M. *The Book of Costume.* Vol. 1. New York: Crown Publishers, Inc., 1976.

Daves, J. *Ready-Made Miracle.* New York: G.P. Putman's Sons, 1967.

Daves, J., Bryan Holme, Alexander Liberman, and Katharine Tweed, eds. *The World in Vogue.* New York: Viking Press, 1963.

Davis, B. *Fashion Windows.* "Loewe by Jose Enrique Ona Selfa." March 14, 2002. http://fashionwindows. com/runway_shows/loewe/default.asp. (Accessed November 11, 2008.)

Davis, M. *Fashion Windows.* "Lilly Pulitzer: True American Classic." http://fashionwindows.com/ fashion/lilly_pulitzer/default.asp. (Accessed November 13, 2008.)

———. *Fashion Windows.* "Michael Vollbracht leaves Bill Blass." Fall 2007. http:// fashionwindows.com/ news/2007/bill_blass.asp. (Accessed November 15, 2008.)

Day, E. *The Observer blog. Guardian.co.uk.* "Why racism stalked the London catwalk." February 17, 2008. http:// guardian.co.uk/lifeandstyle/2008/ feb/17/fashion.londonfashionweek. (Accessed November 17, 2008.)

DeGraw, I.G. *25 Years, 25 Couturiers*. Denver Art Museum, Denver, CO., 1975.

De Marly, D. *Costume on the Stage 1600-1940*. Summit, PA: Rowman & Littlefield, 1982.

———. *The History of Haute Couture, 1850–1950*. New York: Holmes and Meir, 1994.

———. *Worth, Father of Haute Couture*. New York: Holmes and Meir, 1991.

Demornex, J. *Madeleine Vionnet*. Translated by Augusta Audubert. New York: Rizzoli International Publications, 1991.

de Osma, G. *Mariano Fortuny: His Life and Work*. New York: Rizzoli International Publications, 1994.

Derrick, R. and Robin Muir, eds. *Unseen Vogue: The Secret History of Fashion Photography*. London: Little, Brown and Company, 2002.

Deschodt, A. *Mariano Fortuny, un Magicien de Venise*. Tours, France: Editions du Regard, 2000.

Deschodt, A. and Daretta Davanzo Poli. *Fortuny*. New York: Harry N. Abrams, 2001.

Deslandres, Y. *Poiret: Paul Poiret 1879-1944*. New York: Rizzoli International Publications, Inc., 1987.

Devlin, P. *Vogue Book of Fashion Photography*. London: Thames and Hudson, 1978.

Downey, L. "Levi Strauss: A Short Biography." 2005. http:// levistrauss.com/Downloads/History-Denium. pdf. (Accessed September 23, 2007.)

Diamonstein, B. *Fashion: The Inside Story*. New York: Rizzoli International Publications, Inc., 1985.

Dior, C. *Talking about Fashion*. Translated by Eugenia Sheppard. New York: G.P. Putnam's Sons, 1954.

———. *Christian Dior and I*. Translated by Antonia Fraser. New York: E.P. Dutton & Company, Inc., 1957.

———. *Dior by Dior*. Translated by Antonia Fraser. London: Weidenfeld & Nicolson, 1957.

Dixon, H.V. *The Rag Pickers*. New York: Avon, 1971.

Dorner, J. *Fashion: The Changing Shape of Fashion through the Years*. London: Octopus Books, 1974.

———. *Fashion in the 40s and 50s*. London: Ian Allen, 1975.

Duncan, N.H. *History of Fashion Photography*. New York: Alpine Press, 1979.

Ehrlich, D. updated by Karen Raugust. *Fashion Encyclopedia*. "Alexander Julian." http:// fashionencyclopedia.com/Ja-Kh/Julian-Alexander. html. (Accessed November 8, 2008.)

Élegance et Création: Paris 1945–1975. Musée de la Mode et du Costume, Paris, 1977.

Emanuel, D. and Elizabeth Emanuel. *Style for All Seasons*. London: Pavilion: Michael Jospeh, 1983.

Erté. *Erté Fashions*. New York: St. Martin's Press, 1972.

———. *Erté—Things I Remember*. London: Peter Owen Limited, 1983.

Estaban Cortazar. "Estaban." http://estebancortazar. com/. (Accessed November 6, 2008.)

Etherington-Smith, M. *Patou*. New York: St. Martin's Press, 1984.

Eubank, K. and Phyllis Tortora. *Survey of Historic Costume, 2nd ed.* New York: Fairchild Publications, 1994.

Ewing, E. and Alice Mackrell. *History of 20th Century Fashion*. Rev. 4th ed. New York: Quite Specific Media Group Ltd., 2002.

Eyewitness to History: History through the eyes of those who *lived it*. http://eyewitnesstohistory.com. (Accessed March 27, 2009.)

Fairchild, J. *The Fashionable Savages*. New York: Doubleday & Company, Inc., 1965.

Family Business Magazine E-Newsletter. "The World's Oldest Family Companies." http://www.familybusinessmagazine.com/worldsoldest/ worldsoldest4.html. August 4, 2009.

Farber, R. *The Fashion Photographer*. New York: Watson Guptill, 1981.

Farrell-Beck, J. and Jean Parsons. *20th-Century Dress in the United States*. New York: Fairchild Books, 2007.

Fashion, 1900–1939. Scottish Arts Council; Victoria and Albert Museum, London, 1975.

Fashion.at. "Andrew Gn." http://fashion.at/collections/ andrewgn12-2002b.htm. (Accessed November 6, 2008.)

Fashion Encyclopedia. http://fashionencyclopedia.com. (Accessed March 27, 2009.)

Fashion-Era. http://fashion-era.com. (Accessed March 27, 2009.)

Fashion Forum. http://fashion-forum.org. (Accessed March 27, 2009.)

Fashion Week Daily. "Nina Garcia to Go From Hachette to . . . Hachette?" May 08, 2008. http:// www.fashionweekdaily.com/news/fullstory. sps?inewsid=2397191. (Accessed November 6, 2008.)

———. "Project Runway Status Confirmed: Nina Garcia to remain as Elle editor-at-large through Season 5." May 15, 2008. http://fashionweekdaily.com/news/ fullstory.sps?inewsid=4354412. (Accessed November 11, 2008.)

Fashion Windows. "Ralph Ricci: Marrying the Discipline of Art & Philosophy." http://fashionwindows.com/ fashion/chado_ralph_rucci/default.asp. (Accessed November 13, 2008.)

———. "Stuart Vevers Replaces Jose Enrique Ona Selfa at Loewe as Creative Director." July 26, 2007. http://blog.fashionwindows.com/?p=160. (Accessed November 11, 2008.)

Ferragamo, S. *Shoemaker of Dreams: The Autobiography of Salvatore Ferragamo*. 3rd ed. Florence: Centro Di, 1985.

Fine Fashion. Philadelphia Museum of Art, Philapelphia, 1979.

Fleischner, J. *Mrs. Lincoln and Mrs. Keckley: The Remarkable Story of the Friendship Between a First Lady and a Former Slave*. New York: Broadway Books, 2003.

Fogarty, A. *Wife-Dressing*. New York: Julian Messner Inc., 1959.

Fortini, A. *Slate*. "Defending *Vogue*'s Evil Genius: The brilliance of Anna Wintour." February 10, 2005. http://slate.com/id/2113278/. (Accessed November 15, 2008.)

Fortuny, M. *Immagini e Materiali del Laboratorio Fortuny*. Venice: Comune di Venezia Marsilio Edition, 1978.

Fortuny. Fashion Institute of Technology, New York, 1981.

Fortuny nella Belle Epoque. Electa, Milan, 1984.

Foxley, D. *New York Observer*. "Calvin Klein Designer Francisco Costa Discusses Inspiration." February 8, 2008. http://observer.com/2008/calvin-klein-designer-francisco-costa-discusses-inspiration. (Accessed November 6, 2008.)

Fraser, K. *The Fashionable Mind*. Boston: David R. Godine, 1984.

Gaines, S. *Simply Halston*. New York: Jove Publications, 1993.

Galante, P. *Mademoiselle Chanel*. Chicago: Regency, 1973.

Galvin, C. *Sunday Times*. "Annie Leibovitz: Nothing left to hide." October 5, 2008. http://entertainment.timesonline.co.uk/tol/arts_and_entertainment/visual_arts/article4860955.ece. (Accessed November 10, 2008.)

Gap Inc. http://gapinc.com. (Accessed March 26, 2009.)

Garland, M. *Fashion*. London: Penguin Books, 1962.

———. *The Changing Form of Fashion*. London: J.M. Dent & Sons, 1970.

Giambattista Valli. "Chronology." http://giambattistavalli.com/. (Accessed November 14, 2008.)

———. "Fashion Designer." http:// giambattistavalli.com/. (Accessed November 15, 2008.)

Giroud, F. *Dior*. New York: Rizzoli International Publications, 1987.

Givhan, R. *Washington Post*. "Back in Fashion/In the church of Saint Laurent, heresy and revival: Can Stefano Pilati convert reverence into relevance?" May 27, 2007.

———. *Washington Post*. "Fashion Sense: Luxury, Pure Style, Understated Eloquence: Akris's Creations for Women of Power." May 31. 2005.

———. *Washington Post*. "Taking Off From the Runway Business: For Blass Designer, the Industry Wore Thin." June 1, 2007.

Glynn, P. *In Fashion: Dress in the Twentieth Century*. New York: Oxford University Press, 1978.

———. *Skin to Skin*. New York: Oxford University Press, 1982.

Gold, A. *75 Years of Fashion*. New York: Fairchild Publications, 1975.

———. *90 Years of Fashion*. New York: Fairchild Publications, Inc., 1990.

Gorsline, D.W. *What People Wore: A Visual History of Dress from Ancient Times to 20th Century America*. New York: Random House Value Publishing, 1987.

———. *One World of Fashion*. 4th edition. New York: Fairchild Publications, 1986.

———. *What People Wore: 1,800 Illustrations from Ancient Times to the Early Twentieth Century*. New York: Dover Publications, 1994.

Gucci Group. http://guccigroup.com. (Accessed March 27, 2009.)

Haedrich, M. *Coco Chanel: Her Life, Her Secrets*. Boston: Little, Brown & Co., 1972.

H&M. "Roberto Cavalli at H&M." http:// hm.com/us/abouthm/robertocavalliathm__designercooperation.nhtml. (Accessed November 17, 2008.)

Hart, A. and Susan North. *Seventeenth and Eighteenth Century Fashion in Detail*. New York: Rizzoli, 1998.

Hartnell, N. *Silver and Gold*. London: Evans Brothers, 1955.

———. *Royal Courts of Fashion*. London: Cassell & Co. Ltd., 1971.

Haute Couture: Notes on Designers and Their Clothes in the Collection of the Royal Ontario Museum. Royal Ontario Museum, Toronto, 1969.

Hawes, E. *Fashion is Spinach*. New York: Random House, 1938.

———. *It's Still Spinach*. Boston: Little, Brown and Co., 1954.

Head, E. *The Dress Doctor*. Boston: Little, Brown and Co., 1959.

Hearst Corporation. "Glenda Bailey Editor-In-Chief, *Harper's Bazaar*." http:// hearstcorp.com/biography_other.php?id=12&cat_id=6. (Accessed November 5, 2008.)

Helmut Newton. "Biography." http://helmutnewton.com/helmut_newton/biography/. (Accessed Novmber 11, 2008.)

Herb Ritts. "Biography." http://herbritts.com/about/. (Accessed November 14, 2008.)

Hibbert, C. and Adam Hibbert. *A History of Costume and Fashion Vol. 8: The Twentieth Century*. New York: Facts on File, 2005.

History Matters. "Dressmaker and Former Salve Elizabeth Keckley (ca. 1818-1907), Tells How She Gained Her Freedom, 1868." http://historymatters.gmu.edu/d/6224. (Accessed October 6, 2009.)

Hommage `a Schiaparelli. Musée de la Mode et du Costume, Paris. 1984.

Horst. *Salute to the Thirties.* New York: Viking Press, 1971.

Horyn, C. *New York Times.* "Citizen Anna." February 1, 2007.

———. *New York Times.* "When Is a Fashion Ad Not a Fashion Ad?" April 8, 2008

Hot Watches. "History of Diesel." http://hotwatches. co.uk/diesel-watches/. (Accessed November 14, 2008.)

Houck, C. *The Fashion Encyclopedia.* New York: St. Martin's Press, 1982.

The House of Worth: The Gilded Age, 1860–1918. Museum of the City of New York, New York, 1982.

Howell, G. *In Vogue: Six Decades of Fashion.* New York: Viking Press, 1979.

Hulanicki, B. *From A to Biba.* London: Hutchinson, 1983.

The Independent. "Herb Ritts Photographer of the famous and fashionable." December 30, 2002.

———. "This man is on fire: Gareth Pugh—Britain's newest star designer." September 15, 2008.

Informat.com. "Lilly Pulitzer." http://infomat.com/ whoswho/lillypulitzer.html. (Accessed November 13, 2008.)

———. "Biography of Peter Som." January 18, 2007. http://infomat.com/whoswho/petersom.html. (Accessed November 17, 2008.)

The Internet Movie Database. http://imdb.com (Accessed March 27, 2009.)

Internet World Stats: Usage and Population Statistics. http://internetworldstats.com. (Accessed March 27, 2009.)

Investors Business Incorporated. 2007. Charles Tiffany Found All That Glitters In Jewelry. http://money.cnn. com/news/newsfeeds/articles/newstex/IBD-0001- 20512044.htm. (November 1, 2007.)

Jachimowicz, E. *Eight Chicago Women and Their Fashion, 1860–1929.* Chicago: Chicago Historical Society, 1978.

Jaeger. 2007. "About Us." http://jaeger.co.uk/index. cfm?page=1024. (October 10, 2007.)

Jenkins, D, ed. *The Cambridge History of Western Textiles.* Cambridge and New York: Cambridge University Press, 2003.

Johnston, L. *Nineteenth-Century Fashion in Detail.* London: V&A Publications, 2005.

Jouve, M. *Balenciaga (Universe of Fashion).* New York: Universe Books, 1998.

Julians. "About Us." http://julianstyle.com/about. php?categorie_id=4. (Accessed November 8, 2008.)

Kansas City Public Schools. Agins, Teri: Wyandotte High School, 1971. http://kckps.org/recognition/ alumni/2005/agins.html. (Accessed November 3, 2008.)

Karan, D. *Donna Karan New York: An American Woman Observed.* New York: Donna Karan Company, 1987.

Keckley, E. *Behind the Scenes or Thirty Years a Slave, and Four Years in the White House.* London England: Penguin Books Ltd, 2005.

Keenan, B. *Dior in Vogue.* New York: Random House Value Publishing, 1988.

Kellogg, A., Amy T. Peterson, Stefani Bay, and Natalie Swindell. *In an Influential Fashion: An Encyclopedia of Nineteenth- and Twentieth-Century Fashion Designers and Retailers Who Transformed Dress.* Westport, CT: Greenwood Publishing Group, Inc., 2002.

Kennedy, S. *Pucci: A Renaissance in Fashion.* New York: Abbeville Press, 1991.

Kennett, F. *The Collector's Book of Fashion.* New York: Crown Publishers, Inc., 1983.

King, N. *J Camp Live!* "Profile: Reporter and author Teri Agins." July 31, 2007. http://lyingisbad.com/ jcamplive/?p=19. (Accessed November 3, 2008.)

Khornak, L. *Fashion 2001.* New York: Viking Press, 1982.

Koenig, G. *WWD.* "Creed Offers a Taste of Florence." July 6, 2009.

Kybalova, L., Olga Herbenova, and Milena Lamorova. *The Pictorial Encyclopedia of Fashion,* 2nd ed. Translated by Claudia Rosoux. England: Hamlyn Publishers, 1968.

Lagerfeld, K. *Lagerfeld's Sketchbook: Karl Lagerfeld's Illustrated Fashion Journal of Anna Piaggi.* London: Weidenfeld & Nicolson, 1988.

Lakewood Public Library. "Women in History. Elizabeth Keckley biography." March 9, 2009. http://www. lkwdpl.org/wihohio/keck-eli.htm. (Accessed October 6, 2009.)

Lambert, E. *World of Fashion: People, Places and Resources.* 2nd ed. New York: R.R. Bowker Company, 1979.

Funding Universe. "Lane Bryant, Inc." http://www. fundinguniverse.com/company-histories/Lane- Bryant-Inc-Company-History.html. (Accessed March 27, 2009.)

Langlade, E. *Rose Bertin: The Creator of Fashion at the Court of Marie-Antoinette.* Adapted from the French by Dr. Angelo S. Rappoport. New York: Charles Scribner's Sons, 1913.

Larocca, A. *New York.* "The Dapper Mr. Browne." August 20, 2006.

———. *New York.* "Straight Shooter." August 17, 2008.

Latour, A. *Kings of Fashion.* Translated by Mervyn Saville. London: Weidenfeld & Nicolson, 1958.

———. *Paris Fashion.* London: Michael Joseph, 1972.

Laver, J. *Taste and Fashion.* London: George G. Harrap & Co. Ltd., 1937.

———. *A concise History of Costume.* New York: Oxford University Press, 1988.

———. *Fashion, Art and Beauty.* New York: Costume Institute, Metropolitan Museum of Art, 1967.

Laver, J. et. al. *Costume and Fashion: A Concise History.* 4th ed. London: Thames & Hudson, 2002.

Lavine, W.R. *In a Glamorous Fashion.* New York: Charles Scribner's Sons, 1980.

Lee, S.T., ed. *American Fashion: The Life and Lines of Adrian, Mainbocher, McCardell, Norell & Trigére.* New York: Quadrangle/The NY Times Book Co., 1975.

Leese, E. *Costume Design in the Movies.* New York: Frederick Ungar Publishing Co., 1977.

Lewis, J. *Artinfo.com.* "Artist Walk: Annie Leibovitz." October 19, 2006. http://www.artinfo.com/news/story/22798/artist-walk-annie-leibovitz. (Accessed October 6, 2009.)

Levi Strauss & Co. http://levistrauss.com. (Accessed March, 26, 2009)

———. 2007. "Jacob Davis: His Life and Contributions." http://levistrauss.com/Downloads/History_Jacob_Davis_Biography.pdf. (Accessed October 3, 2007.)

Levin, P.L. *The Wheels of Fashion.* New York: Doubleday & Company, Inc., 1965.

Ley, S. *Fashion for Everyone: The Story of Ready-to-Wear.* New York: Charles Scribner's Sons, 1975.

Leymarie, J. *Chanel.* New York: Rizzoli International Publications, 1989.

Lincoln Institute, The. "Abraham Lincoln's White House: Elizabeth Keckley (1818–1907)." http://www.mrlincolnswhitehouse.org/inside.asp?ID=60&subjectID=2. (Accessed October 6, 2009.)

Liz Claiborne Group. http://lizclaiborne.com. (Accessed March 27, 2009.)

Loughran, M. *Suite101.com.* "Elsa Peretti Jewelry Icon Designer for Tiffany & Co." October 27, 2007. http://jewelry-makers.suite101.com/article.cfm/elsa_peretti. (Accessed November 18, 2008.)

LVMH Group. http://lvmh.com. (Accessed March 27, 2009.)

Lynam, R., ed. *Couture: an Illustrated History of the Great Paris designers and Their Creations.* New York: Doubleday & Company, Inc., 1972.

Madsen, A. *Chanel: A Woman of Her Own.* New York: Henry Holt and Co., Reprint, 1991.

———. *Living for Design: Yves Saint Laurent Story.* New York, 1979.

———. *Chanel, A Woman of Her Own.* New York: Henry Holt Co., 1990.

Mahoney, M. and Vladimir Dusil. *Purse Blog.* "Meet Monica Botkier." http://purseblog.com/meet-monica-botkier/. (Accessed November 13, 2008.)

Tomas Maier. http://www.tomasmaier.com. (Accessed October 6, 2009.)

Mario Testino. "Mario Testino Bibliography." http://mariotestino.com/. (Accessed November 14, 2008.)

Marsh, S. *The Times.* "Mario Testino: A portrait of celebrity." June 30, 2008. http://entertainment.timesonline.co.uk/tol/arts_and_entertainment/visual_arts/article4227229.ece. (Accessed November 14, 2008.)

Martin, J.J. *Harpers Bazaar.* "Tomas Maier: Dreamweaver." http://www.harpersbazaar.com/fashion/fashion-articles/tomas-maier-0208. (Accessed October 6, 2009.)

Martin, R. and H. Koda. *Giorgio Armani: Images of Man.* New York: Rizzoli International Publications, 1990.

Maxwell, E. *R.S.V.P. Elsa Maxwell's Own Story.* Boston: Little, Brown & Co., 1954.

McCall Pattern Company. "Butterick: Our History." http://butterick.com/bhc/pages/articles/histpgs/about.html. (October 20, 2007.)

McCardell, C. *What Shall I Wear?* New York: Simon & Schuster, 1956.

McConathy, D. with Diana Vreeland. *Hollywood Costume.* New York: Harry N. Abrams, 1976.

McDowell, C. *McDowell's Directory of Twentieth Century Fashion.* New Jersey: Prentice-Hall, Inc., 1985.

Mendes, V.D. *Twentieth Century Fashion: An Introduction to Women's Fashionable Dress, 1900–1980.* London: Victoria and Albert Museum, 1996.

Mendes, Valerie D. and Amy de la Haye. *20th Century Fashion.* London: Thames & Hudson, 1999.

Menkes, Suzy. *International Herald Tribune.* "The High-Octane Liz Tilberis." April 27, 1999.

———. *International Herald Tribune.* "Renzo Rosso takes control of Viktor & Rolf label." July 21, 2008.

———. *New York Times.* "Missoni's Next Generation." September 28, 2009.

Micheletti, E. *All About Romance Novels.* "Charles Frederick Worth: The Father of Haute Couture." http://likesbooks.com/charlesworth.html. (Accessed September, 23, 2007.)

Milbank, C.R. *Couture: The Great Designers.* New York: Stewart, Tabori & Chang, Inc., 1997.

———. *New York Fashion: The Evolution of American Style.* New York: Harry N. Abrams, 1989.

Milinaire, C. *Cheap Chic: Update.* Rev. ed. New York: Outlet Book Company, 1978.

Miller, B.M. *Dressed for the Occasion: What Americans Wore 1620–1970.* Minneapolis, MN: Lerner Publications, 1999.

Mirabella, G. *In and Out of Vogue*. New York: Doubleday, 1995.

Missoni. http://www.missoni.com. (Accessed October 6, 2009.)

Miyake, I. *Issey Miyake Meets West*. Tokyo: Heibonsha, 1978.

———. *Issey Miyake Bodyworks*. Tokyo: Shokagukan Publishing Co. Ltd., 1983.

Miyake, I, Kazuko Sato, Herve Chandes, Fondation Cartier, and Raymond Meier. *Issey Miyake: Making Things*. New Zurich: Scalo Verlag, 1999.

Modaitalia.net. "Roberto Cavalli Biography." http://modaitalia.net/robertocavalli/bio.htm. (Accessed November 17, 2008.)

Moffitt, P. et al. *The Rudi Gernreich Book*. New York: Taschen America, LLC. 1999.

Mohrt, F. *30 Ans D'Elegance et de Créations 1925–1955*. Paris: Jacques Damase, 1983.

Moore, B. *Los Angeles Times*. "The Obama effect on Thakoon Panichgul." September 21, 2008.

Morris, B. *The Fashion Makers: An Inside Look at America's Leading Designers*. New York: Random House, 1978.

———. *Lookonline.com*. "Fashion Roundtable: An Interview with Three Leading Black Fashion Journalists." Novemeber 14, 2002. http://lookonline.com/fashion-roundtable-1.html. (Accessed November 4, 2008.)

Mugler, T. *Thierry Mugler*. New York: Rizzoli International Publications, 1988.

Muir, R. (2007, April 11). Patricia Creed: 'Vogue' model and fashion editor. *The Independent*. http://www.independent.co.uk/news/obituaries/patricia-creed-444144.html. (Accessed October 6, 2009.)

National Institute of Standards and Technology Virtual Museum. http://museum.nist.gov/. (Accessed March 27, 2009.)

Naughton, J. *WWD*. "Halston's New Scent Formula." July 1, 2009.

Naumann, F.M. *Conversion to Modernism: The Early Work of Man Ray*. New Jersey: Rutgers University Press, 2003.

Neal, T. *Stylelist*. "Confirmed: Monica Botkier for Target." March 18, 2008. http://stylelist.com/blog/2008/03/18/confirmed-monica-botkier-for-target/. (Accessed November 11, 2008.)

Nemy, E. *New York Times*. "Sybil Connolly, 77, Irish Designer Who Dressed Jacqueline Kennedy." May 8, 1998.

New York Magazine. "Andrew Gn." http://nymag.com/fashion/fashionshows/designers/bios/andrewgn/. (Accessed November 8, 2008.)

———. "Bottega Veneta." http://nymag.com/fashion/fashionshows/designers/bios/bottegaveneta/. (Accessed October 6, 2009.)

———. "Chado Ralph Ricci." http://nymag.com/fashion/fashionshows/designers/bios/chadoralphrucci/. (Accessed November 13, 2008.)

———. "Derek Lam." http://nymag.com/fashion/fashionshows/designers/bios/dereklam/. (Accessed November 8, 2008.)

———. "Lilly Pulitzer." http://nymag.com/fashion/fashionshows/designers/bios/lillypulitzer/. (Accessed 13, 2008.)

———. "Peter Som." http://nymag.com/fashion/fashionshows/designers/bios/petersom/. (Accessed November 17, 2008.)

———. "Roberto Cavalli." http://nymag.com/fashion/fashionshows/designers/bios/robertocavalli/. (Accessed November 17, 2008.)

———. "Thakoon Panichgul." http://nymag.com/fashion/fashionshows/designers/bios/thakoon/. (Accessed November 13, 2008.)

New York Magazine, The Cut blog. "Derek Lam Doesn't Knock Knockoffs." March 7, 2008. http://nymag.com/daily/fashion/2008/03/derek_lam_doesnt_knock_knockof.html. (Accessed November 10, 2008.)

———. "Marc Jacobs and Renzo Rosso Team Up on Menswear." November 10, 2008. http://nymag.com/daily/fashion/2008/11/marc_jacobs_and_renzo_rossi_te.html. (Accessed November 14, 2008.)

———. "Why Everyone's Watching Gareth Pugh." September 15, 2008. http://nymag.com/daily/fashion/2008/09/why_everyones_eyes_are_on_gare.html. (Accessed November 13, 2008.)

Nicolson, N. *Mary Curzon*. New York: Harper & Row, 1977.

Niles, L. "Sarah Josepha Hale. Domestic Goddesses." http://womenwriters.net/domesticgoddess/hale1.html. (October 10,2007.)

Norma Kamali: "Home: Bio." http://normakamalicollection.com/customer/bio.aspx. (Accessed November 17, 2008.)

O'Hara, G. Dictionary of Fashion and Fashion Designers. New York: Thames and Hudson, 1998.

———. *The Encyclopedia of Fashion*. New York: Harry N. Abrams, Inc., 1986.

Odell, A. *New York Magazine, The Cut Blog*. "Is Anna Wintour Retiring?!" November 18, 2008. http://nymag.com/daily/fashion/2008/11/is_anna_wintour_retiring.html. (Accessed November 18, 2008.)

Olsen, K. *Chronology of Women's History*. Westport, CT: Greenwood Publishing, 1994.

Onyewueny, I. *My Fashion Life*. "The Gareth Pugh Aesthetic: Can you handle it?" October 14, 2008.

http://myfashionlife.com/archives/2008/10/14/ the-gareth-pugh-aesthetic-can-you-handle-it/. (Accessed November 13, 2008.)

Orecklin, M. *Time.com.* "The Power List, Women in Fashion : Anna Wintour." http://time.com/ time/2004/style/020904/power/3.html. (Accessed November 15, 2008.)

Paperpast Yearbook. http://paperpast.com/. (Accessed March 27, 2009.)

Payne, B. *History of Costume: From the Ancient Egyptians to the Twentieth Century.*

New York: Harper & Row, 1965.

Payne, B., Geitel Winakor, and Jane Farrell-Beck. *History of Costume: From Ancient Mesopotamia through the Twentieth Century.* 2nd ed. Boston: Addison-Wesley, 1992.

Pelle, M. *Valentino: Thirty Years of Magic.* New York: Abbeville Press, 1991.

Perkins, A. *Paris Couturiers & Milliners.* New York: Fairchild Publications, 1949.

Perschetz, L., ed. *W: The Designing Life.* New York: Clarkson N. Potter, Inc., 1990.

Peter Som. "About." http://petersom.com/about.html. (Accessed November 17, 2008.)

Picken, M.B. *A Dictionary of Costume and Fashion: Historic and Modern.*

New York: Dover Publications, Inc., 1998.

Poiret, P. *En Habillant l'Epoque.* Paris: Grasset, 1930.

——. *King of Fashion* (autobiography). Translated by Stephen Haden Guest. Philadelphia: J.B. Lippincott Company, 1931.

——. *Revenez-Y.* Paris: Gallimard, 1934.

Polan, B, ed. *The Fashion Year, 1938.* London: Zomba Books, 1983.

Prabhakar, H. *Forbes.com.* "Tastemakers: Fashion Design." March 14, 2007. http://forbes.com/ style/2007/03/13/tastemaker-designer-fashion-forbeslife-cx_hp_0314fashion.html. (Accessed November 5, 2008.)

Prada Group. http://pradagroup.com. (Accessed March 27, 2009)

Prichard, S. *Film Costume: An Annotated Bibliography.* Metuchen, NJ: Scarecrow, 1981.

Prince, D. 2007. Louis Vuitton: The History Behind the Purse. http://associatedcontent.com/pop_print. shtml?content_type=article&content_type. (November 2, 2007.)

Quant, M. *Quant by Quant.* London: Cassell & Co. Ltd., 1966.

Quant, M. and Felicity Green. *Color by Quant: Your Complete Personal Guide to Beauty and Fashion.* New York: McGraw-Hill, 1985.

Rhodes, Z. and Anne Knight. *The Art of Zandra Rhodes.* London: Michael O'Mara Books, Ltd., 1995.

Ridley, P. *Fashion Illustration.* New York: Rizzoli International Publications, 1980.

Riley, R. *Givenchy: 30 Years.* Fashion Institute of Technology, New York, 1982.

Roberto Cavalli. "Company Profile." http:// robertocavalli.com/en/companyProfile/mission.do. (Accessed November 17, 2008.)

Robinson, J. *Fashion in the Forties.* New York: St. Martin's Press, 1976.

——. *Fashion in the Thirties.* New York: Oresko Books, 1978.

Rooney, A. *A History of Fashion and Costume Vol. 5: The Eighteenth Century.* New York: Facts on File, 2005.

Rochas, M. *Twenty-Five Years of Parisian Elegance, 1925–1950.* Paris: Pierre Tisne, 1951.

Roshco, B. *The Rag Race.* New York: Funk & Wagnalls, 1963.

Ross, J. *Beaton in Vogue.* New York: Outlet Book Company, 1988.

Rykiel, S. *And I Would Like Her Naked.* Paris: Bernard Grasset, 1979.

Salomon, R.K. *Fashion Design for Moderns.* New York: Fairchild Publications, 1976.

Sanderson, L.A. *LifeinItaly.com.* "The Romantic Origins of Missoni." November 2008. http://www.lifeinitaly. com/fashion/missoni.asp. (Accessed October 6, 2009.)

Saunders, E. *The Age of Worth: Couturier to the Empress Eugenie.* Bloomington, In: Indiana University Press, 1955.

Schiaparelli, E. *Shocking Life.* New York: E.P. Dutton & Co., Inc., 1954.

Schreier, B. *Mystique and Identity: Women's Fashions of the 1950s.* Norfolk, VA: Chrysler Museum, 1984.

Seckington, M. *Miss Geeky.com.* "Annie Leibovitz's Disney Dream Portrait Series." January 29, 2008. http://missgeeky.com/2008/01/29/annie-leibovitzs-disney-dream-portrait-series/. (Accessed November 10, 2008.)

Seebohm, C. *The Man Who Was Vogue: The Life and Times of Condé Nast.* New York: Viking Press, 1982.

Severa, J.L. *Dressed for the Photographer: Ordinary Americans and Fashion, 1840 – 1900.* Kent, OH: Kent State University Press, 1997.

SHOWstudio. "Contributors Stefano Pilati." http:// showstudio.com/contributors/16343. (Accessed November 13, 2008.)

——. "Gareth Pugh." http://showstudio.com/ contributors/4252. (Accessed November 13, 2008.)

Smithsonian Institution Press. *Legacies—From Artifacts to America.* "Gown made by Elizabeth Keckley for Mary Todd Lincoln, about 1864." http:// www.smithsonianlegacies.si.edu/objectdescription. cfm?ID=258. (Accessed October 6, 2009.)

Snow, C. and Mary Louise Aswell. *The World of Carmel Snow*. New York: McGraw-Hill Book Co., 1962.

Somerstein, R. *American Masters*. "Annie Leibovitz Life Through A Lens." http://pbs.org/wnet/americanmasters/episodes/annie-leibovitz-life-through-a-lens/16/. (Accessed November 10, 2008.)

Spencer, C. *Erté*. New York: Clarkson N. Potter, Inc., 1970.

Stegemeyer, A. *Who's Who in Fashion, 4ed*. New York: Fairchild Books, 2004.

Steele, P. *A History of Fashion and Costume Vol. 7: The Nineteenth Century*. New York: Facts on File, 2005.

Steele, V. *MSN Encarta*. "Fashion." http://encarta.msn.com/text_761585452___0/Fashion.html. (Accessed September 25, 2007.)

———. *Women of Fashion*. New York: Rizzoli Books International, 1991.

International Center of Photography. "Steven Meisel Applied Photography." http://www.icp.org/site/c.dnJGKJNsFqG/b.2079967/k.A4A8/Steven_Meisel.htm. (Accessed September 22, 2008.)

Stone, E. *The Dynamics of Fashion, 3ed*. New York: Fairchild Books, 2008.

Strom, S. *New York Times*. "Alexander Julian Licensee Liquidated as Rescue Falters." March 1, 1995.

Target. (2009, February). *McQ Alexander McQueen for Target* [Press release]. Retrieved from http://pressroom.target.com/pr/news/fashion/collaborations/mcq-for-target.aspx.

Taschen. "Helmut Newton's SUMO . . ." http://taschen.com/pages/en/catalogue/photography/all/02601/facts.helmut_newtons_sumo.htm. (Accessed November 11, 2008.)

Teboul, D., Christine Baute, and Pierre Berge. *Yves Saint Laurent: 5 Avenue Marceau, 75116 Paris, France*. New York: Harry N. Abrams, Inc., 2002.

Thomas, P.W. *Fashion Era*. "Antique Fashion & Costume plates Part 5—Godey's Fashion Plates." Fashion-Era. http://fashion-era.com/fashion_plates_old/0005_godeys_ladys.htm. (Accessed October 10, 2007.)

Thornton, N. *Poiret*. New York: Rizzoli International Publications, 1979.

Tkacik, M. *New York Magazine*. "America's Next Top Fashion Editor." August 17, 2008. http://nymag.com/fashion/08/fall/49259/index4.html. (Accessed November 6, 2008.)

Tice, B. *Enticements: How to Look Fabulous in Lingerie*. New York: The MacMillan Company, 1985.

Time. 1935. "Patterns." http://time.com/time/magazine/article/0,9171,748881,00.html. (November 1, 2007.)

Toklas, A. *A New French Style*. Paris: J.F. Verly, 1946.

Tolstoy, M. *Charlemagne to Dior: The Story of French Fashion*. New York: Michael Slains, 1967.

Tortora, P. and Keith Eubank. *Survey of Historic Costume, 4ed*. New York: Fairchild Books, 2005.

———. *Survey of Historic Costume, 5ed*. New York: Fairchild Books, 2010.

Tom Ford. "The Brand." http://www.tomford.com/#/en/thebrand/tomford (Accessed October 5, 2009.)

Tory Burch. "About." http://toryburch.com/about.aspx. (Accessed November 5, 2008.)

Trachtenberg, J. *Ralph Lauren—Image-maker. The Man Behind the Mystique*. New York: Little, Brown and Co., 1988.

Trahey, J., ed. *Harper's Bazaar: 100 Years of the American Female*. New York: Random House, 1967.

Trina Turk. "About Us." http://www.trinaturk.com/about.aspx. (Accessed November 15, 2008.)

Tsong, N. *Seattle Times*. "Fashion designer Trina Turk makes it work." August 31, 2008.

Tuohy, L. *Craftstylish.com*. "We're Biased: Couture Designer Charles Kleibacker's Gowns on Exhibit in Ohio." June 7th, 2008. http://craftstylish.com/item/2980/were-biased-couture-designer-charles-kleibackers-gowns-on-exhibit-in-ohio. (Accessed November 8, 2008.)

Tyrnauer, M. *Vanity Fair*.(2008, September) "Less is Maier." http://www.vanityfair.com/style/features/2008/09/maier200809. (Accessed October 6, 2009.)

Ulaby, N. *NPR*. "Esteban Cortazar: Young, Veteran Fashion Designer." September 8, 2004. http://npr.org/templates/story/story.php?storyId=3894400. (Accessed November 6, 2008.)

United Colors of Benetton. http://benettongroup.com. (Accessed March 27, 2009.)

U.S. Census Bureau. http://census.gov. (Accessed March 27, 2009.)

U.S. Department of Labor. http://bls.gov. (Accessed March 27, 2009.)

Vanderbilt, G. *Woman to Woman*. New York: Doubleday, 1979.

Vecchio, W. and Robert Riley. *The Fashion Makers: A Photographic Record*. New York: Crown Publishers, Inc., 1968.

Vickers, H. *Cecil Beaton*. New York: Sterling Publishing Co., 2002.

Victoria and Albert Museum. "V&A: The Golden Age of Couture." http://www.vam.ac.uk/vastatic/microsites/1486_couture/. (Accessed March 27, 2009.)

———. "Fashion in Motion Live Catwalk Event: Missoni." http://www.vam.ac.uk/collections/fashion/fashion_motion/missoni/index.html. (Accessed October 6, 2009.)

Viladas, P. *New York Times Magazine*. "STYLE MATTERS; Designed For Living." April 29, 2001.

Von Furstenberg, D. *Book of Beauty*. New York: Simon & Schuster, Inc., 1977.

Vreeland, D. *D.V.* New York: DeCapo Press, 1997.

Vreeland, D. and Christopher Hemphill. *Allure*. Boston: Bulfinch Press, 2002.

Walden, C. *Telegraph*. "Patrick Demarchelier: 'I don't like exhibitionist women . . .'." September 2, 2008.

Waldren, G. *The Independent*. "Thom Browne: The long and the short of it (an interview)." February 25, 2008. http://www.independent.co.uk/life-style/fashion/features/thom-browne-the-long-and-the-short-of-it-786667.html. (Accessed November 5, 2008.)

Walkley, C. *The Way to Wear ' Em: One Hundred Fifty Years of Punch on Fashion*. Chester Springs, PA: Dufour (P. Owen Ltd.), 1985.

Watson, L. *20th Century Fashion: 100 Years of Style by Decade and Designer, in association with Vogue*. Buffalo, NY: Firefly Books, 2004.

Weitz, J. *Man in Charge*. New York: The MacMillan Company, 1974.

———. *Sports Clothes for Your Sports Car*. New York: Arco Publishing Co., Inc., 1958.

Weston-Thomas, P. *Fashion-Era*. "The Aesthetic Dress Movement: Fashion History of Aesthetics." http://www.fashion-era.com/aesthetics.htm. (September 25, 2007.)

White, E., ed. *Fashion 85*. New York: St. Martin's Press, 1984.

White, P. *Elsa Schiaparelli: Empress of Paris Fashion*. New York: Rizzoli International Publications, Inc., 1986.

———. *Point*. New York: Clarkson N. Potter, Inc., 1973.

Whiteman, V. *Looking Back at Fashion, 1901–1939*. West Yorkshire, England: EP Publishing, 1978.

Whitley, Z. *Answers.com*. "Photography Encyclopedia: Alexander Liberman." http://answers.com/topic/alexander-liberman. (Accessed March 27, 2009.)

Wilcox, R. *The Mode in Costume, 2ed*. London: MacMillan Publishing Co., 1983.

Williams, B.E. *Fashion Is Our Business*. Philadelphia: J.B. Lippincott Co., 1945.

———. *Young Faces in Fashion*. Philadelphia: J.B. Lippincott Co., 1945.

Wilson, E. *New York Times*. "Lilly, 50, Hasn't Aged a Day." November 5, 2008.

The World of Balenciaga. Costume Institute, Metropolitan Museum of Art, New York, 1972.

Worsley-Gough, B. *Fashions in London:* Allan Wingate, 1952.

Worth, J.P. *A Century of Fashion*. Translated by Ruth Scott Miller. Boston: Little, Brown & Co., 1928.

Wunderkind. "About." http://wunderkind.de/flash.htm. (Accessed October 5, 2009.)

WWD. "Andrew Gn RTW Spring 2009." October 1, 2008.

WWD. "Chloé RTW Spring 2009." October 4, 2008.

WWD. "Luther and Cunningham Honored by France." October 7, 2008.

Yarwood, D. *The Encyclopedia of World Costume*. London: MacMillan Publishing Co., 1979.

Yohannon, K. *John Rawlings: 30 Years in Vogue*. Santa Fe, NM: Arena Editions, 2001.

Yoxall, H.W. *A Fashion of Life*. New York: Taplinger, 1967.

Yves Saint Laurent. "Stephano Pilati: Portrait." http://ysl.com/INT/en/index.aspx. (Accessed November 23, 2008.)

Yves Saint Laurent. Costume Institute, Metropolitan Museum of Art, New York, 1983.

Zimbio.com. "100 Most Influential People in Fashion." http://zimbio.com/100+Most+Influential+People+in+Fashion. (Accessed March 27, 2009.)

Index

Credits

Courtesy of Fairchild Publications, Inc.

2; 3; 4; 8 (bottom left); 9 (bottom left); 11 (top left); 13 (bottom right); 14; 15 (bottom left; bottom right); 20; 21 (top right); 22; 30; 31 (top right); 32; 33 (bottom left); 36 (top right); 39; 42 (bottom right); 43; 46; 50; 52 (bottom left); 54 (top left; top right); 55; 57 (bottom left; bottom center); 59; 64 (bottom left; bottom right); 72; 73 (bottom right); 74; 77 (bottom left); 82 (bottom left); 83 (bottom right); 84 (bottom left; bottom right); 85 (top left); 88; 89 (top right; bottom left); 91 (top right); 92; 93; 96 (bottom left; bottom right); 98 (top right); 100; 105; 107 (bottom left); 108; 109; 112; 114; 115; 116 (bottom left); 118; 121 (bottom left; bottom right); 128; 131; 136; 140 (top right; bottom right); 143 (bottom left; bottom right); 144 (bottom left; bottom right); 145; 146; 149 (bottom right); 150 (top left); 151 (bottom right); 154 (top right); 155; 156 (top right); 159; 161; 166; 169 (top right); 170; 179; 180 (top right; bottom left); 187; 188; 190 (bottom left); 193; 198; 199 (top left); 200; 201; 202; 205; 207; 209 (top left); 210 (top left); 213 (top right); 214; 215 (bottom right); 219; 220; 221 (top right; bottom right); 222 (top right; bottom right); 223; 226; 227 (top left); 228; 236; 237; 242; 243 (top left); 244; 249; 258 (bottom center; bottom right); 260; 261; 262 (top right); 265; 266; 268; 269; 271; 272 (bottom right); 277; 280 (top right); 281 (top left); 282; 283 (bottom right); 286; 293; 296 (top right); 297; 298 (top right); 303; 305; 306; 307; 309; 317; 318 (top right); 320 (top right); 322; 323; 324; 325; 327; 328; 329; 332; 336 (top left); 337 (top right); 338; 339 (top right); 343; 344 (top left); 348 (top right; bottom right); 349; 350; 353; 354 (top right; bottom right); 355 (bottom right); 356; 358; 362; 363; 364; 366; 367 (top left); 373; 378; 379; 380; 381; 382; 384; 386 (top right); 390 (bottom right); 391; 392 (bottom left); 396; 397; 398; 399; 402 (bottom right); 403; 404 (bottom left); 405; 409 (bottom left; bottom right); 412; 413; 414 (bottom left; bottom right);

Courtesy of Condé Nast Publications

5 (top left, Dominique Nabokov © 1987; bottom right, Karen Radkai © 1960); 6 (top right, Kourken Pakchanian © 1973; bottom left, Pierre Venant © 1972); 7 (bottom right, Horst P. Horst © 1948); 11 (bottom right, Francesco Scavullo © 1977); 12 (Antonio © 1973; 23 (bottom left, John Rawlings © 1946; bottom right, Henry Clarke © 1951); 24 (bottom left, Frances Mclaughlin-Gill © 1952); 25 (bottom left, Jerry Schatzberg © 1960); 26 (bottom left, Barry Lategan © 1981); 28 (top right, Caponnier © 1921); 31 (bottom left, Francesco Scvaullo © 1974); 34 (top right, Traeger © 1966; bottom left, Cecil Beaton © 1963); 35 (top right, Horst P. Horst © 1979; bottom left, Bert Stern © 1968); 36 (bottom left, Denis Peal © 1985); 38 (top right, Cecil Beaton © 1936; Christian Bérard © 1935); 44 (bottom left, Francesco Scavullo © 1974); 45 (top right, Bert Stern © 1970; bottom left, Horst P. Horst © 1965; bottom right, David Bailey © 1972); 49 (top left, Robert Picard © 1972; top right, Francesco Scavullo © 1974; bottom right, David Bailey © 1972); 51 (Cecil Beaton © 1935); 53 (top left, William Bell © 1960; bottom right, John Rawlings © 1953); 54 (bottom right, Henry Clarke © 1967); 67 (bottom right, Bert Stern © 1967); 68 (bottom left, John Rawling © 1953); 78 (top right, Horst P. Horst © 1937; bottom left, Edward Steichen © 1928); 80 (Brown Brothers © 1918); 81 (top right, Edward Steichen © 1927; bottom, Baron Adolphe De Meyer © 1921); 85 (bottom right, Kourken Pakchanian © 1972); 97 (bottom left, Bert Stern © 1967); 102 (top right, John Rawlings © 1946; bottom left, Erwin Blumenfeld © 1945); 103 (bottom left, Louise Dahl-Wolfe © 1959); 106 (Cecil Beaton); 110 (top right, George Hoyningen-Huene © 1934); 111 (top left, Karen Radkai © 1958); 113 (bottom left, Irving Penn © 1993); 117 (bottom left, Cecil Beaton © 1951); 134 (top right, Carl Oscar August Erickson; bottom left, Carl Oscar August Erickson); 139 (bottom right, John Rawlings © 1951); 143 (top right, Oliviero Toscani © 1989); 147 (top left, Henry Clarke © 1966; bottom right, Irving Penn © 1967); 148 (bottom left, Wanda Gawronska © 1954); 151 (top left, Richard Rutledge © 1953); 154 (bottom left, Henry Clarke © 1965); 158 (bottom, Henry Clarke © 1967); 160 (top right, Luis Lemus © 1940); 163 (top left, John Cowan © 1969; bottom right, William Klein © 1966); 164 (top right, John Rawlings © 1953; bottom left, Bert Stern © 1969); 167 (top right, Irving Penn ©

443

1964); 168 (bottom right, Henry Clarke © 1955; bottom left, Karen Radkai © 1955); 169 (bottom right, Horst P. Horst © 1956); 172 (bottom left, Raymundo De Larrain © 1971); 181 (top left, Horst P. Horst © 1951; bottom right, Horst P. Horst © 1961); 183 (bottom left, George Hoyningen-Huene © 1930); 189 (bottom right, Cecil Beaton © 1948); 192 (top right, J. P. Zachariasen © 1972); 199 (top right, Paul Amato © 1981); 206 (bottom left, Arnaud De Rosnay © 1970); 209 (bottom right, David Bailey © 1967); 224 (bottom right, Horst P. Horst © 1961); 230 (Robert Doisneau © 1949); 233 (bottom right, Tom Palumbo © 1959); 235 (© Frances Mclaughlin-Gill); 245 (top left, Horst P. Horst © 1963); 252 (top right, Frances Mclaughlin-Gill © 1957; bottom left, Frances Mclaughlin-Gill © 1955); 256 (top left, Sam Haskins © 1968; bottom right, Ishimuro © 1977); 267 (top right, Dick Dormer © 1948); 272 (bottom left, © Guy Marineau); 273 (bottom left, Bob Richardson © 1976); 278 (The Helmut Newton Estate/Maconochie Photography); 279 (top left, Bert Stern © 1963; bottom right, Bert Stern © 1962); 280 (bottom left, John Cowan © 1964; bottom right, Irving Penn © 1967); 281 (bottom right, Hans Feurer © 1992); 287 (top left, Edward Steichen © 1928); 288 (bottom left, Irving Penn © 1966); 289 (Arnaud De Rosnay © 1968); 291 (John Rawlings © 1945); 292 (Duane Michals © 1974); 295 (bottom right, Horst P. Horst © 1935); 304 (top right, Serge Balkin © 1948; bottom left, John Rawings © 1943); 308 (bottom left, Henry Clarke © 1966); 314 (bottom right, Gosta Peterson © 1966); 315 (top left, © 1947; bottom right, John Rawlings © 1943); 321 (top left, Harry Meerson © 1936); 335 (top left, Jacques Malignon © 1976; bottom right, Albert Watson © 1977); 339 (bottom left, Horst P. Horst © 1966); 341 (top left, Fredrich Baker © 1940); 345 (Patrick Demarchelier © 1988); 347 (top right, Leombruno-Bodi © 1955; bottom right, Francesco Scavullo © 1974); 357 (top left, Irving Penn © 1948; bottom right, Edward Steichen © 1928); 365 (David Bailer © 1967); 383 (bottom right, Dominique Nabokov © 1987); 388 (top left, George Hoyningen-Huene © 1931; top right, John Rawlings © 1945; bottom right, Carl Oscar August Erickson © 1937); 400 (bottom right, Irving Penn © 1968); 415 (top left, Pierre Scherman © 1984; bottom right, Denis Piel © 1985);

Getty Images
7 (top left, General Photographic Agency); 10 (Evening Standard); 15 (top right, David Lees/Time & Life Pictures); 16 (bottom left, David Montgomery; top right, David Teuma); 23 (top right, Lipnitzki/Roger Viollet); 24 (top right, Gjon Mili/Time Life Pictures); 25 (top right, Reg Lancaster/Express); 26 (top right, Kimberly Butler/Time Life Pictures); 37 (Katy Winn); 40 (top right, Kurt Hutton/Picture Post/IPC Magazines; bottom

left, Kurt Hutton/Picture Post); 41 (bottom left, DAMIEN MEYER/AFP); 44 (top right, Michael Tighe/Hulton Archive); 47 (top left, Jamie McCarthy/WireImage; bottom right, Fernanda Calfat); 48 (top right, Dan Kitwood; bottom left, Karl Prouse/Catwalking); 56 (top right, Eugene Gologursky/WireImage; bottom left, Photo by JP Yim/WireImage); 63 (Giuseppe Cacace); 64 (top right, Vittorio Zunino Celotto); 65 (top center, Alfred Eisenstaedt/Time & Life Pictures); 68 (top right, George Karger/Time Life Pictures); 71 (top right, Leonard McCombe/Time Life Pictures; bottom left, Hulton Archive); 73 (top right, Chris Jackson); 77 (top left, SHAUN CURRY/AFP); 79 (bottom left, Lipnitzki; bottom right, Popperfoto); 82 (top right, Eric Ryan); 83 (top left, Gareth Cattermole); 86 (top right, Evening Standard; bottom left, Frank Barratt); 87 (top left, FRANCOIS GUILLOT/AFP; bottom right, Fernanda Calfat); 90 (top, Terry Fincher/Express); 96 (top right); 98 (bottom left, Popperfoto); 103 (bottom right, Yale Joel/Life Magazine/Time & Life Pictures); 111 (bottom left, Henry Clarke/Musee Galliera/ADAGP/Collection Vogue Paris); 113 (top right, Randy Brooke/WireImage); 117 (bottom right, Steve Granitz/WireImage); 119 (top right); 124 (bottom left, Reutlinger/Mansell/Time Life Pictures; bottom right, Boissonnas/Taponier/Mansell/Time Life Pictures); 126 (top left, Foc Kan/WireImage; bottom left, S. Benhamou/Prestige); 127 (top left, Frazer Harrison; top right, Frazer Harrison; bottom right, Steve Grantiz/WireImage); 135 (Bernard Gotfryd); 138 (Bob Peterson// Time Life Pictures); 144 (top right, Jason LaVeris/FilmMagic); 174 (bottom left, Picture Post/Hulton Archive); 175 (top right, Hulton Archive); 176 (top right, Henry Clarke/Musee Galliera/ADAGP/Collection Vogue Paris); 182 (top right, Thos Robinson); 186 (top right, Hulton Archive); 189 (top left, Eliot Elisofon/Time & Life Pictures); 191 (top left, Maurits Sillem; bottom right, Karl Prouse/Catwalking); 203 (top right, Hulton Archive; bottom left, Library of Congress); 206 (top right, Foc Kan/WireImage); 210 (bottom right,); 211 (bottom right, JON LEVY/AFP); 212 (bottom left, Mark Mainz); 222 (bottom left, SOTHEBY'S/AFPSOTHEBY'S/AFP); 233 (top left, Jerry Cooke/Time Life Pictures); 238 (top right, Peter Stackpole/Time Life Pictures); 245 (bottom right, Keystone); 267 (bottom right, Paul Schutzer/Time Life Pictures); 270 (Tim Graham); 273 (top right, Jill Kennington/Hultin Archive); 276 (Thos Robinson); 283 (top left, DAMIEN MEYER/AFP); 288 (top right, Bob Peterson/Time Life Pictures); 290 (top left, Seeberger Freres); 298 (bottom left, Amanda Edwards); 300 (top right, Lipnitzki/Roger Viollet); 311 (Terry Smith/Time Life Pictures); 314 (top right, Keystone); 321 (bottom right, Imagno); 326 (top left, Henry Clarke/Musee Galliera/ADAGP/Collection Vogue Paris; top right, David E. Scherman/Time & Life Pictures; bottom right, Henry Clarke/Musee Galliera/ADAGP/ Collection Vogue Paris); 336 (bottom right, PAOLO COCCO/AFP); 344 (bottom center, Slaven Vlasic; bottom right, Slaven Vlasic); 352 (Walter Sanders/Time & Life Pictures); 354 (bottom left, Brian Ach/WireImage); 355 (top left, Vittorio Zunino Celotto); 369 (bottom left, Zack Seckler); 371 (top right, Chris Jackson); 374 (bottom left, Carlo Buscemi/WireImage); 376 (top right, K. Terrell/WireImage); 386 (bottom left, PIERRE VERDY/ AFP); 387 (top right, Laure Albin-Guillot/Roger Viollet); 390 (top left, Bernard Gotfryd); 393 (Bernard Gotfryd); 401 (bottom right, Fred Lyon/Time Life Pictures); 402 (top right, Mark Sullivan/WireImage; bottom left, Toby Canham); 404 (top right, Steve Mack/FilmMagic); 409 (top left, Mark Wilson);

Corbis

8 (top right, © Isabelle Weingarten/Sygma); 9 (bottom right, © Pierre Perrin/Sygma); 27 (© Bettmann); 28 (bottom left, © Stapleton Collection); 29 (top right, © Peter Ross); 41 (top right, © Daniel Dal Zennaro/epa); 42 (bottom left, © Carlo Ferraro/epa); 52 (top right, © CORBIS SYGMA); 57 (top right, © Lucas Dolega/epa); 66 (top right, © Federico Patellani/Studio Patellani; bottom left, © Massimo Listri; bottom right, © Massimo Listri); 67 (top left, © Pierre Vauthey; top right, © Bettmann); 75 (top right, © Sergio Gaudenti/Kipa); 77 (bottom right, © Kim Kyung Hoon/Reuters); 87 (top right, © Rune Hellestad); 90 (bottom right, © Norman Parkinson Limited); 97 (top right, © Pierre Vauthey); 99 (© Norman Parkinson Limited); 107 (top right, © Kurt Krieger/Corbis); 110 (bottom left, © Christie's Images); 114 (© Franck Seguin); 117 (top left, © Bettmann); 120 (top right, © Hulton-Deutsch Collection); 122 (Jack Robinson/Hulton Archive); 126 (bottom right, © PIERRE VAUTHEY); 135 (bottom right, © Bettmann); 139 (top left, © Genevieve Naylor); 140 (bottom left, © Andreea Angelescu); 141 (top left; bottom right, © PIERRE VAUTHEY); 142 (top right, © David Lees; bottom left, © Massimo Listri); 148 (top right, © Bettmann); 156 (bottom left, © John Van Hasselt/Sygma); 157 (bottom left, © Bettmann); 160 (bottom left, © Bettmann); 162 (top left, © Zhang Yuwei/XinHua/Xinhua Press; bottom right, © Benoit Tessier/Reuters); 169 (top left, © David Lees); 172 (top right, © Andy Warhol Foundation); 174 (top right, © Norman Parkinson Limited); 176 (top left, © Bettmann); 192 (bottom left, © Bettmann); 194 (top left, © Rune Hellestad); 204 (© Julio Donoso); 206 (bottom right, © Pierre Vauthey); 212 (top right, © Mark Savage); 215 (top left, © Eric Robert); 225 (top left, © James Andanson/Sygma;; bottom right, © Bettmann); 238 (bottom left, © Bettmann); 240 (top right, © Bettmann; bottom right, © Hulton-Deutsch Collection); 243 (bottom right, © Phil McCarten/

Reuters); 251 (top left, © Bettmann); 253 (© Gregory Pace); 255 (top, © Roger Ressmeyer); 258 (top left, © Matt Dunham/Reuters); 259 (© Mitchell Gerber); 262 (top left, © Gregory Pace); 264 (top right, © William Coupon); 272 (top right, © Ethan Miller/Reuters); 294 (© Odile Montserrat/Sygma); 295 (top left, © Hulton-Deutsch Collection); 300 (bottom right, © Underwood & Underwood); 308 (top right, © David Lees); 310 (REUTERS/Mike Segar); 314 (top left, © Eric Robert/ VIP Production); 318 (bottom center, © Rune Hellestad); 320 (bottom left, © Beth Herzhaft); 333 (top left, © Andy Warhol Foundation; bottom right, © Hulton-Deutsch Collection); 334 (top left, © WWD/Condé Nast; bottom right, © Reuters); 337 (bottom left, © Condé Nast Archive); 340 (top left, © Pool/For Picture; bottom, © Pierre Vauthey); 341 (bottom left, © Philadelphia Museum of Art; bottom right, © Philadelphia Museum of Art); 348 (bottom left, © Frédéric Huijbregts); 351 (top left, © Bettmann; bottom right, © Bettmann); 368 (Lynn Goldsmith); 369 (bottom right, © Bettmann); 370 (bottom left, © Tannen Maury); 371 (bottom left, © Rune Hellestad); 372 (© Bettmann); 374 (top right, ADD CREDIT); 376 (bottom left, © Eric Cahan); 377 (top right, © Bettmann; bottom left, © Photo B.D.V.); 385 (top left, © Toni Thorimbert/Sygma; bottom right, © Photo B.D.V.); 389 (top right, © Deborah Feingold); 400 (top right, © Condé Nast Archive); 401 (top left, © Bettmann); 414 (top right, © Zack Seckler);

Courtesy of Catwalking

13 (top left); 21 (bottom left); 33 (top right; bottom right); 91 (bottom left; bottom right); 107 (bottom right); 210 (bottom right); 227 (bottom right); 234; 296 (bottom left; bottom right); 367 (bottom right); 386 (bottom right);

AP Images

17 (Kathy Willens); 65 (bottom right); 71 (bottom right, John F. Kennedy Library and Museum); 89 (bottom center, PRNewsFoto/Kenneth Cole Productions, Inc.); 116 (top right, Jennifer Graylock); 121 (top right); 177 (Richard Drew); 178 (top left, Stuart Ramson; bottom right, Matt York); 347 (bottom left); 383 (bottom left, Mark Lennihan);

Courtesy of the designer/editor/photographer

21 (bottom right); 29 (bottom left); 69 (Courtesy of the Stephanie Lake Foundation); 70 (Courtesy of the Stephanie Lake Foundation); 76; 94; 95; 104; 125; 130; 132; 133; 142 (bottom right); 149 (bottom left); 165; 173; 190 (top right); 194 (top right; bottom left); 195; 196; 208; 213 (bottom left); 218; 229; 231 (Photography by Maria Valentino); 232; 246; 248; 250; 254 (bottom left); 255 (bottom right); 257; 263; 264 (bottom left); 359; 392 (top right);

Reuters
42 (top left, Charles Platiau);

Art + Commerce
58 (© John Huba); 84 (© Jason Frank Rothenberg); 149 (top left, © Sølve Sundsbø); 221 (bottom left, © Jason Frank Rothenberg); 254 (top right, © Craig McDean); 370 (top right, © Steven Meisel);

Art Resource
62 (© The Metropolitan Museum of Art); 119 (bottom left, © The Metropolitan Museum of Art); 123 (© The Metropolitan Museum of Art); 167 (bottom left, © The Metropolitan Museum of Art); 247 (bottom left, CNAC/MNAM/Dist. Réunion des Musées Nationaux); 290 (bottom right, ADD CREDIT); 300 (bottom left, © The Metropolitan Museum of Art); 301 (bottom right, V&A Images, London); 387 (bottom left, © The Metropolitan Museum of Art); 407 (bottom right, © The Metropolitan Museum of Art); 408 (© The Metropolitan Museum of Art);

The Picture Desk
75 (bottom, TOUCHSTONE/WARNERS/THE KOBAL COLLECTION); 186 (bottom left, MGM / THE KOBAL COLLECTION); 346 (top right, 20TH CENTURY FOX / THE KOBAL COLLECTION; bottom left, MIRISCH-7 ARTS/UNITED ARTISTS / THE KOBAL COLLECTION);

V&A Images
120 (bottom left); 319 (© John French); 342; 389 (bottom left);

Mary Evans Picture Library
123 (bottom); 287 (bottom right);

The Metropolitan Museum of Art
150 (bottom right, 1972.209.28);

Everett Collection
175 (bottom left); 299 (bottom right);

Courtesy of Macy's, Inc.
180 (bottom right);

Bridgeman Art Library
183 (top right, Sievers, Wolfgang (1913-2007) / National Gallery of Australia, Canberra / © DACS); 301 (top left, © DACS / The Stapleton Collection); 407 (top left, Bibliotheque des Arts Decoratifs, Paris, France / Archives Charmet);

Courtesy of the Advertising Archives
211 (top left);

Courtesy of the Library of Congress
239;

Redux Pictures
406 (Mark Peterson);